MARKETING

MARKETING

AN INTRODUCTORY TEXT

Martin Christopher

and

Malcolm McDonald

First published 1995 by
MACMILLAN PRESS LTD
Houndmills, Basingstoke, Hampshire RG21 2XS
and London
Companies and representatives
throughout the world

ISBN 0–333–62586–2 hardcover
ISBN 0–333–62587–0 paperback

A catalogue record for this book is available
from the British Library.

10 9 8 7 6 5 4 3 2 1
04 03 02 01 00 99 98 97 96 95

Copy-edited and typeset by Povey–Edmondson
Okehampton and Rochdale, England

Printed in Great Britain by The Bath Press, Avon

Contents

List of Figures and Tables

Figures

Tables

Preface

There has probably never been a time when effective marketing has been more crucial than at the present. The search for competitive advantage has taken on the equivalence of the search for the Holy Grail in the turbulent business environment of the 1990s. The role that marketing plays in guiding corporate strategy is crucial and yet it is still the weak link for so many companies in the process that binds the customer to the organisation.

Marketing in the past has often been misinterpreted and over-simplified. It has been confused with selling – itself a crucial activity – or with a naïve concept of 'giving the customers what they want'.

Through our work as teachers and consultants we have come to the strongly held view that marketing's role in the business is to find opportunities that allow the organisation to reap a greater return on its assets, in particular its marketing assets. The marketing assets of a business include such things as corporate image, brand names, sales and distribution networks, supplier and customer relations and, of course, its people. Incorporated as part of total corporate strategy, marketing becomes a powerful machine for building and developing these crucial assets.

This book is designed to explore these ideas in a simple-to-read format. Whether you are an experienced marketing professional or entering marketing for the first time, or if your work is in a non-marketing function but you need to know more about marketing, we believe you will find this book helpful.

Whilst we have sought to put our own interpretation on the marketing concept and techniques described in this book we owe a large debt to many marketing professionals and teachers, including our past and present colleagues at the Cranfield University School of Management, for their pioneering work in developing the large body of knowledge that now exists in the area. An equal debt is owed to Dorothy Hendry, Lee Smith and Kate Brazier for typing the manuscript.

Cranfield University School of Management

MARTIN CHRISTOPHER
MALCOLM MCDONALD

MODULE 1

The Role of Marketing in Business

CHAPTER 1

Introduction: Marketing's Role in the Organisation

After dominating the world motor-bike market for the best part of fifty years, with famous names like Norton, Triumph and BSA, the British volume motor-bike industry is dead. Similarly, the British ship-building industry is a shadow of its former self, with yards that were known around the world now closed and derelict. On the other hand Jaguar Cars, Rolls-Royce Engines and ICL Computers, having at one time all been close to collapse, have strengthened their positions and survived, albeit under new management and ownership. What are the factors that lead to success or failure in the market place? Why is it that companies in the same industry have widely differing success in achieving sales?

This book seeks to explain the roots of success to show quite simply that the difference between success and failure in the market place is due to something that can be termed 'competitive advantage' and that marketing is ultimately about how that advantage is achieved.

■ What is Marketing?

Marketing is often misunderstood. To many it is just a fancy word for 'selling'; to others it is about advertising and promotion. Still other people think of marketing as market research – finding out what customers want. In a sense, marketing is about all of these and yet it is much more. Marketing is not selling, yet the culmination of successful marketing is a sale. Likewise advertising and promotion may be a highly effective means of communicating with potential customers to inform them about our product or service and to convince them of its merits. Similarly, without an understanding of real customer needs, provided perhaps by market research, we are unlikely to be successful in the market place.

Clearly marketing is concerned with customer satisfaction and with the identification of marketing opportunities; it is also concerned with the harnessing of the firm's resources and the focusing of those resources upon the most appropriate opportunities.

The simplest definition of marketing is that it is the process of matching the resources of the business with identified customer needs. In other words, marketing is concerned with customer satisfaction and with the focusing of the organisation's resources to ensure that the customer is satisfied – at a profit to the business. The idea of customer satisfaction is a basic article of faith in marketing. The marketing-oriented company is one which 'puts the customer at the centre of the business' and seeks to focus all its activities towards creating satisfied customers.

Philosophically there is little to argue with in this notion. However it must be recognised that in any business the ability of the organisation to produce offerings that meet real needs will generally be limited to some very specific areas. More particularly, what we find is that an organisation's skills and resources are the limiting factor determining its ability to meet market place needs. For example, a slide rule manufacturer would find it difficult to compete in the age of electronics with pocket calculators. The strengths and skills of that company, whatever they may be, are quite definitely not in the manufacture of electronic calculators, whereas they may well have a strength in marketing and distribution in specialised markets – thus possibly providing an opportunity to distribute other manufacturers' products aimed at those markets.

What we are in effect saying is that marketing should really be seen as the process of achieving *the most effective deployment of the firm's assets* to achieve overall corporate objectives. By assets in this context we refer specifically to those assets which might best be described as 'marketing assets'.

■ The Company's Marketing Assets

What are marketing assets? Typically when we talk about assets we think first of financial assets, or more precisely those assets that are recognised in the balance sheet of the business. So fixed assets, such as plant and machinery, and current assets, such as inventory or cash, would be typical of this view of assets.

In fact the marketing assets of the business are of far greater importance to the long-run health of the business and yet paradoxically would not appear in the balance sheet. Ultimately the only assets that have value are those which contribute directly or indirectly to profitable sales, now or in the future. Included in our categorisation of marketing assets would be such things as:

- *Brand name:* what is the strength of the image or the 'values' that are created in the market place by the brand name (for example, Schweppes or IBM)?
- *Market 'franchise':* are there certain parts of the market that we can call our own? (The loyalty of customers and distributors will be a factor here.)
- *Distribution network:* do we have established channels of distribution that enable us to bring products or services to the market in a cost-effective way?
- *Market share:* the 'experience effect' and economies of scale mean that for many companies there are substantial advantages to being big. For example, costs will be lower and visibility in the market place will be higher.

- *Supplier relationships:* the ability to have access to raw materials and low-cost components, for example, can be of substantial advantage. Additionally, close cooperation with suppliers can frequently lead to innovative product developments.
- *Customer relations: 'close to the customer'* has become the motto of the 1990s and many organisations can testify to the advantage of strong bonds between the company and its customers.
- *Technology base:* does the company have any unique skills, processes or 'know-how' strengths that can provide a basis for product/market exploitation?

It is only through the effective use of these and any other marketing assets that the company can build successful marketing strategies.

Asset-based marketing should not be confused with that hallmark of the past – the 'production orientation'. A production orientation typifies those businesses so wrapped up in their own processes and technology that they ignore the customers' real needs. Many companies that were once customer-focused have gradually lost that focus because they have failed to recognise changes in the market place and have continued to look inwards rather than outwards. On the other hand, asset-based marketing seeks constantly to identify opportunities for exploiting skills and resources rather than products. Products are simply the vehicle whereby the needs of the customer are met. Indeed, in the growing service sector of the economy there is no physical product in any case, but rather an 'encounter'. To encompass this idea of the product or the encounter as a vehicle for achieving both customer satisfaction and corporate goals (for example profitability) we will be using the concept of 'the offer' throughout the book. The offer represents the totality of elements that the company provides and that the customer perceives himself to be receiving. As Figure 1.1 suggests, there has to be a match between the offer and the need if corporate goals and objectives are to be met.

Essentially the offer is a 'promise of benefits'. In other words, the customer is induced to buy the product or service in the expectation of acquiring desired benefits. It is an old saying in marketing that, 'people don't buy products, they buy benefits'. So people might buy a TV set to be entertained, to be informed or

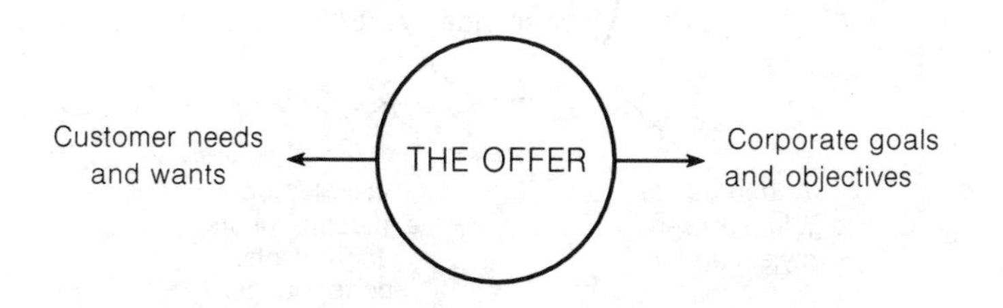

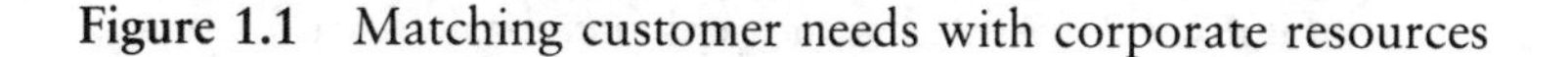
Figure 1.1 Matching customer needs with corporate resources

even to *keep up with the Jones*; but not because they want to buy a cathode ray tube and all the electronics that go with it.

Many companies still fail to recognise this basic fact and continue to focus upon features rather than on benefits. This is particularly true in industrial marketing. Pick up any trade magazine in, say, the engineering field and examine the advertisements. Mostly these advertisements will highlight the technical aspects of the product rather than what the product will do for the customer. Thus a manufacturer of roller bearings might stress the 'track and roller profile' whereas the customer benefit is actually less friction and greater efficiency. This is not to say that technical information is unimportant, but rather that successful marketing is based upon selling solutions to perceived problems.

The same principle applies if we are marketing to another company rather than to the end customer – what is sometimes called 'business-to-business' or 'industrial' marketing. Buyers in such organisations are also seeking benefits or, put another way, they seek solutions to problems. To succeed in the market place therefore our offer has to provide desired benefits or solutions. If it does not, or is not perceived to do so, no amount of high-pressure selling will persuade people to buy it.

Thus the offer should be viewed as a bundle of benefits and/or solutions and not merely as a set of product features. One way of expressing this idea is as a 'halo' or 'surround' that encircles the core product or service (Figure 1.2). In effect, this 'surround' reflects the added values for the customer and thus will provide a means of differentiating the core product or service from competitive offers. The surround comprises such sources of added value as the corporate image, the customer service that is provided, any financial 'packages' that assist the purchase, technical support, after-sales service and, of course, brand or corporate image. This whole bundle of benefits is often referred to as the 4 'P's (Product, Price, Place, Promotion) which are discussed in more detail in Chapter 2.

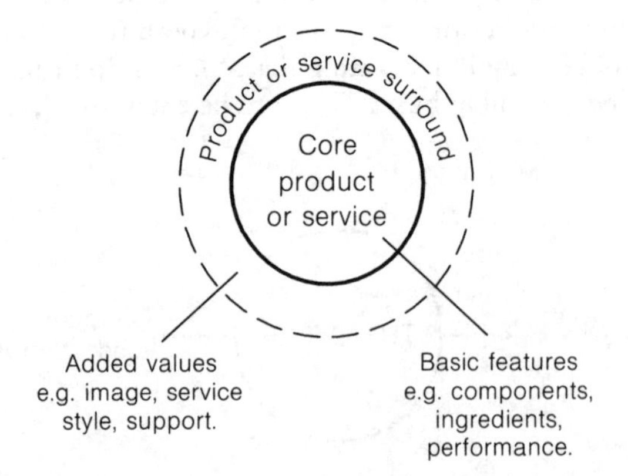

Figure 1.2 Added values enhance basic features

The larger the surround in relation to the core, the more likely it is that the offer will be strongly differentiated from the competition. If, on the other hand, we only emphasise the core product in our promotion, then we are encouraging the customer to see it purely as a 'commodity'. It is relatively easy for competitors to imitate the core product – even if we think we have a patent protection. In so many markets there has been a convergence of technology; for example in hi-fi, in personal computers, in compact disc players and in digital watches. The way in which companies such as Bang & Olufsen, Apple, Sony and Seiko differentiate themselves is not through technology – good though it may be – but through the wider dimensions of design, user-friendliness, quality reputation and breadth of range.

■ The Search for Differential Advantage

Why does Coca-Cola outsell Pepsi, even though in many cases 'blind' tests have shown that people prefer the taste of Pepsi? Why do large numbers of people pay more for a sports shirt with a designer label than one of equal quality from Marks and Spencer? Indeed why, in most markets, is there a 'brand leader'?

The answer is simple: successful companies are those which have worked to produce strongly differentiated offers. Their products or services are not 'me toos'. Customers recognise the added value that, in their minds, enhances the product. Sometimes that added value may be psychological or emotional, as in the case of Coca-Cola; other times it will be because there are specific benefits that are perceived to attach to one offer as compared with that of its competitors.

The strength of Coca-Cola's emotional appeal was well illustrated in 1985 when, after ninety-nine years, the Coca-Cola Company decided to counter the competitive threat in the USA from Pepsi-Cola by introducing an improved formula with a taste that tests had shown was judged superior to that of Pepsi. The new formula was thoroughly researched – about $4 million was spent on taste tests and research with nearly 200,000 consumers. Some of the tests were 'blind tests', that is, the consumer did not know the name of the product. Other research asked the question 'What if this were a new Coke taste?' But none of the questions addressed the issue: 'What if the old familiar Coca-Cola you have known and loved for years were to be removed from the market and replaced by something called "New Coke"?'

When the product was launched in the USA as a replacement for the traditional Coca-Cola there was a national outcry. Sales fell away, pressure groups were formed, primetime TV news programmes reported the issue in great detail. Within months Coca-Cola were forced to bring back the old formulation, now called Coca-Cola 'Classic', complete with the traditional script and logo.

What Coca-Cola had failed to realize was that customers were not primarily buying a taste but an *experience*. Coca-Cola's strength – its source of differential advantage – was its image and the customer values that were delivered by the traditional name and logo. The issue of brands is dealt with in detail in Chapter 11.

The concept of *differential advantage* lies at the heart of strategic marketing. Indeed it could be argued that the ultimate role of marketing management is to achieve and maintain maximum positive differentiation over and above the competition in the eyes of customers.

In seeking to differentiate its products the company needs to recognise that the potential customer is concerned with *benefits* rather than *features per se*. Theodore Levitt, one of marketing's most original thinkers, once wrote 'people don't buy ¼″ drills, they buy ¼″ holes'. The essence of that statement is that the drill is purely a vehicle for the provision of the benefit – a means of solving a 'buying problem'. What this means is that the successful offer is one which promises to deliver *solutions* to customers' buying problems in a superior way to competitive offers.

It is important to recognise that different people will react in different ways to benefit propositions. Take, for instance, non-drip paint. The covering power of non-drip paint is less than regular paint. However, to the do-it-yourself painter the promise of 'non-drip' is a key benefit proposition. On the other hand the primary benefit sought by the professional painter is cost per square metre and thus this part of the market is unlikely to respond to that particular benefit proposition.

In 'high-tech' marketing there is a similar need to focus upon customer benefits rather than upon the technology. For example, computer-integrated manufacturing (CIM) is making slow progress in terms of widespread adoption in the manufacturing industry. One of the reasons for this is the apparently high costs involved. Using traditional investment appraisal techniques such as payback period or discounted cash flow (DCF) it often appears to be uneconomic in terms of the cost reduction it promises. However, the major benefits of CIM, as the Japanese are demonstrating, exist primarily not in terms of reduced costs but rather in the greater manufacturing flexibility it provides, the shorter throughput times and the reduction in working capital. This translates into direct marketing benefits to the manufacturing company. For example, companies using this technology can respond more rapidly to customer needs; they can produce greater variety with little or no cost penalty; they can reduce inventories and thus boost return on investment (ROI).

Thus to convince the potential customer of the advantages of this type of investment requires a focus upon that customer's market place and its characteristics. Rather than selling cost reduction *per se* the CIM equipment manufacturer must sell enhanced market share, even survival. Careful research of the market and an understanding of the 'problems' that customers seek to solve will assist in the process of achieving differential advantage by selling benefits rather than features.

A useful concept here is the idea of the 'benefit proposition'. That is: 'What does our offer promise to deliver by way of benefits and solutions that makes it different from competitive offers?'

Marketing and the Bottom Line

A frequent criticism of western management is that it is too short-term in its thinking and its focus. There is still a tendency, it is argued, to seek to maximise this year's profit – even at the expense of longer-term development of the business. Part of the blame must be placed on the general financial orientation of many senior managers. This is reflected in the accounting mentality whereby costs in general, and product costs in particular, are paid greater attention than the means of revenue improvement. This is not to say that costs are unimportant, but rather to assert a basic truth: products don't make profits, but customers do. The search for long-term profitability must therefore focus as much upon the customer as it does upon the product.

Whilst profitability can be increased in the short term by productivity improvements – that is, by producing the same sales volume at less cost – long-term growth in profitability can only be achieved by increasing volume. *Volume growth together with productivity improvement holds the key to profitability.*

Figure 1.3 summarises the options that are available to the business in its search for sustainable profit improvement. Let us explore some of these ideas in more detail.

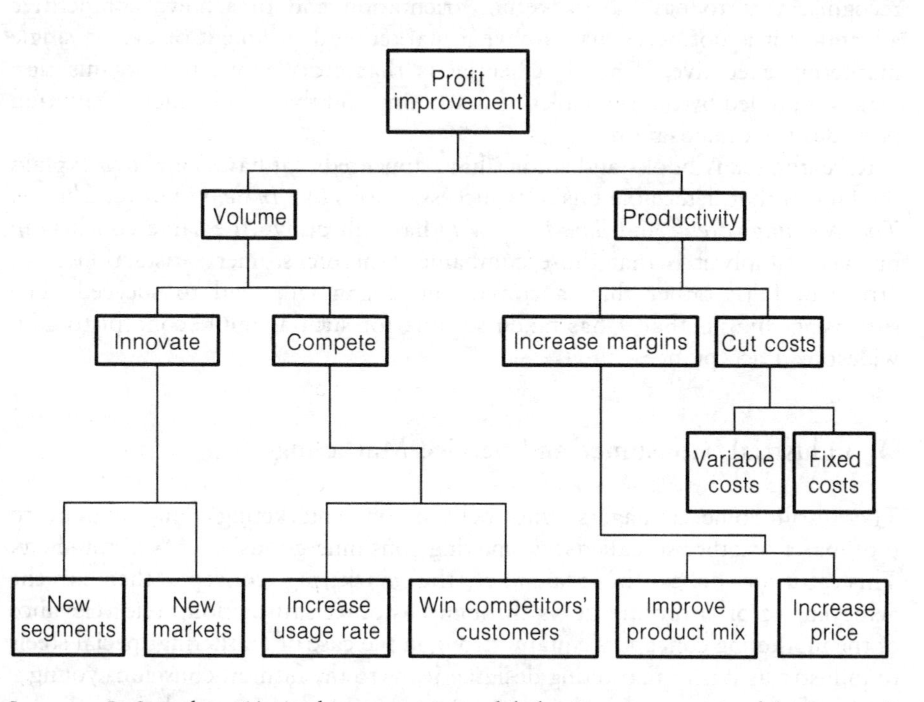

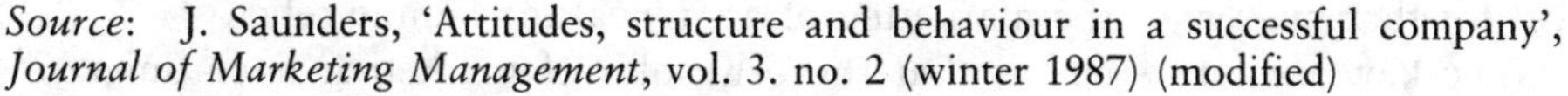
Source: J. Saunders, 'Attitudes, structure and behaviour in a successful company', *Journal of Marketing Management*, vol. 3. no. 2 (winter 1987) (modified)

Figure 1.3 The sources of long-run profit improvements

Opportunities for productivity improvement tend to be self-limiting, in the sense that costs can only be cut so far and price and product mix adjustments can only be made with limited frequency. On the other hand the opportunities for innovation and improved competitiveness are limited only by imagination and creativity. A primary concern of the marketing task within the business is to seek to innovate through product and market development and to strive to enhance competitive performance.

In both cases it is only by placing the customer at the centre of the business that success can be achieved. Innovation that is not based upon the satisfaction of a customer need, either existing or latent, will not succeed – the world is littered with 'better mousetraps'. Similarly the search for competitive advantage will only be successful if based upon a strategy of meeting customer needs more effectively than competitors.

Ultimately, therefore, the role of marketing in the organisation is firstly to ensure that the orientation of the business is towards the customer, and secondly to seek to marshall the resources of the business in such a way as to be perceived by the market as providing superior benefits than are available elsewhere.

There are thus two aspects to marketing. The first is about corporate values and culture and the second is about strategy and execution. It is important to recognise that to have a marketing orientation and to achieve competitive advantage it is not necessary to have a marketing department or even a single marketing executive. What is essential is that every move the organisation makes is guided by the principles of marketing and that a customer orientation pervades the organisation.

Recently, many books and studies have appeared that have sought to explain the factors that determine business success. Books like *In Search of Excellence*, *The Winning Streak* and *The IBM Way* have all drawn the same conclusion: put very simply it is that those companies where customer satisfaction is an article of faith rather than a convenient slogan will tend to succeed. The surprising thing is that it has taken so long for such a simple concept to gain widespread acceptance!

■ Industrial, Consumer and Service Marketing

There still some managers who believe that 'marketing' only applies to toothpaste or other so-called 'fast moving consumer goods' – FMCG for short. This attitude belies the reality of the marketing concept, that is, the achievement of corporate goals through customer satisfaction. The relevance of the marketing concept is equally strong in the case of marketing special steels to industry as it is to marketing designer jeans to the fashion-conscious young – or, for that matter, to the marketing of an appeal for famine relief.

The key point to stress is that the principles of marketing have universal application; what does differ is the way in which the implementation is achieved.

Typically, in *industrial markets* there will be fewer buyers making purchases less frequently, and at higher prices, than will be found in consumer markets. Often the buyer will be a professional purchasing manager, sometimes with specific training in negotiation skills and with detailed product knowledge. However, it can be argued that these differences are only a matter of degree. What, ultimately, is the difference between a housewife shopping on behalf of a family and a purchasing officer buying on behalf of a corporation?

Where there *is* a difference between consumer and industrial marketing is in the emphasis placed upon the different elements of the marketing mix. Thus in the case of marketing special steels the role of TV advertising may be limited in contrast with that of marketing designer jeans. On the other hand there will be a greater emphasis placed upon personal, technical selling in the former case compared to the latter.

The distinctions between *services marketing* and *consumer marketing* are equally blurred. What makes marketing a service different is that the product on offer is 'intangible'. It is based upon a relationship, an experience, an encounter. It quite clearly is focused upon people rather than upon things. However, in reality there are few industrial or consumer products that do not have a personal or 'relationship' dimension involved somewhere along the line. Indeed, a point that was made earlier in the context of the discussion of the 'product surround' was that service is a powerful means of differentiating the product.

Again it is sometimes suggested that services are different because they are perishable and cannot be stored. In other words, a hotel bed, if not sold today, cannot be sold tomorrow; a professional accountant cannot hold his time in 'inventory' whilst he goes on holiday. Once more though, if we reflect on this issue, we will recognise that the distinction is again one of degree. A newspaper, a popular record or this season's fashion have very short lives and the service offer in a sense is just an extreme case of a 'time sensitive' product.

■ International Marketing

International marketing is the performance of the marketing task across national boundaries. As such, the principles are the same. However, the environment in which international marketing takes place is different from the domestic environment; the control it is possible to exercise over the four 'P's is different, and there is a different dimension of complexity to planning the marketing function internationally.

The most critical determinant of the way an organisation markets abroad is its method of entering a foreign market.

The key questions in international marketing are concerned with whether to market abroad, where to market abroad, what to market abroad, and finally how to market abroad.

However, perhaps the best way of answering these questions in more detail is to remind ourselves that marketing is the way in which an organisation matches its capabilities to the wants of its customers against the background of a dynamic environment. International marketing is simply the performance of the marketing task across national boundaries. Marketing research still has to be carried out, appropriate products developed, realistic pricing, packaging and branding policies adopted, sales forecasts made, effective communication with customers has to take place, and distribution policies still have to ensure that the product gets to the right place at the right time.

So, in principle, international marketing is no different from domestic marketing.

Yet, in reality, whenever a company begins to operate outside its domestic market, it is in the field of marketing that it most commonly stumbles. This has forced both academics and practitioners to pay increasing attention to the subject of international marketing, and they have begun to focus more and more on the differences rather than the similarities as a means of improving performance.

International marketing has three unique elements:

- the control which it is possible to exercise over the four 'P's is different.
- there are additional environmental variables.
- there is a different dimension of complexity to planning the marketing function internationally.

The second of these is dealt with in some detail in Chapter 6, Scanning The Environment. The third is dealt with in Chapter 20, Marketing Planning.

Let us look at the first of these in some detail to see in what ways any differences there are have an impact on the marketing mix.

International Control

Without doubt, the most critical determinant of the way an organisation markets abroad is its method of entering a foreign market, for this above all else decides the degrees of freedom it has over the management of the four 'P's.

Straightforward exporting can be either indirect or direct. Indirect exporting is when a third party arranges the documentation, shipping and selling of a company's goods abroad, and this usually represents the smallest level of commitment to international marketing. As foreign sales grow, however, the company begins to make a limited commitment, usually in the form of taking on the documentation task itself. It is often at this stage that overseas agents or distributors are appointed to carry out the selling task abroad, with the result that the company is now a direct exporter, although it is likely that the commitment is still limited to marginal production capacity, with no additional fixed investment.

Recognition of the importance of overseas trading really happens when a limited fixed investment occurs, not just in the form of production capacity, but often also in the form of a marketing subsidiary abroad in recognition of the need for a more aggressive marketing approach.

Foreign production can take the form of licensing, contract manufacturing, local assembly or full manufacture, either by joint ventures or wholly owned subsidiaries. With licensing, the company is hiring out its brand name, technical expertise, patent, trademark, or process rights. The licensee manufactures and markets abroad for the licensor. Whilst this avoids the need for a heavy investment, it can lead to an over-dependence on the licensee, who quickly builds up both manufacturing and marketing expertise. Associated Engineering, the largest engine-components manufacturer in the world, and Pilkington Glass are just two examples of successful licensing abroad.

Contract manufacturing is merely using someone else's production capacity and is usually only possible for technically simple products such as food. It is a useful way of getting round tariff barriers, as well as of gaining experience of a foreign market, without the need for investment in capital and labour.

Similar advantages apply to local assembly, which is also a learning device, as well as enabling a company to avoid paying the higher tariffs on assembled goods, because bringing in unassembled goods helps local employment.

Sometimes, laws forbid 100 per cent foreign ownership of assets, especially in the less developed countries. So many companies set up joint ventures either with a foreign government or with local partners. It is certainly a way of sharing risk and of gaining experience using local expertise, but its major disadvantage lies in the loss of complete control, hence freedom of action, especially in the field of marketing.

One-hundred-per-cent ownership of foreign production plants represents a major commitment to international marketing and should only be done after much research. Most overseas manufacturing is related to where the markets are. ICI built a polyethylene plant in the south of France because this was the only way to get into the market. Likewise GKN's big stake in the German components industry gave it a market share that could not be achieved by direct export from the UK.

From this discussion it will be clear that there is a big difference between the marketing task of a company selling to a middleman as a final customer, with little concern about what happens to the product after the sale, and the task facing the company that assumes full responsibility for all stages of marketing right through to final user satisfaction. Regardless of the level of involvement in foreign marketing, companies are more and more finding it necessary to become marketing oriented in their international efforts.

The important point is that each of the options described above should not be considered as a series of steps to be followed en route to becoming a multinational company (in which all opportunities are assessed from the world-wide viewpoint, and in which the terms 'home' and 'foreign' are meaningless), but more as strategic alternatives. And since the method of market entry is the major determinant of the degree of control a company has over its marketing, each of the different options should be carefully considered before a decision is made.

A precision-components manufacturer appointed a distributor for Europe with a seven-year agreement. Whilst at first this provided some useful additional sales, when a downturn in the UK market took place the company found itself at the mercy of an inefficient and unsympathetic distributor. Territorial expansion therefore ceased to be an option and the company had to initiate a very expensive diversification programme into new products.

To summarise, the key questions in international marketing concern the following issues:

- Whether to sell abroad: geographical diversification may be more desirable than product diversification, depending of course on circumstances; however the decision to sell abroad should not be taken lightly.
- Where to sell abroad is one of the major decisions for international marketing; choosing foreign markets on the basis of proximity and similarity is not necessarily the most potentially profitable option to go for.
- What to sell abroad and the degree to which products should be altered to suit foreign needs is also one of the major problems of international marketing.
- How to sell abroad is concerned not just with the issue of how to enter a foreign market, but also with the management of the four 'P's once a company arrives. Finally, there is the difficult question of how to coordinate the marketing effort in many foreign countries.

■ Is Marketing Unethical?

In recent years, dissatisfaction has been expressed by increasingly large numbers of people at the structure of a society that seems to have consumption as both its means and its end. Capitalism presents an unacceptable face, some believe, inasmuch as it promotes the growth of an acquisitive and materialistic society.

In the late 1960s and early 1970s there was a growing consciousness of the problems that the age of mass consumption brought with it. A quite new awareness of alternatives that might be possible, indeed necessary, became apparent. This movement quickly found its chroniclers: books such as Charles Reich's *The Greening of America*, Alvin Toffler's *Future Shock* and Theodore Roszak's *The Making of a Counter Culture* appeared on book shelves throughout the world. The message articulated in these and other testaments of the movement was basically a simple one: that people could no longer be thought of as 'consumers', as some aggregate variable in the grand design of market planning. They were individuals intent on doing their own bidding.

Feelings such as these have led in the late 1980s and early 1990s to critical examination of commercial activity of all kinds. As one of the more visible manifestations of such activity, marketing has been singled out for special attention. One criticism frequently brought against marketing is that it plays on people's weaknesses. By insidious means, it is claimed, marketing attempts to persuade the consumer that he or she must smoke this brand of cigarette or use this brand of deodorant; that without them their lives are somehow incomplete. This argument involves the notion of the defenceless consumer, a person who is like clay in the hands of a wily marketer and thus in need of protection. Such a view of marketing tends to exaggerate the influence the marketer can bring to bear on the market place. It implies that consumers' powers of perception are limited in the extreme and that consumers' intelligence is minimal. It further suggests that skilful marketing can create needs.

This last point deserves close examination. Marketing may well be able to persuade people that they want a product; but that process should not be confused with creating a need. The sceptic might respond to this view by claiming, for example, that, 'Nobody wanted television before it was invented; now it is a highly competitive market. That market must have been created'. This argument confuses needs and wants. Clearly nobody wanted television before it was invented; but there has always been a need for home entertainment. Previously that need had been met by a piano, a book of parlour games, or something of that kind. Now technology has made available a further means of satisfying the basic need for domestic entertainment – television. Many consumers find that television better satisfies their need for home entertainment than did the piano.

A further example of how new technology can be used to extend an already existing market can be found in the spread of photocopying as the most common method of copying documents. The need to take copies of documents had already existed, but had been largely met by the use of carbon paper. When photocopying was introduced as an alternative, it was soon recognised that the new method had many advantages over the old and that it enabled consumer needs to be met more exactly.

In these examples, as so often, the role of marketing has been to identify in as much detail as possible what the customer needs and then to persuade him or her that a specific product or brand will provide the most effective means of satisfying the expressed need. Underlying this view of marketing is the belief that consumers have certain perceived buying problems. They have needs that can be satisfied only through the acquisition of specific goods and services. Consumers seek satisfactory solutions to their buying problems, first by acquiring information about available goods and services and their attributes, and eventually by choosing that product which comes closest to solving the problem.

Any argument that depends on a view of the defenceless consumer must be rejected by a scrupulous marketer. The consumer is still sovereign as long as he or she is free to make choices – either choices between competing products or the choice not to buy at all. Indeed it could be argued that by extending the range of choices that the consumer has available to him or her, marketing is enhancing consumer sovereignty rather than eroding it. It should be noted, too, that although promotional activity may persuade an individual to buy a product or service for the first time, promotion is unlikely to be the persuasive factor in subsequent purchases, when the consumer is acting from first-hand experience of the product. Although promotion may sell an unsatisfactory product the first time round, it cannot do so on future occasions.

Nevertheless, as we have observed, commercial activities of all kinds, including marketing, are being reappraised in the light of society's current criticisms. It is necessary, therefore, that we look very closely both at the ethics of marketing and at the kind of role that marketing assumes within the social and economic systems supporting it.

■ Some Ethical Concerns

Several specific issues have formed the focus of the debate on the ethics of marketing. The main issues to be discussed include marketing's contribution to materialism; rising consumer expectations as a result of marketing pressure; and the use of advertising to mislead or distort. Let us look at some of the arguments involved in these discussions.

Marketing, it has been suggested, helps feed and in turn feeds on the materialistic and acquisitive urges of society. Implicit in such criticism is the value judgement that materialism and acquisitiveness are in themselves undesirable. Whether or not one holds with this view, there would seem to be a case here that marketing must answer. The prosecution in the case would argue that marketing contributes to a general raising of the level of consumer expectations. These expectations are more than simple aspirations: they represent on the part of the consumer a desire to acquire a specific set of gratifications through the purchase of goods and services. The desire for these gratifications is fuelled by marketing's insistent messages. Further, if the individual lacks the financial resources with which to fulfil these expectations, then this inevitably adds to a greater awareness of differences in society and to dissatisfaction and unrest among those in this situation.

The counterargument that can be used here is that marketing itself does not contribute to rising expectations and thus to differences in society; it merely makes people aware of, and better informed about, the differences that already exist in society. Indeed the advocates of the cause of marketing could well claim that in this respect its effects are beneficial since it supports, even hastens, pressures for redistribution. The defence in this case could also usefully point out that materialism is not a recent phenomenon correlated with the advent of mass marketing.

Much of the criticism levelled at marketing is in fact directed at one aspect of it: advertising. Advertising practitioners themselves are fully conscious of these criticisms. One booklet published by the advertising agency, J. Walter Thompson, was entitled: 'Advertising – Is this the sort of work that an honest man can take pride in?'. Within that publication were summarised six of the major arguments used by the critics of advertising:

That advertising makes misleading claims about the product or service advertised.
That by implication or association it offers misleading promises of other benefits which purchase and use of the product will bring.
That it uses hidden, dangerously powerful techniques of persuasion.
That by encouraging undesirable attitudes it has adverse social effects.
That it works by the exploitation of human inadequacy.
That it wastes skills and talents which could be better employed in other jobs.

Supporters of advertising would point to the fact that advertising in all its forms is heavily controlled in most western societies, either by self-imposed codes (such as the British Code of Advertising Practice) or by legislation (such as the Trade Description Acts). It could also be claimed, on behalf of advertising, that you might be able to persuade people to buy something once through subtle advertising claims, but that sustained patterns of repeat purchase cannot be built up if the product itself is not perceived by the consumer to provide the gratifications he or she seeks. For example we might be persuaded that Martini is indeed 'The Right One', as its promoters claim, and we might give it a trial. However if it fails to do the things we want it to do (that is, meet the needs we wish to satisfy) we will quickly turn to drinking something else and/or seek to gratify our needs in another way.

The debate about the ethics of marketing often confuses marketing institutions with the people who work in them. Clearly there are dishonest business people who engage in activities that are detrimental to their fellow citizens. These activities include dubious trade practices, misleading advertising, unsafe products and various unethical practices that are harmful to consumers. However it seems a grave error to criticise marketing institutions because of the practices of a small number of unethical marketers. It is clear, for example, that there are advertisers who engage in deceptive practices designed to mislead and possibly defraud consumers. Nevertheless the institution of advertising can be used not only to inform consumers about potentially beneficial new products, such as new energy-saving technologies, but also to promote non-profit community services, such as theatres and symphonies. This argument can, of course, be applied to all marketing activities.

■ Marketing and Society

Any critical appraisal of marketing as an activity must take place within the context of the social and economic systems in which it is practised. A leading marketing scholar, the late Wroe Alderson, suggested the concept of marketing ecology as a useful approach to interpreting marketing's wider role. By this he meant the study of the continual adaptation of marketing systems to their environments; his suggestion was that the marketing systems in existence at any one time are simply reflections of the contemporary value system dominant in society. In systems technology, this approach would involve seeing marketing as an 'organised' behavioural system that sustains itself by drawing on the resources of the environment and survives only by adapting to changes in that environment. The environment represents not only the immediate surroundings of our customers and suppliers, but also the wider phenomena that are embodied in technological, ideological, moral and social dimensions.

The environment exerts a number of continual pressures on a marketing system. Technology alone constantly demands change in any marketing activity; shortening life-cycles in all product fields bear witness to its clamorous effects. Many commentators have claimed that the rate of technological development is one of the most forceful catalysts for marketing change. Even greater perhaps than this pressure, however, has been the impetus for change provided by a radically different moral and ideological climate in society at large. The basic purpose of business activities today has come to be questioned, and not only by those committed to alternative systems of exchange.

As has already been briefly discussed above, marketing has been caught up in the broader issue of the social responsibility of business. Although there is a wide range of opinion about the meaning of 'social responsibility', the implication is always that the organisation must look beyond the profit motive. Recent studies have shown that the vast majority of company executives acknowledge the interests of employees and consumers as well as the interests of shareholders. Executives are now being asked to acknowledge the interests of a 'fourth estate', that is, society.

Although unlikely to abandon the profit motive as the primary focus of their attention, company executives are now increasingly exploring ways of conducting business where 'social responsibility' is a salient criterion of success. The positive acknowledgement of the social dimension of corporate activity is likely to result in the deliberate use of marketing and marketing technology as an agent of social change. Already we have seen the adoption of a marketing approach by government agencies in attempts to gain participation in local planning decisions, to care for the countryside, to discourage the smoking of cigarettes, and so on.

When we talk about marketing, we are referring to more than just a set of techniques and procedures. We are alluding to an organised behavioural system that is constantly changing as it adapts to the evolving requirements of society. It is indeed the case that society gets the sort of marketing systems that it needs.

Closely connected to the issue of ethics of marketing, is the issue of consumerism.

■ Caveat Emptor

In a perfectly competitive market place, all the products or services offered by an organisation would meet the needs of its customers and consumers at the requisite level of profits. As the situation is at present, however, consumers complain with an increasingly strident voice about the way businesses operate. What conclusions are to be drawn from this? Are the major companies not based soundly on a marketing philosophy? Or are the strident voices not representative of the wishes of the vast majority of customers?

Consumerism, the name given to a wide spread of activities in the past decade, focuses our attention on the problem. Is marketing failing to do its job well, or are a small collection of agitators making something of nothing? The truth in most cases is probably to be found in the 80/20 rule: 80 per cent of the problem is poor marketing, and 20 per cent is populist agitation.

Traditionally it has been argued that a bad product will sell only once. Its customers will reject it after unsatisfactory performance, and any organisation that persists in offering such products or services cannot survive for long. Consumerists increasingly argue that a passive approach of this kind amounts to shutting the stable door after the horse has bolted. They usually want to see it made illegal for such products or services to be offered on the market in the first place. Most countries have passed a significant amount of legislation in support of this position. Up to the end of the nineteenth century the doctrine of 'caveat emptor' or 'purchaser beware' was widely accepted, although customers and consumers had always enjoyed a certain amount of protection as a result of regulations imposed on traders. However, since the end of the nineteenth century the responsibility for the quality of the product or service sold has fallen more and more on the shoulders of the vendor.

■ Caveat Vendor

In most countries within the EU today, customer groups have succeeded in obtaining massive legislative support. Sweden is perhaps the most extreme example, with its consumer ombudsman and market court. However the UK has its own director of fair trading and an impressive array of legislation, including the Competition Act, which became law in April 1980 and gives the director of fair trading increased powers of intervention. As an illustration of legislation that supports customers' rights we can perhaps take the concept of 'implied terms of sale'. In 1973 a statutory responsibility was laid upon a supplier of goods in the UK to ensure that any goods were indeed good for the purpose for which they were promoted and sold. This reversed the dictum 'caveat emptor', to 'caveat vendor', or 'seller beware'.

Although many business people resisted this trend, it is difficult to see why they should feel that a change of this kind damaged their interests. No marketer, surely, would doubt that trust was an important element in his or her relationship with a customer. That customer groups, or politicians with or without populist agitation, had to lobby and get laws passed to secure this sort of relationship with suppliers is an indictment of marketing activities throughout Europe and beyond.

The marketing of children's toys provides an example of how customers, consumers and company objectives can all be satisfied by careful business practice. The successful toy companies of today are those which inform parents that their products are not potentially dangerous, not coated with lead paint, and will not be destroyed the hour after they are first pressed into active service. Fisher-Price is one of the most successful toy manufacturers. Since 1968 it has eschewed child-manipulative promotion, carefully tested its products with children for durability, safety and purposeful play, and charged the prices necessary to make and market 'good' toys. Sales and profit margins are impressively good.

■ Consumerism's Way to Better Marketing

Consumerism is pro-marketing; it wants the marketing approach to business implemented in a sincere rather than cynical spirit. The cynical implementation that consumerists claim has been all too widely practised, is no better than high-pressure salesmanship or misleading puffery. The sincere implementation of the marketing approach entails respect for each individual customer. Indeed the consumerist argues eloquently that the sort of relationship found between a manufacturer and a customer in, say, a capital-goods market, should be created in consumer markets. And, insofar as that is both economically feasible and what the consumer really wants, marketers must surely want it also.

Broadly, consumerists argue that recognition of the following consumer rights would ensure that a more satisfactory relationship would be built up between organisation and customer (Figure 1.4).

The right to be informed of the true facts involved in any buyer–seller relationship is clearly a fundamental right. Some of the key aspects, which have already been subject to legislation or regulation in Europe, include the full cost of credit/loans taken up, often known as 'truth-in-lending'; the true cost of an item, under the slogan 'unit pricing'; the basic constituent elements of products,

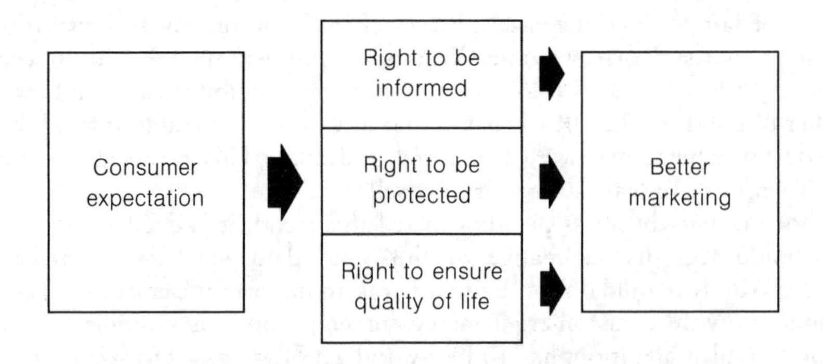

Figure 1.4 Consumerism's way to better marketing

known as 'ingredient informative labelling'; the freshness of foods, discussed generally as 'open-dating'; and 'truth-in-advertising'.

The case against producers is that they either mislead through exaggerated claims or fail to tell the whole truth about their products or services. Consumerists believe that the individual has the right to know these truths. Again, who can doubt that this demand, if sincerely felt, should be met? Who would be unwilling to tell an industrial purchaser the answer to basic questions about any merchandise offered for sale? What other information would our customers like?

The right to be protected is also a major plank in the consumerist platform. All too often at present, consumerists argue, consumers' trust in organisations is abused. Safety standards (which are monitored by government agencies) and the quality of medicines (which are subject to statutory controls) are exceptions that all businesses could learn from. It is certainly the case that the trend within the EU is for many more product fields to be affected by legislative controls. The consumerists' argument that manufacturers should assume liability for any malfunctioning of products offered in the market place would appear to have overwhelmed the opposition. In most cases, however, good marketing will go well beyond the minimum standards required – and will not be slow to tell the customer that it does so.

The right to ensure quality of life is perhaps the most difficult demand for the marketing activity to satisfy. Nonetheless, if a meaningful segment of the market needs to perceive the products it purchases as furthering the quality of life, then that is a need that should be respected. The non-biodegradability of packaging, for example, has been shown on occasion to offend substantial numbers of customers. If a sufficiently large group of these customers is prepared to meet an organisation's research and development costs, along with the costs involved in changing to a preferred alternative, then good marketing should lead the organisation to work with these customers towards a change in its methods of packaging.

It should be emphasised that none of these rights is unfamiliar to the marketer of industrial or consumer products. He or she has been accustomed to responding to similar demands. What is different today is that the process of marketing is no longer done on the initiative of the marketer in a framework of caveat emptor. The framework is no longer paternalistic. Today the customer works through representative institutions, even unions – and the cry is caveat vendor.

Consumerism will affect marketing by bringing into being a more informative approach to all forms of marketing communication. It must, and will, give rise to a greater integrity in the advertising and promotional puffery of our profession without, one hopes, making life too dull, too much like a company share-issue prospectus. It will give rise to a greater concern amongst all levels of business management with the long-term social implications of the materialistic bias of our society. Does the continual emphasis on immediate material expectations bear some responsibility for the level of delinquency in our society? What are the implications for tomorrow of our present pattern of usage of raw materials or pollution of the environment?

The consumerist argues that in present-day Europe we can certainly afford to trade off some of today's advantages for the longer-term interests of society.

■ Consumerism as an Opportunity

The social emphasis of consumerism, particularly its demands for an enhanced quality of life, is no threat to profitable enterprise. In considering this point, organisations might find it helpful to draw an analogy with changing attitudes to social factors at work. From the mid-nineteenth century, manufacturers were compelled by law to ensure that unsafe machinery was fenced in; considerable cost was, of course, incurred in carrying this out. Within the office, modern times have seen a concern to obtain office furniture and equipment designed to promote comfort at work; again, the introduction of such equipment has been an expensive business. It may well be that, in the long term, fewer accidents and a happier work force will help improve an organisation's overall profitability. Even if this does not happen, however, the organisation should bear in mind that society expects the cost of safety at work to be included in the price of a product or service. Consumerism, like safety at work, presents an opportunity to adjust its approach in accordance with changing social standards. As an articulate expression of customer needs, consumerism demands a marketing response.

Consumerism calls out for the reformulation and development of products and services to meet the requirements both of short-term satisfaction and longer-term benefits. A closer look must be taken at the system of marketing values that asserts that immediate consumer satisfaction and longer-term consumer welfare may be opposing goals for an organisation's marketing activity. It is now necessary – and good marketing practice – to promote products that provide consumers with both short- and long-term satisfaction.

In consumer-goods markets, for example, marketing specialists have devoted most of their efforts to promoting desirable and pleasing products. They have tended to ignore the long-term disadvantages to society that often accompany such products. Consumerism has reminded us vociferously of these disadvantages and, in a very real sense, has given us the opportunity to be better citizens. It is possible now to design and sell a motor car that is considerably safer than its equivalent in 1960. At that time attempts to sell safety were conspicuously unsuccessful, even though car makers emphasised safety factors in their promotional literature. It is possible now to design and sell an effective flameproof fabric for children's wear because an awareness of the need for it has been created. Consumerism, in other words, opens up market opportunities that the astute marketing-based organisation will wish to take up. Other examples that can be cited are phosphate-free detergents, lead-free petrol, degradable plastic containers for a host of products, synthetic tobaccos, new nutrient-based breakfast cereals and low-polluting manufacturing systems.

The articulate customer movement known as consumerism is here to stay as a force acting on organisations in their market place. If respectfully used, it can provide a significant further input of information in the process of matching the resources of the organisation with the needs of its customers.

■ Summary

For many years marketing was thought by many to be just another word for 'selling' or, at best, an activity that was appropriate for fast-moving consumer goods but not for the world of industrial products. Recently, however, this attitude has changed and there is now a greater recognition of the fundamental importance of marketing as the keystone for business success. Marketing, as we have seen, is more than simply 'giving the customer what he or she wants'. It requires a clear understanding of the asset base of the business and the means whereby it can differentiate itself from its competitors.

The process of marketing is universally applicable, irrespective of whether it takes place in consumer, service, or international contexts. There are merely some important differences in emphasis to be noted.

The ethics of marketing were discussed, along with consumerism. The conclusion reached is that consumerism offers nothing but opportunities to the firm that puts the interests of the customer at the centre of their business philosophy.

The remainder of this book focuses upon the frameworks and techniques through which the marketing concept can be made a reality in your business.

CHAPTER 2

Managing Marketing

There are two major facets to marketing: firstly there is marketing as an orientation and a philosophy, and secondly there is marketing as a set of tasks and actions. The difference is between creating a marketing *culture* within the organisation on the one hand, and managing the marketing *function* on the other. The responsibility for creating and maintaining the marketing culture is essentially that of the chief executive, for it is he or she who sets the style within the organisation. However, the responsibility for managing and controlling the marketing function will normally require the attention of designated executives with specific skills.

This chapter is concerned with the marketing management process and with the issues and challenges facing the marketing executive. How does a marketing-oriented company take the concept of marketing and turn it into a reality?

The Marketing Mix

Perhaps the most fundamental task of the marketing executive is the management of the *marketing mix*. The marketing mix is the name given to the main *demand-influencing variables* that are available to the company. The classic description of the marketing mix, although something of a simplification, is as the four 'P's. What are the four 'P's?

- *Product*: What decisions relate to the product or service range?
- *Price*: What price should we set for each product or service?
- *Promotion*: How do we communicate with our target market and persuade them to buy our offer?
- *Place*: What channels of distribution, what levels of service, are appropriate?

Each of these elements is capable of influencing demand either separately or together with the other marketing-mix elements. Later chapters in this book will explore each marketing-mix element in more detail, but at this stage it is appropriate to look at some of the general principles underlying decisions on the actual marketing mix that a company might choose to implement.

■ Product/Service

Although customers and their needs are the focal point of the marketing process, few companies started with this in mind. Invariably somebody had a good idea for a product or service and this became the germ of the business idea.

Not surprisingly, then, many businesses see the product or service to be at the heart of the firm's marketing efforts. There may be nothing intrinsically wrong with this attitude as long as business people can see that their product or service does not have to remain as a fixed, unchanging entity – a sort of organisational straitjacket.

Instead, the company must learn to see its output as flexible, being subject to development and adaptation, just like any other component of the market mix. Because the business world is never static the company should keep asking itself the question: 'Does each product/service we offer provide relevant and desired benefits for today's customers' needs?'

Furthermore, it should not mislead itself into thinking that customers buy the product or service as an end in itself. They do not; they buy a whole package of things when they make a purchase. Here are just some of the factors that make up the 'product package':

- Technical features
- Packaging
- Design
- Image
- Functional performance
- Quality
- Availability
- Reputation
- Before-sales service
- After-sales service
- Range of sizes, colours, and so on
- Running costs
- Ease of maintenance
- Ease of use
- Training provided/simple instructions
- Compatibility with existing equipment/services
- Safety
- Pollution hazard reduction

Clearly there is more to a product or service than meets the eye. You cannot force customers to buy your product or service, they must *want* the benefits the purchase will bring them. For companies, this means finding out what particular benefits are wanted by different customer segments. Then the company should choose its customers rather than wait for customers to choose them. It is this knowledge that enables a company to offer a more attractive 'package' than its competitors. This might or might not mean modifying the actual product or service itself.

■ Price

Pricing is an area of marketing with a tremendous potential for increasing short-term profits, but unfortunately if it is done badly it can equally quickly bring a business to its knees.

Is pricing an art or a science? The short answer is that it is probably a bit of both, as we shall see when we come to examine pricing in more detail later. For now, let us just consider what options are open to us for using pricing as a flexible 'connector' that helps to match our efforts to the needs of the customers.

There is a fear amongst many business people that unless they offer the lowest possible price they will not win the order. Whilst this can be true for some businesses, it is rarely the case with market leaders. Take the case of the really successful builder who has built his reputation on quality workmanship. His business continues to thrive and prosper, whilst many other builders with poorer reputations have gone bankrupt through quoting low prices to get a job and then doing poor-quality work to make it pay.

Also, take the example of the housewife who prefers to buy goods from a local shop rather than a supermarket where she can get them at a cheaper price. Why? Quite apart from the convenience factor, she knows she can get personal service from her local shop.

As we suggested earlier, the customer buys a 'package' of benefits and the price ought to reflect the value of the *total package*.

Clearly, price is an important element of the business transaction and, appropriately chosen, it can have not only a big impact on a company's marketing strategy in the long term but can also help to differentiate the product or service from those of competitors.

■ Promotion

The promotion element of the marketing mix is concerned with how to communicate with customers and potential customers. In practice the promotion element of the marketing mix falls into two broad categories:

- Personal promotion (face-to-face dealing with customers)
- Impersonal promotion (for example advertising, sales promotion)

□ *Personal Promotion*

This is the role of selling, which might be accomplished through a sales force. Face-to-face selling has a number of advantages over impersonal methods:

- It is a two-way process that gives the prospective purchaser the opportunity to ask questions about the product or service.
- The sales message can be tailored to the needs of individual customers.
- The salesperson can use his in-depth knowledge about product or service to identify new customer needs and overcome objections.
- The salesperson can ask for an order.
- The salesperson can negotiate price, delivery or special requirements.
- The salesperson can build a relationship with customers and thereby lay the foundations for longer-term business.

However, selling also involves a lot of 'dead' time such as preparing sales aids, phoning for appointments, travelling, failing to win an order, administration and research. Therefore it is a costly business, and needs to be regularly monitored to ensure that it provides a good return for the cost and effort that goes into it.

□ *Impersonal Promotion*

Typically, this area of promotion takes the form of advertising and sales promotion.

Advertising Many companies believe that this is the province of only the very large companies and that it is something best left to the 'experts'. It doesn't have to be like this. Rather than looking at advertising as a *cost*, look upon it as an *investment*; like any other investment it is only going to be any good if it makes money for you.

Spots on television or billboards throughout the country; local radio; leaflets, brochures, stories in the papers and trade journals; cards on newspaper display boards; advertisements in the local paper, yellow pages and local buses, and on gifts such as calendars and pens are all examples of advertising. Even a company's letterheads and the appearance of its vans or trucks convey something about itself.

All advertising needs to address itself to these questions:

- At whom is it aimed? (target customers)
- What should it say? (message)
- How should the message be communicated? (medium)
- How will the result be measured?

These questions can only be answered if a company has a good understanding of its customers and potential customers – what interests them, what would motivate them to buy and what they are likely to read.

Although the various advertising media mentioned above vary in terms of their costs and potential for reaching customers, we can see that combinations of message and media will provide a company with a very flexible advertising repertoire – one that can be tailored to fit your budget.

Sales promotions Sales promotions are essentially short-term campaigns to influence customers (perhaps a competitor's customers, or even intermediaries) to buy more of your product or to use it faster. Some companies use promotions to encourage their own salesforce to sell more.

Generally, promotions take the form of offering a *money* incentive, such as a price reduction or coupon against next purchase, *goods* such as two for the price of one, or *services* such as free estimates and holidays.

■ Place

As we have indicated, the essential task of marketing is to match a firm's resources to customer needs in a way that gives satisfaction to both parties. However it also means that companies have to search continuously for something that will give them a competitive advantage. We have looked briefly at how this might be achieved in the other parts of the marketing mix, but how might it be done in the frequently overlooked area of making goods or services available in the right place and at the right time?

A market gardener started a business of farming organically-grown vegetables. Immediately he was faced with several different ways of getting them to the consumer, some direct, some through intermediaries.

- Producer — 'pick your own' — consumer
- Producer — farm shop — consumer
- Producer — mail order — consumer
- Producer — specialist shops — consumer
- Producer — wholesaler — retailers — consumer
- Producer — restaurants — consumer
- Producer — health farms — consumer

This example also gives a good illustration of the 'place' element of the marketing mix and how that needs to be integrated with delivery and consignment 'packaging'.

Clearly the cheapest channel is 'pick your own', where getting the consumer to come along to bear the harvesting costs will save the farmer money. But suppose that doesn't appeal to people in his catchment area, or suppose he is in a sparsely populated area? A farm shop would have the advantage of appealing to passing trade as well as to regular customers, but distribution costs are already escalating.

On analysis each option offers commercial possibilities; equally, each one involves costs. Also within any particular channel there are areas for cost management. For example, with the penultimate option, should the farmer deliver to the restaurants or should they collect from him?

The essential decision for the company is to decide on distribution channels that give it a sizeable element of control at a reasonable cost. It might also want to safeguard its interests by using more than one channel to reach different customer segments. The choice of channel can also help the company to differentiate its product. A classic example of this was when Avon Cosmetics took their products into the home of the consumer, while the competition continued to trade in department stores and chemists.

Many firms make the mistake of sticking to the traditional distribution channels they know best, even though new channels are opening up all around them. The message is clear. The company must keep an open mind about distribution channels. It should evaluate its existing channels on a regular basis, and not be afraid of investigating or experimenting with new ones.

■ Programming the Marketing Mix

At the outset of this chapter we identified marketing's role as ensuring that the four 'P's – product, price, promotion and place – were successfully managed. Success means that the customer is satisfied and that the organisation's resources are effectively deployed to that end.

Marketing's job is to generate the right mix of sales to customers at the right price, with the right promotion, and at the right time and place. This means that the marketing department must be organised in such a way that these are appropriately mixed together and properly and effectively coordinated in a marketing plan. Later chapters of the book will explore the components of the marketing mix in detail.

Not only must each of the four 'P's be managed separately, but also as they interact with each other in the marketing mix. Furthermore, an adequate answer in terms of a specific mix for this year's marketing problems is unlikely to be adequate for next year's. Products will be improved or made obsolete, new ones launched; prices will need to change; promotion can be upstaged or drowned out; the place of sale can become less satisfactory as alternative opportunities and challenges develop. For example, to what extent might a higher price with more effective promotion improve the overall profit contribution and what effect will this have on market share? To what extent can increased stock availability more than recoup the extra costs in terms of sales and profits? These are marketing-mix problems.

To wrestle with such mix problems and to plan for and implement such solutions most medium-sized and large organisations establish a marketing department and appoint someone to coordinate all such activities at director or boardroom level. This is the role of the marketing function.

To compound the problem of identifying the appropriate marketing mix there are a series of fundamental changes that have taken place in the competitive environment. These changes present significant challenges to the way in which marketing strategies are formulated.

The Challenges to the Corporation

The market place has never been static, and the need to anticipate and respond to change has been a basic prerequisite for survival since business first began. However it can fairly be said that marketing management today faces a greater number of challenges of a more complex nature and from a wider number of sources. Let us examine some of these challenges.

The Impact of Technology

Whilst it has become something of a cliché to refer to the quickening pace of technological change, there is no denying its impact on marketing. The introduction of new technology will tend to render obsolete that which it succeeds. Products based upon yesterday's technology will normally die. Thus the impact of a faster rate of technological change is to reduce dramatically the viable life of a product. In other words, technological change affects the product life-cycle.

An example of this is provided by the typewriter. The mechanical typewriter had a life-cycle of thirty years; in other words a model introduced in 1920 would still be available, little-changed, in 1950. Electromechanical typewriters had a life-cycle of ten years, electronic typewriters five years and now word processors one or two years.

Technology development tends to follow the classic 'S-shaped' curve, with especially rapid change taking place after a period of relatively little development. Similarly this period of rapid change is followed by a period of little change before the next quantum step onto the next S-curve. Figure 2.1 illustrates such a progression in the development of lighting technology.

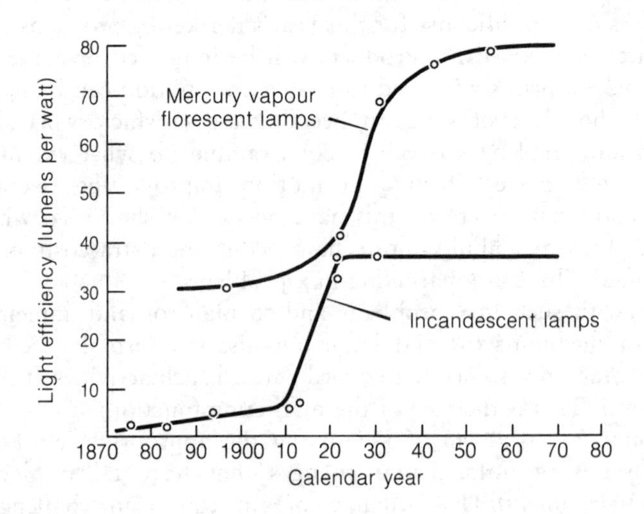

Figure 2.1 S-curves and technology change

The electronics industry provides many examples of shortening life-cycles where technology changes follow each other rapidly. For example from 1964 to 1976 IBM only introduced two families of mainframe computers. As technology changed so did the rate of new product introduction – there were four in the period 1976 to 1980. In the electronic calculator market Hewlett-Packard did not begin selling calculators until 1972 but the technology evolved so quickly (232 models in eight years) that calculators had entered their mature phase by 1980.

It is not only in electronics and advanced engineering that the effect of technology is felt. Video games, which took companies such as Atari to dizzy levels of profitability, dropped rapidly in popularity as 'new generation' electronic games were introduced by companies such as Nintendo.

Clearly marketing in a period of rapid technology change needs to be far more responsive, far quicker to spot trends and take decisions than in those markets where change is relatively slow.

■ The Fragmentation of Markets

In the past we used to talk of the 'mass market'. In other words there was a large volume demand for a standard product. The Model T Ford is perhaps the classic example of a product aimed at such a market. Now though, through wider choice, greater disposable income and customers seeking greater individuality, we have seen the replacement of the mass market with a highly-fragmented market based upon distinct segments and niches. Later in the book we will discuss market segmentation in greater detail, but in essence the idea is that the majority of markets comprise a number of 'sub-markets' which are characterised by customers that share common characteristics. Some of these segments might be distinguished by the age or sex of their customers; in industrial markets it might be by the size of company or the end use of their products. Often it will be the case that a market segment is best described by more than a single dimension.

The basic principle of segmentation, however, is that the greatest chance of market success will occur through the careful matching of the precise needs of that customer group with a 'tailored' marketing mix of product, price, promotion and place.

In consumer markets it has been suggested that there has been a fundamental change in the 'shape' of the market. Figure 2.2(a) depicts the market as it was in the immediate postwar years when customers were first confronted with consumer marketing as we then knew it. This was the era of 'keeping up with the Jones' and the almost universal desire to acquire a TV, a family car and, perhaps, the first package holiday. In the thirty years or so that have followed that era we have seen a greater concern on the part of consumers to express their own individual aspirations through purchases that reflect that individuality. Figure 2.2(b) suggests that the mass market has been 'squeezed' to produce a diversity of fragmented niche markets. There still remains a

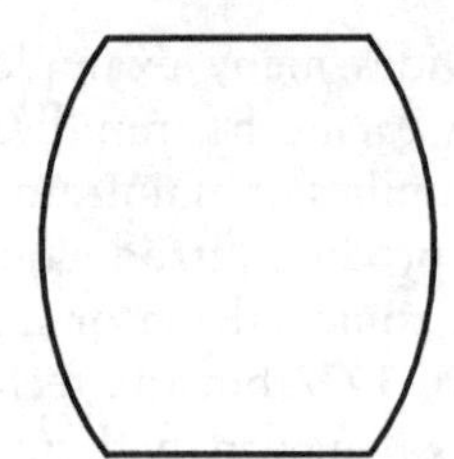

(a) The mass market

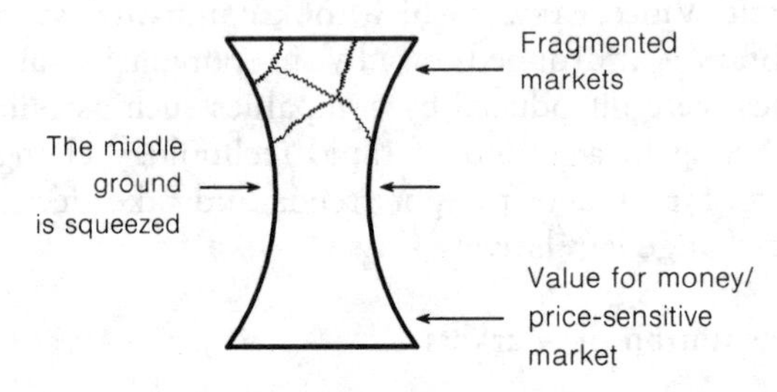

(b) The polarised market

Figure 2.2 The change in consumer markets

sizeable market for 'value for money' at one end of the spectrum, but at the other end we see a multitude of customer requirements, each different from the other. Nowhere is this better typified than in the retail fashion market, with stores that cater specifically for particular age groups, life-styles and income groups.

This phenomenon is not limited to consumer markets. In industrial and service markets we see a similar pattern. There is no mass market for industrial lubricants or for robotics but instead very precisely expressed requirements for specification, for service and for price.

The challenge in today's market place is therefore quite different from that of the 1950s, the 1960s, the 1970s and even the 1980s. The name of the game today is variety.

■ The Globalisation of Markets

One of the major characteristics of the late twentieth century is the trend towards the globalisation of markets. Whilst the global brand is commonplace, for example Coca-Cola, Marlboro cigarettes and IBM computers, the phenomenon of the global company is more a reflection of the drive for economies of scale and scope than of a growing convergence of customer requirements.

A global company is more than a multinational company. In the global business materials and components are sourced world-wide, manufactured offshore and sold in many different countries, perhaps with local customisation.

Such is the trend towards globalisation that it is probably safe to forecast that by the year 2000 most markets will be dominated by global corporations. The only role left for national companies will be to cater for specific and unique local demands, for example in the food industry.

The global corporation seeks to achieve competitive advantage by identifying world markets for its products and then developing a manufacturing and distribution strategy to support its marketing strategy. So a company such as Caterpillar Tractor, for example, has dispersed assembly facilities to key overseas markets. It uses global logistics channels to supply parts to offshore assembly plants and aftermarkets. Where appropriate Caterpillar will use 'third-party' companies to manage distribution and even final finishing. So, for example, in the US a third party company, Leaseway Transportation, in addition to providing parts inspection and warehousing, actually attaches options to fork-lift trucks. Wheels, counterweights, forks and masts are installed as specified by Caterpillar. Thus local market needs can be catered for from a standardised production process.

Even in a geographically compact area such as the EU we find that there is still a significant need for local customisation. A frequently cited example is the difference in preference for washing machines. The French prefer top-loading machines; the British go for front-loaders; the West Germans prefer high-speed spins but the Italians prefer a lower speed! In addition there are differences in electrical standards and differences in distribution channels. In the UK most washing machines are sold through national chains specialising in white goods. In Italy white goods are sold through a profusion of small retailers and customers bargain over price.

The challenge to a global company such as Electrolux, therefore, is how to achieve the cost advantage of standardisation whilst still catering for the local demand for variety. Electrolux is responding to that challenge by seeking to standardise parts, components and modules and then through flexible manufacture and local assembly to provide the specific products demanded by end markets.

■ Time-based Competition

Perhaps the greatest change to impact upon the business environment in recent years has been the growing demand by the customer for service. This phenomenon is explored in detail in Chapter 19, but one particular facet justifies a mention now.

Put very simply, today's customer has become time-sensitive. Because the level of competition in most markets is greater than it was, and because substitutes are almost always available, the customer is not prepared to wait. If the shop is out of stock of Heinz Baked Beans only the most brand-loyal customer would look in other stores or would agree to come back in a week's time! Research shows that most customers in situations like this simply reach out for a competitive brand or even an own label. In service markets, such as hotels, car-hire firms or hairdressers, almost by definition the customer wants immediate gratification with minimal waiting time. In industrial markets the picture is the same – a car manufacturer operating 'just-in-time' assembly lines will only carry a few hours of stock of components and will therefore insist that its suppliers provide delivery on time.

Recognising the importance of time and convenience, companies such as Federal Express, Domino's Pizzas and Tie Rack have developed strong competitive positions. Another example is provided by Benetton, the Italian-based global fashion manufacturer and retailer.

Benetton's order system is 'just-in-time' as production runs are not started until orders have been received. A key aspect of its system is the dyeing of knitted goods after production, rather than dyeing yarn prior to knitting. This allows Benetton outlets to delay commitment to particular colours until later in the production cycle. Since each selling season typically begins with about ten alternative colours, with only about three usually resulting in high demand, the delay in colour choice affords Benetton an opportunity to respond directly to market demand. A retail information system provides valuable information to Benetton for production planning via daily feedback on sales. This updates production on current demand, upon which replenishment schedules for designs and colours may be used. The timeliness of this order data is crucial since popular colours will often sell out in the first ten days of a new season. This rapid response system gives Benetton a competitive edge over the less responsive competitors. Further, Benetton uses CAD/CAM (computer-aided design/computer-aided manufacturing) for design and cutting in order to respond to dynamic demand as rapidly as possible. Finally, the company's marketing strategy promotes simple colour fashion with heavy advertising support, which in turn maximises the benefits from the flexible production process.

Meeting the Challenge

We have indicated just a few of the challenges that face marketing in the closing years of the twentieth century. What should be the response?

The common element in each of the challenges we have discussed has been *change* and in particular the speed of that change. This change has been influenced by technology, by market fragmentation, by globalisation and by customer demands for service. The marketing response therefore has to be appropriate; specifically the marketing organisation of the 1990s must be tuned in to the market and be highly sensitive to trends. It must be capable of fast reaction to those trends and it must be global in its reach.

How might the organisation acquire these characteristics?

Monitoring and Researching the Market

Later in this book we will explore the marketing environment in detail. However, a prerequisite for monitoring environmental change is an effective marketing information system. The use of market research on an ongoing basis is vital to an understanding of the changing requirements of the customer.

The nature of business necessitates that the future is under constant review and is taken into account in forward planning. Markets are perhaps one of the most difficult business areas to forecast because there can be so many variables affecting them. They can be influenced by government legislation, competition, new technology, the economy at large and changing fashions. However, the fact that movements in markets can be more volatile and unpredictable than movements in other areas is not a justification for avoiding methodical analytical techniques. Equally, we might have to recognise when situations defy strict analysis, or the cost of in-depth research would be prohibitive. Then we must fall back to using our best judgement but still, hopefully, in a focused and methodical manner.

Herman Kahn, the American 'futurologist', is quoted as saying 'The only good thing about the future is that it comes one day at a time'. In order that – even at this speed – it doesn't arrive before the company is ready for it, the marketer must develop forecasting procedures that generate a high level of confidence in the prognosis.

Instinctively we know many of the questions to which we seek answers:

- Who are the customers?
- What are they buying?
- Where are they buying?
- When are they buying?
- Why do they buy from us?
- If they didn't buy from us from whom would they buy?
- Are our customers growing or shrinking as a 'group'?
- What are the general growth trends in the total market?
- How do our customers perceive us?
- What threats might change the market situation?
- What new opportunities are beginning to emerge?

Most of these questions can only be answered properly if we have knowledge about our customers, their behaviour, their beliefs and their reaction to our marketing effort. As we have stressed, the whole basis of the marketing concept is grounded in the notion that the profitable development of the company can be ensured only through a constant attempt to match the capabilities of the company to the needs of the customers. So that these needs may be identified, and the suitability of the company's market offering assessed, it is necessary that some type of information flow should be instituted between the customer and the company.

The key task facing the researcher is to understand what sort of decisions require what sort of information. At its simplest, we can identify three levels of marketing decisions that could require an investment in terms of market research:

- Information for strategic, long-term decisions.
- Information for tactical, short-term decisions.
- Information for specific, one-off marketing problems.

The first two situations require a continuous *ongoing* input of market information, whereas the last needs a speedy, *ad hoc* response from the market researcher.

Today the more sophisticated companies have set up systems that provide their executives with market intelligence on a weekly and sometimes even daily basis. They will be provided with information about the level of sales, by product or by market area; levels of inventory throughout the distribution channels; work in progress; trend data and market-share estimates. Very often all this information existed previously within the organisation, but in a fragmented and uncoordinated form. By constructing a *market intelligence system* (MIS) it is possible to provide management with a *data bank* that is designed to meet clearly specified information needs.

Companies that take this route need not limit their MIS to the analysis of current and historical data. Now it is becoming possible to incorporate data about customer attitudes and competitor activity, for example, alongside the more conventional information. Using on-line search facilities it is possible for even the smallest company to access commercial data bases covering every aspect of market information.

The benefits arising from an integration of marketing information through a formal MIS lie chiefly in the 'direction' that is given to otherwise uncoordinated data. The requirements for such a system do not necessarily imply the use of a computer, although of course the power and flexibility of any MIS can be greatly enhanced by such means.

However, for the system to work well, management must be clear about the decisions they have to make and define their information needs, both those that are ongoing as well as *ad hoc*. Without this step being taken much valuable time and effort will be wasted.

■ 'Fast Track' Marketing

It will be apparent that with the rate of technology change and the reduction in the length of the product life-cycle companies can no longer proceed at a leisurely pace from product development through to product launch.

Figure 2.3 reflects the penalty of lost profit and obsolete stock that has to be carried by the company that is slow to market.

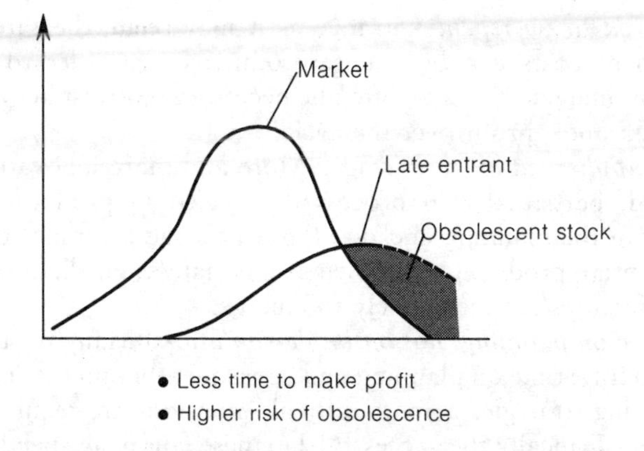

Figure 2.3 Shorter life-cycles make timing crucial

In this case the product was launched too late into a short life-cycle market and was only becoming established as the market for that technology or product variant was turning down. For example, with personal computers, where the market cycle for a particular technology may only be eighteen months, to get to the market six months late means a one-third reduction in profit opportunity.

To respond to this challenge many organisations have focused on reducing the time taken from the drawing board to the market place. Some of the best examples come from Japan, where companies such as Honda, Canon, NEC and Fuji Xerox have been able to reduce dramatically the new product development process. In the West there are other good examples of fast response. IBM, although a late entrant into the personal computer market, made up for lost time by halving the usual industry product development time. Compaq, also in the personal computer market, even beat IBM by creating new machines in less than a year. In Europe companies such as Philips, Volvo and Rolls-Royce have also successfully driven down the time to market.

What are the differences in approach that 'fast track' marketing requires?

There seem to be a number of basic lessons to be learned from the companies who have mastered this new style of marketing.

- *Manage in parallel, not sequentially.* Instead of product design, engineering, market testing and manufacturing following one after the other, they work together – thus eliminating delays and identifying problems at an early stage.
- *Use multidisciplinary venture teams.* Clearly related to the previous lesson is the idea of the venture team. IBM developed its personal computer by putting a multidisciplinary team together and gave them complete autonomy to bring the product to market.

- *Be prepared to overspend.* Strange as it may seem, the careful control of development costs can be counterproductive. In order to speed up the process of innovation it may often be necessary to invest heavily at the front end to guarantee profit over the cycle.
- *Involve suppliers at an early stage.* More and more innovation is supplier-originated, particularly in processes but also in products. By involving suppliers in the planning and development stage leadtimes can be reduced and potential production problems eliminated. Furthermore, innovative product features are more likely to emerge.
- *Spend time on planning, not on implementation.* Many western companies spend too little time on planning and consequently find that implementation of marketing strategies is more difficult, revisions are required and failures are higher. Typically the successful Japanese company spends longer at the planning stage, but once the decision is taken there is immediate action – no committees, no steering groups, no bureaucracy.

■ Make Strategic Alliances

The challenge posed by globalisation presents a major problem, particularly to companies who are not established on the international scene. It may not always be feasible or appropriate for such companies to contemplate overseas expansion – and yet that will be the price of survival in the years ahead. Acquisition or merger may also be neither possible nor desirable.

Many companies in recent years have instead sought out global partners with whom they can form *strategic alliances*. The purpose of these alliances is to create complementary portfolios of marketing skills. This is a development on the old idea of 'synergy', or the '2 + 2 = 5' effect. Sometimes the alliance may be more concerned to share technology, as in the case of the Rover Group and Honda, or ICL and Fujitsu. However strategic alliances can also be effective in extending global market coverage. So, for example, British Airways was able to have an enhanced market presence in the USA through its strategic alliance with US Air. The alliance offered an alternative to takeover or merger, which in any case was not permitted under US law. More recently, other British Airways alliances include one with Qantas. Under such arrangements, passengers enjoy shared terminals as well as coordinated schedules and joint pricing.

Similar strategic alliances include SAS and Continental Airlines in the USA and between KLM, Air UK and Northwest Airlines, also in the USA, so giving airlines greater presence in parts of the world previously less accessible to them.

Whilst these examples are all of companies of substantial size they provide guidelines for others. The general principle of the strategic alliance is to seek out opportunities to enhance and extend marketing skills on a global scale.

■ Summary

In this chapter we have explained the concept of the *marketing mix* and looked in brief detail at the component elements of that mix. We also highlighted the particular challenges that the company must confront that emanate from technology, market fragmentation, globalisation and the 'time-sensitivity' of markets.

The ultimate task of marketing management is to construct a strategy for the marketing mix such that it is capable of overcoming these challenges to achieve competitive advantage.

CHAPTER 3

Relationship Marketing

Whilst it has long been acknowledged that the fundamental purpose of marketing is the 'getting and keeping of customers', the truth is that more attention has been paid, typically, to attracting customers than to keeping them. More recently there has emerged a recognition that marketing needs to encompass not only those activities necessary to capture business in the first place, but also to develop processes that will enhance long-term customer loyalty. This viewpoint is the foundation for the development of the concept of relationship marketing, at the heart of which lies the proposition that the fundamental purpose of marketing is the creation and development of long-term, profitable relationships with customers.

It should not be thought that relationship marketing is a replacement for marketing as it has been practised to date. Rather it is an augmentation and a refocusing of the marketing concept with the emphasis placed upon strategies to enhance customer retention and loyalty. Some of the major differences in emphasis between the traditional approach, which we label 'transactional', and the 'relationship' focus are shown in Table 3.l.

Table 3.1 The shift to relationship marketing

Transactional focus	*Relationship focus*
• Orientation to single sales	• Orientation to customer retention
• Discontinuous customer contact	• Continuous customer contact
• Focus on product features	• Focus on customer value
• Short time scale	• Long time scale
• Little emphasis on customer service	• High customer service emphasis
• Limited commitment to meeting customer exceptions	• High commitments to meeting customer expectations
• Quality is the concern of production staff	• Quality is the concern of all staff

It will be seen from Table 3.1 that the major difference between the relationship focus and the transactional focus is the emphasis upon continuous commitment to meeting the needs of individual customers, and that service and quality are particularly stressed.

Many marketing practitioners might justifiably protest that they have been practising relationship marketing for years but did not realise it! In truth, however, many others have failed to recognise the importance of customer loyalty as a driver of profitability and hence have tended to concentrate their effort on a single-minded pursuit of market share. Relationship marketing as a philosophy is concerned with the 'quality' of market share, not just its absolute level, in other words the minimisation of customer defections and the building of long-term partnerships with customers who willingly repeat purchase from us.

■ Marketing as a Process

One of the distinguishing characteristics of the relationship marketing approach is that it places the emphasis upon the need to take a cross-functional, business-wide approach to customer satisfaction. It sees marketing as a process rather than a function. Figures 3.1(a) and (b) highlight this difference.

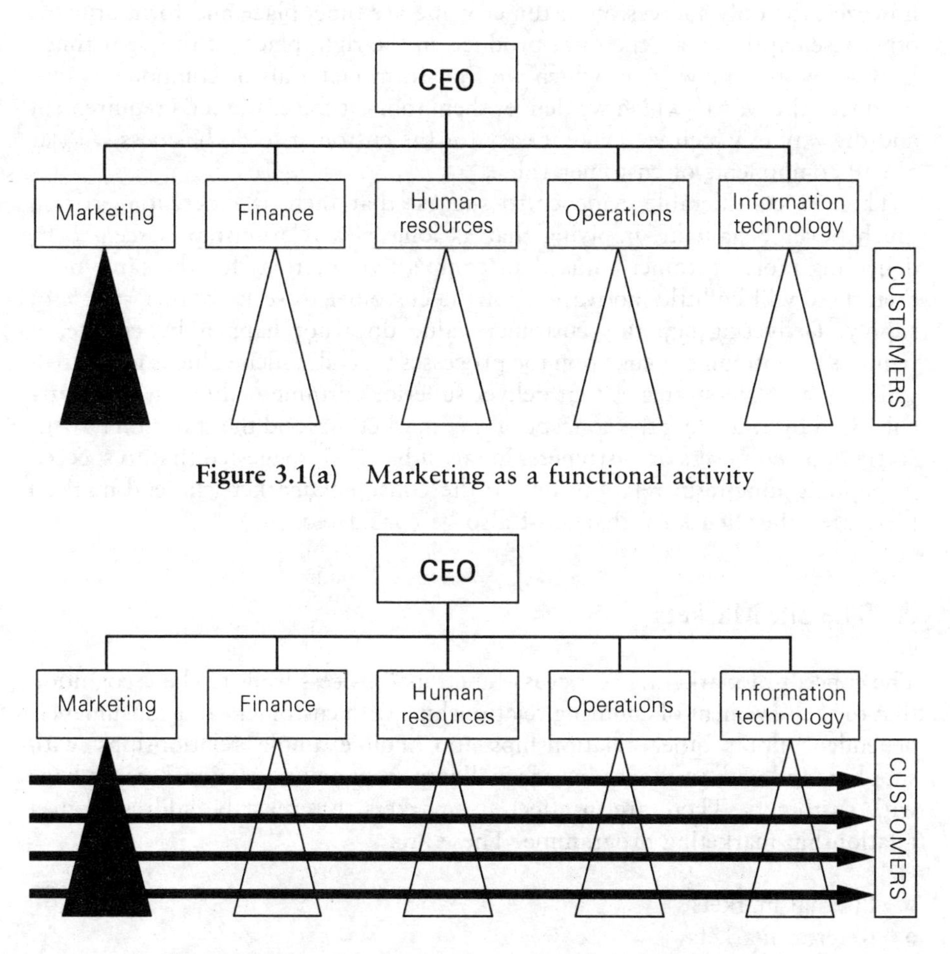

Figure 3.1(a) Marketing as a functional activity

Figure 3.1(b) Marketing as a cross-functional activity

Clearly there will always be a requirement for the marketing function to manage such tasks as advertising, market research, pricing, and so forth. However overlaying the traditional vertical organisation are a number of cross-functional processes that must be managed if the business is to be truly market-facing.

These processes include such activities as new product development, order fulfilment (that is, the physical satisfaction of demand), marketing planning and the management of customer relationships. Obviously this view of marketing has many implications for the organisational structure of the business and these issues are further addressed in Chapter 21.

A fundamental aspect of marketing processes is that they add customer value. What this means is that the product or service on offer becomes more attractive to the customer because of the way we do things. Customer value is perceptual and different customers clearly will place value on different things. Essentially, however, the only sources of customer value are time, place and form utilities, otherwise expressed as 'the right product, in the right place, at the right time'. In other words the ways in which we transform materials or components into products, the way in which we deliver them to meet the customer's requirement and the way in which we make it easy for the customer to do business with us are all components of customer value.

There is considerable evidence to suggest that there is inherent inertia in much buyer behaviour, implying that as long as a relationship is seen to be delivering more customer value than competitive offerings for the same price then there will be little motivation for the customer to seek another source of supply. Delivering superior customer value does not happen by chance, it requires a continuing focus upon the processes whereby such value is generated.

This search for strategies that deliver superior customer value can be greatly enhanced by extending the concept of the 'market' beyond the traditional focus solely upon end-users or customers. In fact it has been suggested that to succeed in building long-term relationships in the consumer market (the end-market) there are other 'markets' that must also be considered.

■ The Six Markets

The concept of marketing as a cross-functional process leads to the recognition that the achievement of enduring relationships with customers and consumers is dependent upon other relationships too. For example relationships with suppliers and with employees clearly will impact upon the relationships we have with customers. There are in effect six markets that must be addressed in a relationship marketing programme. These are:

- Internal markets
- Referral markets
- Influencer markets

- Employee markets
- Supplier markets
- Customer markets

Internal Markets

There is now widespread recognition that one of the major determinants of marketing success is the existence of a strongly felt and unanimously accepted 'corporate culture' within the business. Sometimes this set of commonly held beliefs is termed 'shared values', reflecting the commitment to customers subscribed to by the entire workforce.

The creation of such a culture requires vision and leadership at every level in the organisation, but it also requires open channels of internal communication. This is the realm of internal marketing. An internal marketing programme should seek to inform and motivate all the members of the organisation towards defined goals of customer satisfaction. If an internal, service-oriented 'climate' can be generated and sustained then the evidence is that customer satisfaction is more likely to result.

Seminars, workshops, team-building exercises, continuous and good two-way communication channels, newsletters, quality-improvement groups and, above all, a focus upon the idea that everybody in the organisation has a 'customer', are the ingredients of a successful internal marketing programme.

Referral Markets

The power of word-of-mouth is substantial. A recommendation from a respected source is often worth more than any media advertisement. Referrals can also come from sources of professional advice such as doctors, lawyers, bank managers and accountants as well as from existing satisfied customers.

Referral markets are often difficult to identify but a start can be made by asking new customers what influenced them to purchase from us. Referral markets must be researched and the factors that influence their recommendations must be clearly understood. Specific communication programmes with these sources of referrals should be developed.

Existing customers can be encouraged to act as 'recruiting agents' for the business. Often a small incentive is all that is needed to persuade a satisfied customer to encourage others also to patronise the business. Once again, however, such strategies need to be planned and programmed so that they are not left to chance but form a defined part of the overall relationship marketing plan.

Influencer Markets

Clearly there are many sources of influence on buyer behaviour and so the definition of an 'influencer market' is not straightforward. In the context of relationship marketing an influencer is an organisation, entity or individual that directly or indirectly might cause a customer to buy our product or service. A critical part of a relationship marketing programme may therefore involve seeking to work more closely with the influencers. An example might be a margarine producer that seeks to encourage an interest in low-cholesterol diets by supporting the research of heart disease. Another example might be manufacturers of domestic smoke alarms lobbying government to invest in public-information programmes on fire protection.

Much of what we call 'public relations' is often focused upon developing a positive attitude amongst critical influencer markets. The ultimate aim is to seek to ensure that the environment in which we market our offer is as favourable as possible.

Still other sources of influence are the 'innovators' or 'early adopters', who are often used by others as a point of guidance. Drug companies have long recognised the importance of building close relationships with general practitioners who have a position of influence amongst other doctors when it comes to prescribing practice.

■ Employee Markets

'Good people are hard to find'. Because every organisation is highly dependent upon the quality of the people it employs, it is imperative that a high priority be given to recruiting and retaining employees who are likely to assist the company in achieving its overall marketing objectives. The aim should be to make the company into an organisation that is attractive to people who share the values the company espouses.

Companies as diverse as Disney and the Ritz-Carlton chain of hotels have built up a reputation for service quality that owes a great deal to the care that is put into employee recruitment. Given the high costs of training new recruits in any business, it makes a lot of sense to ensure that the right people are recruited in the first place, and that once in place a strong emphasis is placed upon minimising employee turnover. Companies with higher than the industry average of staff turnover will often be poor performers in terms of customer service.

Evidence exists in many markets that a 'virtuous circle' can be created whereby committed and satisfied employees lead to loyal and satisfied customers, which further encourages and reinforces customer orientation amongst the employees (Figure 3.2).

■ Supplier Markets

In the past, relationships with suppliers were often adversarial. It was thought to be good practice to have several suppliers for a single item and to 'play one off against the other'. Negotiation on price was the chief focus of the buyer-

Figure 3.2 Employee satisfaction leads to customer loyalty

supplier contact and there was little recognition of the connection between supplier relationships and success in the end market. Happily this point of view is now changing.

Many companies have found that closer relationships with suppliers can lead to innovation in product design and functionality, quality improvements and lower purchasing costs. The move towards 'single sourcing' is also a part of this trend. The idea here is that the best way to gain the benefits of buyer-supplier collaboration is through working closely in a spirit of trust and long-term mutual commitment – a spirit that is unlikely to be engendered if the buyer insists on splitting his business between several competing suppliers.

■ Customer Markets

In a sense the customer market is affected by the organisation's success or failure in all the other markets (Figure 3.3). The customer market represents all the people or organisations that buy goods or services from us. They can be either end-users/consumers or intermediaries.

In this, the sixth market, the impact of customer service can be profound. Often the only source of differentiation is the quality of service provided. This is particularly the case when dealing with intermediaries or distributors. For example, the amount of shelf-space a retailer is prepared to give to one brand as against another brand in the same category will often be determined, for instance, by the supplier's ability to operate a just-in-time delivery system or by the supplier's ability to receive orders electronically and to link information systems together, and so on.

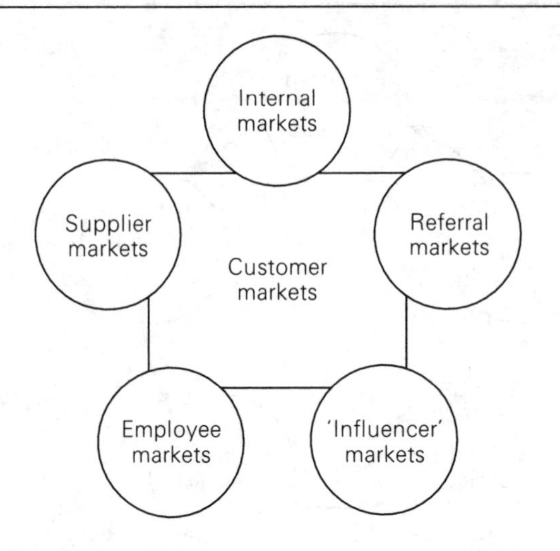

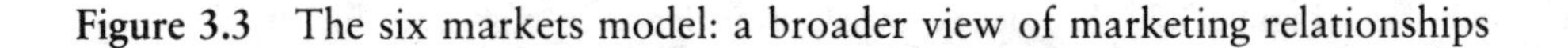

Figure 3.3 The six markets model: a broader view of marketing relationships

Even when marketing to end users, the service and quality dimension can be critical. When faced with the decision as to which television set or word processor to buy, the consumer will be partly influenced by the brand name, but issues such as guarantees, after-sales service, customer support and off-the-shelf availability are increasingly the determinants of customer choice.

■ Relationships as Partnerships

The basic philosophy underlying relationship marketing is that the goal of all marketing activity should be the establishment of mutually beneficial partnerships with customers. If customers perceive there is greater value in staying with a particular supplier than in moving to any other, then clearly they will stay. Hence the challenge to management is to develop marketing strategies that are designed to create enduring customer partnerships.

Ideally the concept of partnership should be applied to each of the six markets. Hence partnerships with employees, with influencers, with suppliers, as well as with customers, will ensure greater long-term profitability for the business.

For example many companies are benefiting from closer relationships with suppliers. What they are discovering is that by working alongside suppliers they can find ways to take costs out of the supply chain by focusing on such things as just-in-time delivery systems, linking ordering procedures through Electronic Data Interchange (EDI) and eliminating the need for rework by quality-improvement programmes. In addition they can build customer value by working together on product improvements and new product development. Indeed some studies suggest that a major source of innovation is the upstream supplier.

Emerging from this concept of partnership is the idea of the 'extended supply chain'. Whilst traditionally companies have tended to see their strengths in terms of their own capabilities and resources, the notion of the extended supply chain looks beyond the legal boundaries of the company for new sources of competitive advantage. Supply-chain management can be defined as the management of upstream and downstream relationships with suppliers, distributors and customers in such a way that greater customer value-added is achieved at less total cost. The result of a successful supply-chain management programme should be enhanced profit for all the partners in the chain.

Already many companies have found considerable benefit in developing partnerships in the supply chain. The Rover Group has achieved a significant improvement in its competitive position through developing a strategy based upon what it calls 'the extended enterprise'. The aim is to seek to develop a seamless pipeline that cost-effectively moves and converts materials and components into customer-specific finished products in the shortest possible time. To achieve this requires close relationships with a reduced supplier base, just-in-time assembly and a responsive, centrally managed, distribution system with on-line information links with dealers. The result is that a customer can walk into a Rover outlet, sit down at a computer screen and literally 'design' the car he or she wants from the options available. Once the decision to buy has been made, the order can be transmitted directly to Rover and the car delivered from a central distribution facility if available from stock and, if not, the order can be included in the production schedule.

Rover's partnership strategy was partly inspired by the success of their alliance with Honda. In 1981 Rover signed an agreement with Honda to begin a number of collaborative programmes in research and development, production and joint sourcing. For Rover, this relationship led to significant benefits in terms of access to superior engine technology and exposure to Japanese manufacturing management methods.

The advantage to Honda of this collaboration was an accelerated entry into Western European markets, lower costs of purchased materials through joint procurement programmes, access to design and styling skills with a European focus and a large growing market for its engines. Other car manufacturers around the world are following similar strategies based upon partnership and collaboration as they see the mutual advantages that can accrue.

In other industries the benefits of partnership arrangements are being discovered. Laura Ashley, the fabric and clothing manufacturer and retailer, was losing money and customers as it encountered growing problems in managing its complex global network of material and product flows into and out of its factories. Customers in their retail outlets were frustrated as out-of-stock incidence increased and seasonal styles arrived late, if at all.

To overcome this loss of competitive advantage Laura Ashley decided to focus upon its real strengths, which were essentially design and marketing, and to build a partnership with Federal Express to manage all of its in-bound and out-bound logistics. Federal Express has expertise in managing time-sensitive deliveries world-wide and it has an advanced 'tracking and tracing' information system, which means that product flow can be managed against known requirements in the retail stores.

The Laura Ashley–Federal Express partnership provides a good illustration of the benefits to an organisation of focusing upon that part of the value chain where the firm has competitive advantage and then seeking a partner(s) to manage the other parts of the chain where the partner(s) has superior skills.

One company that has been a consistent advocate of the 'strategic alliance' is the Japanese company Toshiba. Over the years Toshiba has sought out alliances through technology-licensing agreements, joint ventures and partnerships to complement its own internal strengths and resources. These alliances often involve a considerable financial commitment and are long term in their intent. As a result Toshiba has become a world leader in many technologies and markets. For example, through its joint venture with Motorola, Toshiba is now the biggest producer of large-scale memory chips. Its collaboration with IBM in flat-screen colour-monitor technology has given it a significant edge in this fast-growing market. Often in return for the technology it imports from its partners, Toshiba provides access to its manufacturing skills and its product-development capability, whereby technologies can be converted rapidly into marketable products.

Partnerships, whatever the type or the specific arrangements, lie at the heart of relationship marketing and in today's complex business environment may often be the only means whereby competitive advantage can be gained and sustained.

■ Managing Relationships in the Marketing Channel

The stronger the relationship with a partner, the greater the barrier to entry it presents to competitors. Suppliers to Marks and Spencer, who have built up over many years exceptionally close linkages, have little to fear from competitors as long as the product and service they provide continues to meet the stringent requirements placed upon them by Marks & Spencer. This is because of the considerable investment made by both parties in product and process development, in linked logistics systems and in continuous improvement programmes.

The old idea that buyers and sellers should maintain a distance from each other and only concern themselves with 'negotiating a deal' can no longer be sustained. Instead the trend is increasingly towards a much wider, business-development-focused relationship, where the supplier takes a holistic view of the customer's needs. A good example of this is provided by recent developments in what is sometimes termed 'trade marketing'. Whilst much of the emphasis in traditional marketing has been placed upon end-users to 'pull' the product through the marketing channel, trade marketing is concerned to gain access to the marketing channel and to increase the 'opportunities to buy' experienced by end users. In other words to ensure that maximum shelf space, distribution and availability is achieved. Occasionally these strategies are referred to as 'push' strategies, however such a term implies a production orientation and it is probably better to talk simply in terms of a 'relationship strategy'.

Figure 3.4 highlights the difference between the two approaches. The conventional buyer-supplier interface is a fragile connection, easily broken by competitors, based upon a motivation on the part of the buyer to maximise margin, and on the part of the seller a motivation to maximise volume.

In the relationship-based approach the two 'triangles' are invert to bring about a much stronger interface bond. Now there are multiple points of connection between the vendor and the customer. The objectives of the vendor are to develop the customer's business, to focus on the customer's return on investment and enhancing the customer's own competitive capability. The benefit to the vendor if those objectives are achieved is the likelihood that it will be treated as a preferred supplier. At the same time the costs of serving that customer should be lower as a result of a greater sharing of information, integrated logistics systems and so on.

To achieve such multiple 'connections' between the two parties clearly requires a mutual understanding of the benefits that can be achieved though partnership. In reality it will require a proactive approach from the vendor in which business solutions are presented to the customer, rather than a sales proposition. For example many manufacturers marketing to the retail trade now seek to illustrate the impact of a proposed relationship in terms of return on investment within the category in which the product in question competes. Thus the supplier must be able to demonstrate the impact that the relationship can have upon shelf-space profitability, stock-turnover, and so on.

In the USA these closer relationships between suppliers and retailers have led to the development of interlinked logistics and information systems known generically as 'quick-response' systems or 'efficient consumer response'. The underlying principle behind these systems is that information on sales is captured at the point of sale and transmitted directly back to the supplier. The supplier can then schedule production and distribution on the basis of known demand rather than upon orders, which are unpredictable in volume and frequency. The benefits to the supplier are greatly reduced logistics costs and improved production efficiencies; the retailer needs to carry less stock, and yet runs out of stock less often. Such relationships have resulted in the supplier being awarded 'preferred supplier' status, thus gaining increased shelf-space. Within the first year of integrating their information and logistics system in this way with Wal-Mart (America's biggest retailer), Procter & Gamble's business with Wal-Mart grew by 40 per cent.

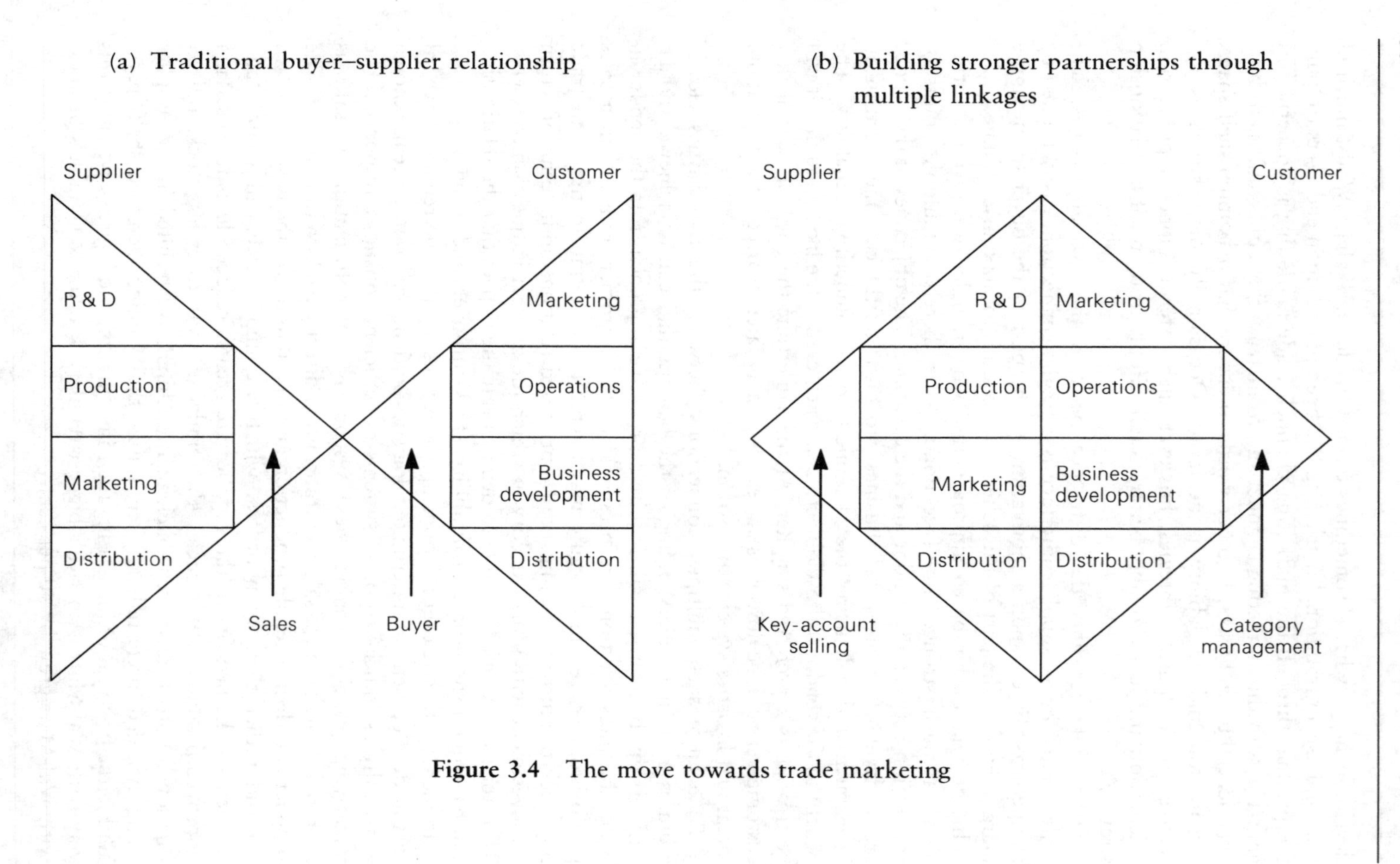

Figure 3.4 The move towards trade marketing

Building End-User Relationships

The ultimate relationship is with the end-user. Even though the business may distribute its products through intermediaries, the challenge will always be to build an enduring relationship with the consumer. Simple satisfaction with the product or service is not enough as there will usually be competitive offers that can match performance on the 'fundamentals'. Later, in Chapter 18, we will discuss ways in which customer retention might be improved, but it is appropriate to stress here the importance of a two-way dialogue with consumers as a critical foundation for long-term relationships.

The 'feedback loop' is not always available in many traditional marketing structures. Opportunities for the consumer to respond to the experience of purchase and consumption should be created on a continuing basis. Customer 'hot lines', 0800 numbers, customer-satisfaction surveys, are all ways in which feedback from the market place can be obtained.

Consumer opinion should be involved at every step in the marketing process. For example, Boeing, the North American aircraft builder, has established extremely strong relationships with customers such as British Airways by involving them in the detailed design of aircraft from the drawing board onwards. Teams of engineers from British Airways worked alongside their counterparts at Boeing and General Electric (the engine manufacturers) to design the new Boeing 777 so that it would be both 'customer friendly' and 'end-user friendly'. Hence British Airways engineering crews worked on improving the maintainability of the aircraft before it even left the drawing board. Likewise luggage stowage in the cabin has been improved through close cooperation between Boeing and British Airways. It is largely because of the strength of this relationship that British Airways have ordered fifteen 777s with General Electric engines with an option for a further fifteen at a price of £100 million each, in the face of stiff competition from Airbus and Rolls-Royce.

On a quite different scale, another example of relationship marketing is provided by Barbour, the UK based manufacturer of outdoor and sporting apparel. Barbour has always sought to build relationships with its end-users. Purchasers of the various garments manufactured by Barbour are encouraged to return them to the factory when they need repair or reproofing. At country fairs and exhibitions, a free refurbishing service is provided. Consumers' views on Barbour products are constantly sought to help it improve the product range. Advertising is also used to underline the theme of the relationship the Barbour user has with the product and, by implication, with the company. Small though the company is, it is highly profitable with sales continuing to grow year by year.

Summary

In this chapter we have described the way in which the conventional approach to marketing needs to take on a broader, relationship-based approach. The suggestion has been that in the changed market environment that exists in most developed economies today, there must be at least as much attention placed upon keeping customers as upon getting them. The development of successful relationship marketing strategies can be enhanced by a focus upon the 'six markets': the internal market, the referral market, the influencer market, the employee market, the supplier market and the customer market. Specific, but complementary, strategies should be designed for each of these markets, the ultimate goal being to create a partnership approach to marketing that transcends the traditional, narrow transaction approach, and embraces the entire supply chain to achieve greater customer value at every level in that chain.

MODULE 2

Understanding Customers and Markets

CHAPTER 4

Buyer Behaviour

At its most simplistic level, business could be described as some kind of popularity contest in which products and services all vie for attention, buyers voting for the winners with their chequebooks.

Since few businesses offer unique products or services, and as few buyers have unlimited finance at their disposal, every purchase decision is, in reality, a *choice* decision:

- Should we spend our hard-won savings and buy that dream kitchen? Company A are more expensive than Company B, but they offer more attractive designs, don't they? Might we do better if we bought do-it-yourself kitchen units . . . could save some money that way? How about getting it on credit and paying back by instalments? But what about that exotic holiday we promised ourselves? We couldn't have that and a new kitchen. . . . Or could we somehow manage both? And what about the car? It's reaching a state where we ought to think of getting a newer model . . .

Such thinking could typify almost any purchase decision, and we know this to be true because we are all buyers ourselves. In the end we make our choice using a combination of rational judgements, based on facts and previous experience, and subjective feelings that determine our likes and dislikes. Factors such as our upbringing, values, stage of life, the situation in which we find ourselves and the pressures we are under can all have some bearing upon our purchase decision.

As Man is a thinking, feeling creature, before he takes any action it has to seem to be logical and to feel right. Both the 'head' and the 'heart' need to sanction any commitment to action. Successful marketers know this to be true and use this knowledge to their advantage.

In this chapter we will look at some of the useful behavioural models that have been developed and can help marketers to understand the very bedrock of the marketing process – the preferences, prejudices, motivations and buying habits of their customers.

We will also consider what different pressures exist if the buyer is buying on his own behalf, or for an organisation. Equally we will look at differences in industrial buying decisions and consumer purchases.

Buyers and Consumers: Know the Difference

Often the person who buys a product or service is also the consumer, but this is not always the case. For example, in an industrial setting a buyer might be ordering vast shipments of raw materials that go to different parts of the organisation to be processed. He doesn't use these materials personally. On the domestic front, a housewife might buy articles of food or clothing for her family that she will never use herself.

Clearly it is in the marketer's interest to know all about his buyers *and* consumers. If he has both, then inevitably they may have different needs that have to be satisfied. However, for simplicity's sake, in this chapter we will confine ourselves to talking about buyers only. The lessons we learn about them will in most cases be just as applicable to consumers.

■ A General Model

Whenever we try to predict human behaviour we must never forget that we are dealing with an extremely complex phenomenon. Many scientists claim that the main challenge facing Man is not to understand and conquer outer space, but to explore inner space; to find out how the brain works, how memory functions and so on. Even experts in this field claim there are vast grey areas when it comes to understanding the inner working of Homo sapiens.

Nevertheless, from the work that has already been done in the behavioural field, we believe it is possible to draw a general model of the influences on consumer behaviour. In this model we show the influences on the buyer as coming from two sources, personal and external.

The personal influences are those which are characteristics or traits of the buyer as an individual. Thus he will have hopes, fears, ambitions, doubts, perceptions, beliefs, attitudes, values, knowledge and experience. The buyer faces the world with a 'persona' or personality that is his alone, and only he knows how much energy and hard-earned wealth he is prepared to put into the buying transaction.

However, the individual does not operate within a vacuum; there are always external influences which can have a bearing on his behaviour. Is the transaction legal? How will peer groups or the family respond? Is the general economy such that it is wise to buy now? How much is the buyer's behaviour conditioned by his situation, social class or culture? None of us is as free as we might choose to believe.

Figure 4.1 shows these two sources of influence feeding through 'hoppers' on to the 'pans' of a balance. Clearly, if for a particular type of purchase the personal factors far outweigh the external ones, then the marketer needs to know this – and also what these factors are. If the balance swings the other way, the marketer should be just as interested in understanding the reasons why.

At the end of the day it is this balance between personal and external forces that characterises how the buyer interacts with the buying process. In simple terms this process can be described in three stages.

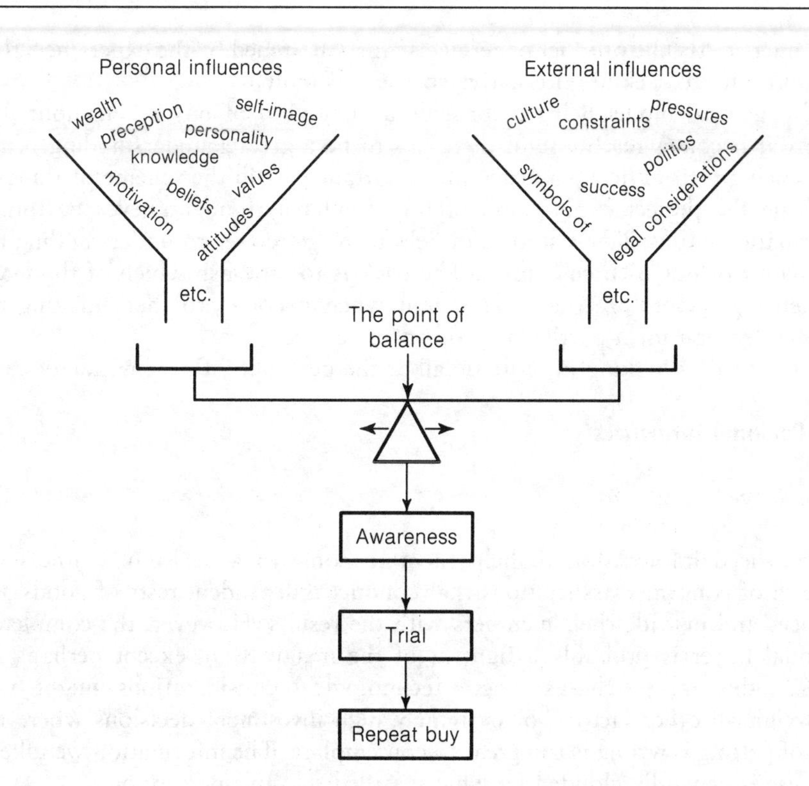

Figure 4.1 Influences on consumer behaviour

1. *Awareness.* The buyer becomes aware of a product, service or new brand through some sort of communication. This might be in the form of advertising or some other type of promotion controlled by the marketer. Equally, awareness might be established by word of mouth, which is clearly not under his control. The most that can be accomplished at this stage of the buying process is that the buyer will decide to give the product or service a trial.

2. *Trial.* Here the customer uses and evaluates the item and decides if it performs in a satisfactory way. Whether or not the buyer will decide to repeat the purchase will depend upon how well the product or service met his needs and how far it conferred non-functional benefits on the user. So, for example, a sports car is often bought not just as a means of transportation but for a host of other reasons, not least among them some form of social recognition, self-image enhancement and prestige. The trial is therefore not an entirely rational process because the buyer is making up his own mind using many subjective criteria.

3. *Repeat buying.* The decision to rebuy depends largely upon what happened during the trial phase. Various elements of the marketing mix, especially advertising, can be used to remind the buyer of the benefits he derived from the trial. Obviously, it is extremely difficult to persuade disappointed

customers to try the product or service again. Chastened by the experience, they would prefer to seek an alternative source of supply.

This general model helps to provide an overview of buyer behaviour, but before it becomes really useful there has to be a greater understanding of the influencing factors that play such an important part in the scheme of things.

While the perfect explanation of buyer behaviour might never be found, systematic and intelligent study can help us to get closer to understanding the behaviour of our own customers. The trick is to establish which of the many influencing factors are the most potent when it comes to them making the buying decision for a particular product or service.

Let's start by looking in more detail at the personal influencing factors.

■ Personal Influences

Knowledge

Buyers need information to help them to come to a decision. Witness the growth of consumer associations that conduct independent tests of goods and services and provide their members with the results. However, the completely rational buyer is probably a figment of the imagination, except perhaps for some industrial purchases where technological considerations might well outweigh all other factors, or extremely high investment decisions where the risk of getting it wrong is too great to contemplate. The information we take in and use is generally clouded by what is called selective perception.

In a recent product test in France, two well-established brands of margarine were evaluated by four hundred households. One was the brand leader, the other was much smaller in terms of market share. Half of the sample was provided with the two brands in anonymous wrappers marked simply X and Y, the other half received its margarine in the usual brand wrappers.

When asked to state which brand they preferred, there was approximately a fifty-fifty split between the anonymous brands. Surprisingly, the other half of the customer sample, who knew the identity of the product, voted sixty-five to thirty-five in favour of the brand leader.

This illustrates how perhaps the most rational reason for buying food – its taste – can be distorted by other considerations. Selective perception has the effect of getting us to 'massage the facts', or even screen them out, so that the information we receive is what we want to hear. In many ways we are the promoters of self-fulfilling prophesies.

At an American university a guest speaker had been invited to give a talk to the senior students. As an experiment, half of the students about to attend the lecture had been informed that this particular speaker was a last minute stand-in and had a poor reputation in his specialist field. In contrast, the other students were told how lucky they were to have such an eminent authority to come to the university and that they would be witnessing something special. On evaluating the speaker's lecture, those who had been 'conditioned' to expect the worst were highly critical, whereas those going in with high expectations largely found them fulfilled.

What messages might the marketer draw from these stories?

- Getting knowledge about our products or services over to customers is not easy.
- We need to think about effective learning mechanisms to 'educate' our customers.

It is a fact that many of the things we know today are a result of continued repetition . . . just think of poems you know, or multiplication tables! Therefore customers can also learn about our products and services if we continually repeat simple and memorable messages to them, whether from face-to-face salespersons or through advertising. How many of us can honestly say that when we hear the beginning of a jingle on a TV commercial something in our brain doesn't sing along with it?

The second theory about learning is to appeal to as many of the senses as possible. We take in information through sight, sound, touch, taste and smell, and to this list some would add a sixth sense, some form of intuitive process. It can be shown that although we might remember something by seeing it, our chances of recall are enhanced if we can hear it as well. Better still, using it or handling it makes the learning a totally sensory experience.

□ *Motivation*

At first sight the field of motivational studies can be quite confusing. For some psychologists words such as 'motive', 'drive', 'urge', 'wishes', 'needs' and 'wants' have a particular meaning of their own. For others, they can be used interchangeably. Fortunately there is general agreement on the concept of motivated behaviour, as is the observable response to a felt need.

Figure 4.2 shows how the 'motivation' process works. A need is said to exist until action has been taken to satisfy it.

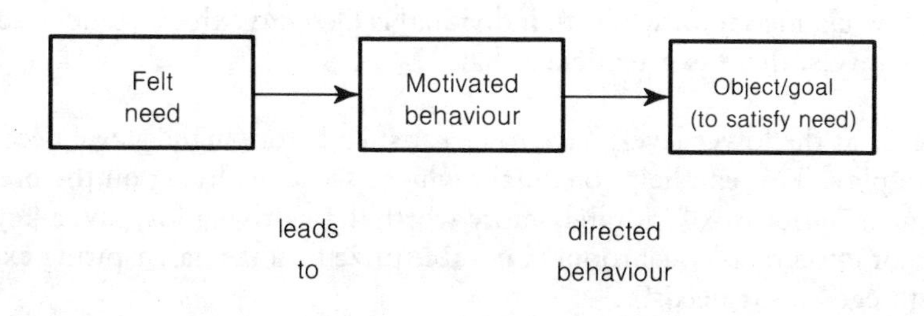

Figure 4.2 The process of motivation

One of the most significant figures in the study of motivation is Abraham Maslow. As a result of his studies he saw Man as a perpetually wanting creature. Moreover, he concluded that human needs develop in a sequential way, from what he termed 'lower' needs to 'higher order' ones. He identified five main categories.

At the lowest level, Man's actions are driven to satisfy what Maslow termed 'basic needs'. These are mainly physiological in nature, such as the need to satisfy hunger and thirst, and to stop feeling cold.

Needs at the next level are termed 'safety' or 'security needs' and are largely concerned with protection from physical or psychological loss.

After that are 'belonging needs', the needs for affection and affiliation, to be part of a group and enjoy all the social contact that goes with it.

Next are what he described as 'ego-status' needs, which are concerned with the need to feel important in the eyes of others, to have self-esteem, recognition, success and prestige.

The highest level of needs Maslow described as 'self-actualisation'; the need for challenge, personal fulfilment, to be creative and to realise one's own potential. Conventionally this hierarchy of needs is shown as in Figure 4.3.

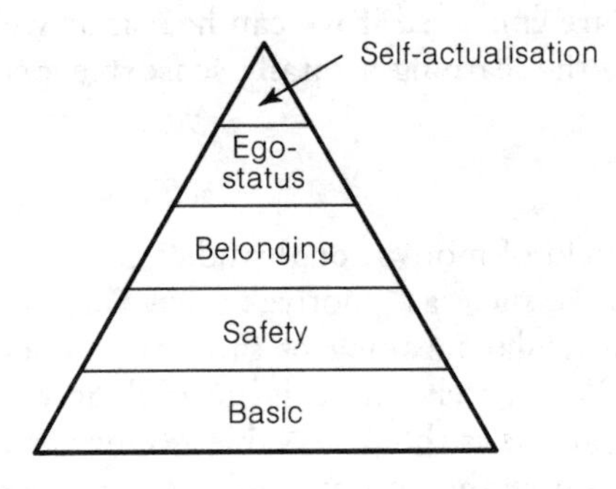

Figure 4.3 Maslow's hierarchy of needs

Maslow claimed that, while an individual is likely to exhibit some needs at all of these levels, there is a tendency that:

- Needs at the lower levels have to be satisfied before higher-level needs come into play. This can help to explain why to someone living on the breadline, regular meals are of infinitely more worth than striving for, say, a key to the senior executives' washroom (a notable prize for many an aspiring executive with ego-status needs!)
- This hierarchy of needs is situational, in the sense that if circumstances change, or if one is threatened at one's existing level, it is possible to 'slide'

back to a lower level. For example, someone who is a cooperative and sociable team member (satisfying his belonging needs) might become withdrawn and uncommunicative, keeping information to himself, when it is rumoured that there will be some lay-offs in his department. (Safety needs are now paramount.)

- It is possible that some individuals might be influenced by higher-level motives even when lower needs have not been fully satisfied. So, for example, they might cut back on food they can ill afford in order to sustain an activity that to them is self-actualising. (The starving artist syndrome.)

Some critics of Maslow have commented that in the western industrialised societies the basic needs are largely covered by the state or by various welfare organisations, as perhaps are many of the safety needs. However this argument doesn't really invalidate his proposition, it just serves to provide another perspective (Figure 4.4).

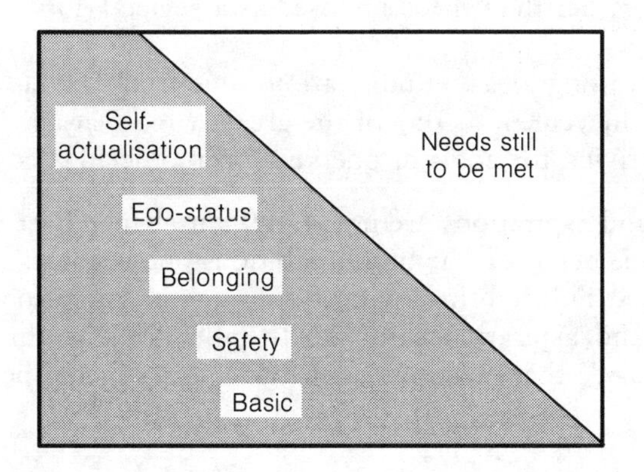

Figure 4.4 Unmet deeds in developed markets

For the marketer, the implications of Maslow's work are far-reaching. Imagine that we had to market Bicko Biscuits. These are the various messages we might convey to our customers if we could identify them in the hierarchy of needs:

5 Self-actualisation	'A new experience. Tease your taste buds with our biscuits'
4 Ego-status	'Not for the *hoi polloi* these Bickos'
3 Belonging	'Join the in-crowd, have a Bicko'
2 Safety	'Our biscuits are pure, through and through'
1 Basic	'Bickos fill you up'

At a more serious level we might note that:

- At the creature-comforts level (because that is what the basic needs might amount to in industrialised societies) there might be a demand for cheaper commodities or smaller packs, in order to save money and at the same time afford to run a car or buy a video-recorder.
- Here there will be a preference for the familiar; for life assurance, burglar alarms and so on.
- These needs might materialise as demands for distinctive styles of clothing, various group activities from holidays to team sports, romantic greetings cards and gifts of all shapes and sizes.
- This level will be concerned with anything that conveys non-spoken messages about power, prestige, achievement, strength, recognition and importance.
- The final level is not always easily distinguishable from the previous level, but deep down it is to do with living to one's own standards and aspirations, rather than those imposed as a societal norm.

Some other interesting ideas on motivation came from David McClelland who came to view achievement as one of the greatest motivators. For him, Man is motivated by striving for goals of one kind or another. He concluded that:

- Ambitions and aspirations are not static, but change over time.
- The more one achieves, the more ambitious one becomes (the corollary to this being that failure brings with it a decline in aspirations).
- Ambitions and aspirations are largely influenced by the behaviour and performance of other members of the group to which a person belongs.

□ *Personality*

There have been many studies about personality and its influence on subsequent behaviour, although not all of these have been adopted by marketers. One of the earliest ways of personality 'typing' was to ascertain whether people were inclined to be *introverts* (inward-looking, quiet, thoughtful, and so on) or *extroverts* (outward looking, gregarious, socially skilled). Using this basic typology it is suggested by some that it is possible to identify differences in life-styles, job preferences, hobbies, and so on.

Another way of looking at personality type is to consider the extent to which a person is 'compliant', 'aggressive' or 'detached':

- *Compliants* like to be needed and appreciated; they seek to avoid conflict and are unlikely to upset others; they are loving and unselfish.
- *Aggressives* believe in the survival of the fittest; they need to be the best and to achieve recognition even if they have to exploit others to do so.
- *Detacheds* tend to be self-sufficient and private; they want minimal interference from others and place high value on their independence.

Some tentative results have been obtained by behavioural researchers using this framework, but the extent to which purchasing behaviour is influenced by personality variables is still not clearly understood. Some thought-provoking work has been done by Everett Rogers, who was interested in how personality type might influence a person's readiness to buy a new product or service. He identified five 'types', as Figure 4.5 shows.

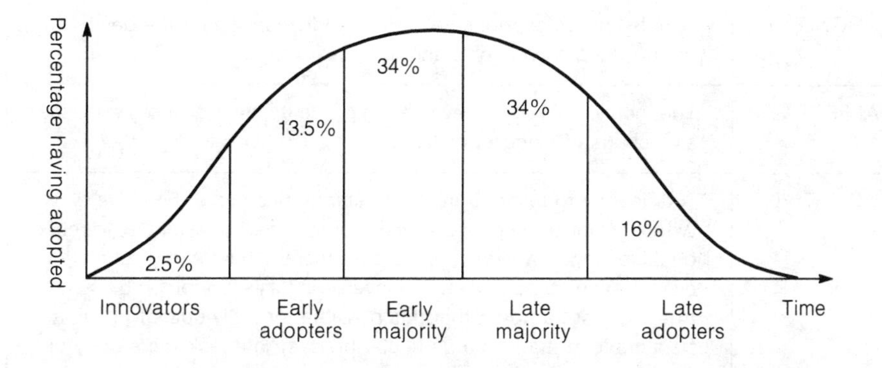

Source: After Everett Rogers, *Diffusion of Innovations* (New York Free Press, 1962).

Figure 4.5 The adoption and diffusion process

For any new product or service, someone somewhere has to be adventurous enough to buy it first. These are the innovators, who in any market are likely to comprise about 2.5 per cent of the buying population. What appeals to these people is novelty and a sense of pioneering. To lead fashion, whether in clothes or anything else, is highly attractive to innovators and as a consequence they are not as price-sensitive as other buyers might be.

If the product or service lives up to its expectations it is taken up by the early adopters. These are slightly more cautious than innovators and don't like the idea of being guinea pigs for new ideas. Nevertheless, as soon as they are satisfied that the new product works, they are happy to buy.

Gradually, by this process of people buying, using and talking about the product or service, it reaches all types of buyers – even the late adopters.

This simple model of innovation is of great use to the marketer because it can give him some insights about his customers and the best ways of communicating to them. For example:

Innovators 'It's new and technologically light years ahead'
Early adopters 'Things are changing, catch the wave'
Early majority 'Look at the benefits you could gain'
Late majority 'Look at the benefits that have been gained'
Late adopters 'You can't beat a tried and trusted idea'

□ *Attitude*

While attitude is not an easy concept to define, there is some agreement that it refers to three elements that are assumed to predetermine behaviour, as summarised in Figure 4.6.

COGNITIVE	Beliefs and perceptions held by an individual about the benefits of the product, service or brand in question.
AFFECTIVE	The individual's overall evaluation of the item in question, expressed as feelings of liking or disliking.
CONATIVE	A tendency to respond in a consistently positive or negative way with respect to the product, brand or service. For example, to reflect one's feelings towards a brand by generally buying it, if one's evaluation of it is positive. The reverse of this situation would also be true. It must be noted that it is possible for individuals to have a favourable attitude to a particular product, but lack the money or need to take any action.

Figure 4.6 Elements of attitude

Attitudes develop over life as people gain experience and change their responsibilities. While in theory attitudes ought to be very personal and individualistic, in practice they can be similar to those held by many others. This is because attitudes are modified by many societal influences such as interaction with other people or groups, exposure to information, the current values in the environment at large and emerging wants or needs.

Much corporate advertising and image projection is designed to encourage positive attitudes towards the company. In this way, instead of treating each buying decision as a separate evaluation, the customer will more or less automatically approach the supplier to which he is favourably disposed.

While attitude can influence purchasing behaviour, favourable performance of the product or service has the effect of reinforcing the attitude. Equally, many customers seek reassurance that they have done the right thing by making the purchase and so after-sales communication – through personal contact or advertising – will also help to strengthen positive attitudes.

Up until now we have concentrated on the 'personal influences' side of our general model about buyer behaviour. We have looked at some of the key factors that help to determine behaviour – knowledge, motivation, personality and attitude. But, as we have seen, even these factors are affected by some influences external to the buyer. Let us now switch our attention to this other equally important set of factors.

External Influences

Culture

This is one of the most persuasive influences on customer choice; the sum total of social and spiritual beliefs, technologies, values and actions that impinge upon all individual and group behaviour. Culture can have a general effect upon whether or not entire product classes, such as washing machines, are purchased at all in certain societies.

Although there are many superficial similarities between the French and Belgian cultures, such as the French language, there are significant differences in the ways certain products are purchased. The French prefer to purchase alcohol in the form of wine, for example, whereas Belgians show a greater propensity for drinking beer.

Numbers, colours, symbols, style of dress, body language and methods of greeting may also have quite distinctive meanings in various cultures. If the marketer is unaware of these then his consequent embarrassment will be measured not only in blushes, but in lost sales. There are many examples where multinational marketers have failed to appreciate the effects on customer behaviour of using words that turned out to be either obscene or meaningless.

However, even at the more limited level of marketing at home, one has to be sensitive to the different 'subcultures' that can typify certain regions of the country. For example, in the UK, patterns of family life and social activities can vary tremendously between, say, the south-east and the north-east regions.

□ *Economic*

Economic factors are of great significance in deciding whether a particular purchase takes place at all, when it occurs, and how payment is made. Clearly changes in people's incomes have direct consequences for their purchasing behaviour. Therefore national trends and government fiscal policy can be useful in building formal economic models that can help to predict aggregate demands for products and services, that is, the amounts that will be bought throughout the economy.

Marketers must use such models with caution, however, because they often cease to be of value if they are applied too rigidly, except in the most general, commonsense way. As we have seen, individuals and small groups might be driven to behave in quite idiosyncratic ways, as the following example demonstrates.

A company launched a new health-type apple drink, and, because of new manufacturing technology, was able to price it as low as ordinary lemonade. The launch was accompanied by extensive advertising, which described the product-benefits and stressed its quality. Despite all this the response was very disappointing. Subsequent research showed that potential customers did not believe that the benefit and quality claims could be genuine at such a low price.

The company therefore increased the price by 20 per cent and, sure enough, demand rose. In fact over the following two years the price was increased in stages until it was double the original launch price – and with every increase sales rose too!

Economic theorists would tell you that both buyers and sellers are rational in an economic sense; that is, producers of goods and services always maximise their profits, while customer choice is determined by the extra utility or satisfaction derived from the purchase compared with the final outlay. Also, it is generally assumed that there is such a thing as a 'demand curve', which dictates that as price goes up, the quantity demanded will fall.

Of course both these economic theories hold true in many cases, but in life there are many exceptions to the rule and the apple-drink story is one of them. The moral of the story is that economic factors may not explain the totality of customer behaviour. Price carries quality connotations for the customer, which the marketer must carefully take into account. It is the customer's perception of price that matters, not the abstract economic notion.

□ *Social Context*

In consumer markets we are all familiar with the idea of 'keeping up with the next-door neighbours'. Behaviour in which the individual takes the responses of others into account is in fact not just confined to consumer markets; social context also influences much industrial purchasing. For instance, research in Europe and North America has shown that although an objective cost–benefit analysis, based on economic and technical performance factors, is said to dictate the industrial purchasing process, other notions are also taken into consideration. These include the size of the supplier, the perceived quality of its staff, the marketing policies it pursues and the creativity of the sales contacts.

A British manufacturer of defence equipment selling to the Middle East has found that price is of little importance. Quality is taken for granted. Performance is assumed to be as specified. The crucial determinant of the purchase order is the ability to establish a personal rapport with the buyer. There have been occasions where orders have been awarded to the most expensive tenderer, whose performance levels have been lower, rather than to the cheaper bidder.

□ *Situation*

Situations exert more specific influences on customer choice than perhaps any other factor. Births, marriages, deaths, unexpected guests, things breaking down or wearing out, sudden illnesses, holidays, hobbies, pastimes – the list is almost endless. Every change of situation can stimulate a new set of needs and generate a new group of potential customers.

At first sight such events appear random and haphazard. Yet astute marketers have noted that many of life's events come to all of us, regardless of the uniqueness of our personal biography. That patterns exist can be illustrated by the concept of the family 'life-cycle' (Figure 4.7).

Stage	Characteristics
Young dependants	Little purchasing power, but can influence family buying decisions.
Young singles, not living at home	Few financial burdens; fashion opinion leaders; recreation orientation. *Buy:* basic kitchen equipment, basic furniture, cars, holidays.
Young newly marrieds, no children	Better off financially than they will be when family arrives; high purchasers; above average purchase of durables. *Buy:* cars, refrigerators, cookers, furniture to last, holidays.
Full nest I, youngest child under 6	Home purchases at a peak, financial assets low; few savings; interested in new products; like advertised products. *Buy:* washers, driers, TVs, videos, baby foods, cough mixture, vitamins, toys.
Full nest II, youngest child over 6	Better off financially; some wives work; less influenced by advertising; buy large size, economy packages. *Buy:* many foods, cleaning materials, bicycles, music lessons, pianos.
Full nest III, older marrieds with dependent children	Financial position improving; more wives work; some children work; hard to influence with advertising; high purchase of durables. *Buy:* new, more tasteful furniture, replacement refrigerators, and so on, non-essential appliances, magazines.
Empty nest I, married couple, children departed, one partner still working full time	Home ownership at peak; most satisfied with financial situation and money saved; interested in travel, recreation and self-education; make gifts and contributions; less interested in new products. *Buy:* holidays, luxuries, home improvements.
Empty nest II, marrieds, no children at home, retired	Drastic cut in income, stay at home. *Buy:* medical appliances, health-care products that aid sleep and digestion.

Figure 4.7 The family life-cycle

☐ *Socioeconomic Grouping*

A popular way to categorize buyers is by using a combination of social and economic factors. This gives rise to the following general classification:

- *Class A* (approximately 3 per cent of population): usually live in large detached houses or in the better parts of town. The head of the household is likely to be a successful business or professional person, for example a senior civil servant, or have considerable private means.
- *Class B* (approximately 12 per cent of population): Head of household quite senior, but not top of his or her business or profession. Quite well-to-do, respectable life-style without being luxurious. Non-earners will live on modest private incomes or pensions.
- *Class C1* (approximately 23 per cent of population): Head of household will be small tradesperson or non-manual worker carrying out what are usually termed 'white-collar' jobs.
- *Class C2* (approximately 32 per cent of population): Head of household will be skilled manual worker who will have served an apprenticeship or equivalent. Typical jobs could be foreman, electrician, plumber, carpenter.
- *Class D* (approximately 21 per cent of population): Head of the household will be a manual worker, generally semi-skilled or unskilled, such as machinist, bus driver, shop assistant, process worker.
- *Class E* (approximately 9 per cent of population): Mainly old age pensioners, widows, casual workers and any others who for reasons of illness, disability or unemployment are dependent on social security schemes.

This particular grading system is long-established and, while it has served its purpose and been particularly useful for targeting for advertising, many marketers are looking for ways to improve upon it. In many countries it has been recognised that buying decisions are no longer clearly correlated with social class. Instead the concept of 'life-style' has moved to the fore.

☐ *Life-style*

The concept of life-style is based upon the values and aspirations that individuals hold. It is suggested that such factors can provide a better indication of likely purchase behaviour. One such life-style typology is shown below:

- *Self-explorers* (approximately 15 per cent of population; this group is forecast to grow slowly) Motivated by self-expression and self-realization; have broad horizons, high tolerance; see global picture; hold spiritual values (but shun organized religion); reject doctrinaire solutions in favour of holistic, evolutionary growth based on individual awareness.

- *Social resisters* (14 per cent of population). Caring group, believing in fairness and quality of life for all; altruistic; concerned about social and ecological issues; can be intolerant and moralistic.
- *Experimentalists* (11 per cent of population; slowly growing). Highly individualistic, they are motivated by fast-moving enjoyment; materialistic and pro-technology but against traditional authority (like the self-explorers).
- *Conspicuous Consumers* (19 per cent of population; slight growth). Motivated by acquisition, competition and getting ahead. They are traditional, pro-authority and support law and order. Concerned about appearance and position; pushy.
- *Belongers* (18 per cent of population; shrinking slightly). Seek quiet, undisturbed, conventional family life; conservative, traditional rule-followers. Tend to be against change; interest in future revolves around the security of the family.
- *Survivors* (17 per cent of population; shrinking slightly). Strongly class-conscious and community spirited. If not taken advantage of, will be hardworking, traditional and cheerful. Their motivation is to 'get by'; often active trade unionists.
- *Aimless* (5 per cent of population; [a] will remain stable [b] will increase). [a] *Young unemployed* motivated by short-term pleasure or 'kicks'; often anti-authority. [b] *The old* whose motivation is day-to-day existence, often in trying circumstances.

We have looked at some of the more pertinent factors that act as external influences on the buyer's behaviour; namely culture, economy, social context, situations, 'life-cycle', socioeconomic factors and life-style groupings. From what has been discussed it is clear that to get anything like a perfect understanding of a buyer's behaviour is not easy; at best we get tantalising insights into elements of behaviour. Indeed, comprehensive models of buyer choice must seek to combine all these elements of behavioural influence if they are to provide a useful base for marketing strategy.

Consumer versus Industrial Purchase Decisions

Earlier we talked about the buying decision process as having three stages; awareness, trial and repeat buying. It is perhaps more accurate to describe this process as being typical of most consumer purchases. For industrial purchases the buying process can be more complex and involve more stages, as Table 4.1 shows.

The need for the purchase invariably starts from within the buyer's organisation as some kind of problem or need. The remaining 'buy stages' gradually unfold, sometimes over a period of weeks or even months. This process is clearly very different to walking into a shop and saying 'I'll have one of those please!', paying, and walking out.

Table 4.1 Industrial buying process

Stage	*Description of industrial buyer's actions*
1	Recognizes needs or problems, works out general solution.
2	Works out the characteristics and quantity of what is needed.
3	Prepares detailed specification.
4	Searches for and locates potential suppliers.
5	Analyses and evaluates tenders, proposals, plans, etc.
6	Selects 'best' supplier.
7	Places trial order.
8	Evaluates trial order.
9	Negotiates main contract subject to trial results.
10	Monitors deliveries, quality etc.

What makes the industrial buying decision more complex is the fact that rarely is just one person involved. Because of the technological, production, financial, safety and quality ramifications of buying a new piece of plant or machinery, for example, a number of people have to be satisfied that the correct buying decision is being made.

The Decision-Making Unit (DMU)

The individuals who are involved to one extent or another in the decision-making process are known as the DMU. In practice the size of the DMU tends to be in proportion to the size of the buying company, as Table 4.2 implies.

Table 4.2 Decision-making unit

Number of employees	*Size of DMU*	*Average number of contacts made by salesman*
0–200	3.42	1.72
201–400	4.85	1.75
401–1000	5.81	1.90
1000+	6.50	1.85

Clearly we are talking here about important buying decisions, but what is interesting to note is how salesmen rarely make contact with all those who influence the purchase. In effect they are missing opportunities to explain how their product or service will benefit each person in the DMU – and experience tells us that all members need to feel favourably inclined towards the purchase, especially those with organisational status.

Pressures on Industrial Buyers

When we buy things for ourselves, often we have only ourselves to satisfy. At most only our partners or close family are likely to be concerned. For the industrial buyer the situation is very different. He finds himself, as one member of the DMU, perhaps involved with senior executives of higher status to himself; almost certainly working with people who are technically more competent. Sometimes there is not enough, or confused, information about what is required, and some of his colleagues might be trying to score points over others because secretly they would prefer to see another supplier with the contract. Much human interaction and behaviour can be at work in these situations and the official 'buyer' can feel himself pulled this way and that – and on top of all this are all the external factors we have already discussed.

Little wonder, then, that those involved like to maintain that they are being strictly rational and analytical in their approach to the buying decision. It certainly helps to keep the decision-making on track, but consider this example.

A pump manufacturer, with a reputation for making robust and reliable pumps, called in an industrial designer to improve their appearance. Engineers at the company were shocked: 'You won't improve our pumps' performance; anyway, who sees them? They're installed underground' was their cry. 'Ah,' said the chief executive, 'but they are not *bought* underground, are they?'

Summary

1. All buying decisions are choice decisions.
2. The marketer has to try to understand the buyer's motivations and behaviours if he is going to influence the buyer.
3. The buyer's behaviour is rich and complex and emanates from many sources, some personal to the individual, some external.
4. While every buyer is different, it is possible to establish patterns of 'sameness'.
5. All patterns of behaviour are partly rational, partly emotional, depending on the nature of the product or service and the buyer's situation.
6. The industrial buying situation is more complex than the typical consumer situation because it has more stages, more people get involved and, as a result, the quality of their interaction can confuse matters.
7. By analysis and creative research it is possible for marketers to get closer to understanding buyers. Knowing how people buy makes it easier to sell to them.

CHAPTER 5

Market Segmentation

We have seen so far that marketing is an attitude of mind concerning customer satisfaction rather than a set of techniques to simply 'sell' products or services. No matter how good the product or service on offer, if there are not enough customers to buy it then there is no business.

Equally, when an organisation starts giving customers the consideration they deserve and finds out more about them and their needs, it often discovers that they do not possess the resources or skills to take advantage of *all* market opportunities. In other words, a particular organisation may not be as competitive as others when it comes to some *particular types* of customer, whereas it might be very competitive when it comes to others.

For example, we might consider the way in which numerous variations of domestic appliances, such as refrigerators and washing machines, are aimed at different customers and consumers depending upon their needs, motives for buying and social and economic characteristics. In consumer and industrial markets it is increasingly necessary to create and present a different offer to each group of customers, or, in the language of marketing, *market segments*. Therefore the theme for this chapter is the customer – the most important person in the life of any business.

For reasons of clarity we have chosen to talk about customers and their needs throughout this chapter, although, as we have already seen, sometimes the *customers* are not the *consumers* of our products or services. For example, if we ran a small bakery most of the bread might well be bought by the housewife; yet it would be her family who are the main *consumers*.

Similarly, manufacturers of expensive toys will have to understand all about the needs of the consumers – small children – but all the sales will be made to parents or adult relatives, and so *their* motivations must be equally understood.

Having two levels of 'customer' in this way does not invalidate any of the principles outlined in this chapter. It just means that extra thought has to be given to such situations to ensure that the marketing activity is focused in the right place.

Customers as Sources of Profit through Segmentation

It should be stressed that the strength and value of the marketing process hinges on how well we handle the process of customer segmentation. Get it wrong and it is likely that there will be a 'mismatch' between our offer and the needs of the customer.

The concern, therefore, is to seek ways of classifying customers so that, whatever the nature of our business, we will be in a position to offer a product or service to them that will enable us to differentiate ourselves from everyone else. This is the way to increased profitability.

Conceptually, it is easy to grasp that markets don't buy anything – it is people who buy things. It is only when we can identify *groups* of buyers that we can begin to talk about markets. Such markets can be further classified into submarkets, or segments. There are many different ways of approaching segmentation; how can we be sure we are using the best one?

Unfortunately it is impossible to be prescriptive about this because some creative insight is necessary to provide us with the very method of segmentation that is right for our company. Remember, the purpose of segmentation is to find the best ways to match our capabilities with groups of customers who share similar needs and thereby gain some commercial advantage.

There are, however, some generally accepted criteria concerning what constitutes a viable market segment. These are as follows.

■ Criteria for Viable Market Segmentation

■ Identifiability and Measurability

The segment must be clearly identifiable and measurable in terms of the variable chosen as the basis of segmentation. Marketing managers often get a hunch that their customers belong to groups that have specific attributes, but there may be no objective evidence to support a differentiated marketing programme.

■ Relevance

The basis of segmentation (age or social status, for example) must be relevant to the purchase or use of the product. Customers of a particular brand might well share all sorts of personal characteristics, but these can only form the basis of effective market segmentation if they can be related to buyers' behaviour.

■ Potential

The segment should be of sufficient potential size to ensure that an adequate return can be obtained from any marketing investment made in it. Over-segmenting the market results in trying to serve many small submarkets without being able to reap the advantages of long production runs and distribution economies.

■ Accessibility

An identified market segment can be exploited commercially only if it can be reached. It must be accessible to one or other element of the marketing mix, usually but not exclusively the media. It must also be capable of being serviced through available marketing channels.

Although there are many methods of segmentation, they are basically variations of just two approaches. Both of these need to be considered.

- Analysis of the way customers respond or behave.
- Analysis of customer characteristics.

■ Analysis of the Way Customers Respond or Behave

This is essentially a description of the way customers actually behave in the market place, and falls into two parts: *what* is bought; and *why*.

In respect of *what* is bought, we are talking about the actual structure of markets in the form of the physical characteristics of products – place of purchase and price paid, for example. This information tells us if there are any groups of products (or outlets, or price categories) that are growing, static, or declining, thus indicating where there are opportunities and where we might be faced with problems. Consider the following example.

A very small carpet company, whose sales were declining, discovered on analysis that, although the market for carpets was rising overall, the outlets to which they had traditionally sold (that is, specialist carpet shops) were accounting for a declining proportion of sales. Furthermore, the analysis disclosed that demand for higher-priced carpets was falling and there was a switch towards fibre types not manufactured by this company. Knowing this information, the company was able to revise its production plans and change its traditional distribution outlets, which had the effect of reversing the decline in sales and profitability.

Although this example might appear to be elementary, it is surprising to find even today how many companies plan ahead on information that is little more than a crude extrapolation of past sales trends. Clearly, such approaches are fraught with danger and can cause serious commercial problems when market structures change, as in the case of the carpet company.

The second part of analysing customer behaviour is to understand *why* customers behave the way they do. If we can understand the behaviour of our customers we are in a better position to sell to them. However, when it comes to predicting human behaviour, we know from experience that people do not always behave in the expected manner.

One behavioural theory is that customers are rational when it comes to making a purchase and therefore seek to maximise their satisfaction with that purchase or in its utility value when compared with the financial outlay or effort put into the transaction.

However, this theory only helps up to a point. While it might work quite well in some markets, it is well known that other markets can exhibit increase in demand with increase in price. This will be particularly true of goods or services that appeal to the vanity or ego of the purchaser, such as cars, beauty-care products and clothes.

As we have seen, there are also a number of theories based on the idea that a customer's behaviour is largely conditioned by the psychological or social pressures exerted by those around him or her. Thus their attitudes and behaviour can be influenced by family, work colleagues, cultural patterns, personal aspirations and life-style. Such socio-psychological dimensions can provide many opportunities for successful segmentation strategies.

One such strategy that has proved highly successful in consumer markets is the idea of life-style segmentation.

■ Life-Style Segmentation

'We are what we eat' is a point of view that has been around for some time and, in a sense, its extension to 'we are what we consume' is the basis for life-style marketing.

Essentially the life-style concept relates to individual aspirations, personal role models (and role playing) and statements that people want to make about themselves. Much of modern consumer advertising is based on the principle of life-style *aspirations*. Very few of the consumers of Marlboro cigarettes, for example, are going to find themselves on a horse in the Arizona desert rounding up steers! Similarly, most users of certain hair shampoos that are currently advertised are unlikely to live the exotic lives that are featured in those advertisements.

In life-style marketing the reality is less important than the aspiration and the self-image. Because different people will have different aspirations and self-images, then it is logical that this should form the basis for a segmentaion of the market.

Thus, in life-style segmentation the aim is to group consumers on the basis of 'shared values'. So, for example, one group of potential customers for a financial service may be typified by their traditional, family-oriented life-style, in which savings are synonymous with security. Another group however, thinks in terms of consumption, rather than saving, and is concerned to maximise short-term gain from any investment they might make. Clearly such different groups need to be addressed in quite different ways. The following provides a particular segmentation analysis of life styles in a consumer goods market.

- *The Status Seeker* A group which is very much concerned with the prestige of brands purchased
- *The Swinger* A group which tries to be modern and up to date in all its activities
- *The Conservative* A group which prefers to stick to larger successful companies and popular brands
- *The Rational Man* A group which looks for benefits such as economy, value, durability, etc.

- *The Inner Directed Man* A group which is especially concerned with self-concept: members consider themselves to be independent
- *The Hedonist* A group which is concerned primarily with sensory benefits

Benefit Segmentation

It will be recalled from Chapter 1 that one of marketing's basic principles is: customers don't buy products, they buy benefits. A corollary of this tenet is that not all customers seek the same benefits. In other words, an opportunity might exist to segment the market according to the *benefits* that customers seek.

This is based on the notion that when customers buy a product or a service they do so because they wish to acquire the benefits the product or service will bring them. In this sense, the physical features or characteristics of what is purchased do not motivate buyers. What does motivate buyers is what the product will do for them.

The difference between the *features* of a product or service and the *benefits* that product or service gives to the customer is not just a question of semantics. It is crucial that the company seeking success should be aware of this difference. Too often companies fall into the trap of talking about what their product or service is or does (*features*) instead of what the customer will get out of it (*benefits*).

Benefit Analysis

The best starting point for a company is to undertake a detailed analysis to establish the full range of benefits it can offer to its customers. This can be done by listing the major features of the product or service, and then working out what these mean to the customer. However, we will first say a little more about the different kinds of benefits that exist.

Standard Benefits

These are basic benefits that accrue from the product or service. They will not be unique because our competitors can, in all probability, claim similar benefits for their goods or services. However, it is important for us to work out the standard benefits because customers are often not as knowledgeable as they appear to be. If we do not communicate the standard benefits, customers might well believe that our offer is in some way inferior to that of our competitors. The following are examples of standard benefits:

- 'Our product meets all the Safety Legislation requirements, *which means that* your staff will be at no risk when they use it.'
- 'Our service has a money-back guarantee, *which means that* if we don't do the job to the standards we claim it doesn't cost you a penny.'

□ *Company Benefits*

These are the benefits the customer will receive by dealing with a company. Remember the customer is not just buying your products or services, he is also buying a relationship with a company. The more it is possible to convince him that there are additional benefits to be gained from entering into a business relationship with one particular company, as opposed to competing ones, the more persuasive the argument becomes. Look at the following examples:

- 'We've been specialising in this technical field for longer than anyone else in this area, *which means that* you have the best possible expert advice close at hand whenever you need it.'
- 'We are a small family business, *which means that* you get individual and personal attention when you deal with us.'

□ *Differential Benefits*

Without doubt, the benefits that offer the greatest prospect of a competitive 'edge' over competitors are *differential* benefits. Here we are looking for benefits that cannot be provided by others. If you think about this for a moment, it is obvious that if a company is offering more or less the same as everyone else in the business, chances are that it can only compete by offering a lower price.

If a company cannot identify any differential benefits, then it is either providing a product or service that is identical in every way to the offerings of the competition (which is most unlikely), or the benefit analysis has not been done thoroughly enough. Some examples of differential benefits are:

- 'We are the only supplier who genuinely provides a round-the-clock service, *which means that* your machinery will never be out of service.'
- 'We use a unique hardening process on our machine tools, for which we have the patent, *which means that* our tools last longer and that saves you money.'

You will have noticed that all the examples given above state a feature of the product, service, or company and then turn this into a benefit for the customer by using the expression 'which means that . . .' Sometimes it isn't easy to decide if the product of the expression 'which means that' is genuinely a benefit. In these cases, challenge the supposed benefit with 'so what!' One of two things will happen:

- the 'so what' test will reveal that the benefit is real and has substance for the customer; or
- the 'so what' test will reveal something with little benefit for the customer, in which case continue with another 'which means that' until a real benefit is reached.

The following example shows the 'so what' test in operation:

- 'Our components are fully tested, which means that every single one will perform to the specification laid down.'

  Response: So what!

  '. . . which means that they have a guaranteed life of twenty thousand hours and will not let you down.'

  Response: So what!

  '. . . which means that your production lines can run continuously without the inconvenience of sudden breakdowns, thus giving you savings on both production and maintenance.'

  This would seem to be a very worthwhile benefit.

Clearly, to be useful for segmentation a benefit has to appeal to a significant number of customers. The benefit analysis process described here not only enables us to make a comprehensive list of all benefits, but also to see how they relate to what different customers seek. It thus makes it possible to emphasise product benefits with a high level of appeal for any particular customer segment.

So far we have looked at customers in terms of *what* they buy and *why* they buy it. It is also possible to segment markets by the characteristics of customers.

■ Analysis of Customer Characteristics

This approach to segmentation seeks to find ways of describing groups of customers in terms of their predominant characteristics. There are a number of different ways of approaching this type of analysis. The most frequently used methods are based on what are called 'demographics'.

■ Consumer Markets

For consumer markets, these demographics are likely to be age, gender, education, stage in the family life-cycle, and social status in life represented by jobs, residence, and income. The following summarises these categories:

- *Socio-economic*: for example social class, status, income.
- *Psychographic*: for example personality, attitudes, motives.
- *Demographic*: for example age, gender.
- *Geographic*: for example country, region, urban or rural dweller.

By knowing about these characteristics of our customers it is possible, through research, to find out more about what they read, what they watch on television, how they spend their leisure time and how much disposable income they have.

All of this information can assist with our choice of methods to reach various customer groups and influence the tone of what we wish to say to them. Some simple examples are as follows:

- Retired professional and business people often have a high disposable income and tend to spend more money on specialist services like health care. They will probably spend more on things such as hobbies and holidays. Less well-off retired people will obviously have less disposable income and will devote more of their resources to the basics of life.
- Young families with one or two young children, particularly those in the managerial classes, will tend to live on private estates. They have an above-average income; they often commute long distances to work and for shopping, and have high expenditure on furniture, entertainment, kitchen equipment and domestic appliances.
- Often, certain kinds of people tend to be located in certain types of location. For example, our first group (above) tend to live in private flats, or in detached or semi-detached houses in seaside areas; whereas the second group are more likely to be found in modern, cheaper, private housing estates. Today it is possible to be very specific about consumer purchasing habits according to the type of accommodation and area in which people live. One such method is known as ACORN (A Classification Of Regional Neighbourhoods), which breaks down the whole of the UK into thirty-eight neighbourhood types, all of which can easily be identified by their postcodes.

Industrial Markets

For industrial markets, demographics are likely to be: type of industry, company size (by number of employees), turnover, main production processes, level of technology, purchase quantity/frequency, type of buyer (for example research chemist, production engineer) and level of after-sales service requirements.

Imagine a small businessman with a specialised reclamation and repair service for machinery. It would obviously be quite useful for him to classify potential customers using what is called the *Standard Industrial Classification*. This is a government publication that analyses industry, forming a number of broad categories and then a number of sub-categories within these broad groups. It is then a comparatively simple task for the businessman to ascertain which categories are likely to have a demand for his particular services.

Our small businessman may now be able to classify potential customers by using some, or a combination, of the following:

- Company size.
- The nature of the firm's production processes.
- Levels of expenditure on specific areas such as distribution, research and development.

■ International Market Segmentation

Typical segmentation models in international marketing consist of geographical groups, such as Western Europe, Eastern Europe, North America, ASEAN, Australasia and so on. Such groupings, however, are of very limited value as actionable marketing propositions, as they bear little relationship to actual consumption/usage patterns.

Taking Europe as an example, there are typically three discrete groupings: EC, EFTA, Eastern Europe. Within Eastern Europe, however, there are at least three subgroups: the 'strong' group (Czechoslovakia and Hungary), the 'middle' group (Poland, Bulgaria, Romania and 'Yugoslavia'), and the 'poor' group (the former Soviet republics).

Even within Western Europe, however, there are significant differences due to natural phenomena. For example Scandinavia has short summers and long winters; Greece, Portugal, Italy and Spain have long summers and short winters. Netherlands has low plains; Switzerland has mountains. The per capita GDP of Switzerland is seven times that of Portugal. There are significant communication and distribution differences. For example there is virtually no TV in Norway, whilst it is very strong in Italy. Retail channel concentration is very dense in Northern Europe, whereas there is a preponderance of small, independent outlets in Southern Europe. There are also significant cultural and linguistic differences, and so on.

If, therefore, geography is to be relevant, it is more sensible to think in terms of the Anglo-Saxon North, the Latin South, North East France, Benelux, North West Germany, and so on.

Even this, however, is simplistic, in the sense that there are basically three kinds of 'products':

- *Truly global products.* These are: either products or services that are inherently global, such as international services, world-standard industrial products, high-technology products and the like; or they are fashion products or national products that have become global, such as Chivas Regal, Coca-Cola, Rolls-Royce, McDonald's, Remy Martin, and so on. These have become global because of their image or positioning.
- *National products.* These typically depend on strong market responsiveness, client relationships, national preferences, and where global efficiencies are less critical.
- *Hybrid products.* Here adaptation across countries is possible and this requires a rethinking of simple geographical segmentation bases, such as customer groups with similar needs across national boundaries. For example JWT discovered three broad breakfast types across Europe; there is a fashion lager market across Europe; there are commonalities in computer software applications across Europe; and so on.

To summarise, there are significant legal, regulatory, linguistic, communication media, distribution channel differences throughout the world and even across

Western Europe. There are, consequently, few truly global products and many traditional habits remain deep-rooted, militating against international segmentation.

On the other hand (and this applies particularly to Western Europe) there are a number of growing trends that suggest that the need for international market segmentation will become increasingly important. These are:

- The desire for monetary union, social-affairs union, foreign-affairs union, defence-policy union, and so on.
- increasing product/technical standardisation.
- Deregulation of transportation, telecommunications, pharmaceuticals, and so on.
- Attitude convergence towards work, individuality, materialism, the environment, and so on.
- Pan-European buying.
- Mergers, acquisitions, joint ventures.
- Increased travel, education, media exposure, fashion, and so on.

The bases for international market segmentation are likely to be specific groupings of countries, such as the new 'Euro Regions' outlined above, or customer groups across selected countries.

Summary

A useful summary of the issues relating to market segmentation is shown in Table 5.1.

Table 5.1 Bases for market segmentation

What is bought	• Price categories
	• Outlets used
	• Physical characteristics of different products
Who buys	• Demographic factors
	• Socio-economic factors
	• Geography
Why	• Benefits
	• Attitudes/beliefs
	• Personality/lifestyle

To summarise this chapter on customer segmentation, look at Figure 5.1 and the following:

- Very few companies can afford to be 'all things to all people'.
- Customer segmentation enables the firm to target its limited resources on the most promising opportunities.

- What is an opportunity for firm A is not necessarily an opportunity for firm B, since the two companies will have different strengths and weaknesses.
- A company needs to develop the customer segments it understands, and for which its offer is best suited.
- Segmentation can be based on many factors, but, as we have seen, the segments should be:
  (a) large enough to ensure that they are economic to service;
  (b) defined in such a way that the company can develop specialised skills in serving them;
  (c) described in terms that are relevant to actual purchase behaviour.

When tackled intelligently, customer segmentation will help to determine a company's marketing and sales objectives, and also help to improve decision-making in complex business situations.

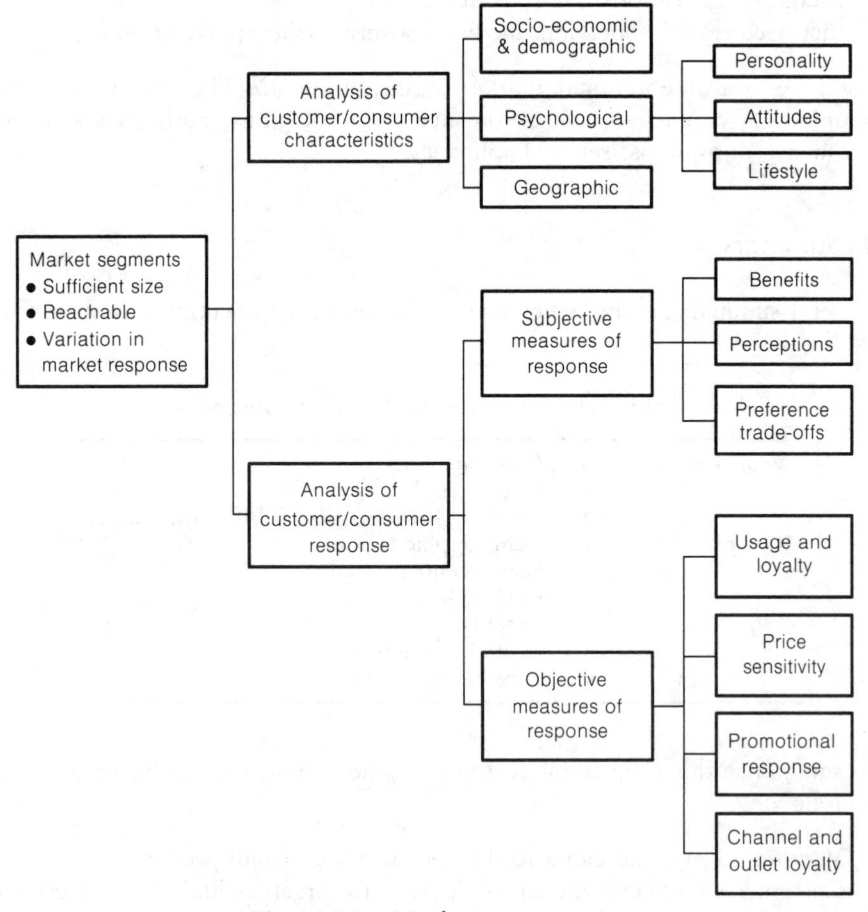

Figure 5.1 Market segmentation

CHAPTER 6

Scanning the Environment

So far in this book we have looked at marketing, both as a concept and as a process. We defined marketing as matching the abilities of the supplying company with the needs of the customer so that they both get what they want. The limitations that militate against this matching process working well are likely to be weaknesses within the company and external factors, which can be seen as threats. However, on the positive side, companies also possess strengths and the business environment is rarely completely hostile. As one commercial opportunity dies, another will appear. The successful company plays on its strengths, which it tries to build, and tries to reduce its weaknesses. At the same time it identifies and concentrates on the available opportunities, while consciously negotiating a way through the threats.

The Marketing Environment

There are likely to be several important factors that can affect the extent to which it is possible for an organisation to balance its resources and efforts with customer needs. This milieu in which the organisation is operating is referred to as the *marketing environment* and consists of the following components:

- Customers
- Competitors
- Social and cultural trends
- Political, fiscal, economic and legal policies
- Technology
- Institutional patterns

It is our intention to examine in much more depth elsewhere in this book the two most obvious components of the marketing environment – customers and competitors. The ability to know who our actual and potential customers are and to understand in what ways different groups of customers have different needs is obviously central to any organisation's success. Equally, since what competitors do will always affect a business, it is necessary to find ways of monitoring their activities and of building that information into decision-making.

This is why these two crucial components of the marketing environment are treated in more depth elsewhere in this book. This, however, is not to imply that the other elements listed are not important. Indeed, it is the purpose of this chapter to examine their impact on the organisation and to look at ways of monitoring them, starting with social and cultural trends.

Cultural Trends

Different countries – and, in domestic markets, different regions – have different preference patterns that spring from culture and tradition. For example, preference shown by customers for one product over another may be based purely on cultural traditions or trends. Consider for a moment European breakfast habits. The Dutch prefer cheese, the British like toast and the Danes enjoy crispbread. If there are problems when marketing domestically, the problems are that much greater when it comes to differentiating between cultures. Intuitive skills in domestic markets can make a great contribution to marketing programmes, but behaviour according to the same cultural criteria in foreign markets can lead to the most elementary and expensive marketing mistakes.

Material Culture

This is often responsive to increased national wealth and its consequent rewards, as well as the current state of discretionary income and its impact on purchasing inclinations and abilities. Language is another aspect of culture that requires the most careful attention in the choice, for example, of brand names and in the communication of ideas. Different cultures respond differently to the acquisition of conspicuous wealth, towards changes in life-styles and towards taking social risks.

Education

This determines whether or not written communication is possible. High levels of illiteracy make instructions on packaging pointless; training programmes for distributors and agents must take careful cognisance of the problems that result. The conduct of marketing research will also pose its own problems which can be severely restricting because such a high premium must, of necessity, be placed on objectively collated data in the face of an uncertain cultural situation.

Religion

Like language, religion is a readily identifiable aspect of cultural differences that we find both within and across national boundaries. Its taboos and predilections must be ascertained and their impact on economic behaviour studied with care. For instance, anything to do with liquor in some Muslim countries must be handled with great sensitivity. Attitudes and values, most especially towards marketing, advertising and sales, will need to be ascertained and understood.

☐ *Business Practices*

These vary between cultures and nations, as do acceptable modes of dress. For example, the conventions for making business appointments in South America and the Middle East not only vary but are alien to most European businessmen. Punctuality, or at least respect for this convention, is interpreted differently across national boundaries. Whilst a safari suit and long socks might be acceptable business dress for men in many hot climates, exposed knees and lower arms would be considered a mark of disrespect by many native businessmen of the Gulf states. Contract negotiation, itself an art, must be adapted accordingly. What may be common negotiating practice 'at home' may be wholly unacceptable to businessmen in the country in which you are trying to develop a commercial presence.

☐ *Social Organisation*

This can be seen most clearly at work in the family or in the company's purchasing department. Certain cultures respect age and status, whilst others have developed a more meritocratic stance. Some have a greater respect for womenfolk than others. Some operate through a greatly extended concept of family, whereas in other cultures the family has almost broken down as an effective social institution, even for bringing up children.

Ultimately, successful intercultural marketing activity is built upon an understanding of how local culture interacts with the four 'P's.

■ Political, Fiscal, Economic and Legal Policies

The political, fiscal, economic and legal policies of the governments of the countries in which we sell our goods also determine what we can do. For example, inflation reduces the discretionary spending power of consumers, and this can result in market decline. Legislation concerning such things as labelling, packaging, advertising and environmentalism all affect the way in which we run our businesses, and all these things have to be taken into account when we make our plans.

One of the most obvious and visible examples of government policies has been the impact in certain countries of heavy taxation on tobacco and the banning of cigarette advertising. This has forced tobacco companies to seek less hostile markets in other parts of the world, but most have also diversified into other products and services in order to continue their historical growth in turnover and profits. Also, publicity about, and in many cases legislation against, unhealthy ingredients in food has caused significant changes in purchasing behaviour. In the USA and the UK, for example, per capita consumption of chicken now exceeds that of beef. This is a prime example of an industry not being sufficiently aware of changing environmental trends and allowing a competitive industry to overtake them.

Turning for a moment specifically to the internal environment, *tariffs* are taxes on imports levied in order to earn revenue and protect home industries. They affect the price of imported goods, making them less competitive than locally produced goods. Companies affected by tariffs often react by using marginal cost-pricing policies, by modifying the product, by repositioning the product in a high-priced market segment or by CKD shipping (completely knocked down) for local assembly, thus attracting a lower rate of duty.

Quotas are direct barriers to imports. They are much more serious because the firm has less flexibility in responding to them. Apart from attempting to obtain a fair share of quotas, virtually the only response is to set up local production if the market size warrants it.

Exchange control means that foreign exchange is in short supply and the government is rationing it. If a company is manufacturing in a country with exchange controls, it has to make sure it is able to obtain exchange for imported supplies of raw materials or component parts; or else develop local supplies irrespective of possible higher costs and indifferent quality. Also, such a country is unlikely to give high priority to profit remittance, whilst currency fluctuations can either wipe out a company's profit or create a windfall virtually overnight.

Non-tariff barriers in the form of customs documentation, marks of origin, product formulation, packaging and labelling laws can similarly have a dramatic effect on a company's freedom over the management of its marketing effort.

Political instability, boycotts, customs, unions and other environmental factors can also have a drastic effect on a company's marketing policy. For instance, one German company selling consumer products in Latin America lost most of its market share when the tariff was raised from 20 per cent to 50 per cent. The options discussed by the local management at an emergency meeting were: to continue paying the high duty and change the product positioning to a high price segment; to import the primary ingredients and assemble locally; to ask for a lower price from the home factory; or to give up the market completely. Eventually, the company realised that it had to take a longer-term view that took account of the potential in the total Latin American Free Trade Area (LAFTA), and that this should have been done at the market entry stage rather than after a heavy investment had been made in only one market. Eventually the company set up manufacturing facilities in one of the LAFTA countries and South America is now a profitable market for the company. But, above all, the company learned the hard way that it just did not enjoy the same degree of control over its international marketing as it did over its home market.

■ Technology

Technology is constantly changing. We can no longer assume that our current range of products will continue to be demanded by our customers. For example, the introduction of non-drip paint had a profound effect on what had traditionally been a stable market. People discovered that they could use paint without causing a mess, and eventually the product was demanded in new kinds of outlets such as supermarkets. Those paint manufacturers who continued to make only their traditional kind of paint and to distribute it through traditional outlets went into decline very quickly.

More recently, companies such as Gestetner have been badly affected by the encroachment into their traditional areas of business by more effective small photocopying machines, whilst the printing industry is being affected by the development of desktop publishing. The advent of the computer, of course, has revolutionised just about every facet of business life, whilst the merging of telecommunications and computer technology is causing a fundamental reappraisal of a whole host of industries, with new ones springing up to replace those that do not keep abreast of changing technology.

Technological change is now such an accepted facet of business life that no organisation can afford to ignore it. British Cellophane Limited, part of the Courtaulds group, dominated the European cellophane packaging market for many years until the invention of oriented polypropylene, based on oil. Since BCL had such a hold on the market they chose to ignore this technological development, until before long major oil companies entered traditional cellophane markets with a lower-priced product. It was only then that the company decided to embrace the new technology, via an acquisition. The result was that the company lost its dominant position in the market, and, whilst it has recovered well there is no doubt that many years of difficulties could have been avoided given a more perspicacious approach to technological change.

■ Institutional Patterns

Institutional patterns are another aspect of the marketing environment that contemporary marketers have inherited from previous years of trading activity. Since we have been talking about food and technology, this point can be illustrated by two well-known examples.

Until the late 1960s, the major pattern of food distribution throughout Europe was for relatively small grocers or multiple stores to operate through highly local retail outlets. The advent of mass car ownership has transformed this pattern in two decades to one of large-scale supermarkets in almost every developed country. In so doing, several other traditional retail institutions have been undermined – the pharmacist, the butcher, the greengrocer, the fishmonger, the dairy, the hardware merchant, and even the baker.

But even today changes are taking place. Supermarkets that present themselves only as discount retailers are losing out to those who are making more specialised offers to a more discerning public. The result is that in the UK, for example, Boots, St Michael and Sainsbury have become brand names in their own right, whilst a whole new generation of specialist retailers are beginning to emerge.

The Giro method of banking, invented in Austria and widely practised throughout Europe for half a century, only reached the UK in the 1960s. It is only now that the Giro system is beginning to make any real impact on the pattern of banking behaviour amongst the two thirds of the population who made no use at all of the clearing banks at the time of Giro's introduction, and to whom the convenience of banking services had hitherto not been effectively available.

The essential point is that the environment in which we operate is not controlled by us. It is dynamic, and hence must be monitored constantly. Let us turn briefly to the methods that are available to us to help monitor the environment.

Means of Scanning the Environment

In looking at formal approaches to scanning the environment we should look first at *marketing research*.

It is sometimes said that a prime management concern in marketing is the *conversion of uncertainty into risk*. Uncertainty implies an inability to state the likelihood of any possible outcome occurring. By implication all outcomes must be treated as equally likely. Under *uncertainty* the manager must consider, say, the chance of failure in a new product launch to equal the chance of success. *Risk*, on the other hand, suggests that the likelihood of outcomes might be assessed more precisely. The marketing manager might feel that a particular new service launch has only a 5 per cent chance of failure. Our ability to make successful decisions is enhanced if we are operating under conditions of known risk rather than uncertainty. If this conversion of uncertainty into risk is the prime marketing management task, the second is surely the reduction or at least the minimisation of that risk.

To achieve either of these goals the manager requires information. Good information is a facilitator of successful marketing action. Seen in this way, marketing management becomes essentially an information-processing activity. Marketing research is therefore concerned with much more than simply telling us something about the market place. Rather, it is a systematic and objective search for, and an analysis of, information relevant to the identification and solution of marketing problems. Marketing research can be classified as being either ad hoc or ongoing.

Ad hoc marketing research refers to situations where the identification of a research problem leads to a specific information requirement. So when a French manufacturer of proprietary pharmaceuticals found that sales of its long-established cough remedy were falling, it decided to conduct a study of consumer attitudes and beliefs about cough remedies and used the information gained to relaunch the brand.

Ongoing marketing research, as the name implies, provides more of a monitoring function, resulting in a flow of information about the market place and our performance in it. The Confederation of British Industry (CBI) maintains a regular monitor, based upon surveys, of business confidence and investment intentions in the UK, for example.

Sometimes there is a dichotomy between two other forms of marketing research, *external* and *internal*. Much valuable intelligence can be gained from internal marketing analysis, and external information gathering should be seen always as a complement to such internal information and not an alternative.

External marketing research is conducted within the market and the competitive environment in which the company exists.

Internal marketing research is based upon an analysis of company data gained from information such as sales trends, changes in the elements of marketing – price, for example – and advertising levels.

There are a number of headings under which the methods of marketing research might usefully be examined. Figure 6.1 provides a summary and useful framework for discussing the forms of marketing research activity that are encountered most frequently.

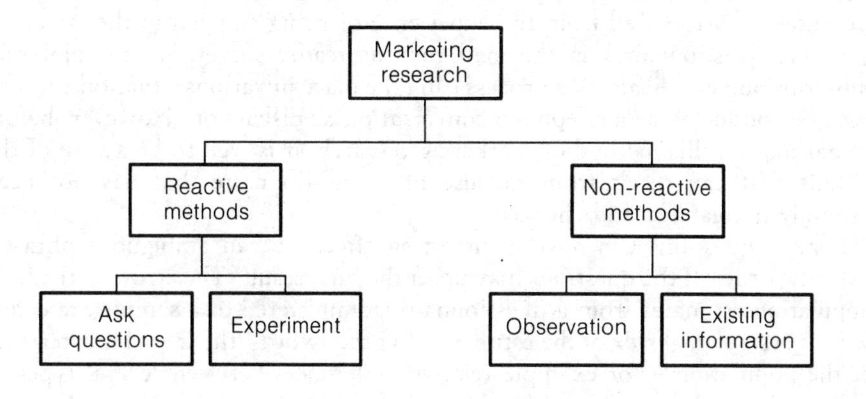

Figure 6.1 A framework for marketing research

■ Reactive Marketing Research

As the term implies, *reactive* marketing research is information about the market place and the customers who inhabit it. It can involve us in asking questions, such as in a survey or during an interview. Equally it can involve experiments. Figure 6.2 summarises the principal options.

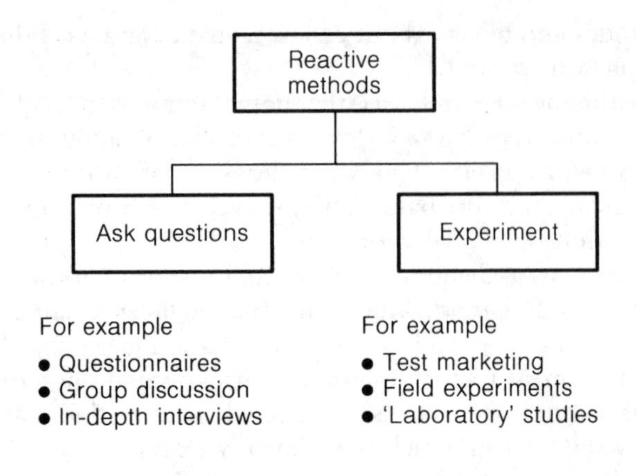

Figure 6.2 Forms of reactive marketing research

■ Questionnaires

Questionnaires are the favoured means of data gathering. They are a flexible instrument and can be administered by an interviewer or by the interviewee. As we know only too well from the experience of being stopped in the street, or receiving questionnaires in the mail such as reader survey questionnaires in subscription periodicals, this process can take place in various situations. It may even be conducted as a telephone conversation or discussion. However, before embarking on this method of marketing research, it is well to be aware of the pitfalls that can result from the use of a questionnaire that has not been carefully preplanned and checked.

Loaded questions can have a distorting effect, as can ambiguous phrases. Even the order of the questions may upset the final result. The errors in the final population estimates from a questionnaire administered to a sample are called *bias* or *systematic error* of the estimates. In other words, the true characteristics of the population – for example relative preferences between several types of industrial compressor – may be different from the estimate produced by the sample survey. This bias may result from the way in which the sample was chosen or from the means by which the survey data were collected.

Such pitfalls can be reduced by carefully designing the questionnaire and then *pilot testing* it. In other words, give the survey a trial run on a subgroup of the intended sample to isolate any problems, ambiguities or omissions that may arise in the responses.

■ Group Discussions

Group discussions may be a more appropriate way to gather market information as they attempt to draw insights for marketing action from smaller-scale, more detailed studies. Such studies are intended to provide qualitative cues, rather than quantitative conclusions.

In such circumstances a group discussion is a loosely structured format where the leader – often a trained psychologist – attempts to draw from the group their feelings about the subject under discussion. The group is chosen to be representative of the population in which the researcher is interested, although naturally any conclusions emerging from the discussions can only form the basis of qualitative generalisations about that population. Such interviews need not be conducted in groups. They can be equally effective in pairs or alone with the interviewer.

■ Single Interviews

Single interviews are an alternative way of deriving information. Sometimes they are extended or in-depth interviews and have the advantage that both the interviewer and interviewee can explore certain lines of discussion more rigorously if this is perceived as being of mutual benefit, whereas a group discussion must always maintain a degree of structure if it is to be meaningful. Such a form of single in-depth interview will be used more often when information regarding specialised markets is required in industrial marketing research.

■ Experiments

Experiments are another type of reactive marketing research. Earlier in this book we assessed the benefits of test-marketing new products. Marketing experiments can also help us to gain a better understanding of how marketing processes work.

For example, a manufacturer of confectionery wanted to know if the effect on sales of a 'money-off' offer was greater than spending a similar sum on in-store merchandising improvements. The information he needed to answer the question could only be obtained from the experiment, whereby a number of stores were selected in different areas of the country and used as the testing ground for these alternative promotional approaches. The stores chosen for the experiment were as near alike as possible in terms of turnover on the brand in question and served similar types of customers.

One-third of the stores ran the 'money-off' promotion, one-third used the improved in-store merchandising, and the remaining third carried on selling the product without any changes. After a period of two months the manufacturer felt able to draw conclusions about the relative effectiveness of the two promotional methods by comparing store results with those stores where no changes were made.

Market experimentation need not necessarily involve the setting up of large-scale experimental designs such as the one just discussed. Sometimes laboratory-type situations can be used to test marketing stimuli. Often advertisements will be pre-tested in such laboratory conditions. Samples of the target audience for an advertisement will be exposed to the advertisement and their reactions to the sample will be sought. Eye cameras, polygraphs and tachistoscopes are just some of the devices that have been used successfully to record physical reactions to marketing stimuli.

Whilst the theory of experimentation in the marketing context is sound enough, there are a number of drawbacks to its operation in practice. It is very often difficult to set up experimental situations that are microcosms of the total market. There is always the problem of controlling all the variables in the experiment, for example the actions of competitors, and of course the cost of setting up and maintaining market experiments can be prohibitive.

■ Non-Reactive Marketing Research

These methods are based upon interpretation of *observed phenomena* or extant data. By definition, they do not rely upon data derived directly from respondents. Figure 6.3 summarises the main forms of *non-reactive* marketing research.

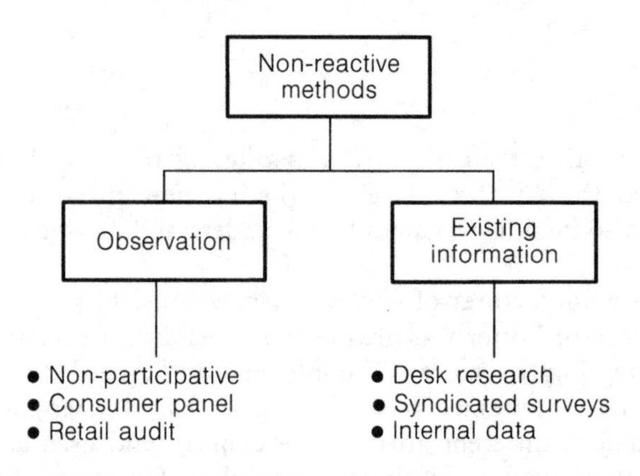

Figure 6.3 Forms of non-reactive marketing research

■ Desk Research

Desk research should in fact be the *starting point* of any marketing research programme. Desk research involves the use of existing information for determining the extent of prior knowledge about the subject being studied. There is often a wealth of material to be obtained from published and unpublished sources, which can reduce the need to 'rediscover the wheel'.

Official statistics such as those published by governments, OECD, the EU and the UN, can provide detailed data on markets and patterns within those markets. Other sources such as newspapers, technical journals, trade association publications and published market studies will provide a 'fill-in' to any later field work that might be needed. *Internal data* derived from sales figures and salesmen's reports can also be a guide to the direction that later studies might need to take.

Observation

Observation can be a very effective marketing research technique. How people behave in the real world and how they react to stimuli can often be discovered best of all through watching and interpreting their reactions. Some observational methods, such as a camera in a supermarket, do not involve the direct participation of the researcher and this can be a limiting factor. Often the areas of activity in which we are most interested may only occur infrequently and the observation must be sustained over a period in order to capture a single activity.

Participant Observation

'Participant' observation, a phrase borrowed from anthropology, involves the observer in attempting to become a part of the activity that is under observation. This form of marketing research is very limited in its scope, although one British research organisation, Mass Observation, did some early pioneering work in this area in a number of studies, a famous example being a major study of consumer behaviour in public houses.

Retail Audit

Retail audit is widely used as a secondary source of observation data. This has been developed and perfected as a technique over a period of time and, properly controlled, it can be a very accurate source of marketing information on brand shares, market size, distribution coverage and sales trends.

The audits conducted by A. C. Neilsen Ltd are perhaps the most widely known, and work on a simple basis. Within a particular product field a representative sample of stockists is chosen and their cooperation obtained. At regular periods the investigator visits the stockists and notes two things; the current levels of stock of the product group being audited, and the invoices or delivery notes for any goods in that group delivered since the last visit. With the information on stock levels obtained on the *last* visit, it is a simple matter to determine sales of each item being audited during the period between visits – that is, opening stock plus deliveries between visits less closing stock = sales during period.

The Consumer Panel

The consumer panel is another similar source of data. This is a sample group of consumers in a particular product field who record in a diary their purchases and consumption over a period of time. This technique has been used in industrial as well as consumer markets and can provide continuous data on patterns of usage as well as other data such as media habits.

Integrating Marketing Research with Marketing Action

How should managers approach this issue? In the first place it is necessary to view marketing information as a resource. This means that we must be concerned with the problems of producing, storing and distributing it. Marketing information has a limited shelf life – it is perishable. Like other resources, information has a value in use. The less the manager knows about a marketing problem, and the greater the risk attached to a wrong decision, the more valuable the information becomes. This latter point is an important consideration in assessing marketing research budgets. It implies the need for a cost–benefit appraisal of all sources of marketing information. There is no point in investing more in such information than the return on it would justify. Naturally, it is easier to determine the costs than the benefits. The managerial benefits of marketing research are difficult to pin down. They can be expressed in terms of additional sales or profits that might be achieved through the avoidance of marketing failures that could otherwise result if there is a lack of information.

One company involved in the development of an industrial application of heat exchangers in West Germany believed that there was a 20 per cent chance that the product might not succeed, leaving them with a development and marketing bill of DM 2 million. From this they inferred that the maximum *loss expectation* was DM 400 000 (that is, 20 per cent of DM 2 000 000) and that it was worth paying up to this sum to acquire information that would help them avoid such a loss. Such a cost–benefit calculation implies that the information they could acquire would in itself be totally reliable. Because such *perfect information* is rare, and in this case could not be obtained, they budgeted a smaller sum for marketing research, which effectively discounted the likely inaccuracy of the information. Such an approach can be a valuable means of quantifying the value of marketing research in a managerial context.

The use of marketing research by European companies has grown considerably in the last decade or so. Its use is not confined to manufacturers selling into consumer markets; some of the most interesting work to have been conducted in recent years has been on behalf of industrial marketing organisations, service companies such as banks, and social organisations such as voluntary and government agencies.

With this growth of marketing research has come an increasing sophistication in the use of the techniques available to the researcher, now a professional whose advice is looked for more and more in marketing decision-making. Likewise, the growth of companies that provide specialist marketing research services has multiplied so that it is now a major industry in its own right. This means that the manager has the facility available to him or her to monitor the effectiveness of their marketing performance and also to gain a better feel for what opportunities exist in the market place.

Finally, let us have a brief look at the difficulties of marketing research in the international context.

International Marketing Intelligence

International marketing intelligence is simply the systematic gathering, recording and analysis of data about problems relating to the marketing of goods and services internationally. It is concerned with the following:

- Where to go.
- How to enter.
- How to market the 4 'P's.
- Traditional marketing research questions within each market.

International marketing intelligence involves marketing research covering additional factors not usually present in domestic marketing; and studies of many foreign markets individually.

This form of marketing research is often referred to as *comparative analysis*. It is a way of organising information on international markets and involves comparing and grouping countries in ways useful to decision-making, thus maximising the use of a company's international experience. For example, grouping countries according to their geographic proximity, which some companies do for the purpose of marketing control, can be a mistake if they are not homogeneous in characteristics important to the company's marketing. Grouping countries according to stage of economic development, for example, can be a useful way of filling data gaps, for the missing values can be assumed to be similar to those available in the small group. Also, the expense of researching in many small markets can often be avoided by carrying out research in a sample of countries and extrapolating the results to other countries in the same group.

A large electronics company carried out a comparative analysis of its markets worldwide by first identifying the characteristics that were important to its international marketing decisions, then grouping different countries according to their similarity in these dimensions. They found three distinct groupings and began to develop marketing strategies for these three groups, rather than developing separate marketing strategies for each individual country as previously. The result was reflected in great savings for the company and also an improvement in the company's control.

There are a great number of problems in international market research not normally present in domestic research. These centre around cultural problems and economic problems. In some parts of the world only oral communication is possible, with several languages being spoken. Quite apart from these considerations, it is often almost impossible to interview women. For example in most Islamic countries women are not allowed to talk to men without their husbands being present. Mail and telephone surveys are impossible in some countries, either because they are illegal, or because they are impractical. This leaves virtually only personal interviews, often difficult because of geographic and cultural problems.

Published data is less available and often unreliable, whilst different base years and different definitions are often used. Add to this the cost of researching foreign markets, and it will be seen at once that international market research is not just a simple extension of domestic techniques; although it must be said that as far as questionnaire design and sample sizes are concerned, exactly the same rules apply.

■ Preparing the Marketing Research Brief

■ Do We Need a Research Brief?

Regardless of who carries out the work, it is important that a clear brief should be produced against which the subsequent work will be undertaken and judged. The research brief – which should be produced in both written and verbal form – is a key document and the starting point. In its preparation it is important that the following questions are to the fore:

- What do we want to know?
- What will we do with the information when we get it?

In this way, clearly defined objectives will be set and adhered to.

■ What Should it Contain?

First, the commissioning company should think very carefully about what and how much it wishes to tell in the brief. Ideally the brief should be open, precise and factual – but there may be particular points that are best omitted, for example the precise budget.

A good briefing document, preferably accompanied by product/service literature, may span 1–5 pages. Its elaboration/discussion at a briefing meeting should clarify points, confirm contents and remove any written ambiguities. At the end of the meeting, if a quotation is to be submitted, the consultant/agency should both see and show a firm commitment to the project.

A good research brief should contain the following:

- Background information on the market, the company, its products/services, market standing and so on.
- Research objectives – perhaps both primary and secondary. In this section it may be useful to define precise question areas to be covered by the research.
- Desired time scale: overall project completion date, together with any interim report times or key decision dates (for example product development stages or interfaces with other departments).
- Report format/presentation requirements (if defined): this is a good opportunity, if the commissioning company wishes, to indicate preferences.
- Company liaison/contact; information to be made available in support of the research.
- Market-place confidentiality or openness required from the research.

It is not suggested that the briefing document be seen as a 'straitjacket', but as a series of well thought-out guidelines. As such, the expertise of the agency/consultancy should be sought in the briefing meeting, both with regard to the information and requirements of the brief, as well as in discussion of the best methods of achieving the brief's objectives.

■ What Else Might We Do?

Whilst it is not suggested that the brief should exactly define some areas – for example research methodology or precise budget allocation – it could be helpful if some verbal discussion on these points takes place during the briefing meeting. Given the expected expertise of the agency/consultancy, it is a very fair approach to provide a comprehensive briefing and ask for a written proposal offering the best solutions, including recommended methodologies, expected time frames and costs involved.

Whilst guidelines as to the probable research budget are very helpful, indications of precise budget allocations frequently tend to be met by proposal documents/terms of reference just under or exactly equal to the figures given!

Some commissioning organisations set a proposal deadline or tender-submission date. At the briefing stage it may be best to indicate the competitive quoting levels involved without necessarily defining or naming these precisely.

This stage should be seen as a further opportunity to confirm importance and commitment. Remember, the client retains the prerogative to reject all proposals or require modifications to them. Normally the costs involved in the briefing meeting and preparation of the research proposal are seen by consultants/agencies as part of their prospecting/business development costs and involve no client charges (whether the proposal is accepted or not) unless specifically previously agreed (and then, best in writing).

Preparing the Research Proposal

What is the Research Proposal?

Basically the proposal – a written document and personal presentation – is a best response to the marketing research brief. As such it represents an ability to communicate and this should be a selection factor – remember that the organisation subsequently commissioned to carry out the research is providing an indication or preview of its listening, communication and presentation skills. This assessment opportunity for you, the client, should not be overlooked!

The research proposal should provide a specification of what the research organisation will do, how it will carry out the work and what it will cost. It is important that it conveys its understanding of what is expected and its competence to provide the work most efficiently. This understanding and competence should be in both written and verbal form if personally presented.

What Should it Contain?

A good research proposal should include:

- Background information: to convey a clear understanding of the project and the issues involved.
- Objectives: these should be clearly listed and very precisely defined against the needs of the problem.
- Work programme and methodology: these should cover how the objectives will be achieved and the way the work programme will be completed; it should detail sample size, research stages and questionnaire methods.
- Fees/payment terms and time scales: these should be clearly stated and broken down to show expenses and the work schedule.
- Company details and research personnel involved: to include research company competence and brief biographies of personnel, plus, if relevant, any business terms.
- Summary of research project benefits and agency's confidence in its competence to 'deliver' what is required.

How Should the Sponsoring Organisation Respond?

Acceptance of the proposal should be in writing. It should authorise the work and confirm the points of agreement and costs involved. This should provide a binding agreement as to what is to be done and at what cost – hopefully eliminating any subsequent disagreement between the two parties.

■ Summary

From this brief summary of research methods and techniques in marketing it can be seen that the scope of marketing research can be considerable. Yet, at the same time, we must recognise that even the most carefully designed and conducted studies can at best only provide *imperfect information* of market phenomena. However, that being said, marketing research remains the link between the identification of market opportunities and successful exploitation of them by organisations, whatever their specialism or function. It is the principal means of monitoring the environment in which the matching process takes place.

CHAPTER 7

Competitive Analysis and Strategy

Success in the market place is dependent not only upon identifying and responding to customer needs but also upon our ability to ensure that our response is judged by customers to be superior to that of the competitors. In other words, the development of marketing strategies must be based around both customer satisfaction and competitive differentiation.

Just as we can remember the key components of the marketing mix by the shorthand of the 'four P's', so too can we focus upon the basic elements of competitive strategy by reference to the 'three C's'. The three C's in question are the Customer, the Competition and the Company. Figure 7.1 illustrates the triangular relationship that exists between the three 'C's.

Competitive strategy, therefore, can be seen as a search for differential advantage as perceived by customers. The key here is *perceptions* since the ultimate test question is: How does the customer evaluate our offer compared with competitive offers?' This basic principle is the foundation for market *positioning*. A key component of the strategic process in marketing is the identification of an appropriate competitive 'position' in the market place. In essence the position of a brand or offer is simply the customer's perception of

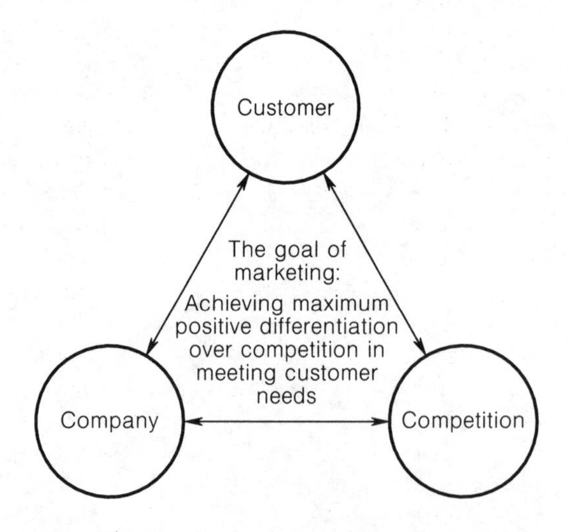

Figure 7.1 Marketing and the three 'C's

the similarity or dissimilarity of our brand in relation to competitive offerings. As such it will be influenced by the particular marketing mix of product features, promotional appeals, price level and place (distribution) factors that the company selects.

How do companies achieve this competitive advantage? Many commentators and academics have investigated this fundamental question and their findings tend to point in the same direction. Put very simply, successful companies have a cost advantage or they have a 'value' advantage – or a combination of the two. The cost advantage means that the company can produce and distribute its products at a lower cost than the competition, whilst the value advantage means that the company's offer is perceived as providing differentiated benefits to customers – the product has greater 'added values'.

Let us examine briefly these two fundamental sources of competitive advantage.

■ Cost Advantage

In many industries there will typically be one competitor who will be the low-cost producer, and more often than not, that competitor will have the greatest sales volume in the sector. There is substantial evidence to suggest that 'big is beautiful' when it comes to cost advantage. This is partly due to economies of scale, which enable fixed costs to be spread over a greater output, but more particularly to the impact of the 'experience curve'.

The experience curve is a phenomenon that has its roots in the earlier notion of the 'learning curve'. Researchers discovered during the last war that it was possible to identify and predict improvements in the rate of output of workers as they became more skilled in the processes and tasks on which they were working. Subsequent work by Bruce Henderson, founder of the Boston Consulting Group, extended this concept by demonstrating that *all* costs, not just production costs, would decline at a given rate as volume increased. In fact, to be precise the relationship that the experience curve describes is between *real* unit costs and *cumulative* volume. Further it is generally recognised that this cost decline applies only to 'value added', that is costs other than bought-in supplies. The experience curve in its general form is shown in Figure 7.2.

There are many implications of this relationship for the development of marketing strategy, not least in the determination of pricing strategy. However, its importance in this current discussion is in the fact that if one company's relative market share is greater than that of its competitors then, other things being equal, it should be further down the experience curve. In other words it will have a cost advantage. Such a cost advantage can either be used to lower price, thus putting the squeeze on competitors, or to earn higher margins at the same price as competitors.

Later in this book it will be suggested that it will generally be preferable to use such a cost advantage to reinvest in the product rather than use it to initiate

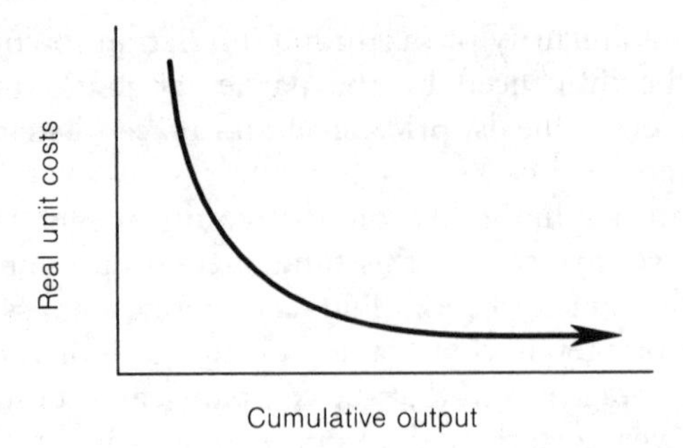

Figure 7.2 The experience curve

price wars and thus run the risk of reducing the product to the status of a 'commodity'.

Value Advantage

We have already observed that 'customers don't buy products, they buy benefits'. Put another way the product is purchased not for itself but for the promise of what it will 'deliver'. These benefits may be intangible, that is, they relate not to specific product features but rather to such things as *image* or *reputation*. Alternatively, the delivered offering may be seen to outperform its rivals in some functional aspect.

Unless the product or service we offer can be distinguished in some way from its competitors there is a strong likelihood that the market place will view it as a 'commodity' and so the sale will tend to go to the cheapest supplier. Thus the importance of seeking to attach additional values to our offering to mark it out from the competition.

What are the means by which such value differentiation may be gained?

Essentially the development of strategy based upon additional values will normally require a more segmented approach to the market. When a company scrutinises markets closely it frequently finds that there are distinct 'value segments'. In other words different groups of customers within the total market attach different importance to different benefits. Market segmentation is discussed in greater detail in Chapter 8 but its importance here lies in the fact that often there are substantial opportunities for creating differentiated appeals for specific segments. Take the motor car as an example. A model such as the Ford Sierra is positioned in the middle range of European cars; within that broad category specific versions are aimed at defined segments. Thus we find the basic, small engine, two-door model at one end of the spectrum and the four-wheel drive, high performance version at the other extreme. In between are a whole variety of options, each of which seeks to satisfy the needs of quite different 'benefit segments'. Adding value through differentiation is a powerful means of achieving a defensible advantage in the market.

In practice what we find is that the successful companies will often seek to achieve a position based upon *both* a cost advantage *and* a value advantage. A useful way of examining the available options is to present them as a simple matrix as in Figure 7.3.

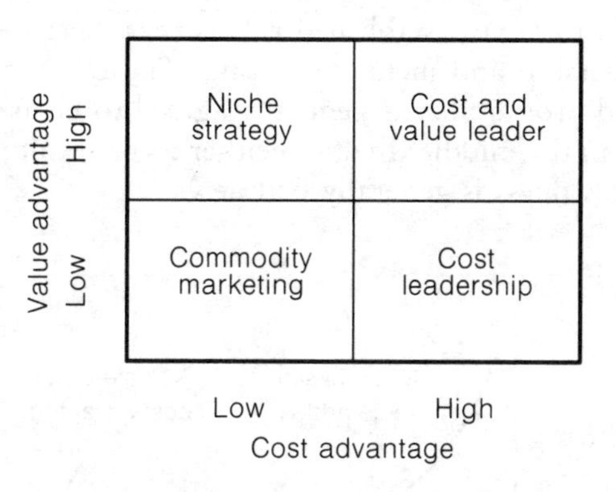

Figure 7.3 The sources of competitive advantage

Let us consider these options in turn.

For companies who find themselves in the bottom left-hand corner of our matrix the world is an uncomfortable place. These products are indistinguishable from their competitors' offerings and they have no cost advantage. These are typical 'commodity' market situations and the only ultimate strategy is either to move to the right on the matrix, that is, to cost leadership, or upwards into a 'niche'. Often the cost leadership route is simply not available. This will be the case particularly in a mature market where substantial market share gains are difficult to achieve. New technology may sometimes provide a window of opportunity for cost reduction but in such situations it is often the case that the same technology is available to competitors.

Cost leadership, if it is to form the basis of a viable long-term marketing strategy, should essentially be gained early in the market life-cycle. This is why market share is considered to be so important in many industries. The 'experience curve' concept, briefly described earlier, demonstrates the value of early market share gains – the higher your share relative to your competitors, the lower your costs should be. This cost advantage can be used strategically to assume a position of price leader and, if appropriate, to make it impossible for higher-cost competitors to survive. Alternatively price may be maintained enabling above-average profit to be earned, which is potentially available to develop further the position of the product in the market.

The other way out of the 'commodity' quadrant of our matrix is to seek a 'niche' or segment where it is possible to meet the needs of customers through offering additional values. Sometimes it may not be through tangible product features that this 'value added' is generated, but through service. For example, a steel stockholder who finds himself in the commodity quadrant may seek to move up to the niche quadrant by offering daily deliveries from stock, by providing additional 'finishing' services for his basic products or by focussing upon the provision of a range of special steels for specific segments.

What does seem to be an established rule is that there is no middle ground between cost leadership and niche marketing. The relationship between size, differentiation and profitability is generally agreed to be as depicted in Figure 7.4. Being caught in the middle (that is, neither a cost leader nor a niche-based provider of added values) is generally bad news.

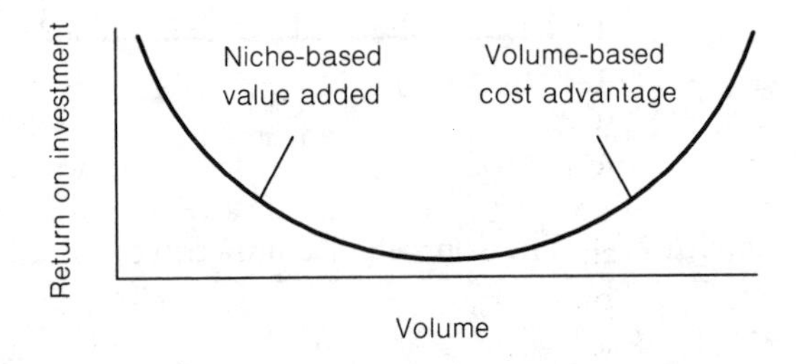

Figure 7.4 The dangers of the middle ground

Finally, perhaps the most defensible position in the matrix is the top right-hand corner. Companies who occupy that position have products that are distinctive in the values they offer and are *also* cost competitive. Arguably, many Japanese products, particularly in consumer markets, have achieved this position. Clearly it is a position of some strength, occupying 'high ground' that is extremely difficult for competitors to attack.

■ Market Share Strategies

In discussing the advantages and disadvantages of pursuing niches or volume it is important that the issues surrounding 'market share' be fully understood. That there is a strong relationship between market share and return on investment has been confirmed by the analysis of data from thousands of companies participating in the PIMS study (Profit Impact of Market Strategy). This study, in searching for explanations of variations in profitability between firms, identified a strong correlation between market share and ROI.

However, a warning should be sounded: it may well be that profitable companies have high market shares, but it does not follow that all high market share companies will be profitable. Quite simply this is because market share can be 'bought'. It can be bought through price reductions, increased marketing effort and product development. All of this can be good practice unless it is at the expense of long-term profit. Some companies have failed to recognise that investing in market share is really only viable early on in a product/market life-cycle. Likewise, other companies have been caught out when the product/market life-cycle turns out to be much shorter than was anticipated. In summary, market share strategies are long-term, and in volatile markets such strategies must be pursued with care.

A further issue surrounds the question, 'share of *which* market?' In other words, of what is market share a measure? The answer is that it all depends on how we define the total market. A holiday tour operator specialising in the organisation of cultural tours of sites of antiquity, accompanied by a professor of archaeology, is not operating in the same market as a tour operator offering ten days in Majorca for two hundred pounds. Yet they both offer holidays.

The definition problem is helped if we use the concept of the 'served' market. The served market is best described in terms of the specific needs that we seek to meet rather than some generic product category. Some have called market share in this context 'share of mind', meaning that when potential customers are contemplating a purchase to meet a specific need they limit their choice to offerings they consider competitive. The marketing challenge may thus be seen as one of how to increase 'share of mind' amongst specific target groups.

■ Competitive Analysis

As markets mature, as growth rates stabilise or markets enter recession, the only way to grow a business faster than the growth of the market is at the expense of the competition. This implies a need to understand in the greatest possible detail the competitive context and the characteristics of specific competitors. Here the work of Michael Porter, a Harvard Business School professor, is particularly valuable in providing a framework for the systematic exploration of the competitive context. Figure 7.5 summarises the main forces driving industry competition. These key determinants of competitive position are as follows:

■ Market Competition

Obviously the more numerous or equally balanced the competitors, the more intense will be the rivalry within the market. If this is combined with a slow industry growth rate, and if fixed costs relative to variable costs are high, then the prognosis is for a high level of aggressive competition, probably accompanied by severe price cutting. A further influencing factor will be the

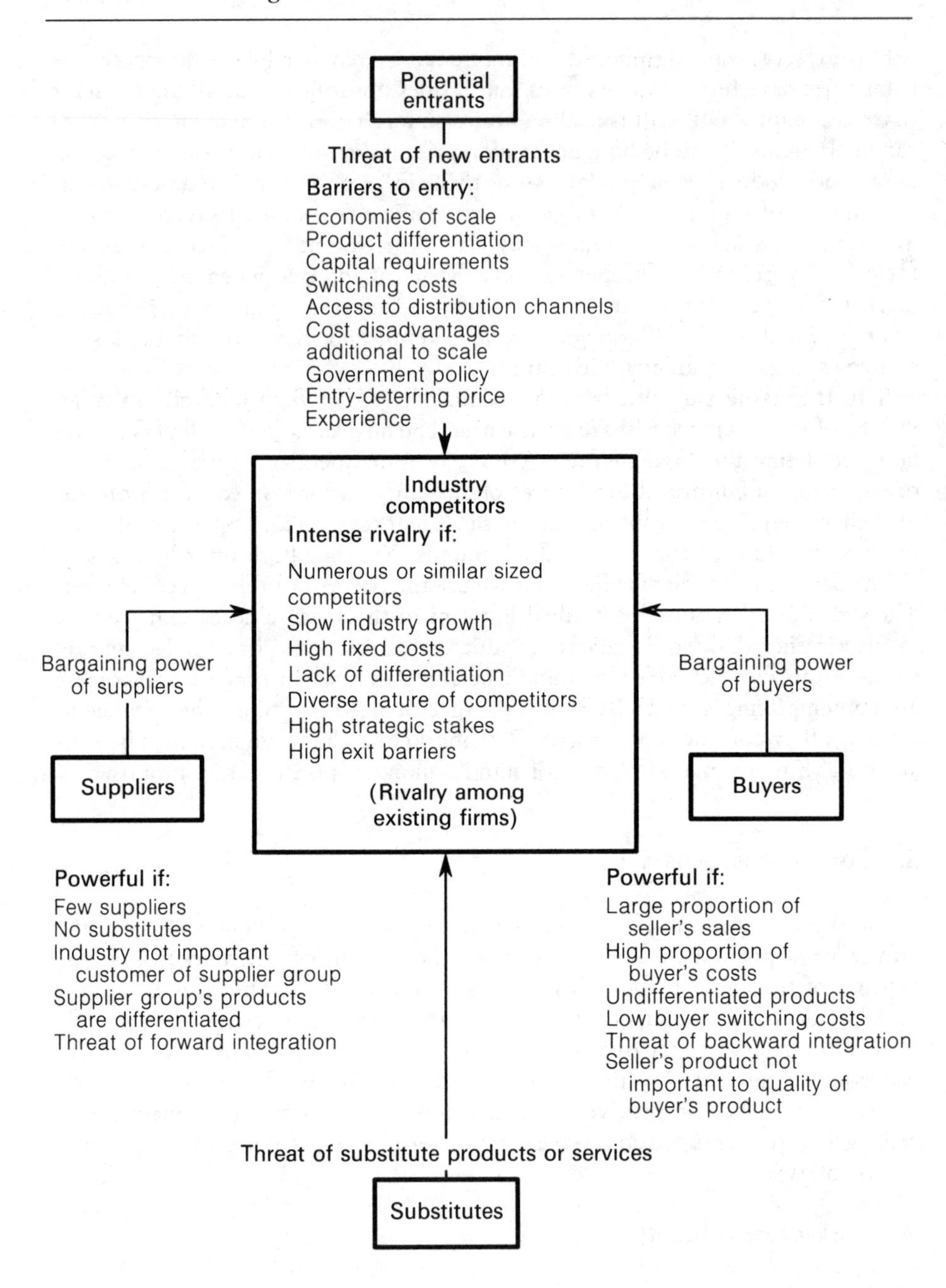

Source: Michael E. Porter, *Competitive Strategy* (New York: Free Press, 1980).

Figure 7.5 Forces driving industry competition

extent to which the competing products on offer are seen as substitutes by the market place with few switching penalties for buyers.

Of key importance will be the relative cost structures of the major players in the market; these will be determined not just by market share but by capacity utilisation and production technology.

■ Threat of New Entrants

In analysing markets one of the factors to be appraised is the existence, or absence, of 'barriers to entry'. In other words, how easy is it for new entrants to enter the market? Typically barriers might be provided by economies of scale so that without a minimum market share unit costs will be uncompetitive. Similarly heavy start-up costs – whether through the need for capital investment or high levels of marketing expenditure – can provide a barrier. Government regulation, as for example in the telecommunications industry, might also prove an effective barrier.

Conversely markets may be easy for new competitors to enter where product differentiation is low or where technology changes can overcome cost barriers. In the latter case a good example would be the way in which new technology has made it possible for new daily papers to be launched in an industry that previously had high entry barriers.

■ Substitute Products

One factor that can considerably alter the strategic balance in a market place is the development of products that meet underlying customer needs more cost-effectively than existing products. The development of synthetic fibres had a major impact upon the demand for natural fibres, for example. Similarly, the advent of home video recording through video cameras has virtually eliminated the demand for home movie products.

■ Bargaining Power of Buyers

The competitive climate of a market will clearly be influenced by the extent to which customers wield power through purchasing strength. Thus a market that is dominated by a limited number of buyers, or where a buyer takes a larger proportion of the seller's output, will substantially limit the seller's opportunities for individual action or development. The UK grocery market illustrates this situation well, with a handful of major retail chains being able to exert considerable influence over manufacturing suppliers' marketing policies and thus their profitability. Another source of competitive threat from buyers will exist when opportunities arise for backward integration up the value chain by buyers.

Bargaining Power of Suppliers

Many of the threats that potentially exist from buyers can also come from the suppliers to an industry. If the supply of critical materials is controlled by a few suppliers, or if an individual company's purchases from a supplier constitute only a small part of his output, then freedom of manoeuvre may be limited. Again, if opportunities exist for forward integration by suppliers, this constitutes a further source of potential competitive pressure.

Competitive Information

Competitive analysis at this level requires access to a wide range of information, necessitating a continued monitoring of all sources of data. The range of competitive intelligence that should be gathered is listed below. Some of the issues listed appear to be obvious and yet it is surprising how often we lack accurate information on them. Ideally a 'data bank' on the competitive environment should be established; use should be made of annual reports, annual statutory returns, Dun & Bradstreet reports or their equivalent, trade press and financial reports, publications from trade associations as well as company catalogues and advertisements.

- Who are the competition . . . Where?
- Who else might become a competitor?
- Their shares of market segments and trends.
- Their product line, performance, quality, service.
- Their management, its skill, philosophies.
- Size and development of their sales force and how they organise the sales effort.
- Their promotion strategy.
- Their pricing policy, terms, discounts.
- Their technological capability.
- Their financial strength.
- Their objectives.

Information can often be gathered from customers and suppliers about competitor's actions or intentions. If personnel are recruited from competitors they should be debriefed as far as professional ethics allow. In fact it is often surprising to see just how much openly available competitive intelligence can be gathered by making use of the sources described above.

Table 7.1 gives some indication of the sources of competitor information, most of which is readily accessible. What organisations typically lack is an effective *marketing intelligence system* that collects, interprets and disseminates this information on a regular and systematic basis. This is not so in the case of the Japanese External Trade Organisation (JETRO), a subsidiary of the

Table 7.1 Sources of competitor information

	Public	*Trade/Professionals*	*Government*	*Investors*
What competitors say about themselves	• Advertising • Promotional materials • Press releases • Speeches • Books • Articles • Personnel changes • Recruitment advertisements	• Manuals • Technical papers • Licences • Patents • Courses • Seminars	• Company House reports • Lawsuits • Office of Fair Trading and Monopolies Commission	• Annual meetings • Annual reports • Prospectuses • Stock/Bond issues • Speeches to security analysts
What others say about them	• Books • Articles • Case studies • Consultants • Newspaper reports • Environmental groups • Unions • Ex-employees	• Suppliers/Vendors • Trade press • Industry studies • Customers • Sub-contractors	• Lawsuits • Government ministries • National plans	• Security analysis • Reports • Industry studies • Credit reports

Ministry of International Trade and Industry (MITI), which has eighty offices around the world all of which gather competitive and relevant information for transmission back to Japan. The larger Japanese companies also operate worldwide monitoring systems, which, quite legally, screen and index all material, patents, licences and academic journals in their fields of interest.

To be a viable basis for marketing strategy, competitive analysis must be organised and managed as an ongoing activity – not just an *ad hoc* response to a particular circumstance.

■ Competitive Benchmarking

The ultimate test of the efficiency of any marketing strategy has to be sales – not just measured against volume targets, but rather in terms of profit. Those companies who strive for market share, but who measure market share in terms of volume sales, may be deluding themselves in that volume can be bought at the expense of profit. The only market share measure that counts in the long run is the *sterling share* of the market. In other words, what percentage of the total expenditure made by customers in this market ends up in our sales revenue?

Because market share is an 'after the event' measure we need to utilise continuing indicators of competitive performance; this will highlight areas where improvements in the marketing mix can be made.

In recent years a number of companies have developed a technique for assessing *relative* market place performance, which has come to be known as 'competitive benchmarking'. Originally the idea of competitive benchmarking was literally to take apart a competitor's product, component by component, and to compare its performance in a value engineering sense with your own product. This approach has often been attributed to the Japanese, but many western companies have also found the value of such detailed comparisons.

However, the idea of benchmarking is capable of extension beyond this simple comparison of technology and cost-effectiveness. Because the battle in the market place for the 'share of mind' that we referred to earlier is essentially concerned with perceptions, it is perceptions that we must measure.

Companies such as Rank Xerox have led the way in conducting regular surveys amongst customers, in which they seek to measure exactly how their customers see them as suppliers not just of a product, but of a total service. Not only does Rank Xerox measure the perceptions of customers concerning the relative performance of Xerox copiers compared with other copiers – it also seeks to measure the image that customers have of it compared with other groups in the 'office automation' field, such as IBM, Digital and NEC.

The measures that are used in this type of benchmarking programme include delivery reliability, ease of ordering, after-sales service, the quality of sales representation and the accuracy of invoices and other documentation. These measures are not chosen at random, but are selected because of their importance to the customer. Market research, often based on in-depth interviews, would typically be employed to identify what these 'key success factors' are. The elements that customers identify as being the most important then form the basis for the benchmark questionnaire. This questionnaire is administered to a sample of customers on a regular basis – for example, British Telecom carries out a daily telephone survey of a random sample of their domestic and business customers to measure customers' perceptions of service. For most companies an annual survey could suffice; in other cases perhaps quarterly, particularly if market conditions are dynamic. The output of these surveys might typically be presented in the form of a competitive profile as in the example in Figure 7.6.

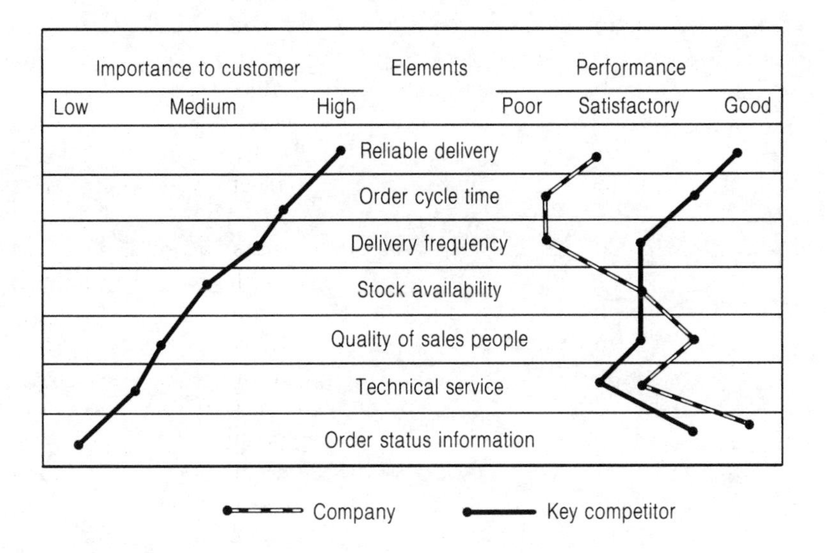

Figure 7.6 Competitive benchmarking

■ Summary

In today's environment the ability to present customers with a total offer that is recognised as superior to competitive offerings has become the prime task of marketing. We have seen that it is possible to gain competitive advantage both through lower costs and through greater product and service differentiation.

Knowledge of the competition is as important as knowledge of customers. Increasingly the leading companies are developing information systems that enable a continuing monitor of competitive strategy and performance to be maintained.

These days, the phrase 'competitive advantage' having become the rallying cry in so many organisations, it has become even more crucial to build marketing strategies that explicitly take account of competitive considerations.

CHAPTER 8

The Marketing Audit

The Auditing Process

A marketing audit is an integral part of the wider *management audit*. In order to explain what a marketing audit is, it is necessary to explain firstly what the audit process is and how it relates to business disciplines other than finance, and secondly to explain what a management audit is.

Auditing as a process is usually associated with the financial side of a business and is conducted according to a tightly-defined set of accounting standards. The conventions of accounting are well documented, easily understood, and consequently lend themselves readily to the auditing process. The total business process, although less formal, more innovative and relying more on judgement than on a set of rules, is still nevertheless capable of being audited.

Basically an audit is the means by which a company can understand how it relates to the environment in which it operates. It can thereby identify its own strengths and weaknesses as they relate to external opportunities and threats. It is thus a way of selecting a position in that environment based on known factors.

Expressed in its simplest form, the purpose of a business plan is to answer three central questions:

- Where is the company now?
- Where does the company want to go?
- How should the company organise its resources to get there?

This being so, the audit is one of the means by which the first of these questions is answered.

Often, the need for an audit doesn't manifest itself until things start going wrong for a company, such as declining sales, falling margins, lost market share and under-utilised production capacity. At times like this, management often attempts to treat the wrong symptoms. For example, changing the product, reorganising the sales force, reducing prices, and cutting costs are often just some of the actions taken by management. But such measures are unlikely to have much effect if there is a much more fundamental problem that has not been identified. Essentially the argument is that the problem has to be properly defined; the audit is a means of helping to define the problem.

Although business problems are far less amenable to the highly structured analytical methods characteristic of the sciences, it is the very complexity of business problems that give rise to the need for some kind of structured procedure to help identify problems. The more complex the problem, the more necessary is a structured approach.

To summarise, the audit is a structured approach to the collection and analysis of information and data in the complex business environment as an essential prerequisite to problem-solving.

■ The Form of the Audit

So far we have considered what an audit is and why it is relevant to problem-solving in business. Before turning specifically to the larger question of what a management audit is and where the marketing audit fits in, it is necessary to describe the form that is common to both the management audit and the marketing audit.

An auditor will be faced with two kinds of variables. All business variables can be split into two kinds. Firstly, there are variables over which the company has no direct control. These usually take the form of what can be described as *environmental* and *market* variables. Secondly, there are variables over which the company has *complete* control. These we can call *internal*, or *operational* variables.

This gives us a clue to the structured way in which an audit should be conducted. That is to say, in two parts:

- The external audit.
- The internal audit.

Figure 8.1 describes in a very simple form the total business process. The white area represents the external variables over which the company has no direct control. The tinted area represents the area over which the company has complete control. The external audit is concerned with auditing the *uncontrollable* variables, whilst the internal audit is concerned with auditing the *controllable* variables.

A central feature of all audits is the external audit and the internal audit. The purpose of the internal audit is to help assess the relative importance of the organisation's internal resources *vis-à-vis* the external environment, and in particular *vis-à-vis* the market in which the company operates and the resources of competitors. This means that whether we are talking about a marketing audit, a distribution audit, a production audit, or any kind of audit, internal resources should always be assessed relative to key external factors.

The term *management audit* merely means a company-wide audit that includes an assessment of all internal resources *vis-à-vis* the external environment. In practice the best way to carry out a management audit is to

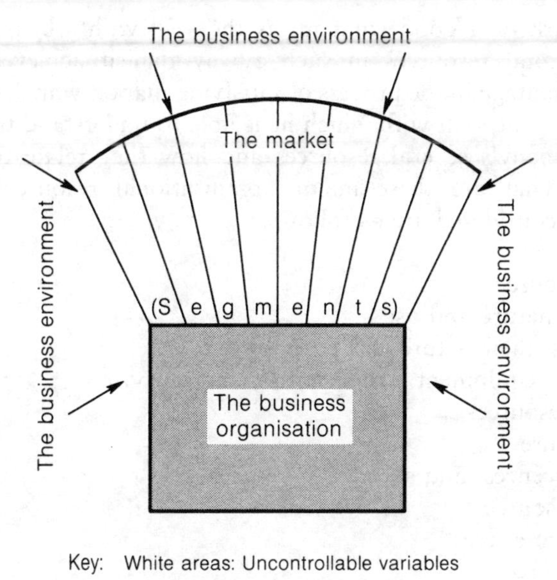

Figure 8.1 Internal and external marketing variables

carry out a separate audit of each major business function. Thus the marketing audit is merely part of a management audit, in the same way that a production audit is part of a management audit. The following illustrates this point:

- Marketing audit
- Distribution audit
- Personnel audit
- Finance audit
- Purchasing/production audit

All of the above add up to a management audit.

■ The Management Audit

Before going on to describe the marketing audit in detail, it is necessary to stress that, although it is easier to carry out a management audit by breaking it down into discrete parts based on the major functional areas of a business, it would be completely wrong to imply that this means that each of the constituent audits is mutually exclusive. In practice this can never be the case, because it is obvious that everything that happens in each major business area has an indirect influence on sales and that all are therefore interdependent.

Just as a mark of a good company is the skill with which it succeeds in organising its total resources in such a way that it achieves a profitable competitive advantage in the process of satisfying market wants, so the mark of a good auditor is the skill with which he is able to understand the relationship between a company's several resources and how they relate to the external environment. What are these major organisational resources? The major headings to be considered are as follows:

- Physical resources:
  - land: its nature and use
  - buildings: their nature and purpose
  - plant and equipment – their nature and purpose
- Technical resources:
  - expenditure
  - plants, licences, and so on
- Financial resources
- Purchasing resources
- Labour resources:
  - Special skills
- Marketing resources
- Distribution resources

It will be obvious from what has been said earlier that consideration of each of the items under these major headings will be of value only when compared with similar data for competitive companies.

Whilst this functional categorisation could be further subdivided, it will be seen from Figure 8.2 how each of these major business functions fits into the conceptual framework of the total business process given in Figure 8.1.

Another way of understanding the marketing audit and its place in the management audit is by reference to the business chain through which raw materials pass en route to final customers. Figure 8.3 shows the relationship of the marketing audit with other functional audits.

■ The Marketing Audit

The external audit starts with an examination of information on the general economy and then moves on to the outlook for the health and growth of the markets served by the company. The competitive environment is also included as part of the external audit.

Whilst the eventual objective of the external audit is to assess the extent to which economic and market factors indicate what the desired course of action should be, the starting point is to consider all possible angles. Some of the key areas to be included in the external market are shown in Table 8.1. The internal audit checklist is given in Table 8.2. To complete the picture of the marketing

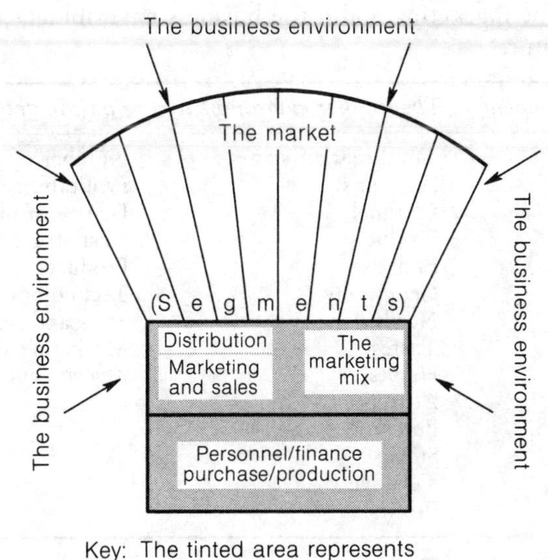

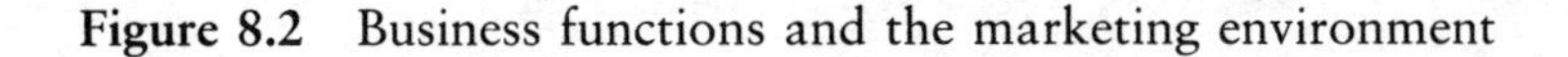

Figure 8.2 Business functions and the marketing environment

audit the information in Table 8.1 and 8.2 are combined in Table 8.3 to show the external audit on the left and the internal audit on the right.

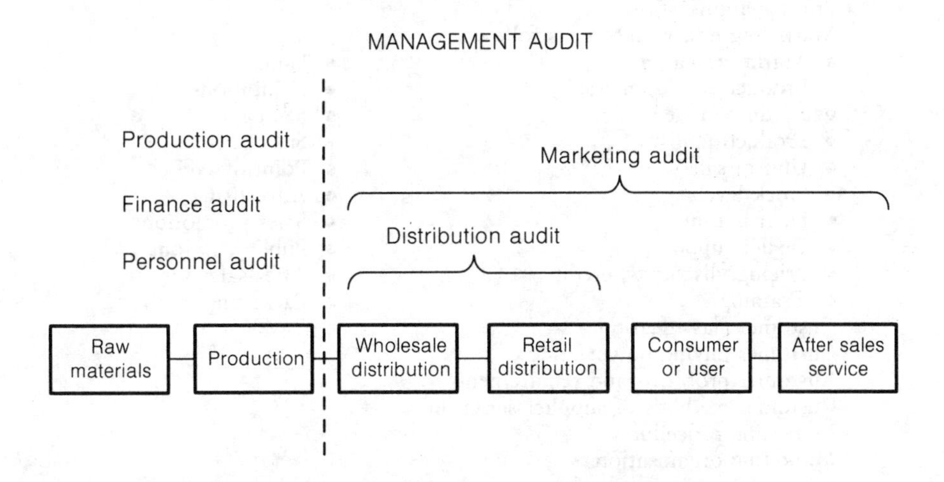

Figure 8.3 The marketing audit in context

Table 8.1 The marketing audit: the business environment (past, present, future)

Economic environment	*The market environment*	*The competitive environment*
Economic	Total market size	Number of competitors
Fiscal	Segments	Profitability
Social	Channel	Degree of integration
Business	Products	Cost structure
Legal	End Use	Products
Technological	Geography	Technology
International	Needs	Sales and market shares
Intra-company	Tastes	Marketing skills
	Habits	Key success and failure factors
	Attitudes	
	Purchasing ability	
	Stocks	
	Turnover	
	Profits	

Table 8.2 Marketing operation variables (past, present, future)

Sales (total, by geographical location, by industrial type, by customer, by product)

Market shares
Profit margins
Marketing mix variables, as follows:

- Market research
- Product development
- Product range
- Product quality
- Unit of sale
- Stock levels
- Distribution
- Dealer support
- Pricing, discounts, credit
- Training
- Samples
- Exhibitions
- Selling
- Sales aids
- Point of sale
- Advertising
- Sales promotion
- Public relations
- After-sales service
- Packaging

Customer classification
Customer buying power
Customer problems and requirements
Customer methods of supplier selection
Marketing procedures
Marketing organisation
Sales/marketing control data

Table 8.3 The marketing audit: external and internal variables combined

External audit *The business environment* *(past, present, future)*	*Internal audit* *Marketing operational variables* *(past, present, future)*
Economic environment:	*Own Company*:
Economic	Sales (total, by geographical location, by
Political	industrial type, by customer, by product)
Fiscal	Market shares
Social	Profit margins
Business	Marketing mix variables, as follows:
Legal	• Market research
Technological	• Product development
International	• Product range
Intra Company	• Product quality
	• Unit of sale
The market environment:	• Stock levels
Total market size	• Distribution
Segments	• Dealer support
Channels	• Pricing, discounts, credit
Products	• Packaging
End use	• Samples
Geography	• Exhibitions
Needs	• Selling
Tastes	• Sales aids
Habits	• Point of sale
Attitudes	• Advertising
Purchasing ability	• Sales promotion
Stocks	• Public relations
Turnover	• After sales service
Profits	• Training
	Customer classification
The competitive environment:	Customer buying power
Number of competitors	Customer problems and requirements
Profitability	Customer methods of supplier selection
Degree of integration	Marketing procedures
Cost structure	Marketing organisation
Products	Sales/marketing control data
Technology	
Sales and market shares	
Marketing skills	
Key success and failure factors	

■ When Should the Marketing Audit be Carried Out?

A mistaken belief held by some is that the marketing audit should be a last, desperate attempt to define a company's marketing problems in such a way that a solution suggests itself that is within the capability of the firm to implement; or at best something that is carried out by an independent body from time to time to ensure that a company is getting the optimum utilisation from its resources.

However, marketing is a complex function, with many interrelating parts that themselves interface with the market place and the actions of competitors. Thus it seems illogical not to carry out a thorough situation analysis at least once a year. This is especially so when it is considered that the rate of technological advance, improved communications and increased competition make it increasingly difficult to retain a secure position in traditional markets.

Fundamentally there is no difference between a situation analysis and a marketing audit, except that the actual term 'marketing audit' implies a formal, periodic review by an independent body. As such, it is not uncommon for companies to subject themselves to such an audit by an outside firm of consultants from time to time; whereas a situation analysis may be considered to be a continuous, internal process of self-appraisal and evaluation culminating in a summary marking the beginning of a new planning cycle and forming the basis of the next decision-making stage.

In an ongoing situation, a company will constantly review its marketing organisation and operating effectiveness and adapt gradually to changing circumstances. Some companies, however, particularly those new to marketing planning, will adopt a more formal, major audit-type approach and then may make a number of far-reaching changes in the organisation and its policies as a result. The purpose of both the situation analysis and the marketing audit, however, is the same; their purpose in relation to marketing planning is to help the company to understand the dynamics of its business and its markets, and how they interrelate.

There is much evidence to indicate that many highly successful companies, as well as using normal information and control procedures and market research reports throughout the year to adapt to their changing environment, also start their planning cycle each fiscal year with a formal review through an audit-type process of everything that has had an important influence on trading activities. Certainly in many leading consumer goods companies the self-audit approach is a tried, tested and thoroughly understood self-discipline that is built into an integrated management process. The recommendation, then, is that the marketing audit should be institutionalised as part of an annual planning system.

This brings us to the more difficult question of who should carry out the marketing audit, for surely it is difficult for any manager to be completely honest and impartial when reviewing his or her own departmental operations? It may well be advisable to have someone from outside carry out an audit every so often to check that a company is getting the most out of its resources. However outside studies often suffer from a lack of internal ownership.

The answer, therefore, is to have the audit carried out by the company's own line managers. Problems usually centre around lack of time and lack of objectivity. The best way to overcome these problems is firstly by institutionalising auditing procedures in as much detail as possible, and secondly by thorough training in the use of the procedures themselves.

However, even this will not result in the achievement of the objectives of an audit unless a rigorous discipline is laid upon management from the highest down to the lowest levels involved in the audit. Such a rigorous discipline is usually successful in helping managers to avoid the sort of tunnel vision that often results from a lack of critical appraisal.

■ What Happens to the Results of the Audit?

The major question that remains to be answered centres around what happens to the results of the marketing audit. In the same way that some companies waste considerable time and effort developing marketing plans that cannot be used, so other companies consume valuable resources carrying out audits that bring very little by way of actionable results.

Much of the literature indicates that marketing plans are developed in three major phases: a searching analysis of the industry and the company (the marketing audit); the formulation of objectives and strategies upon the basis of the audit; the development of programmes to implement the strategies.

There is grave danger that at the marketing audit stage, which provides the foundations upon which the whole planning edifice is built, insufficient attention is paid to the need to concentrate on analysis that determines which trends and developments will actually affect the company. The list in Table 8.3 merely demonstrates the completeness and logic of analysis. But whilst the planner should consider every heading, he should discipline himself to omit from the plans that will eventually be prepared all information that is unrelated to the company's specific problems. Inclusion of such things as brand-switching analyses, or over-detailed sales-performance histories by company and product that lead to no logical actions whatever, only serve to rob the marketing plan of focus and reduce its relevance. All analysis should be assessed on the basis of what it means in terms of the company's future development.

The next step is to sift and organise the information in a logical manner, followed by a review of the information to identify those factors and conditions that appear to be pertinent to the future of the company. In other words, situations, trends, facts, information and opinions that appear to have a bearing on the problems facing the company in getting and retaining customers. Judgement has to be used so that anything that is not relevant is omitted, the end result being a condensed statement of market information that is pertinent to the company's problems, with all extraneous information removed. Often this end result is referred to as *intelligence* as opposed to *data* or *information.*

■ How to Organise the Findings of the Audit

Since the objective of the audit is to help indicate what a company's marketing objectives and strategies should be, it follows that it would be helpful if some format could be found for organising the major findings of the marketing audit. Indeed, the key to the successful completion of this stage of the marketing planning process is an ability to organise major findings into a logical and usable format as an aid to setting objectives, just as at the audit stage itself the task is made easier by adopting a structured approach to the task.

It will be recalled that the marketing audit begins with obtaining information on the general economic environment, and then goes on to examine the outlook for the growth and health of the industries served by the company, including a review of competitive activities. The internal audit of the company's own resources can then be made in the light of this background information on the economy, the market, and competitors.

It has also been stated, however, that merely to record information of this kind is not problem-solving. This requires discovery of the extent to which these economic and other factors do actually indicate what the course of the business should be. Economic indicators *per se* cannot be used in plans in any direct way. One way of writing down facts, information and conclusions in such a way that the task of reviewing marketing objectives becomes easier is by summarising the audit under the headings *Strengths*, *Weaknesses*, *Opportunities* and *Threats*, often referred to as a SWOT analysis. Expressed in its simplest form, this means listing the company's key internal strengths and weaknesses as they relate to external opportunities and threats.

This is the most difficult phase in the whole auditing process, for it represents the final focusing of attention on what the auditor considers to be the key issues affecting the business. It will be immediately apparent that several items could be included either as strengths or weaknesses, or as opportunities or threats, depending upon the view of the auditor; for what is seen as a threat by one person is often seen as an opportunity by another.

Whilst this will always be so, it must be said that the actual act of carrying out the marketing audit, if done thoroughly and according to the structured approach suggested here, will go some considerable way towards giving the auditor a comprehensive knowledge of the business, trends in the market, where value is added by competitors, and so on. This should ensure a more realistic assessment of strengths, weaknesses, opportunities and threats, which will eventually form the basis of realistic marketing objectives and strategies.

An initial format for the SWOT analysis is given in Figure 8.4. This will be expanded on in Chapter 20 on marketing planning.

■ Summary

In summary the main point to bear in mind is that by adopting the kind of structured approach to the auditing process recommended in this text, the person carrying out the audit stands a much better chance of a reasonable definition of the key problems facing a company than he would if he relied entirely on a more intuitive approach.

Strengths (internal)	**Weaknesses** (Internal)
Opportunities (External)	**Threats** (External)

Figure 8.4 Initial format for a SWOT analysis

Thus there are basically two phases which comprise the auditing process:

- The identification, measurement, collection and analysis of all the facts and opinions that impinge upon a company's problems.
- The application of judgement to uncertain areas that are remaining following this analysis.

The first step in the auditing process is, therefore, to list all the facts and opinions relating to the problems facing the company. Analysis of these facts and opinions, and the application of judgement to help isolate those factors that are critical to success and the synthesising and sorting process, then follows.

Figure [illegible] Standard format for a SWOT analysis

So, there are basically two phases which comprise the planning process:

- The [illegible] of all the facts and opinions [illegible]
- The [illegible] analysis.

[illegible]

MODULE 3

Managing the Offer

CHAPTER 9

Product Management

The products or services that are offered to the market place are the most visible signs of an enterprise. In all probability they convey to customers more about a company than any other form of marketing activity. Not only are they the source of all revenue and profits today, but they will also be the most important factors in terms of success in the future.

However, continued successful business operations also depend upon the ability of companies to base their products or service offerings on the changing needs of a dynamic market place. Exactly how fast the marketing environment is changing will vary from business to business.

Nonetheless, regardless of its rate, change is a fact of business life and we ignore it at our peril. This means that the product or service element of the marketing mix has to be managed carefully. In turn this means that we have to learn to look at our offering in a new light and begin to understand some of the strategic options open to us if we want to survive and win. Selecting the most suitable strategies for our products or services is what this chapter is all about.

What is a Product/Service?

On the surface this might seem a naïve question, yet its answer is fundamental to successful marketing.

From the ground covered in earlier chapters we know that what we sell has to match up in some way with what the customer wants. The product or service links the customer to us as shown in Figure 9.1.

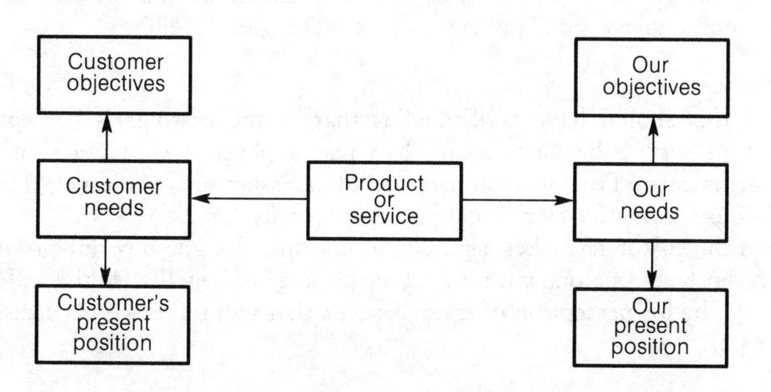

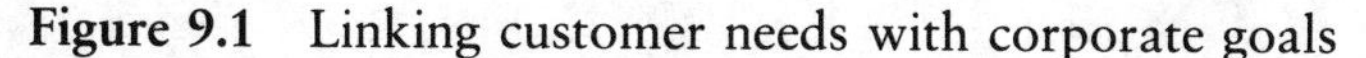

Figure 9.1 Linking customer needs with corporate goals

The customer should need our product or service, either to help solve some current problem he or she is facing, or else to make a contribution in some way to corporate or personal objectives. For our part, we need a viable product or service to help us improve our present position and meet our objectives.

While we should be clear about our own needs and objectives, those of the customers are not always quite so obvious and sometimes we have to make intelligent guesses about them. Even so, we can already see that it will be helpful to look at the product or service we offer through our customer's eyes.

It has been shown that customers buy products or services for many reasons. Different people look for different types of benefits to satisfy their needs. Here are some types of customer benefit:

- Good value for money/competitive price
- Novelty
- Availability
- Good design
- Ease of use
- Fashionableness
- Safety
- Pride of ownership
- Economy in use
- Efficient performance/end results
- Ease of servicing
- Quality
- Packaging
- Prompt delivery
- Choice of colours, sizes, and so on
- Reliability
- Terms available
- Discount available
- Reputable image (of supplier)
- Convenience/minimal disruption of normal routine
- Scarcity value
- Ease of purchase
- After-sales service
- Durability
- Guarantee/warranty available
- Prestige or status
- Labour saving
- 'Storability'
- Space saving
- Return on investment
- Availability of spares
- Range of accessories/peripherals
- Easy to follow instructions
- Made in this country
- Ecologically safe, that is doesn't damage environment
- Freedom from artificial additives
- Designer labelling

What this should have confirmed is that in the customer's perception a product or service becomes more than just a physical entity, a sum of its component parts. For the customer our offer assumes a whole new range of dimensions, some of which might surprise even us.

When the customer makes a purchase, not only does he buy our product or service, but he buys along with it a whole package of benefits. At the end of the day it will be his perception of these benefits that will influence his decision to buy or not.

Thus the situation is not like this:

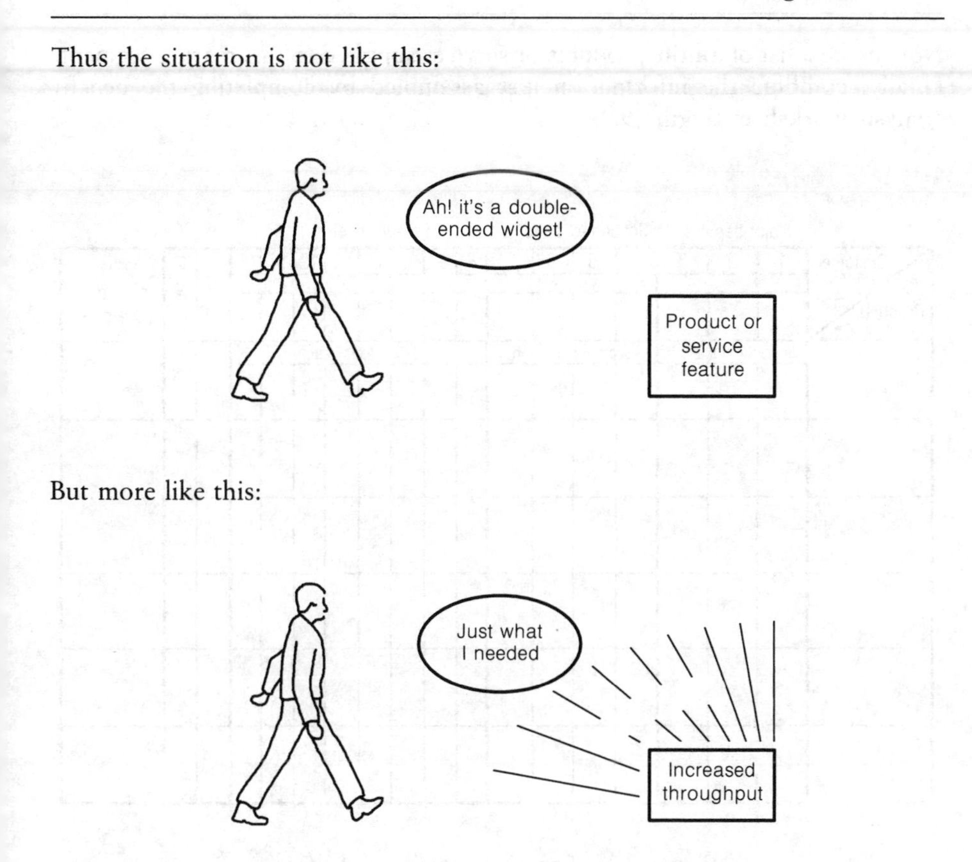

But more like this:

■ The Benefit Analysis Worksheet

The following process describes how we can arrive at a match between the benefits of our major products and selected market segments. Taking a specific market segment, look at the list of possible customer benefits we generated earlier and:

1. Pick out the three major benefits for this customer segment. Identify these in some way on the list.
2. Next, select the four benefits that come after those just selected. Again, mark these in the same way.
3. Finally, identify all the other benefits on the list that are valued to a lesser extent by this key market segment.

Now make a list of all the products or services supplied to this market segment. Finally, combine the information just assembled by completing the benefit analysis worksheet (Figure 9.2).

	Major benefits			Secondary benefits				Lesser benefits										
Customer benefits → / Products or services ↓	1	2	3	4	5	6	7	8	9	10	11	12	13	14	15	Total	Ranking	Notes comments, etc.
	Score 12 max each			Score 6 max each				Score 4 max each										

Figure 9.2 Benefit analysis worksheet

□ *Notes for Completing the Worksheet*

1. Write down the products or services offered in the spaces provided on the left of the worksheet. There are six spaces. If more are needed, extend the worksheet on to another sheet of paper.
2. Write down the benefits identified above so that the three major benefits are put as headings to columns one, two and three of the worksheet.

   The next four benefits are entered as headings for columns four to seven inclusive.

   All other benefits are written as headings to columns eight onwards.
3. Consider the first product or service listed on the worksheet. Score it according to how well it supplies the benefit at the head of each column. It will be noted that the first three benefits can score a maximum of twelve points, the next four a maximum of six points and the remainder a maximum of three points.
4. Repeat this process for the other products or services.

Figure 9.3 is an example, purely for illustration.

	Price	Performance	Safety	Design	Packaging	Durability	Discount	Delivery	After-sales	Instructions			Total	Rank	Comments
Prod A	12	9	9	6	3	4	6	1	3	3			56	1	
B	6	10	7	4	3	6	6	1	1	2			46	3	
C	8	10	10	4	3	3	6	3	3	2			52	2	
D	4	8	12	6	3	6	6	3	1	3			52	2	

Figure 9.3 Benefit analysis worksheet results

☐ *Interpretation of the Worksheet*

The 'total' score is an indicator of how many 'benefit points' each product is providing. In the example shown in Figure 9.3 Product A scores the most points and is ranked first, Products C and D come next to rank equal second, while Product B is ranked third.

Not only does this technique enable products or services to be compared and measured against the benefits they supply, it also gives rise to some very pertinent questions. For example:

- Why are products B, C and D not competitively priced?
- Can the performance of the products, especially A and D, be improved?
- Why are the safety scores of B and A so low?
- Why is packaging so uniformly poor?
- Can the design of B and C be improved?
- What are the immediate steps that might be taken to improve the benefits provided to customers?
- Taking into account the ranking of the individual products or services (that is, their total benefit scores), is the correct allocation of energy and resources being made to each? Might their relative importance be reappraised?

Such questions asked of any company can only lead to a search for improvement. This will be just as true for our products or services as it was in the illustration given here. Moreover, since all such improvements are based on providing greater customer benefits, they hold every prospect of bringing about important changes. This process can be repeated for other market segments of our business.

So far we have returned to the idea that the product or service is the most visible thing connecting the supplier to the customer. We went on to ask a quite fundamental question: 'What is a product or service?' A marketer's response is to define output in terms of how it provides customer benefits. Thus a product or service, as well as being a physical entity, will be perceived by the customer as a 'package' of benefits.

We found that there were a number of sources of potential benefits to customers, but in reality they would not all be equally attractive. Some benefits have more currency than others. Building on this point, we suggested a technique that enables a company to assess its output in terms of the benefits it provides.

■ The Product/Service Life-Cycle

■ The Life-Cycle Curve

The idea of benefit analysis that we have just explored is a very important one. It does have one drawback, however. It is virtually a 'snapshot' of the company's products or services at a given moment, and cannot portray what is happening over a period of time.

Because the product/service life-cycle *does* enable us to understand what happens over time, the concept becomes a valuable marketing tool. Like most good ideas, the life-cycle concept is extremely simple to grasp. What it tells us is that any product or service exhibits a sales pattern as shown in Figure 9.4.

The early part of the sales curve denotes a struggle to get the product or service known; sales were hard to come by and a lot of time and energy went

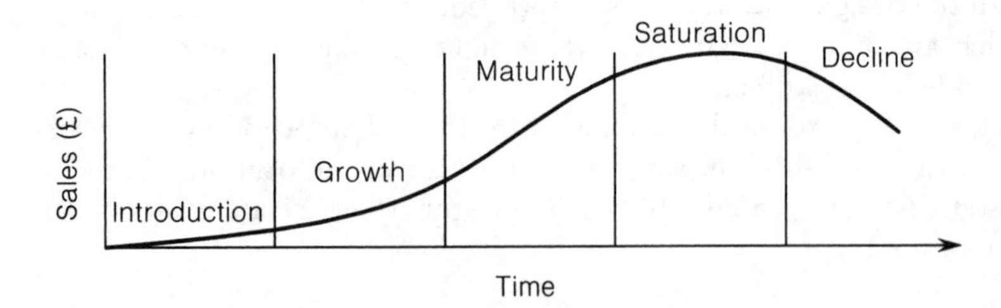

Figure 9.4 Product/service life cycle

into developing contacts in order to create awareness and acceptance of it. It is aptly called the *introduction phase.*

Assuming the product or service is acceptable to its target market, then there comes a time when it 'takes off'; everybody seems to want to buy it. This is the *growth phase.* But no market is infinitely expandable, and eventually the rate of growth slows as the product or service moves into the *maturity stage.*

Eventually a point is reached where there are too many firms in the market; price wars break out and some firms drop out of the market. Sales level off or gradually decline as demand has largely been satisfied, if not by us, then by the many competitors who would have been equally attracted by the growth potential of the market for this product/service. This is the *saturation phase.*

After a period of relative stability, the interest in our product/service wanes and sales start to fall more quickly. This is the *decline phase.* Exactly how far sales are allowed to fall is largely a managerial decision, as we will see.

This then is the product/service life-cycle and it appears to hold true for all products and services. For fashion items and similar short-lived fads, the life-cycle can be quite short; decline is reached perhaps in days. For other items the life-cycle can be measured in decades.

■ What Does the Life-Cycle Curve Tell Us?

- The life-cycle curve can be a predictive device. It can tell us what sales pattern we might expect and allow corrective action to be taken.
- It can be a comparative device, in the sense that it can tell us if we are mirroring the total market experience or somehow falling short. Figures 9.5–9.7 illustrate this point!

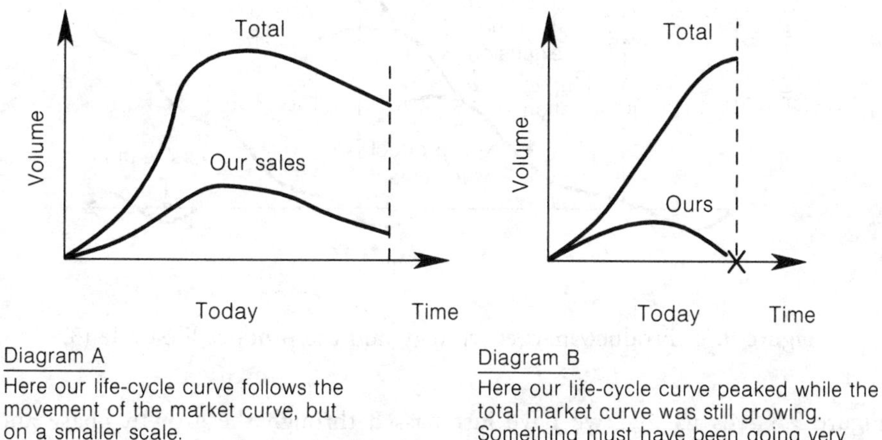

Diagram A

Here our life-cycle curve follows the movement of the market curve, but on a smaller scale.

Diagram B

Here our life-cycle curve peaked while the total market curve was still growing. Something must have been going very wrong for this to happen. What was it? Why are we in decline at this stage?

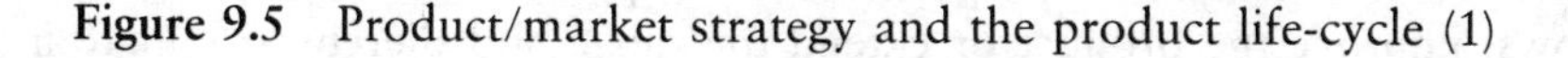

Figure 9.5 Product/market strategy and the product life-cycle (1)

- The life-cycle curve can tell us how we might best support and invest in our product or service, as we shall see in a little while.
- The life-cycle curve can give us important clues about when to use short-term strategies in order to 'distort' the life-cycle to our advantage. For example, suppose this curve represented one of our products or services, as in Figure 9.6.

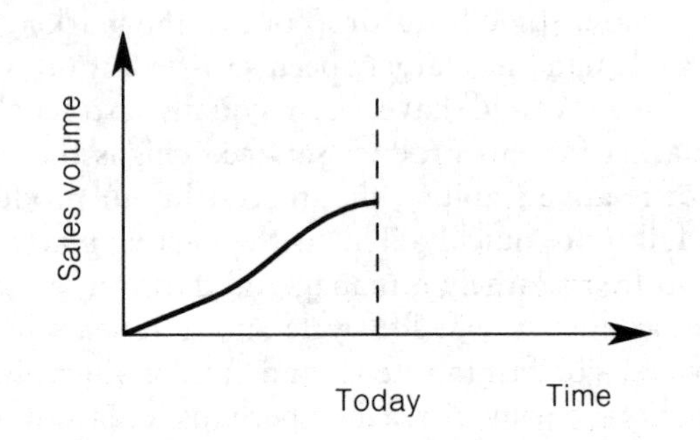

Figure 9.6 Product/market strategy and the product life-cycle (2)

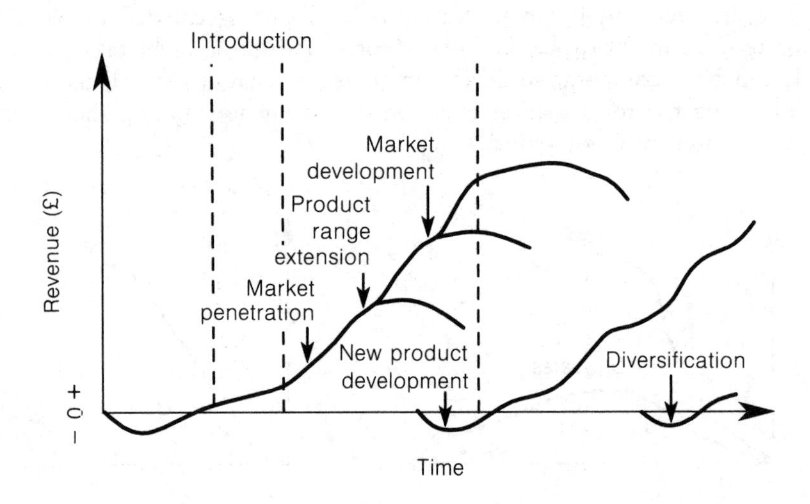

Figure 9.7 Product/market strategy and the product life-cycle (3)

Figure 9.6 tells us that we have just passed through the growth phase and appear to be entering the maturity phase. If we take no action, we could expect the sales curve to level out and eventually decline.

However, we could take steps to delay this process. We could, as Figure 9.7 shows, improve the product or extend the range and thereby stimulate more sales. When that initiative has run its course and sales start to level out again, we could extend the market or develop a new segment. Again this stimulates the sales curve and extends the period of growth.

However, these actions all cost money and so they have to be weighed against the level of increased sales they would expect to generate. Eventually there comes a time when it becomes counterproductive to prop up an ailing product or service in this way. The section on portfolio management in the next chapter will help us in making the go/no-go decision about investing in particular products or services. But, for now, let us concentrate on understanding more about the life-cycle.

■ Life Cycle – Costs and Strategies

As the above example has shown, in respect of product management a company must be prepared to vary its strategies as the product or service moves through its life-cycle. But it is not only in respect of product management that alternative strategies should be considered. Pricing, distribution and promotional efforts also need to be regularly reviewed. For example, early promotional efforts will almost certainly have to concentrate on creating awareness for the product, especially if it is a completely new product or service concept. Later in the life of the product, when awareness levels are high, it is more likely that a company will need to spend more effort on positioning and imagery in what often turn out to be crowded markets during the high growth phase. Likewise, distribution channels are likely to change, as will pricing. Clearly, it may prove fatal to refuse to bow to price pressures as the market reaches maturity, because if hard-won market share is lost at this crucial stage this could well adversely affect profits.

So, market circumstances change over the life of a product or service and a company's policies should also change accordingly. Table 9.1 illustrates a set of guidelines used by one company in the electrical components market to help it determine appropriate marketing strategies at different stages of the life-cycle. In this case, the company combined the two stages of maturity and saturation.

Drawing a product life-cycle can be extremely difficult, even given the availability of some form of time-series analysis. This is connected with the complex question of market share measurement.

Firstly, let us remind ourselves that a firm needs to be concerned with its share (its proportion of volume or value) of an *actual* market. However, in order to measure an actual market, great care must be taken to ensure that a company is measuring the right things. Take the example of the company manufacturing a nylon carpet for institutional markets. It is clearly nonsense to include concrete in their measurement of the floor-covering market because concrete, although a floor covering, does not satisfy the needs that customers have for warmth and colour and therefore is not a part of their market. Neither,

Table 9.1 Life-cycle stages: characteristics and responses

	Introduction	*Growth*	*Maturity/saturation*	*Decline*
Costs	Can be high, due to inexperience in supplying and the cost of promotion.	Increasing due to increased volume and fighting off competition. High growth requires funding.	Stabilising/reducing as experience and reduced competition take effect.	Can be high if not managed due to diseconomies of scale, for example only small runs.
Demand	Unpredictable. Forecasts can vary widely.	Upper limits might be forecast but volatile situation sensitive to prices and competition.	Fairly well defined.	Known and limited.
Competition	Largely unknown.	Many new entrants jump on 'bandwagon'. Competition fierce.	Marginal competitors leave. Remainder tend to specialise with particular segments.	New entrants are unlikely. Competition declines.
Customer loyalty	Trial usage, new relationship, little loyalty.	Some loyalty but to ensure supplies many customers might have more than one supplier.	Well-established buying patterns with high customer loyalty.	Extremely stable. Customers are not motivated to seek new suppliers.
Ease of entry	Relatively easy because market leaders have not yet emerged. Customers feeling their way.	More difficult as some suppliers begin to establish market share and benefit from economies of scale.	Difficult because of established buying patterns. New business has to be won.	Little incentive to enter.
Price	Price to capitalise on newness (high) or to penetrate the market (low).	Price competitively.	Price defensively.	Price according to perceived product life, for example high for milk.
Promotion	Active and aggressive.	Active and aggressive.	Selective and specialised.	Minimal if at all.
Product/service range	Limited and specialised to meet the needs of early customers.	Rapid expansion in order to capitalise on new opportunities.	Range expansion slows down or ceases.	Range narrows as unproductive items are dropped.

probably, should linoleum nor woollen carpets be included. To help with this, let us remind ourselves of the following definitions:

- Product *class*, for example carpets
- Product *form*, for example nylon rolls
- Product *brand*, for example 'X'

'X' as a brand, for the purpose of measuring market share, is *concerned only with the aggregate of all other brands that satisfy the same group of customer wants*. Nevertheless, the manufacturer of 'X' also needs to be aware of the sales trends of other kinds of carpets and floor covering in the institutional market, as well as of carpet sales overall.

So far we have studied the idea of the product or service life cycle. We found that not only do products/services not last forever, but that the pattern of sales over their lifetime is remarkably similar. The life-cycle can be useful in four ways

- It can be a predictor of sales performance.
- It enables us to compare ourselves with our 'industry'.
- It gives us clues about how and when we might use short-term strategies to extend the life-cycle.
- It provides us with clues about the most appropriate strategies to use at different stages of the life-cycle.

The important point to remember at this stage is that the concept of the product life-cycle is not an academic figment of the imagination but a hard reality that is ignored at great risk. It is interesting to see how many commercial failures can be traced back to a naïve assumption on the part of managements that what was successful as a policy at one time will continue to be successful in the future.

Let us now broaden the discussion to a consideration of managing a range of products or services and the ways in which they satisfy market needs.

The art of successful product management must be based on a clear view of just *how* the present and future product range will continue to meet these twin goals of customer and corporate objectives.

As a first stage in successful product management it is important to think of the 'product' as a variable in the marketing mix, in the same way that we consider price or promotion as a variable. The extent of freedom to manoeuvre on the product variable will depend largely upon the internal resources of the firm and where its strengths are in relation to the competition. We shall explore the techniques of *strengths and weaknesses analysis*, often called a SWOT analysis, in more detail in Chapter 20. For now it is sufficient to suggest a number of pertinent questions to help us establish the appropriateness of current product strategy:

- What benefits do customers seek from this type of product?

- Does our product provide these benefits in greater proportion than competitors' products?
- What competitive product advantages are causing us to lose market share?
- Does our product range still provide 'value-in-use' to the customers in relation to its cost to them?
- Does each product in our range still meet the corporate objectives set for it?

The answers to these, and other questions, will provide a firm basis for developing a product/market strategy.

Product/Market Strategy

What is product/market strategy? Very simply it is the totality of the decisions taken within the organisation concerning its target markets and the products it offers to those markets. Strategy implies a chosen route to a defined goal and an element of long-term planning. Thus the product/market strategy of the firm represents its commitment to a particular direction in the future.

The effective company is one that plans for growth, and in terms of its product/market strategy seeks to plan its *product portfolio* well in advance – in terms required or determined by product policy. The company must plan for growth, and both product policy and product/market strategy must be growth-oriented; but clearly the growth must have purposeful direction if future profits and cash flows are to be maximised. This direction is provided through appropriate growth policies, indicating the *vectors* (variable directions) along which the firm is intended to move.

One helpful device for considering product/market strategy is the so-called 'Ansoff' matrix, named after its developer. The Ansoff matrix shown in Figure 9.8 depicts the simple concepts employed.

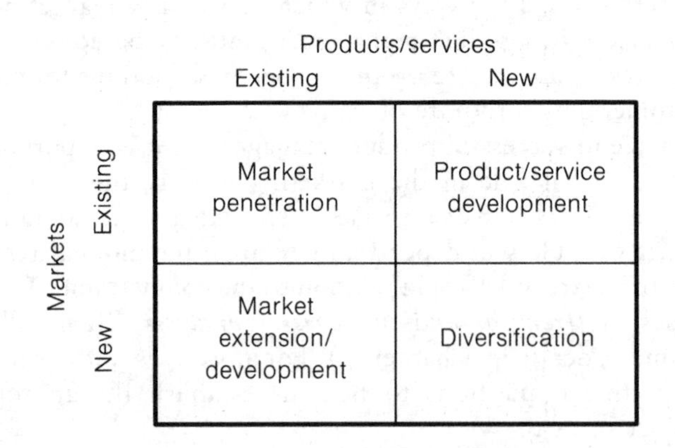

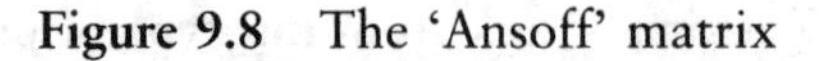
Figure 9.8 The 'Ansoff' matrix

■ Strategy Options

Most companies find that the strategy options open to them can be encapsulated in the Ansoff matrix where the axes are 'products/services' and 'markets'. Businesses have the option of staying with their existing products/services or developing new ones. Equally they can choose to remain in existing markets or develop new ones. The combination of these options gives rise to the following broad strategies.

□ *Market Penetration*

This will involve keeping existing customers and finding new ones in the same market. Thus pricing and promotion will have to be very competitive, because other suppliers are not just going to sit back and let us take their business. However, there are fewer unknowns and therefore in theory fewer risks.

□ *Product/Service Development*

This would involve modification of existing products/services to improve their quality, style, or whatever characteristics are valued by customers. The ultimate goal would be to increase sales or profits, or even reduce costs by taking advantage of new technology.

The implication of this strategy is that the company possesses the technical resources and skills to make it a viable proposition. Given the failure rate of new products/services and the element of the unknown associated with this strategy, it must be considered as slightly risky.

□ *Market Extension/Development*

This involves finding new users for the product/service. This might mean going further afield geographically (even exporting), opening up new market segments, or finding new applications for the products/services.

This strategy implies that the company has marketing strengths and the wherewithal to make inroads into new markets. Again the element of dealing with the unknown makes this a slightly more risky strategy.

□ *Diversification*

The most risky strategy of all, since both markets and products/services will be new. Because of the high risk, such a strategy would need very careful evaluation. However, if we develop a brilliant new idea for a product or service, it might be appropriate for us to move in this direction.

The procedures described in the next chapter provide a means of determining the most appropriate product strategy to follow.

Product Revitalisation versus New Product Development

The Ansoff matrix, referred to earlier in this chapter, whilst having a certain simplicity because it strips marketing down to its basics, does nonetheless tend to over-simplify the issues surrounding product/market strategy. The reason is that there are different kinds of new products and new markets. It is important that we are clear what these are.

There can be degrees of newness of the product:

- It can stay the same.
- It can be extended in some way, for example new colours or sizes.
- It can be redesigned, modified or improved.
- It can be a new product or concept entirely.

A similar analysis can be provided for markets:

- They can be the same.
- They can be broader in terms of how they are defined.
- They can include new coverage, but on related areas.
- They can be totally new.

The trusty Ansoff matrix is good at reminding us that marketing life can become too complicated, but its insistence that things are either old or new, black or white, overlooks all those middling shades of grey. As an aside, when exactly does a new product become an existing one? Is it after a specific time? When it's at a certain stage of its life-cycle? Or when a certain number of people have become aware of its existence? We can see, then, that the straight Ansoff matrix isn't quite as simple as it seems.

A more accurate representation might be to produce a matrix with more than four boxes, built around the degrees of newness of both products and markets listed above. However there is still a problem. What comes first? Should it be a concern for technology? Or markets? This is where market research should help us . . . but does it?

Let us for a moment imagine that we are that ubiquitous buggy whip manufacturer who keeps cropping up in books and articles on marketing. Let us step back in time to the nineteenth century, when his business was at its zenith. Being an advanced sort of chap, he would go out and talk to his customers, the cab and cart drivers, asking what it was they wanted. Had he known it, he was doing market research, but at that time of course it hadn't been invented!

A few he talked to wanted better whips, but most of them were really fed up with horses. What with the price of hay and the smelly and unreliable nature of their charges, what they really wanted was to drive a car. Not any old car, but one with independent suspension and air conditioning. The problem was, like market research, the internal combustion engine had not yet been invented! This, of course, is a silly story, but it is not without value. Firstly, it explodes the myth that marketing is all about asking people what they want and then making it. Taking an extreme stance such as this is shown to be intellectually puerile. Secondly, it throws the nature of technological development into stark relief.

When it comes, technological development provides a quantum leap forward. Just think about the electronics industry. It really all started with the invention of the thermionic valve. This gave way to the transistor, which was superseded by the miniaturised circuit, and most recently by the microchip. Each of these technological breakthroughs spawned in their wake a multitude of technology-driven products that hitherto had been the stuff of science fiction stories.

Clearly, then, there are some markets that have a propensity to be supply-side driven. After the initial breaking of the innovative dam, which owes much to the 'R' of R&D, the new product eventually becomes modified and adapted. In other words, the 'D' of R&D becomes more important. It is in these kinds of businesses where there must be strong links between marketing and R&D.

There are, however, other markets that are fundamentally more stable and customer-driven. Here, marketers can keep their finger on the customer's pulse and respond to changing needs. Even then, it will be important to monitor the product in terms of its position on its life-cycle. Sooner or later, demand will become mature and the market will develop into a replacement market. Just look at what is happening to some of our famous companies at the moment. When it gets to this stage, there are really only three options open to the marketer:

- go for new technology and in effect shift the goal posts;
- do what marketers have always done, segment customers in a more creative way; or
- pray that you have the lowest costs in your field, otherwise you won't survive.

The question of how to manage the new product development process is dealt with in detail in the next chapter.

■ Summary

In managing products or services the marketer must pay due regard to the benefits that customers seek as well as to the position in the product life-cycle.

Marketing strategies will need to be adjusted as the life-cycle changes. The appropriate marketing mix at the point of introduction will not be effective at the maturity stage, for example.

Finally, the Ansoff matrix provides a useful framework for identifying the strategies options available to the company as it seeks to develop its product/market base.

CHAPTER 10
Product Strategy

■ Product Portfolios

Most businesses operate by offering more than one product or service to the market place. They can be said to have a *portfolio* of products or services. Thus, while all the discussion about the life cycle holds true, in reality most companies are managing not one, but a number of different product/service life-cycles.

Ideally these would be managed so that they 'meshed' together in a sensible way, as Figures 10.1(a) and 10.1(b) show.

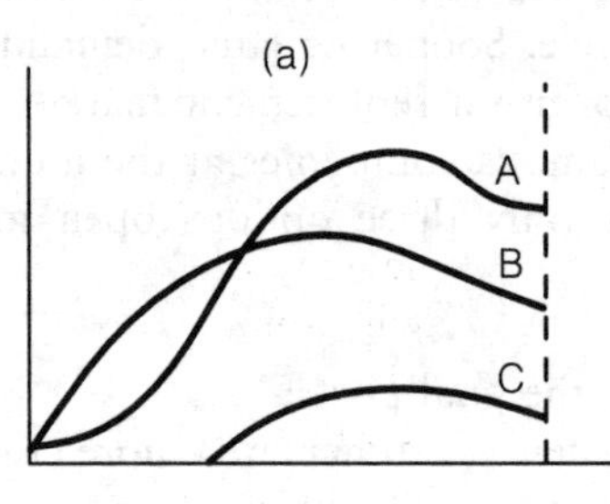

This is not a good pattern. All three products peaked some time ago and are now in decline. There is no new product to offer a promise for the future.

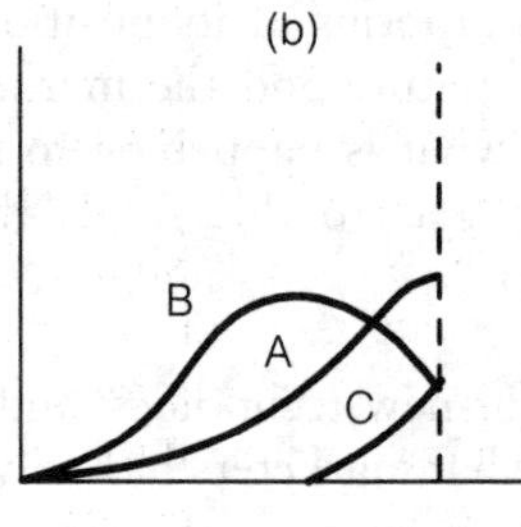

This is a good pattern. Product A, the earlier breadwinner, is in decline; but product B still holds a prospect of growth and product C is in its introduction stage, offering a bright future.

Figure 10.1 A portfolio of several product life-cycles

A successful business would develop a portfolio more like that in Figure 10.1(b). In fact, over the years, its growth could be attributed to a number of well-timed and profitable product/service launches like those in Figure 10.2.

Therefore, in order to achieve a successful product/service portfolio, it will be necessary to manage our existing output and bring it into line with our longer-term objectives. At the same time we will have to be capable of generating not only profits, but also sufficient funds to invest in new products and services.

The idea of a product portfolio is for a company to meet its objectives by balancing sales growth, cash flow and risk. As individual products progress or

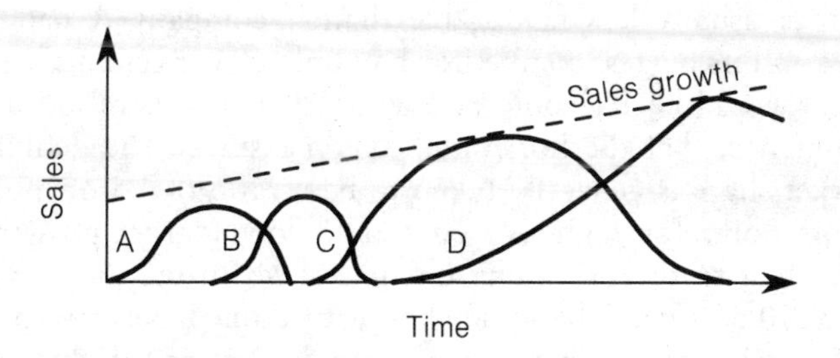

Figure 10.2 Ideal product introduction pattern over time

decline, and as markets grow or shrink, then the overall nature of the company's product portfolio will change. It is essential, therefore, that the whole portfolio is regularly reviewed and that an active policy towards new product development and divestment of old products is pursued. In this respect, the work of the Boston Consulting Group over the past decade has had a profound effect on the way managements think about this subject and about their product/market strategy.

In many respects the idea of the product portfolio is similar to the investor's portfolio of stocks and shares. The investor, for example, may wish to achieve a balance between yield or income and capital growth; some shares might produce more of the latter and less of the former and vice versa. Again, the investor might attempt to achieve a balance in terms of risk – some shares having a higher risk of capital loss attached, against which must be balanced the prospect of higher returns.

Cash flow is a key determinant of the firm's ability to develop its product portfolio. To emphasise this, the Boston Consulting Group developed a means of classifying products within the firm's portfolio according to their cash generation and cash usage.

■ The Boston Matrix

In the Boston Consulting Group's simple matrix, products are classified according to their positions on two dimensions: one is concerned with *relative market share* and the other with *market growth rate*. Market share is used because it indicates the extent to which the products should be capable of generating cash. Market growth is used as an indicator of the product's cash requirements.

The measure of market share used is the product's share relative to the largest competitor. This is important because it reflects the degree of dominance enjoyed by the product in the market. For example, if company A has 20 per cent market share, and its biggest competitor has 20 per cent market share also, this position is usually less favourable than if company A had 20 per cent market share and its biggest competitor had only 10 per cent market share. The relative ratios would be 1:1 compared with 2:1. It is this ratio, or measure of market dominance, that the horizontal axis measures. The definition of high relative market share is generally taken to be a ratio of 1.5 or more.

The cut-off point for high as opposed to low market growth should be defined according to the prevailing circumstances in the industry, but this is often taken as 10 per cent. The somewhat picturesque labels attached to each of the four categories or products give some indication of the prospects for products in each quadrant (Figure 10.3).

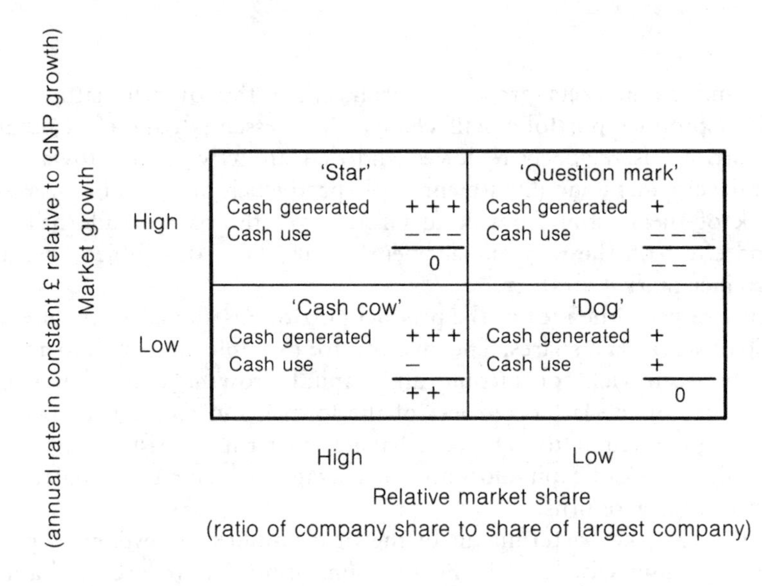

Figure 10.3 The Boston matrix

- *The question mark* is a product that has not yet achieved a dominant market position and thus has a high cash flow; or perhaps it once had such a position and has slipped back. It will be a high user of cash because it is in a growth market. This is also sometimes referred to as a *wildcat*, or *problem child*.
- *The star* is probably a newish product that has achieved a high market share and is probably, on balance, more or less self-financing in cash terms.
- *The cash cows* are leaders in markets where there is little additional growth, but a lot of stability. These are excellent generators of cash.
- *Dogs* have little future and are often a cash drain on the company. They are probably candidates for divestment, although such products often fall into a category aptly described by Peter Drucker as 'investments in managerial ego'.

Since the 'Cash Cow' is the only quadrant that actually generates cash, some very clear messages come from the Boston matrix:

- To manage the product/service portfolio effectively the cash generated by 'cash cows' must be used to invest in 'stars' and selected 'question marks'.
- Investing in 'question marks' with good prospects should lead to them developing into 'stars'.
- Investing in 'stars' should develop them into tomorrow's 'cash cows'.
- The higher the relative market share of a 'star', the better are its prospects as a 'cash cow'.
- High investment in a 'cash cow' should never be necessary.
- Investment in 'dogs' is generally money wasted.

The Boston matrix can be used to forecast the market position of our products, say, five years from now if we continue to pursue our current policies. Figure 10.4 illustrates this process for a manufacturer of plastic valves. The area of each circle is proportional to each product's contribution to total company sales volume.

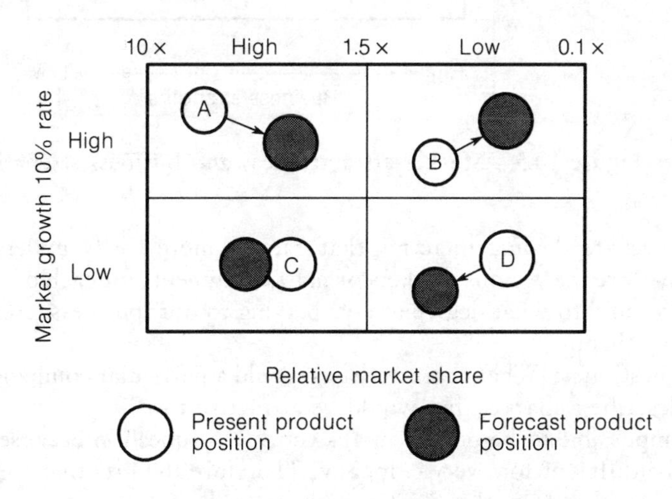

Figure 10.4 The product portfolio, current and projected

■ The Directional Policy Matrix

As a further aid to product strategy, Shell, General Electric, McKinsey and others developed a multi-factor approach to portfolio management. They used industry attractiveness and business strengths as the two main axes and built up these dimensions from a number of variables. Using these variables, and some scheme for weighting them according to their importance, products (or businesses) are classified into one of nine cells in a 3 × 3 matrix. So the same purpose is served as in the Boston matrix, that is, comparing investment opportunities among products or businesses. The difference is that multiple criteria are used.

For the sake of simplicity, the matrix can be constructed in a similar way to the Boston matrix, except it should be noticed that the axes have changed. Also, the labels attaching to each of the Boston boxes have been changed (Figure 10.5).

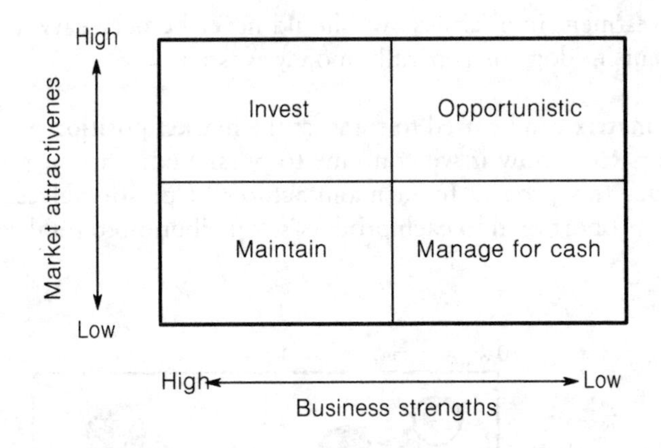

Figure 10.5 Market attractiveness and business strengths

Now we are dealing in terms that can be more easily understood. How 'attractive' are the various markets or market segments for each of our products or services and to what degree are we playing to our 'business strengths' when we supply them?

The question is: 'What characteristics would a particular company be looking for to describe a market that would be attractive to it?'

It is impossible to be precise in answering this question because the answer should be different for every company. Therefore the lists that follow are just some general headings that might be considered.

Market Attractiveness

This could involve:

- The size of the market(s).
- Its 'reachability'.
- The number and quality of the competitors.
- The level of prices that can be charged.
- The profits to be made, versus effort put in.

- High customer loyalty.
- A supportive business environment.
- Has needs that can easily be satisfied.
- Takes more than one product/service.
- There is no difficulty with its technology.
- Its buying patterns and structure are well understood.
- Good prospect for growth.
- Customers pay promptly.

■ Business Strengths

These could include:

- Technical expertise in this area of work.
- Record of meeting delivery promises.
- High quality output.
- Flexibility, that is, to changing requests.
- Good reputation/image.
- Creative, that is, solutions to customers' problems.
- Have a bank of loyal customers.
- Room to grow.
- High quality/loyal staff.
- Some successful products/services.
- Good at small/medium/large production runs.

Having established the criteria for market attractiveness and business strengths, it is now possible to construct a portfolio matrix for the business. However, before doing so, let us look at an example of how a small company set about this task.

■ Sealitt Ltd

This small company makes various types of seals and gaskets. Its original product was rubber trim for fitting motor vehicle windows. These are supplied to motor factories, replacement windscreen specialists and van/caravan converters.

It then developed door trim rubber strips for draught and weather sealing, essentially for motor factories. This venture led to producing draught-excluder strips for DIY outlets. Its latest ideas are to provide seals for double glazing units and also gaskets of all shapes, sizes and application, mainly for engineering companies.

The company buys in most of its materials. Its strengths are the expertise it has developed for buying judiciously, and the ability to cut and shape materials economically but to high standards. Its portfolio matrix looks like that in Figure 10.6.

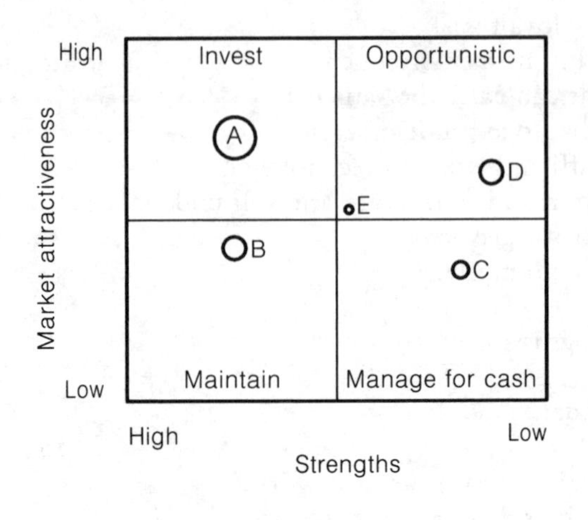

Key: A = window trim (vehicles)
B = door seal strip
C = glazing seals
D = gaskets
E = DIY

The size of each circle approximates to the level of sales for that item.

Figure 10.6 Portfolio matrix for Sealitt Ltd

The company's strengths are geared up to supplying the 'motor trade'; the demand for window trim makes it an attractive market. Similar strengths apply to door seals, but the market is less attractive since there is a smaller demand for replacements. (It would not have the capacity to supply the OEM – (original equipment manufacturer – market, for example Ford, Rover.)

Double glazing seals looked on the surface a good proposition for Sealitt Ltd, but it was found that there was some new expertise to acquire; also several customers went out of business without paying. The well-established double glazing companies either produced their own seals or had approved suppliers. Thus this item, which started as an 'opportunistic development', went almost immediately into the bottom right-hand quadrant.

Gaskets use least of the company's business strengths but seem to be an attractive market. Sales are quite sizeable. DIY insulation is a small business and never seems to have taken off, mainly because the company has too little experience in dealing with that particular market.

■ Analysis of Sealitt Ltd

It would seem that the company has a problem looming in terms of future business prospects. At present the door trim is less attractive than window trim, which has good growth prospects, but where is the next 'invest' product coming from? Since the sales of gaskets are quite good, should the company invest in improving its business strengths in this area and concentrate on developing this part of the business?

Can the DIY insulation find more attractive markets? Is a new opportunistic product required with better 'credentials'? The double glazing sealing appears to be a flop, so should it be discontinued, as it is only getting in the way?

These are serious questions that have to be answered. To help with this, Figure 10.7 presents some strategy options suggested by directional policy analysis.

<table>
<tr>
<td>INVEST
Invest for growth:
• penetrate market
• accept moderate short-term profits
• sell and promote aggressively
• expand: – geographically
– product line
• differentiate product/service</td>
<td colspan="2">OPPORTUNISTIC
Opportunistic development:
• be critical of prospects
• invest heavily in selective products/services</td>
</tr>
<tr>
<td>MAINTAIN
Maintain market position and manage for earnings:
• maintain market position with successful products/services
• differentiate products/services to keep share of key segments
• prune less successful products or services
• stabilise prices, except where temporary aggressive stance is required to deter competitors</td>
<td>SELECTIVE
• live with low growth
• improve productivity
• reduce costs
• look for 'easy' growth segments</td>
<td>MANAGE FOR CASH
• prune aggressively
• maximise cash flow
• raise prices at expense of volume
• minimise expenditure</td>
</tr>
</table>

Figure 10.7 Directional policy analysis for Sealitt Ltd

■ The Directional Policy Matrix as a Predictive Device

So far we have just looked at the portfolio matrix as a static 'snapshot' of the company. However, it is possible to make even greater use of it, as we shall see.

Let's go back to our example of Sealitt Ltd. This time the manager has added more information to the matrix by indicating the trends he expects for each part of the business (Figure 10.8). His two-year forward projections are shown as dotted lines, and again the circles represent sales levels.

We can see that overall the sales from the invest box are going to increase, but that the market growth will slow down slightly.

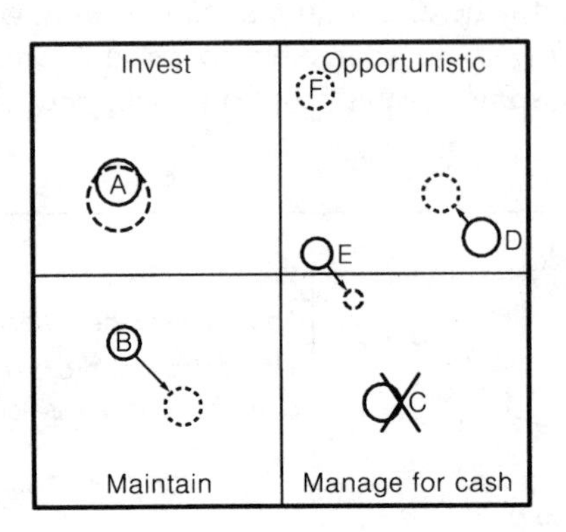

Figure 10.8 Portfolio matrix showing current and forecast positions

The maintain product is planned to keep the same level of sales, but the market is certainly becoming less attractive and matches with fewer of the company's strengths.

Product C, the double glazing seal, will be scrapped. The DIY insulation E is seen to be fading away and is likely to be withdrawn. Gaskets (D) are planned to generate more sales, but the product is still short of being an invest product.

A new product F is scheduled to provide the lost revenue from C and E. This product, with the right investment, has the possibility of becoming a future opportunistic product. It certainly plays to more of the company's strengths than the gaskets business. It is essential for the company to develop a new opportunistic product as the window trim sinks into the maintain quadrant.

■ Developing New Products and Services

So far in this book we have tended to focus on existing products and services. However, experience tells us that nothing lasts forever. Eventually today's breadwinners fall into decline and something else has to be found to take their place.

In practice most new products and services emerge gradually from modifications of existing ideas and technology – from putting together familiar things in a slightly different way. It is this interplay between existing products or services and the search for improvement and innovation that provides the dynamism for the growth-orientated company.

However, the search for growth, prosperity and market opportunity is not without risk. A high proportion of new products and services finish up on the scrapheap without anyone mourning their passing. The road to success is strewn with the smouldering remains of erstwhile 'world beating' ideas developed by bright, intelligent managers. Some businesses stake their all in a new product or service; failure, when it occurs, is often total.

■ Resistance to Change

As if getting the right quality of innovative ideas were not problem enough, there is also the issue of resistance to change, which occurs in all walks of life, the company being no exception. This resistance can derive from a number of factors:

- The desire to maximise returns from existing capacity products and services.
- The desire to defend current patterns of behaviour, systems and procedures.
- The desire to minimise losses on existing plant and equipment (and people) through enforced obsolescence.
- The desire to protect status derived from past experience.
- The desire to avoid risk consequences.
- Fear of the unknown.

However, by personal leadership and demonstrating an openness to change themselves, managers can create the right climate for innovation. In this way the company can capitalise on its strengths by being able to respond to new situations. It is such a flexible approach that is the hidden strength of the small company.

■ Strategy of Minimal Risk

The least risky way of dealing with the development of new products and services is not to innovate but to copy others.

By taking this stance the company avoids all the costs associated with developing new ideas and creating markets for them. Instead, it takes the ideas and modifies them according to its capacity. It then 'surf-rides' the wave in the market place created by the innovator.

The key to success with this strategy is *timing*. To get into the market too early, before the new idea becomes accepted, can put a company in the position of a trailblazer with all the attendant costs. But if a company arrives too late, the market for the idea may have been monopolised by others.

Nevertheless, it does seem that a risk/reward 'rule' appears to operate along a continuum, as in Figure 10.9.

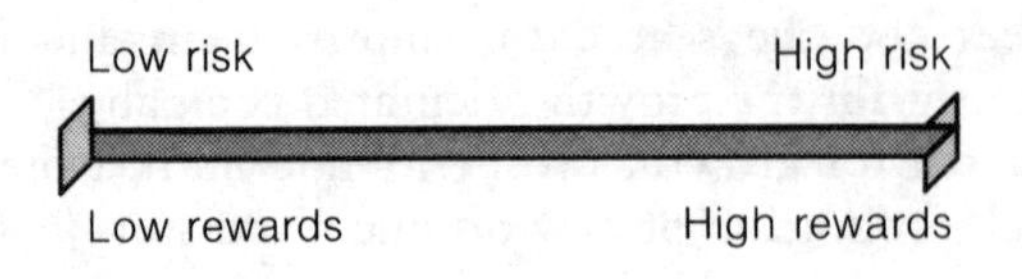

Figure 10.9 Risk/reward continuum

Although this may seem a little prescriptive, such a 'rule' is endorsed by proverbs and sayings such as: 'Luck favours the brave' and 'Who dares wins'. It will therefore be useful to look at other options towards the right-hand end of the risk/reward line.

Creative Ideas

The potential sources of new ideas for products and services are virtually boundless. They can range from the sudden insight, the 'eureka' kind of invention, through to some very analytical techniques.

Here are just some sources of ideas for new products or services. There is no significance in the order in which they are placed:

- Brainstorming – a technique that involves a group of people 'free thinking' about the new uses to which a product or service can be put. The key to brainstorming is that *all* ideas are listed and judgement about their feasibility is suspended. Only when a large number of ideas are generated are they considered in terms of feasibility.
- Talking and listening to customers or intermediaries.
- Monitoring technological developments.
- Monitoring new legislation, for example that which has impact on safety, the environment or crime reduction. These can be potent sources for new products or services.
- Running an ideas scheme among staff.
- Attribute listing – this involves listing the attributes of a product or service and then modifying them in the search for an improved version.
- Carrying out market-gap analysis.
- Keeping in touch with what competitors are doing.
- Setting up a 'think tank' with staff and/or appropriate outsiders.
- Analysing past sales figures for significant trends.
- Making forced relationships – new ideas are listed and then worked at in pairs. Sometimes interesting products or services can emerge from this process. For example separate gramophone turntable, tape deck, amplifier and tuner were put together as a 'music centre'. More recently a TV and video recorder have been integrated into one single unit.
- Conducting specific market research.
- Monitoring customer queries or complaints.

- Lateral thinking – looking at familiar ideas and turning them back to front. For example a small company made glass fibre boats but needed to diversify. It could have looked at other types of craft, but it decided that if its expertise was making structures to 'keep water out' then it also had the expertise to 'keep water in'. By developing this line of thinking the company expanded into making storage tanks and reservoirs, essentially using its existing technology.
- Applying new ideas stemming from the availability or application of new materials. For example new plastic materials are being developed that can make them ideal substitutes for more expensive metal products.

Irrespective of *how* we generate new ideas for products or services, there seem to be three universal 'laws' of which we should be aware:

- Successful innovators have a much better understanding of user-needs than their less successful contemporaries.
- The odds against a new product or service being successful are very high, in the order of thirty to one against. Therefore to have one good idea it is likely that we would need to have considered about thirty. In other words, the quality ideas come from quantity.
- The key sources of new product ideas are likely to be based on research and development and market research. Attractive though they might seem, successful ideas generated by creative-thinking techniques have been fairly limited, because they are likely to be product- rather than market-focused.

■ Other Considerations

Perhaps giving birth to the new idea for a product or service is the most difficult part of the process of innovation, but there are clearly many other factors to take into account before we rush to the market place:

- Is there a need for the new product or service?
- What sort of demand will there be?
- Are the customers likely to be new or existing ones?
- Can I reach the new customers?
- Will the new product/service fit in with the existing range?
- Do we have the resources and expertise to provide it?
- What does the competition provide? How does it compare?
- What will be the costs of providing this new product/service?
- What will be the result if we don't provide it?
- Will it make money?
- Is it what we want to make, or like making?
- Is it consistent with the image of our company?
- What life could we expect from the new product/service?

■ A Screening Procedure for Ideas for New Products or Services

All the considerations we have just raised make it essential that new ideas for products or services are rigorously screened to ensure they will be viable. The screening procedure should look something like that in Figure 10.10.

We have seen that new products are the life blood of a company in its attempt to survive in a dynamic and competitive marketing environment. The search for viable and profitable new products must be a continuing task of marketing management but it is a task that is fraught with risk.

For the majority of companies the introduction of a new product involves a great deal of investment, both in the development process and in the initial introductory stage when market acceptance has to be won if the product is to succeed. This investment can represent a considerable slice of a company's resources, not only financial but also physical and managerial; yet there can be no fail-safe guarantee that the investment will yield the sort of return that the company would consider acceptable. In some cases a single new product failure could bring disaster to a company, especially if it had pinned all its hopes on the new product only to find that the outcome fell far short of expectations.

Consider the case some years ago of the Rolls-Royce RB211 engine. Here the company had committed major resources to an engine that, whilst technically unimpeachable, did not match the wants of a large enough section of the market to recoup the tremendous development costs. Hindsight would suggest that this was an unwise step to take. As it was, it almost led to the collapse of the company.

Another example occurred in the consumer goods market, when a major food manufacturer invested heavily in developing a new dessert. Careful testing indicated that the product would be acceptable to potential customers. However, when the company proceeded to launch the product it found that retailers were unwilling to stock it as the type of packaging developed for the product led to problems of stacking.

These examples can be matched with many others in the consumer, industrial and service markets. Research has indicated that, in some product areas, up to 80 per cent of all new product launches fail, in the sense that they do not meet marketing targets and are withdrawn soon after their introduction. Some product fields, such as grocery or cosmetics, are more prone to early failure than others but, whatever the context, all the evidence seems to suggest a high failure rate for new product introductions.

What then should marketing managers do to reduce the uncertainty that surrounds the new product launch? There are no crystal-ball revelations about prospects for success or failure in this area, but some procedures can be very helpful in quantifying the risks implicit in a new product launch. We shall now go on to explore some of these methods, but, before we do so, we should first look more closely at some other factors involved in the new product-testing decision.

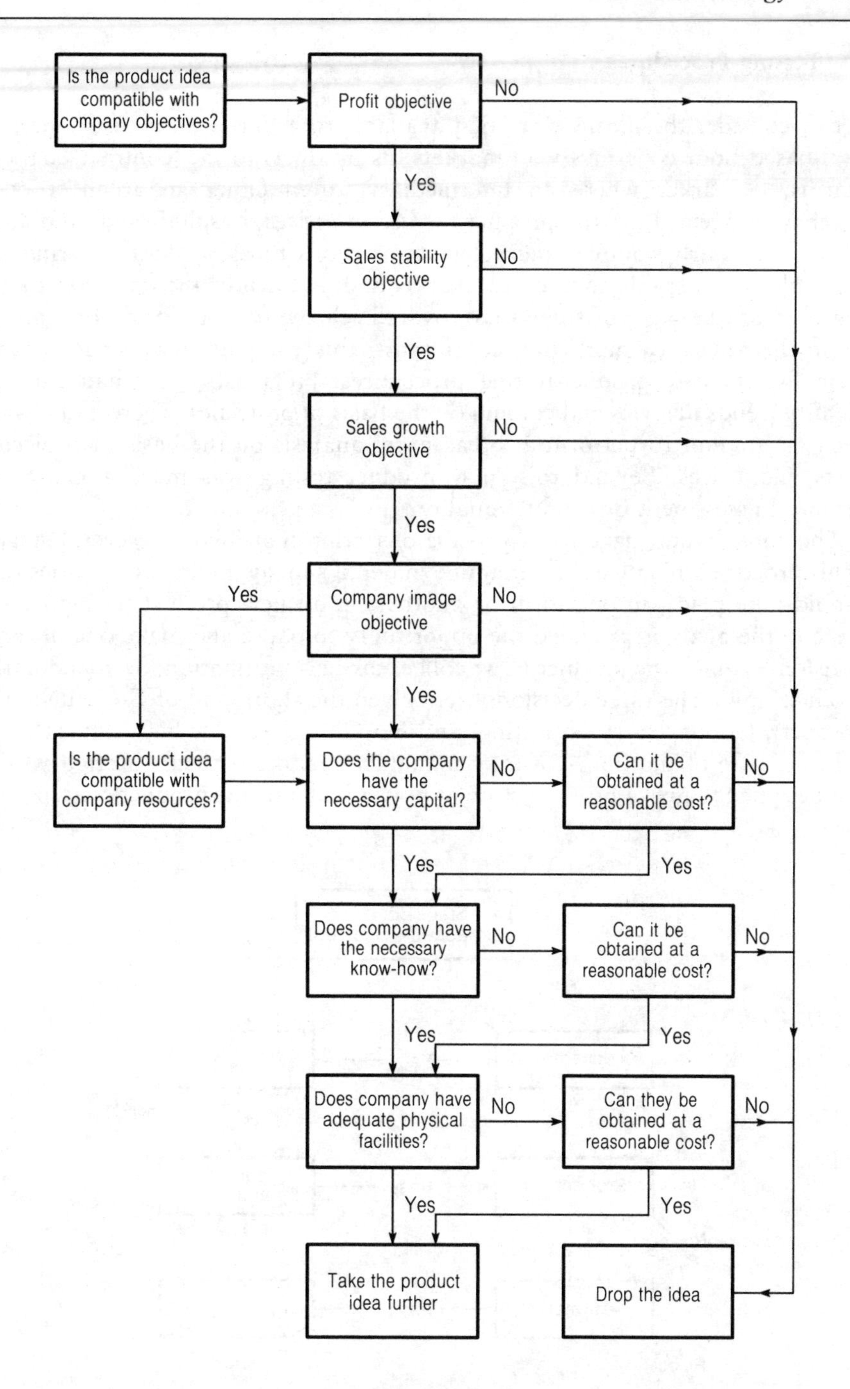

Figure 10.10 Screening procedure for new products

■ Testing Procedures

Let us consider the means of testing available to a European manufacturer of sisal-based floor coverings who markets his products to the 'contract' market; that is, a market where an intermediary, often either an architect or a purchasing agent, buys the product for use in offices, hospitals and schools.

This is a fairly complex market where various types of floor covering are available. It is a highly competitive market and, frequently, the floor covering is specified on the basis of some total, overall scheme for interior decoration.

On the advice of marketing consultants, this company was attempting to formalise its new product-testing procedures. Previously, they had tried to identify trends in styles and colours on the basis of past sales. There had always been an attempt to perform a 'break-even' analysis on the basis of projected costs and prices. Beyond this, new product testing was more a matter of technical assessment or product quality.

The consultants suggested a process of testing that involved several stages. (This process, which we shall examine in detail shortly, indicates activities that should take place, in one form or another, in all new product testing.) Each stage in the analysis provided the opportunity to pause and make one of three decisions: launch the product now; collect further information; or abandon the product now. The three decisions were given the shorthand of Go (launch the product), Go On (carry on testing) and No Go (reject) (see Figure 10.11).

In the case of the floor-covering manufacturer, the sequence started with a test designed to give a broad picture of how acceptable the product concept was

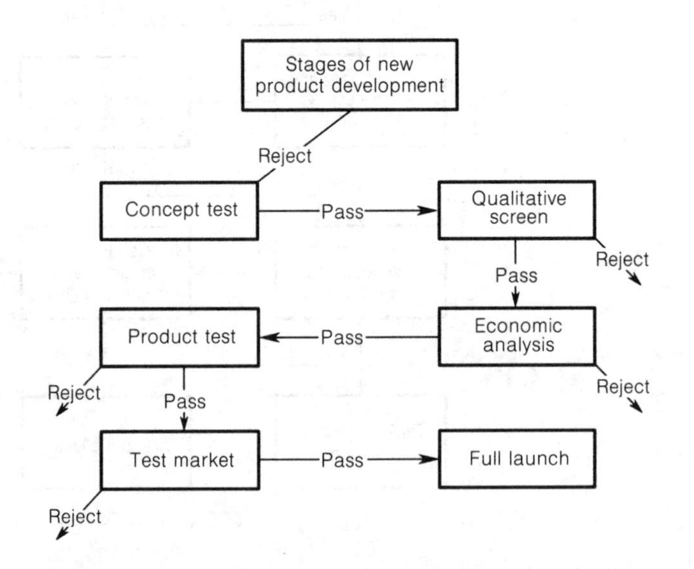

Figure 10.11 Stages of new product development

to its potential market. (This was accompanied by an initial appraisal of how the product might fit into the company's product portfolio.)

□ *Concept Test*

This was administered by means of a dozen interviews conducted by trained interviewers, with architects and purchasing agents representative of the target market. The purpose of the test was to expose them to details of the technical specification, possible colour range and recommended uses of the product. Sometimes artists' impressions of designs and colours were shown. The results of this stage of the test sequence were entirely qualitative but they served to eliminate all those products that were complete non-starters. It was scarcely possible to make a decision to launch the product at this stage.

□ *Qualitative Screen*

This was the next stage, and formed a screening process that posed two basic questions:

First, *is the product concept compatible with company objectives?* Issues involved were, for example:

- Does the concept complement our existing market offering?
- Is it compatible with the image that we seek and the segment of the market with which we identify?

Second, *is the product concept compatible with company resources?* Issues involved here were:

- Does the company have the capital to get this product to market and to develop an initial level of sales?
- Does the company have the necessary know-how and adequate physical facilities to handle the product successfully?

□ *Economic Analysis*

If the product concept survived the screening process it was subjected to this next stage in the testing sequence. This analysis was designed to examine the economics of the project under differing assumptions of costs incurred and revenue achieved.

It was conducted at a fairly simple level as the company at that time had only a limited knowledge of how the market would react to products priced outside the narrow band with which the company was familiar. It was acknowledged that this stage of the testing sequence could be made considerably more sophisticated by applying the methods of investment appraisal that were in common use in other companies.

Once this stage of the testing had been successfully concluded, the company might feel sufficiently confident of the viability of the concept to move ahead to a full-scale market launch. Such a decision would have to be based on some highly positive results from the initial stages of the test sequence since the cost of setting up a promotional programme would be substantial. More often a decision would be taken to go on to the next, more expensive, stage of the analysis.

□ *Product Test*

In this case the product test was designed to gain impressions from a relatively large number of potential customers of how they would react to the physical product when it was compared with competing products. The expense of product testing lies in the fact that considerable quantities of the physical product must be provided. The aim of the test is to identify a representative sample of the target market and to interpret the reactions relative to the competing products. Aspects of the product tested at this stage would be physical characteristics, the range available, the suggested usage, price and image connotations. This company recruited a panel of architects and purchasing agents who were invited to compare, according to a number of appropriate criteria, the proposed new products with selected competitive products. The analysis of these results enabled a picture to be built up of how the proposed new product compared with existing products in a number of key dimensions.

It was at this stage that the company normally made the final decision as to whether or not to launch the new product. Clearly there would still be some uncertainty about the new product's success, but the sequential testing had enabled this uncertainty to be reduced to an acceptable level. The company could have gone on, as many do, to the next test.

□ *Test Market*

This, as the name implies, is an attempt to reproduce the conditions of a full-scale launch but on a much smaller scale. Often a town, or geographical area, is chosen as representing the ultimate market; the product is launched in that town or area alone and its progress observed. As a test of this kind is very much an 'experiment', it is necessary to ensure that conditions within the test market would be such that they could be reproduced on a national scale. For example, no extra promotional effort should be expended other than an amount proportional to the total to be spent in the proposed full-scale launch.

It should be noted, however, that test markets can never be completely reliable indicators of ultimate market performance. Quite apart from the problems of 'grossing up' small-scale test-market results to provide a global picture, there is always the possibility of unusual competitive activities that distort the results.

While we have portrayed these stages of testing as a sequence, it should be clear that some of the stages could be conducted concurrently, as with the qualitative screen and the economic analysis. Whatever the sequence, the purpose of new product testing remains the same: to reduce uncertainty surrounding the new product to a level acceptable to the company whilst still enabling the launch to be made at the earliest possible time.

The methods of product testing might vary from marketing situation to marketing situation but, whether the product be a new airline service, heavy-duty transformers or a vinyl wallpaper, the principles are universal and the benefits considerable.

■ Forecasting Future Sales

The problem of estimating the level of future sales of any product, new or old, is ever-present and may only be imperfectly solved. Knowing in advance what levels of sales could be achieved, given a particular marketing mix and a particular marketing programme, would reduce considerably the complexity of the marketing decision. However, few people can claim the ability to predict the future accurately and in detail and the marketing decision maker has to fall back on other, less precise methods.

Even some of the most carefully prepared forecasts of future sales can be disproved by events. The wider environment in which the forecast is set changes in ways that are not always foreseen and thus are not incorporated in the forecast. Energy crises, crop failures, drought, revolutions – these are just a few of the major events that can upset the forecast. It could be suggested that, if the world is so dynamic, what is the purpose of forecasting anyway? The answer is quite simply that any attempt to reduce the uncertainty that surrounds the future will, if used as a flexible input to the planning process, make us question the appropriateness of what we are currently doing. It must be recognised, however, that forecasts are useful only if they are indeed used in a flexible way. Sales forecasts can too easily become straitjackets which inhibit the organisation's activities, as when they are seen as targets, endowed with all the sanctity that numbers tend to assume in a management context.

Forecasts deal with contingencies, not certainties. The head of planning in a large multi-national chemical company says, 'We have to have alternative plans that can deal with either/or eventualities'. Establishing the nature of the 'either/or' is the task of the market forecaster. Parallel to the need for flexibility is the need to recognise that the output of the forecast should be expressed in terms of a *range* of possible outcomes. Sales estimates share the imprecision of most forecasting methods. Beyond this, however, it must be recognised that the process whereby any sales level is achieved is essentially *probabilistic*. In other words, chance has a central role in the outcome of any marketing process. Our forecasts can, and should, be made to incorporate the probabilities that are implicit in the marketing environment in which we operate.

The successful use of forecasting can be seen in the case of a manufacturer of household durables. Prior to the start of each fiscal year they worked out three different forecasts: 'optimistic', 'pessimistic' and 'most likely'. If taxation levels changed, competitive activity became particularly aggressive, or if some other phenomenon occurred to alter the market, the manufacturer could adopt an alternative plan without having to repeat the forecasting procedure. This approach enabled the company to react to market conditions with immediate flexibility.

But how do we start to grapple with the sales estimation problem?

■ Understanding Market Potential

The distinction between actual and potential customers is vital to successful sales estimation. The forecaster is concerned with establishing what proportion of the total market potential will be represented in his or her sales estimates. Market potential has been defined as the maximum possible sales opportunities for all sellers of a good or service. As such, it refers to the potential sales that could be achieved at a given time, in a given environment, by all the firms active in a specified product/market area or segment. Thus the concept of market potential extends our view of the market for our product, in that we see the product as competing against alternative means of satisfying the same need. Successful sales estimation will, therefore, depend on determining the proportion of the market that can be achieved, given a specific marketing mix and marketing programme. This situation is illustrated in Figure 10.12.

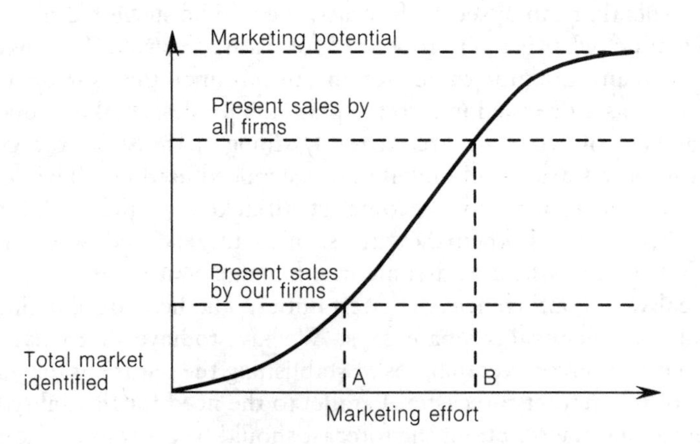

Figure 10.12 Market potential curve

A presentation of this kind, of course, gives a static picture of actual and potential sales at a given time and in a given environment; it could be influenced both by environmental changes and by changes in marketing effort by any of the firms (including ourselves) in that product/market area.

Looking at the sales-estimation problem in this light, we see how it can be possible for estimates to become self-fulfilling prophecies, in that the estimate and the marketing mix/programme are dependent upon each other. In a sense, a given level of market achievement is predicated by what we believe to be potentially achievable.

■ The Forecasting Horizon

Clearly the time period that we select for the forecasting exercise will influence our approach and our choice of estimation techniques. Most managers are accustomed to thinking in terms of short-, medium- and long-term forecasting, the actual length of these periods being determined by the organisation's planning requirements. As an example, a manufacturer of wine bottles in Spain knows that their short-term forecasting requirements are based on their need to plan production schedules on a weekly basis. Their medium-term requirements are determined by the industry demand over the period of time it takes to install and make operational additional production capacity – in this case, a year. And the longer-term forecasting must take account of changing consumer requirements, such as easy-to-open bottles and changing technology in the bottling and packaging fields.

Precise definitions of what constitute the short, medium and long term for any company will clearly vary, but should ultimately depend on the reaction time implicit in a company's activities and its organisation. The reaction time for firms in ladies' fashion markets must necessarily be much shorter than for those companies engaged in the construction of hydroelectric power projects. Their definition of the forecasting horizon will vary correspondingly.

The firm's definition of that horizon will also be influenced by the variability of demand in their markets. For established products, that variability may not be pronounced, particularly if seasonal variations are allowed for. Even though on a week-by-week basis sales may seem to fluctuate widely, there will often be an underlying steady-state or a recognisable upward or downward direction in sales. The forecasting task for the manufacturers of beef stock cubes, a product in a steady-state that has lasted for many years, is quite different from that facing the Swedish firm Uddeholm as they launch on a completely untried market a new grade of stainless steel for use in the processing of fertilisers.

■ The Techniques of Estimation

Two broad approaches to market estimation have been employed by market forecasters in their attempts to estimate future sales levels. These may be termed *macro* (or aggregate product-market) estimates and *micro* (or individual product) estimates. These approaches are not alternatives, but should complement each other in the information they provide. Both approaches can use qualitative and quantitative methods of estimation, depending on their objectives.

□ *The Macro Level of Estimation*

Let us first consider the macro approaches to estimation. Here the emphasis is on observing the broad picture and, from that, deducing the implications for the product/market in which we are interested. Many business forecasters use leading indicators (that is, indices of related or even non-related activities) as aids in estimating changes in market conditions at the macro level. For example, in the UK the *Financial Times* Ordinary Share Index has tended in recent years to signal changes in general economic conditions about six months in advance. Similar UK leading indicators, which would be classified as quantitative methods of estimation, are: new housing starts (a lead of about ten months), net acquisition of financial assets by companies (leading by about twelve months) and interest on three-month bank bills (with a lead of approximately eighteen months).

Such indicators will only provide approximate pictures of general business conditions and cannot be guaranteed to offer consistent correlations. On the other hand the forecaster may discern that there is a close fit between a seemingly unrelated activity and the sales performance of a particular product. One Danish manufacturer of garden furniture has established a satisfactory method of predicting sales on the basis of an apparent correlation between the rise in real wages in Denmark and the sale of their products, with a lag of eighteen months. This does not necessarily imply any causal relationship – simply a statistical association – but it did seem to provide a useful aid to sales estimation.

There has been a considerable growth in recent years in the use of *marketing models* to provide a macro-type basis for sales estimation. Generally these models are based on a number of statistically derived relationships drawn from empirical observations. Some of these can be relatively simple, embodying only a few relationships and requiring nothing more than a calculator to perform the manipulations. On the other hand, one Europe-wide oil company has recently developed a sophisticated energy model to guide it in formulating its strategy on synthetic fuels. The model covers all major energy forms, conversion technologies, transportation modes and demand. It also projects investment, financing and resource depletion to the year 2025 and even attempts to predict prices on the basis of supply and demand. A model of this kind attempts to *explain* the observed market behaviour in terms of marketing trends. This contrasts with the garden furniture example above, where the correlation is not explained, only accepted as an *observable* phenomenon.

Not everybody shares this enthusiasm for large-scale models, because of the problems of quantifying what are often qualitative and intangible relationships.

Such relationships will often change considerably over time, thus making the model obsolete. Another factor weighing against the use of models is the considerable expense involved in collecting the necessary data. In many markets – as in the soup market – for example, it may be more cost-beneficial to employ less sophisticated estimation techniques.

An example of a qualitative macro estimation is the Delphi forecast (named after the Greek oracle who foretold the future). Here a group of experts discuss a problem, such as, 'What will be the major marketing features of the year 2010?', and give their consensus of the answer to this problem.

These macro approaches, it was suggested earlier, are particularly suited to forecasting that is intended, primarily, to depict broad market conditions. In themselves, though, they rarely provide a complete answer to the company's sales estimation problem. The micro level approaches to estimation, which tackle the problem from the other direction, from the study of the sales prospects for an individual product, can often provide the missing pieces of the jigsaw.

□ *The Micro Level of Estimation*

Micro approaches are based on building up, from an individual customer level, an estimate of what total sales of the product could be in a given period. Quantitative micro methods rely heavily on surveys of actual and/or potential customers of the sort we discussed in Chapter 6, which dealt with marketing research. Although the procedures involved may be very sophisticated, these studies basically rely on indications from respondents about their likely purchasing behaviour. For example, a German manufacturer of household electrical goods carries out a regular survey amongst a representative sample of actual and potential customers to ascertain the likelihood of their purchasing particular electrical appliances in the next twelve months. Using this device, they can track the way in which first-time sales will move and also the way in which the replacement market is moving.

At the micro level, many companies rely on forecasts that are based solely on an analysis of past sales. In other words, past sales are charted with a view to identifying patterns and trends that enable projections to be made. The nature of projections must be clearly understood: they are extrapolations from past behaviour and are based upon an assumption that what has happened in the past will be a guide to what will happen in the future. This need not be so. One British firm in the building products market expanded its production facilities on the basis of a sharp upturn in the mid-1980s, only to find that by 1990 the market had collapsed. The collapse lasted long enough to damage the firm's profitability and cast doubt on its chances of long-term survival.

An example of a qualitative micro estimate would be an estimate based on the judgement of members of the sales force concerning future sales.

Successful marketing management must be based upon reliable estimates of market demand. It would probably be true to say that companies pay rather less attention to this crucial input to marketing decisions than they should. Success in the markets of the future will almost certainly require a reversal of this neglect.

■ Summary

The key to successful product strategy is a balanced portfolio of products that includes both established products and a steady flow of new products. The use of the Boston matrix can be helpful in analysing the options for product strategy and in highlighting gaps in the portfolio.

Because the chance of failure is high in new product launches the use of formalised methods of appraisal is advocated, including market research as well as economic analysis.

Sales forecasting takes place against a background of uncertainty, and is therefore largely probabilistic. The task is influenced both by the forecasting horizon and by the stability of the markets in which we operate. Techniques include both macro and micro approaches.

MODULE 4

Positioning the Offer

CHAPTER 11

Branding

What is a Brand?

In Chapter 1 we referred to the organisation's marketing assets. Top of the list was 'brand names'. Figure 1.2, repeated here as Figure 11.1, depicted the nature of the 'offer' made by organisations to their customers.

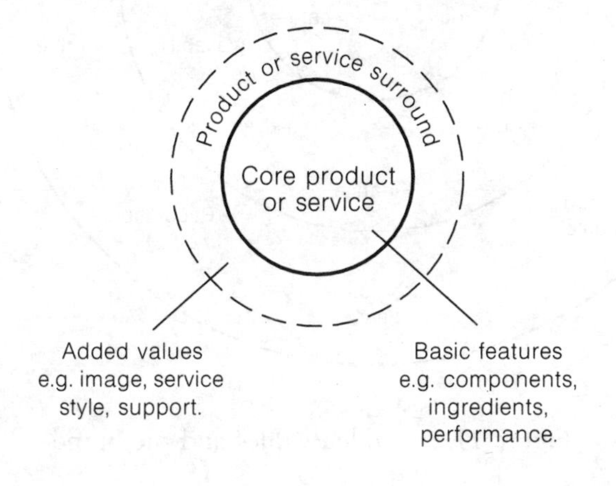

Figure 11.1 Added values enhance basic features

Figure 11.2 is an expanded version of this concept.

As can be seen from Figure 11.2, a product is, of course, a whole package of things, which can be boiled down to three main elements:

- *The Core Product*, that is, what it is, what it does, its efficacy, price and packaging.
- *The Service Surround*, that is, availability, delivery, after-sales service, warranties and accessories.
- *The Intangibles Surround*, that is, quality perceptions, reputation, corporate image, organisation and brand name.

In this chapter we shall be concentrating on the intangible elements, particularly brand reputation and value perception. To underpin the importance of these, let us throw out a challenge. Suppose you and the authors of this book are competitors in the oil market; after all, lots of organisations can make oil and put it into cans. However our cans have a green and red stripe on them, and our

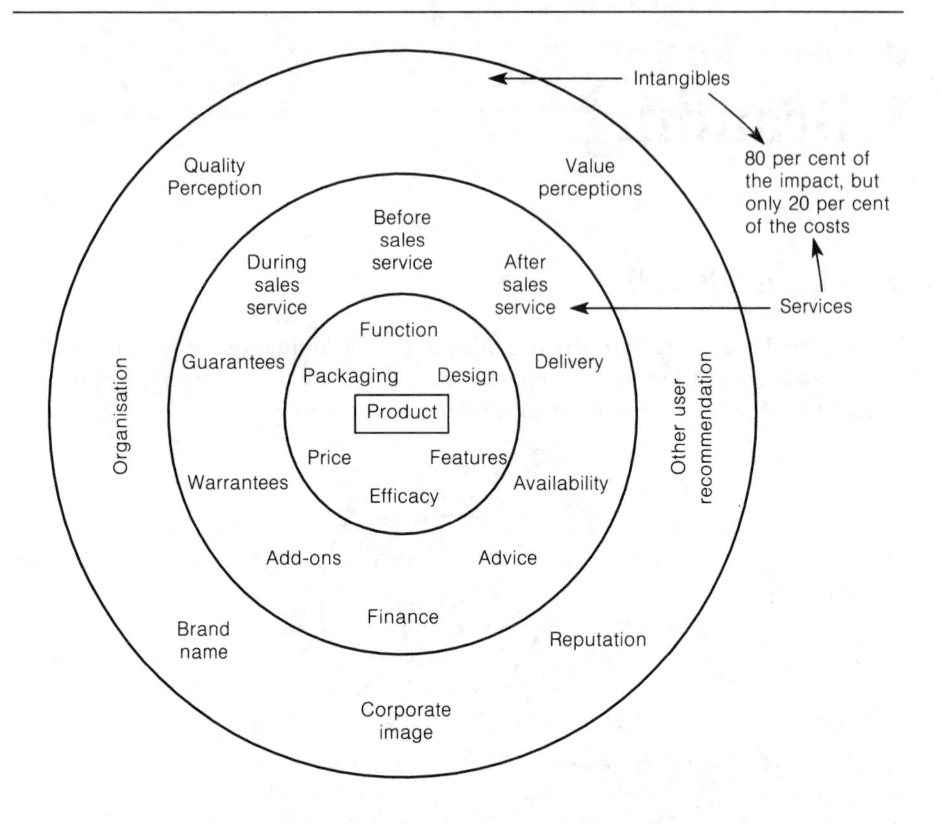

Figure 11.2 Added values and the brand

oil is called Castrol GTX. Need we say more? Although you may have a similar product technically, we will have a very large world market share – and you will be struggling in comparison. Such is the power of brand names.

By way of further evidence, Figure 11.3 shows some research results from the PIMS database (Profit Impact of Market Strategies) of some 3000 strategic business units.

The figures inside the boxes represent return on investment. While not wanting to diminish the role of market share, in this chapter we are concentrating on the other axis, *relative product quality*. Its potency cannot be denied, judging by the results shown here.

Should any proof be necessary, let us look at one of the toughest markets in the world, the grocery market. According also to the PIMS database, the number-one brands have a return on sales of almost 18 per cent, whilst the number two has a margin of around 4 per cent. That is why names such as Heinz, Kelloggs and Mars are so powerful. Rather than envy these types of companies, their competitors ought to spend some time reflecting upon what it is they do to get such spectacular results.

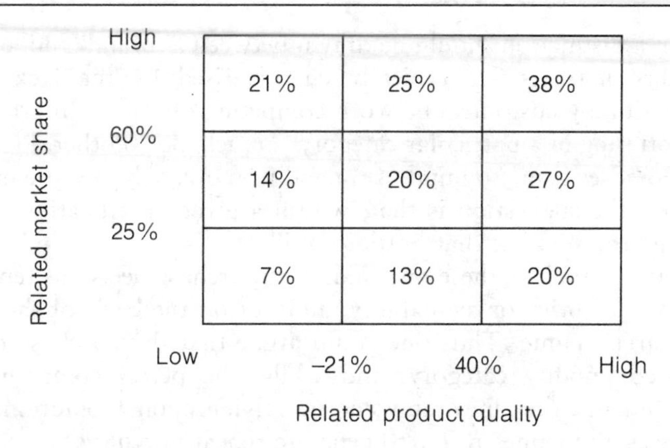

Figure 11.3 The profit impact of market share and quality

Put simply, they have a 'win-win' strategy. They study their consumers and consistently provide them with a product of excellent value, for which they are prepared to pay a premium and create demand pull through the retail chain. For their part, retailers are delighted with the gross margin return they get from their inventory investment in leading brands. This recipe ensures that customer, retailer and supplier all get what they seek from coming together. There are no losers.

The key to success should not really be that elusive, yet it continues to slip through the grasp of so many well-intentioned and aspiring companies. When the chairman of Procter & Gamble states his basic beliefs about marketing and says, 'The successful company is one which is first to identify emerging customer needs and to offer product improvements which satisfy those needs', and 'The successful marketer spots a new trend early and leads it', he is not saying anything that any of us could possibly contradict. Deep down we know this must be the truth. What differentiates the successful companies from the also-rans is that they live out their beliefs and make them reality. Their beliefs do not remain as pious hopes stranded on glossy mission statements, they come alive.

Returning to Figure 11.2, we can see that it also depicts a *relationship* with the customer. This relationship is personified either by the organisation's name or by the brand name on the product itself. ICI, IBM, BMW, Kodak and Cadbury are excellent examples of company brand names. Persil, Nescafé, Fosters, Dulux and Castrol GTX are excellent examples of product brand names.

First, then, it should be stressed, that when we refer to the term 'brand' in this book we use it to encompass not only consumer products, but a whole host of offerings, including people (such as politicians and pop stars), places (such as Bangkok), ships (such as the *Queen Elizabeth*), companies, industrial products, service products and so on.

Second, a distinction should be drawn between a 'brand' and a 'commodity'. Commodity markets are typically characterised by the lack of perceived differentiation by customers between competing offerings. In other words, one product offering in a particular category is much like another. Products such as milk or potatoes come to mind or tin and iron ore. Whilst there may be quality differences, the suggestion is that, within a given specification, this bottle of milk is just the same as that bottle of milk.

In situations such as these one finds that purchase decisions tend to be taken on the basis of price or availability, and not on the basis of the brand or the manufacturer's name. Thus one could argue that the purchase of petrol falls into the commodity category, and whilst the petrol companies do try to promote 'image', they inevitably end up relying upon promotions such as free wine glasses and games to try to generate repeat purchase.

There are examples, however, of taking a commodity and making it a brand. Take, for example, Perrier Water: the contents are naturally occurring spring water, which – whilst it has certain distinctive characteristics – at the end of the day is still spring water. Yet through packaging and, more particularly, promotion, an international brand has been created with high brand loyalty, and consequently it sells for a price well in excess of the cost of the ingredients.

Conversely one can also find examples of once-strong brands that have been allowed to decay and in effect become commodities. This process is often brought about because the marketing asset base has been allowed to erode – perhaps through price cutting or through a lack of attention to product improvement in the face of competition. One market where this has happened in the UK is the fruit-squash drink market. Fifteen or twenty years ago there were a number of very strong brands – Suncrush, Kia-Ora, Jaffa Juice, to name just a few. In this market the quality of the brand had traditionally been stressed, but a switch in promotional emphasis occurred in the 1960s towards promotional offers of one sort or another. Price cutting became prevalent and resources were switched out of advertising that promoted the values of the brand and into so-called 'below the line' promotional activities. The main effect of this, twenty years later, has been to reduce the bottle of orange squash to the level of a commodity to such an extent that the major brands are now retailers' own-label products.

Figure 11.4 depicts the process of decay from brand to commodity as, over time, the distinctive values of the brand become less clear and thus the opportunity to demand a premium price reduces. So, today, we find a bottle of Perrier Water selling at a premium over a bottle of orange squash!

The difference between a brand and a commodity can be summed up in the phrase 'added values'. A brand is more than just the sum of its component parts. It embodies, for the purchaser or user, additional attributes that, whilst they might be considered by some to be 'intangible', are still very real. To illustrate the power of these added values consider the result of a *blind* test (that is, where the brand identity is concealed) in which Diet Pepsi was compared against Diet Coke by a panel of consumers:

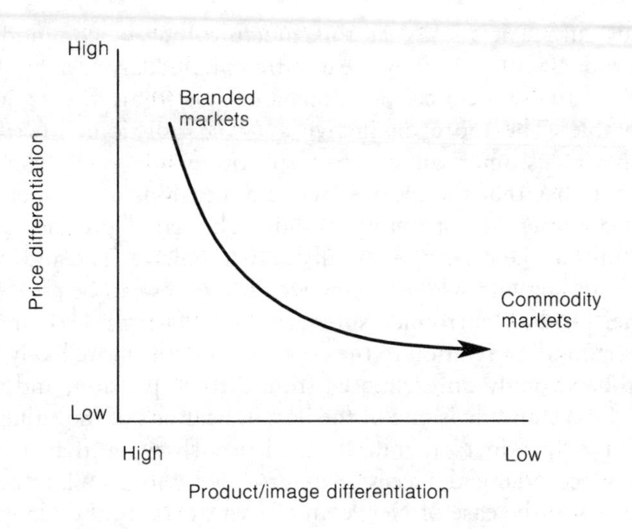

Figure 11.4 From brand to commodity

- Prefer Pepsi: 51 per cent
- Prefer Coke: 44 per cent
- Equal/can't say: 5 per cent

When the same two drinks were given to a matched sample in an *open test* (that is, the true identity of the brands was revealed), the following results were produced:

- Prefer Pepsi: 23 per cent
- Prefer Coke: 65 per cent
- Equal/can't say: 12 per cent

How can this be explained if not in terms of the added values that are aroused in the minds of consumers when they see the familiar Coke logo and pack?

The same phenomenon is also encountered in industrial marketing. In a commodity market such as fertilisers, the initials 'ICI' printed on a plastic sack had the effect of communicating to the purchaser a statement about quality and reliability, giving ICI a considerable advantage over lesser-known brands.

Often these added values are emotional values that customers might find difficult to articulate. These values are given to a product quite simply through the marketing mix of product, packaging, promotion, price and distribution. All of these elements of the mix can be used to develop a distinctive *position* in the customer's mental map of the market. As in all the references to brands thus far, the concept of 'positioning' is developed in greater detail in the following chapters, but suffice it to say at this juncture that in commodity markets competing products, because they are undifferentiated, are seen by the customer as occupying virtually identical positions and thus to all intents and purposes are substitutable. The more distinctive a *brand* position, however, the less likelihood that a customer will accept a substitute.

It is thus the case that the most effective dimensions of competition are the relative added values of competing brands. The 'core' product is purely the tangible features of the offering – usually easy to imitate. The added values that augment the product and where distinctive differences can be created, are to be found in the 'product surround' summarised in Figures 11.1 and 11.2. The larger the 'surround' in relation to the core product, the more likely it is that the offering will be strongly differentiated from the competition, and vice versa.

The Coca Cola example is one of the best indications of the value of what we have called the 'product surround'. Evidence showing that it is a major determinant of commercial success was provided above. When one company buys another, as in the case of Nestlé and Rowntree, it is abundantly clear that the purpose of the acquisition is not to buy the tangible assets that appear on the balance sheet, such as factories, plant, vehicles and so on, but the brand names owned by the company to be acquired. This is because it is not factories that make profits, but relationships with customers, and it is brand names that secure these relationships.

It might be argued, therefore, that if it is possible to value a company for sale, then surely it should be possible to do so on an on-going basis and specifically to recognise the worth of marketing assets as represented by brands.

The question of asset protection and development is in a sense what marketing is all about. The 'stewardship' of marketing assets is a key responsibility that is recognised in many companies by, for example, the organisational concept of brand management. Here an executive is given the responsibility for a brand or brands and acts as the product 'champion', competing internally for resources and externally for market position. It is but a short step from this organisational concept to a system of 'brand accounting', which would seek to identify the net present value of a brand based upon the prospect of future cash inflows compared with outgoings.

One advantage of such an approach is that it forces the manager to acknowledge that money spent on developing the market position of a brand is in fact an investment that is made in order to generate future benefits. There is a strong argument for suggesting that, for internal decision making and on questions of resource allocation, a 'shadow' set of management accounts be used, not the traditional approach whereby marketing costs are expensed in the period in which they are incurred, but an approach that recognises such expenditure as investments.

Buying a major brand nowadays often makes more sense to organisations than launching a new brand, with all the risk and uncertainty that this entails. This is just one of the reasons why brand valuation has emerged as a major issue in recent times and why brands are increasingly sought after as assets.

Some of the more spectacular examples of the value of brands as assets can be seen in acquisitions in which colossal premiums were paid above the balance-sheet asset value. Philip Morris, for example, bought Kraft for $1.29 billion, four times the value of Kraft's tangible assets. Grand Metropolitan bought Pillsbury for $5.5 billion, a 50 per cent premium on Pillsbury's pre-bid value. More recently, AT and T paid a massive premium for the NCR brand. RHM, taking its cue from this trend, more than trebled its asset value when it voluntarily valued its own brands and incorporated them on the balance sheet.

■ The Difference between Successful and Unsuccessful Brands

We hope that we have, by now, provided some initial signals about the increasing importance of brands in business success. The PIMS database, along with other databases, shows conclusively that strong, successful brands enable organisations to build stable, long-term demand and enable them to build and hold better margins than either commodity products or unsuccessful brands. (Brands, of course, can be either successful or unsuccessful. Waterways in the UK is a prime example of an unsuccessful brand.)

Successful brand building helps profitability by adding values that entice customers to buy. They also provide a firm base for expansion into product improvements, variants, added services, new countries, and so on. They also protect the organisations against the growing power of intermediaries. And last, but not least, they help transform organisations from being faceless bureaucracies to ones that are attractive to work for and deal with.

We must not, then, make the mistake of confusing successful and unsuccessful 'brands'. The world is full of products and services that have brand names, but which are not successful brands. They fall down on other important criteria:

- A successful brand has a name, symbol or design (or some combination) that identifies the 'product' of an organisation as having a sustainable competitive advantage, for example, Coca-Cola, IBM, Marks & Spencer.
- A successful brand invariably results in superior profit and market performance (PIMS).
- Brands are only assets if they have sustainable competitive advantage.
- Like other assets, brands depreciate without further investment, for example Hoover, Singer, MG, and so on.

There are many 'products' that pretend to be brands, but are not the genuine article. As the Director of Marketing at Tesco said, 'Pseudo brands are not brands. They are manufacturer's labels. They are 'me-toos' and have poor positioning, poor quality and poor support. Such manufacturers no longer understand the consumer and see retailers solely as a channel for distribution' (reported in *Marketing Globe*, volume 2, number 10, 1992).

Seen in this light, the pseudo brands can never be mistaken for the real thing, because the genuine brand provides added brand values. Customers believe that the product:

- will be reliable;
- is the best;
- is something that will suit them better than product X; and
- is designed with them in mind.

These beliefs are based not only on perceptions of the brand itself relative to others, but also on customers' perceptions of the supplying company and beliefs about its reputation and integrity.

The title 'successful brand' has to be earned. The company has to invest in everything it does so that the product meets the physical needs of customers, as well as having an image to match their emotional needs. Thus it must provide concrete and rational benefits that are sustained by a marketing mix that is compatible, believable and relevant.

By dint of considerable effort, British Telecom is close to changing from a well-known name to a successful brand. It may not quite be there yet, but it is beginning to shake off its erstwhile bureaucratic image and is getting closer to providing a consistent, high-quality service. IBM, despite all its recent trials and tribulations, still has a substantial world market share and that three-lettered logo is still very powerful.

■ The Components of a Brand

There are three principal components: brand strategy, brand positioning and brand personality.

The first of these, *brand strategy*, stems from the position of the brand in the portfolio of the organisation that owns the brand. A quick reference to Chapters 9 and 10 will remind us that some poor brands are competing in high-growth markets, whilst others are competing in mature or declining markets. Thus the objectives for the brand could well call for different levels and types of investment (invest or harvest), innovation (relaunch, augment, cut costs), sales and distribution patterns (extension, reduction, broad, narrow), market share, usage aims (new, existing behaviour), and so on.

The first point to be made, then, is that an organisation must be clear what the appropriate objectives are for a brand.

The second component, *brand positioning*, is concerned with what the brand actually *does* and with what it competes. In other words, brand positioning starts with the physical, or functional aspects of the brand (the centre circle in Figure 11.2). For instance, Canada Dry is positioned in the UK as a mixer for brandies and whiskies, rather than as a soft drink competing with Coca-Cola, Pepsi-Cola and 7-Up. Tide is a tough, general-purpose detergent, rather than a powder for woollens. Tesco is a high-quality grocer rather than a low price supermarket. SAS is positioned as the business person's airline.

There are usually several main motivators in any market, only one or two of which are of real importance. These dimensions are best seen as bipolar scales along which brands can be positioned. For example:

- Expensive/inexpensive
- Strong/mild
- Big/small
- Hot/cold
- Fast/slow
- Male/female

Because they are so obvious, they are easy to research in order to establish which are those that people regard as the most fundamental basis for buying. It will be obvious that not all consumers look for the same functional performance, so market segmentation becomes important at this stage. A useful starting point in this kind of primary market interpretation is to draw a bipolar map, as shown in Figure 11.5. Figure 11.6 shows an actual bipolar map for detergents.

Clearly the physical dimensions of any market will change over time, so this kind of basic research should be conducted on a regular basis to establish, firstly, what the main dimensions are and, secondly, whether the position of any competing product has changed.

In highly mature markets, brands are likely to be positioned close to one another, thus indicating that the basic functional or physical characteristics are less likely to be the sole basis on which a product or service is selected.

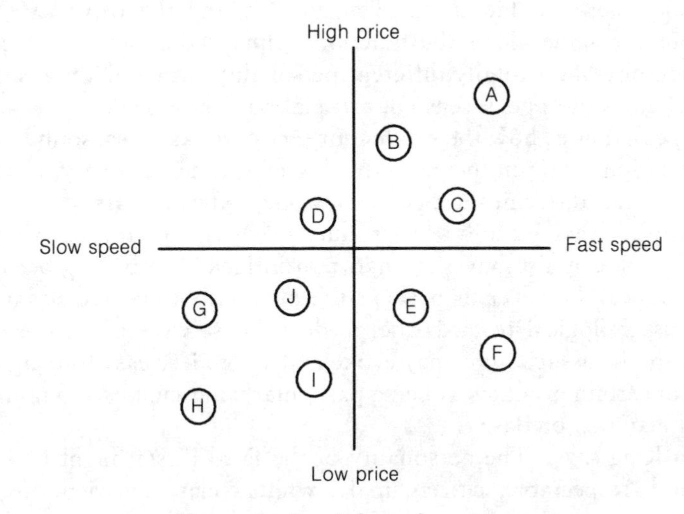

Figure 11.5 A brand position map

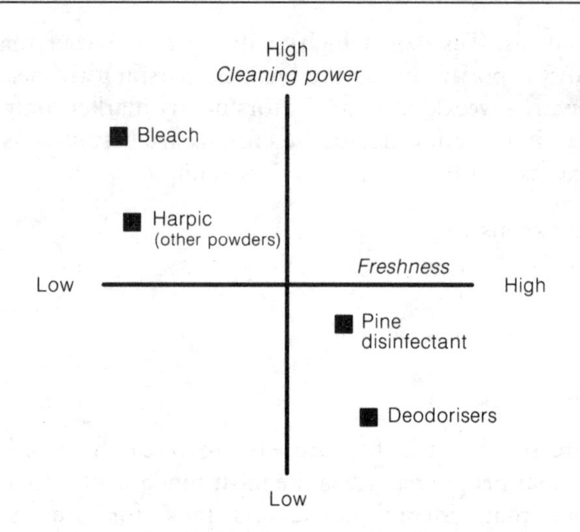

Figure 11.6 Bipolar map for detergents

This brings us to the final component, *brand personality*. Stephen King said that a product is something that is made in a factory; a brand is something that is bought by a consumer. A product can be copied, but a successful brand is *unique* and, particularly in mature markets, is a key discriminator in the market place.

Brand personality is a useful descriptor for the total impression that consumers have of brands, and in many ways brands are like people, with their own physical, emotional and personality characteristics. Brands are very similar, in that they are a complex blend of physical, emotional and personality characteristics. Thus two brands can be very similar in terms of their functions, but have very different personalities.

For example, the Ford Fiesta, the Peugeot 205 and the Rover Metro all perform about the same along the functional dimensions of size, speed and price. Yet each one has a totally different personality, which is the result of a blend of three sorts of appeal: sensual, rational and emotional.

Sensual appeal, that is, how the product or service looks, feels, sounds and so on, can have an important influence on buying behaviour. It is easy to imagine how this appeal can differ in the case of, say, cigarettes, or cars.

Rational appeal, that is, how the product or service performs, what they contain and so on, can also have an important influence on buying behaviour.

Emotional appeal, however, is perhaps the most important and has a lot to do with the psychological rewards the products or services offer, the moods they conjure up, the associations they evoke and so on. It is easy to imagine the overt appeal of certain products as being particularly masculine, or feminine, or chic, or workmanlike, or flashy.

As Stephen King says, 'The personality of the Ford Fiesta might be seen as that of a solid, respectable, citizen, male, white collar, conscientious, hard working, not terribly ambitious, used to play football but now is more likely to spend Saturdays going on shopping expeditions, is proud to vote Conservative and reads the *Daily Mail*. The Renault 5, on the other hand, might be a tentatively dashing girl of 27, who wears what she thinks is the fashion of the moment, reads *Cosmopolitan*, drinks Campari, is a bit muddled about money and votes Liberal. The Fiat Panda might be a teenager, going to be good looking, but still a bit spotty, very uncertain about himself, under the bravado, but a good lad really.' It will be seen from this, that trying to describe a brand is very similar to trying to describe a person. But, each successful brand, like people, is unique. Brand personality, just like people, is the result of a whole gamut of influences, such as the places where it is sold, the price that is charged, other brands from the same manufacturer, how it is used, the kind of people who buy and use it, after-sales service, the name of the brand, advertising, point of sale material, PR, sponsorship and so on. Of all these, advertising is clearly an important one.

The point is that, for any brand to be successful, all these elements have to be consistent, as they will all affect the brand's personality and it is this personality, above all else, that represents the brand's totality and makes one brand more wantable, or appealing, than another. Put at its simplest, it is a brand's personality that converts a commodity into something unique and enables a higher price to be charged for it.

One of the present authors, in another book entitled *Creating Powerful Brands*, combines brand functionality and personality in a matrix. This matrix is shown in Figure 11.7.

The vertical axis refers to a brand's ability to satisfy utilitarian needs, such as quality, reliability, effectiveness and so on, where the consumer's need for such

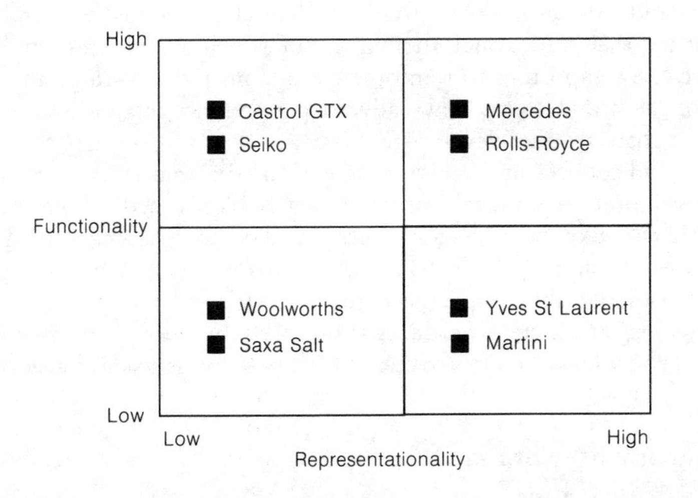

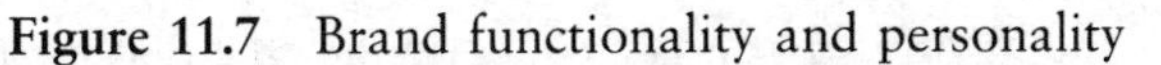
Figure 11.7 Brand functionality and personality
(from *Creating Powerful Brands*, by Leslie de Chernatony and Malcolm McDonald, Butterworth/Heinemann 1992)

benefits is high. The horizontal axis represents the brand's ability to help consumers express something about themselves, be it, for example, their mood, their membership of a particular social group, their status and so on. Brands are chosen on this dimension because they have values that exist over and above their physical values. We call this dimension representationality. For example, products such as Yves St Laurent neckties are effective brands for expressing particular personality types and roles, with functional attributes being secondary.

It is possible, by means of market research, to identify the degree to which consumers perceive a brand as reflecting functionality and representationality and then to plot these on a matrix. Having done this, it is then possible for the marketer to consider how best to use the available resources to support the brand.

For products and services in the top right-hand box (that is, ones that both provide functional excellence and are good vehicles for non-verbal communication about themselves), a creative strategy that reinforces consumers' lifestyle requirements should be adopted, communicated through appropriate media channels. Additionally, the quality of the brand needs to be maintained through high standards of quality control and continuous product development. Also, strict control over channels of distribution should be exercised.

For products and services in the top left-hand box (that is, ones bought by consumers because of a high utilitarian need rather than because of a need to say something about themselves), product superiority needs to be continuously maintained, as 'me-tooism' is a continuous threat to such brands. Also, heavy promotional support is important in communicating the functional benefits of the brand.

For products and services in the bottom right-hand box (that is, ones that are less important for their functional attributes, but which are high as symbolic devices), it is clearly important to reinforce continuously the cultural and lifestyle aspects of the brand and a heavy advertising presence is almost certainly more important than product-development issues.

For products and services in the bottom left-hand box (that is, those that are bought by consumers who are not particularly concerned about either functional differences or self image), successful branding is more difficult, because it is likely that they must have wide distribution and be very price competitive. Cost leadership, then, becomes important to the brand owner, which entails being an efficient producer. Brands in this sector are obviously vulnerable, and to succeed an attractive price proposition is usually necessary.

■ The Company as a Brand

It will, by now, be obvious that it is frequently the case that a company's name is the brand used on different products or services, as opposed to an individual brand name for each product, as in the case of, say, Persil.

To present themselves in the most favourable way, firms develop a corporate identity programme, ensuring that all forms of external communication are coordinated and presented in the same way. Corporate identity can be a valuable asset, which if effectively managed, can make a major contribution to brand success.

Classic examples of this include IBM, ICI, Mercedes, Marks & Spencer with their universal St Michael brand, Sony, Yamaha, JCB and countless others. It works well as a policy, given the prohibitive costs of building individual brands *ab inititio*, providing the product or service in question is consistent with the corporate image. In this respect it is easy to see why Ford has been unable to compete effectively in the high-class car market and was eventually forced to buy Jaguar in order to enter this segment. Equally, it can be seen why Mars was able to enter the ice-cream market using the Mars corporate brand name, but why it uses a totally different brand name, Pedigree, in the animal foodstuffs market. Also, whilst there is a 'halo' effect of using a famous corporate name on a new product or service, there are also risks to the total portfolio, should any one new product prove to be disastrous. For example, Levi Strauss was known and respected for jeans. Their extension into Levi tailored classic suits failed because of wrong associations. Adding the name Pierre Cardin to bathroom tiles in Spain did little for the value of this core brand!

Peter Doyle developed a useful matrix for considering what an appropriate strategy might be towards corporate, as opposed to individual, product branding. This is given in Figure 11.8.

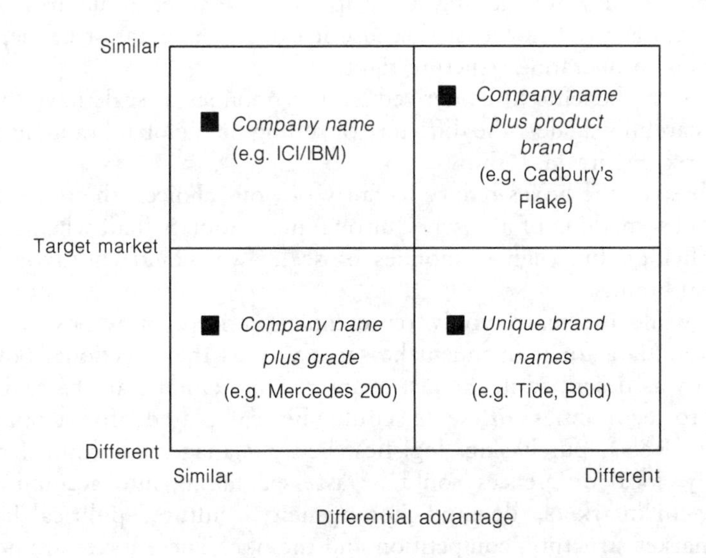

Figure 11.8 Corporate brand positioning

Global versus Local Brands

So, if we can now distinguish between a brand and a pseudo brand, what is a global brand? Here is a definition: *a global brand is a product that bears the same name and logo and presents the same or similar message all over the world*. Usually the product is aimed at the same target market and is promoted and presented in much the same way.

A survey that encompassed ten thousand people in the USA, Japan and Europe discovered that the following were the ten most widely recognised brand names. Top was Coca-Cola, followed by Sony, Mercedes-Benz, Kodak, Disney, Nestlé, Toyota, McDonald's, IBM and Pepsi. Probably there are a few surprises here, but what are the alternative options to having a mass global brand?

There are only two broad counter options:

- develop a global brand, such as American Express, or Coca-Cola; or
- have a local brand in each country of operation.

What fuels the decision making regarding which choice? Clearly, it depends mainly upon the types of customer. However there are some other practical considerations to take into account, such as the cost of production, the distribution costs, promotion, competitive market structure, channels, legal constraints and operational structures.

Procter & Gamble experienced major problems trying to get washing powders and liquids established under one brand name across Europe. For one thing, they had to try to accommodate different types of washing machines, different types of water, different washing habits, and different cultures. Then there was the business of getting to grips with market structures and competition, and, last but not least (because it can be the greatest barrier of all), getting its own operating structure right.

Clearly, then, the benefits to be derived from economies of scale have to be weighed very carefully against the difficulty of setting up a global brand, as the following matrix, Figure 11.9, shows.

Although three of the boxes reduce to fairly obvious choices, the top right-hand box is still something of a poser. Our own inclination is that, when faced with high difficulty, but high economies of scale, we would endeavour to establish global brands.

Of course, while the matrix only represents a concept, it is possible to develop concrete data for it in much the same way as the directional policy matrix, which was described in the last chapter. For example, all the savings attributable to economies of scale could be calculated, for example manufacturing, R&D, purchasing, logistics, better management control and so on. Equally, local differences could be assessed taking into account the infrastructure of markets, demand homogeneity, culture, political/legal framework, market structure, competition and the like. These issues are dealt with in more detail in Chapter 20, Marketing Planning.

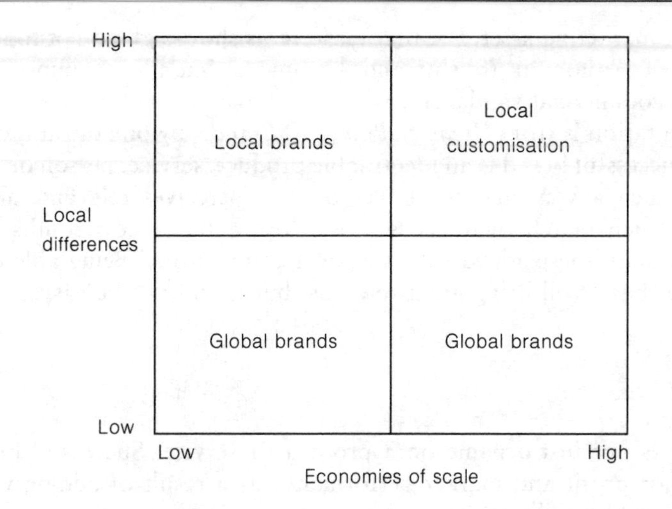

Figure 11.9 Global versus local brands

By looking at international markets in this way, the odds come out very much higher in favour of global brands as against local ones. Predictions about future trends only serve to reinforce this hypothesis. For example, in the European single market it has been predicted that:

- Prices will tend to harmonise towards the lowest levels across Europe.
- Purchasers will tend to buy on a Pan-European basis to gain maximum price advantage.
- Major distributors (especially importers) will operate transnationally and take advantage of remaining price differentials and low-cost suppliers.

There is already much evidence to confirm that these trends are already happening. Donald Casey of Lauder Associates asserts, 'The growth in global branding is a direct result of the explosion of media consumption amongst the young. In every country the data show that the younger consumers are significantly more aware of international brands, particularly in fields like TV, music, video and sports'. Further support is provided by Alan Woofe who says, 'The most fundamental point of all this is that one day there will eventually be a Euro-market, and there may one day be Euro-consumers in the foreseeable future'.

The portents are clear. Already, large Pan-European retailing groups are appearing and if an organisation does not have a European brand, especially if it is in fast-moving consumer goods, it does not appear to have very good prospects. It is brand names that win customers, make a profit and create customer loyalty. As stated earlier, Nestlé wanted to buy Rowntree purely for its brands, not for its factories. A good brand, at the end of the day, is the company's best marketing asset. For that reason it is short-sighted not to invest in the brand. To allow it to slip and become a 'me-too' commodity is tantamount to commercial vandalism.

Our final quotation is from *Creating Powerful Brands*, by one the authors of this book: 'A successful brand is an identifiable product, service, person or place augmented in such a way that the buyer or user perceives relevant, unique added values which match their needs most closely. Its success results from being able to sustain these added values against competitors.' Being able to do this on a global basis will bring great rewards, but it will not be easy.

■ Summary

A brand name is not just a name on a product or service. Successful brands result in superior profit and market performance as a result of adding values desirable to the target consumer.

The three key components of a brand are the brand strategy, the brand positioning and the brand personality. For a brand to succeed, it has to appeal to the senses, have rational appeal and emotional appeal. The degree to which functionality and representationality are important to consumers will determine the brand strategy.

Global branding versus local branding as a strategy will depend ultimately upon the homogeneity of demand patterns in different countries and the concommitant economies of scale to be enjoyed from created global brands.

CHAPTER 12

Pricing Strategy

The pricing decision is one of the most important issues that the marketing executive has to face. Its impact will usually be reflected in the quantity of the product sold, the contribution to profits that the product will make and, even more crucially, the strategic position of the product in the market place. In addition, in a multiproduct company it is frequently the case that a decision taken on the price of one product will have implications for other products in the range. It is not surprising, therefore, that much has been written and discussed on the subject of pricing and that it has created considerable controversy as to how the price decision should be made.

Frequently this controversy has centred around the role that costs should play in determining price. Traditionally, the price of a product is based upon the identification of the costs associated with manufacturing, marketing and distributing the product with the subsequent addition of a mark-up to reflect the desired profitability. Such an approach has been criticised on a number of counts. Firstly, it can prove to be extremely difficult in practice to identify the true costs of a product. In so many cases the company will have joint costs and fixed costs that can only be allocated to a specific product on an arbitrary basis. Secondly, such a cost-plus approach to pricing ignores the demand sensitivity of the market place. It may be that a price determined on a cost-plus basis is higher than the market place will accept, or perhaps it may even be lower than the price that the market can bear. Attempts have been made to overcome these problems by using a *marginal cost* approach rather than a *full cost* approach so that the pricing decision becomes one of attempting to maximise the contribution the product will make – that is, the difference between the *price* and the direct and attributable *costs*.

The basic problem with any cost-based approach to pricing is that it implicitly assumes that the customer is interested in *our* costs, whereas in reality the customer is only concerned with *his own* costs. This can be expressed another way – the customer seeks to acquire benefits and it is in order to acquire those benefits that he is prepared to pay a certain price. Seen from this perspective, the company making the price decision is faced with the need to identify the value – in the customer's eyes – of the benefits inherent in their product. The costs of that product thus become irrelevant to the pricing decision even though they are highly pertinent to the profitability of that decision. In other words *costs determine profits*, not price.

Benefits and Price

Throughout this book we have suggested that in any purchase decision the customer is seeking to acquire 'benefits'. A product must bring with it the promise of performing certain tasks, of solving identified problems, or even of providing specific gratifications. Thus the product is not bought for the particular components or materials that go into its manufacture *per se* but rather it is bought for what, as an entity, it can do.

The implication of the benefit concept from a pricing point of view is that the company must first identify the benefits the customer perceives the product to offer and then attempt to ascertain the value that the customer places upon them. The key issue here is that it is the customer *perception* that is important. It may be, for example, that two competing companies offer products that are technically identical to all intents and purposes and yet one company can command a premium price. Why should this be? It may be that additional benefits offered by one company in the way of technical advice or after-sales service are perceived to be superior to those offered by another. Or it may just be that the 'image' of that company is seen as superior. Whatever the reason, there are many cases of this type of 'differential advantage' that cannot be explained simply in technical or quality terms. One study looked at the price advantage that IBM has traditionally had in computers and found that IBM machines are priced substantially above competing machines of equal performance; this price differential appears to be independent of machine size. Since a substantial percentage of users are still willing to buy IBM machines even though their relative price is high, the implication is that IBM offers customers something to induce them to pay a substantial premium for an IBM machine.

The study identified that this price premium was achieved not through superior hardware or technology, but rather through the image that IBM had for quality, reliability and customer support.

Another way to look at this price advantage is to think of the maximum price at which the product could be sold as being the sum of two elements. Firstly there is the 'commodity price' element; this is the base price for the generic product, which would be determined by supply and demand in the market place. On top of this should then be added the 'premium price differential', which reflects the totality of the benefits that the customer perceives will be acquired through purchase of that product. Figure 12.1 shows this concept diagrammatically.

The existence of this 'premium price differential' can only be explained in terms of perceived benefits. The task of the pricing decision maker therefore becomes one of identifying these benefits and placing a customer value upon them. It is in reality a 'bundle' of benefits and so the first step in this suggested approach to pricing is to 'unbundle' the product and identify the individual benefit components that together constitute the totality.

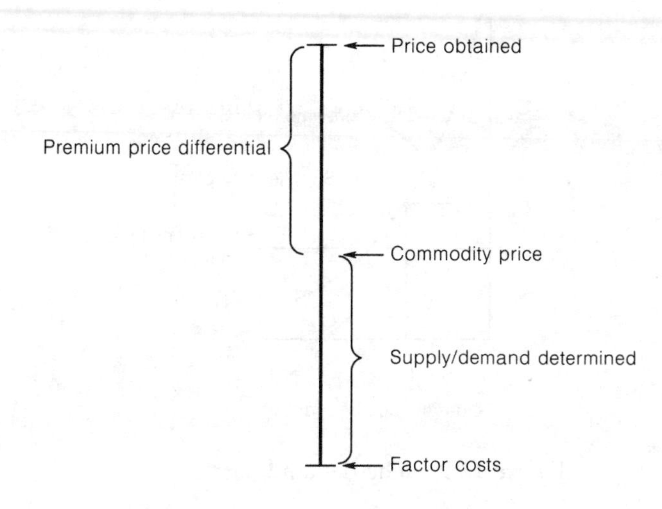

Figure 12.1 The components of price

■ Price and Value

Every purchase by a customer is a 'trade-off'. The trade-off is between the value the customer places on the acquisition of the product versus the costs that are involved in that acquisition, plus any subsequent costs that might be involved, for example maintenance or upgrading costs.

There is nothing new in this idea. Economists have long talked about the concept of 'utility'. Whilst some of their ideas on the relationship between price and demand may seem naïve there is nevertheless an important message for the pricing decision-maker in the recognition that price must be seen in terms of *value*.

The Victorian economist Alfred Marshall was the first really to articulate the idea of price as a reflection of the value placed on a product or service by the consumer. He developed the concept of the *demand curve*, which simply stated that the higher the price charged for a product the lower will be the demand for it as potential consumers see the price exceed the product's perceived value to them. It is interesting to note that this concept suggests that the price charged for a product may be lower than the value placed upon it by some customers. This is the notion of a 'consumer surplus'. In Figure 12.2 a demand curve for a particular product is represented and the price currently prevailing in the market place is P_1.

It can be seen from Figure 12.2 that there are some consumers, albeit fewer in number, who would actually be prepared to pay a higher price. The number of such consumers obviously declines the higher the price that is charged. The consumers who fall into this category are actually paying a price less than the

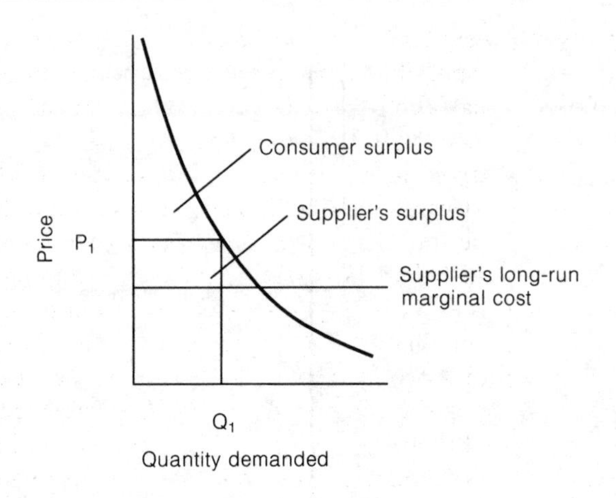

Figure 12.2 The demand curve

value they perceive they are gaining through purchasing the product. They are enjoying a consumer surplus. At the same time, it can also be seen that the price P_1 is actually higher than the supplier's long-run marginal cost. In other words in this case there is a 'surplus' accruing to the supplier as well. This analysis is an over-simplification of the real world but it might be a useful focus for the price decision-maker to think of his problem along the lines suggested by Figure 12.3.

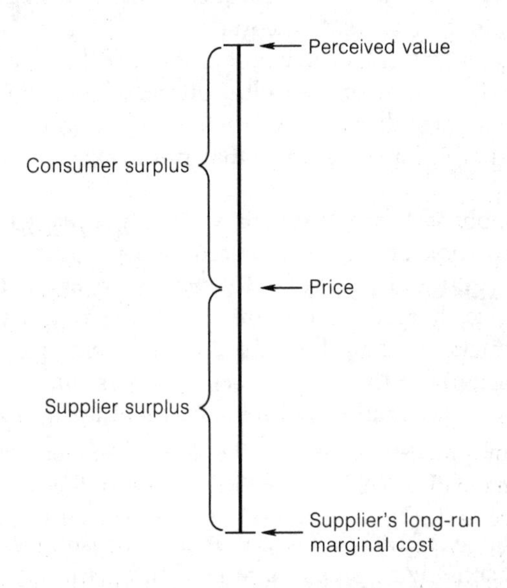

Figure 12.3 Consumer and supplier surplus

The pricing problem can be seen in this way as an attempt by the supplier to achieve the greatest possible 'surplus' over long-run marginal cost whilst still pricing no higher than the perceived value placed on the product by potential customers.

An alternative way of looking at this is to see the problem in terms of the need to identify what value the target market places upon the product and then to convert that value into a market price. The first step towards solving this problem is to recognise that there will be different groupings of customers with different perceptions of a product's value. These groupings are in effect *market segments*. Thus we might identify a specific segment of the market that seeks certain benefits from a product and values them at a particular level.

However, it is not sufficient just to identify the perceived value of a product to the customers and then set a price equal to that value. Frequently there will be costs other than price that face the customer in acquiring that product. These additional costs over and above purchase price could include freight, installation, training, maintenance, service, spares support and other 'life cycle costs', as they are sometimes termed. In addition there may be perceived costs in terms of risk of product failure or, particularly in the case of consumer products, social and psychological risk.

From the customer's point of view therefore it can be argued that the decision to purchase is a trade-off between all costs involved on the one hand and the perceived benefits resulting from acquisition on the other. This relationship may be expressed as follows:

- Highest price the customer will pay =
  perceived benefits-costs other than price

Thus it can be seen that in the pricing decision it is as important to understand the cost structure of our potential customer as it is to know our own! It is essential to the pricing decision to recognise the total cost impact on the customer of the acquisition of our product. Even though the customer may not himself have fully evaluated the implication of the acquisition, the supplier will be better positioned to sell to the customer if these costs are known. The appropriate concept here is that of 'life-cycle costs', which refers to all the customer costs that will be incurred by the customer from the acquisition of the product through to the end of its useful life. For example, in pricing a piece of numerical control equipment the manufacturer should identify the effects that the equipment will have on the customer's manufacturing economics, its likely life, any maintenance and upgrading costs and its disposal value if any.

Given a full analysis of the life-cycle cost implications of the product, the pricing decision-maker can now focus attention upon the identification and quantification of the product's perceived benefits.

Benefit Evaluation

One of the first attempts to break loose from the constraints of cost-oriented pricing and to seek instead to incorporate some recognition of perceived value was the technique developed by the Glacier Metal Company, which it termed 'product-analysing pricing'. This attempted to build up a final price by identifying the physical features that go into the product and then to value these features in customer terms. The method was based upon a statistical analysis of previous prices obtained for similar products to provide quantified estimates of the relative contribution of each physical component to the final price. The analysis was limited as such to the physical attributes of the product and did not quantify non-physical benefits other than by talking loosely about the 'product surround'. Because of these limitations it did not provide the pricing decision-maker with the crucial information on customer evaluation of perceived product benefits – both physical and intangible. To do this we need to seek an alternative approach to benefit evaluation.

Trade-off Analysis

In recent years a number of developments have taken place in the fields of mathematical psychology and psychometrics that have great value in quantifying the relative importance that potential customers place upon the various attributes of a product. These techniques are based upon a type of trade-off analysis called 'conjoint measurement', a powerful device for quantifying the intangible as well as the physical benefits present in a product. The 'trade-off' approach to pricing follows a sequence of logical steps:

Step 1: Identification of Benefit Components

It is important to recognise that the potential customer for a product will have his/her own perceptions of the benefits contained within that product. To identify these perceived benefits it is necessary to conduct a limited, small-scale survey of potential and/or actual customers. The purpose of this study is to elicit the key features or benefits that are expected to be acquired as a result of using the product. Direct questioning can be used, such as, 'What is it that makes Brand X different from Brand Y?' More sophisticated procedures for elicitation of benefits exist but essentially they all have the same purpose: to draw from consumers their own perceptions of product features rather than the manufacturers'. So, in a study of customers for a new chemical compound, the following attributes might emerge:

- Quality
- Availability
- Impact on customer's production economics

- Storage conditions necessary
- Technical assistance

The question is then: 'What relative value is placed upon each of these components?'

Step 2: Quantifying Benefit Values

Because a product is in effect the totality of its component attributes, a way must be found of separating these and measuring their individual value to the customer. It is here that conjoint analysis becomes particularly useful. Using the attributes identified in Step 1, the researcher presents to the sample of customers a variety of hypothetical products that contain different configurations of the previously identified attributes, each configuration having a different price. Thus, for the example of the chemical compound, the hypothetical product configurations in Table 12.1 might be constructed.

Table 12.1 Attribute levels

Attribute	*Product 1*	*Product 2*
Quality	Impurities less than one part per million	Impurities less than ten parts per million
Availability	Make to order	Available from stock
Impact on customer's production economics	No impact	Improves usable output by 10 per cent
Storage conditions	Stable product, long shelf life	Requires high level storage environment
Technical assistance	Manufacturer provides high level technical advice	Weak
Price	£5 a pound	£5.50 a pound

Clearly there are many different combinations of attribute levels. Only two examples are given here but they will be sufficient to demonstrate the concept of trade-off. The question put to the survey respondents is: 'Given that the two alternative products above are available, which would you prefer?' Both products have their advantages and their disadvantages and the final choice will be based upon the trade-off of the pluses and minuses. By extending the questioning to include other configurations of the same attributes it is possible, using conjoint analysis, to produce a numerical 'weight' for each attribute which reflects the relative importance attached to each of the attributes in question. More specifically it enables the researcher to identify for each attribute the weight given to different *levels* of that attribute. Thus for 'quality' it will be possible to determine the extent by which 'impurities less than one part per million' is preferred over 'impurities less than ten parts per million' – or any level of impurity in the range under consideration.

However, the greatest advantage of using conjoint analysis in this context is that it also provides the researcher with *the relative utility of different price levels*. Thus we have a means of interpreting the price equivalence of differences in the perceived values of different combinations of product attributes. Step 3 describes this procedure.

■ Step 3: Determining the Price Equivalence of Value

The output of the conjoint analysis of the data collected in Step 2 might typically appear as in Figure 12.4.

For each level of each attribute a 'utility' is computed and this can be graphed to give a visual indication of the importance of that attribute. More importantly, though, it enables the value of this arbitrary 'utility' measure to be given a price equivalence. It will be seen from Table 12.1 that the difference in utility between a price of £5 and £5.50 is 0.25 (that is, 1.00–0.75); thus the price equivalence of one unit of 'utility' is (£5.50–£5)/0.25, that is, £2.

Using this information we can say, for example, that a 10 per cent improvement in saleable output is worth a price difference of £1 per pound (£2 [1.00–0.5]). Again we can say that the benefit of a stable product with a long shelf life is worth an additional £0.5 per pound (£2 [0.75–0.5]) over a product requiring a high-level storage environment.

Given this information it is clear that the price decision maker has a very powerful insight into the components of value in the customer's mind. The decision-maker can now also identify which product attributes have the biggest influence on value perception. In the case examined here, for example, availability and quality are seen as the two major components of value. A change from Level 2 to Level 1 in availability brings an increase in utility of 1.0 and a change from Level 2 to Level 1 in quality produces an increase in utility of 0.75 (worth £2 and £1.50 per pound respectively).

This information on the 'price-equivalence' of customer values can provide a basis for price determination that reflects the worth the market places upon our offer. Perhaps one of the most important features of the value-in-use approach advocated here is that it focuses our attention upon customer perceptions of product attributes and away from the more narrow production-orientation of suppliers' costs. In this sense it is very much a market-oriented approach to pricing.

There are also certain strategic issues raised by this approach to pricing, particularly with regard to marketing communications. It is well known that in many product/market fields there is a definite relationship between the price obtained and the perception of quality on the part of the customer. In other words, where there is a perception of 'added values' then the demand/price relationship can be radically altered. Where added values are perceived to exist

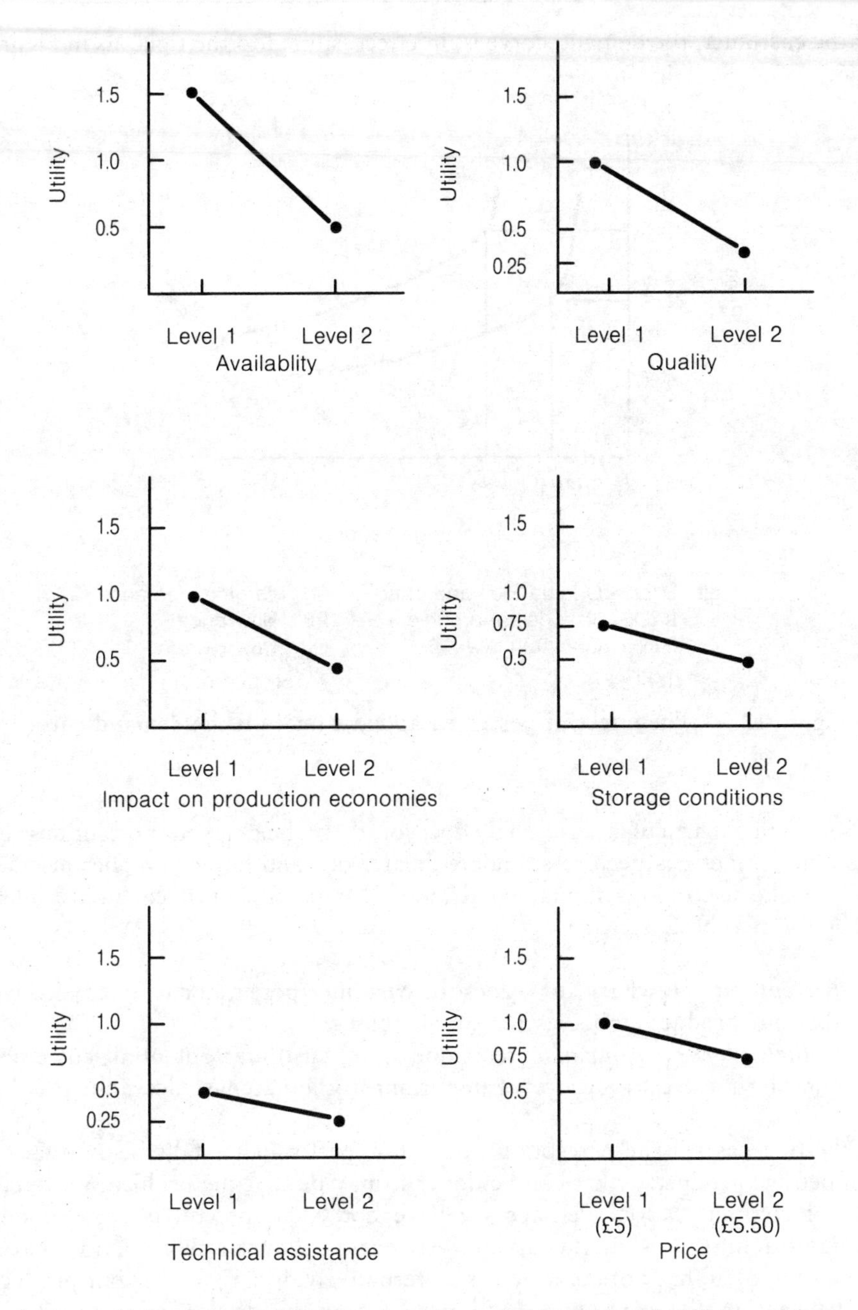

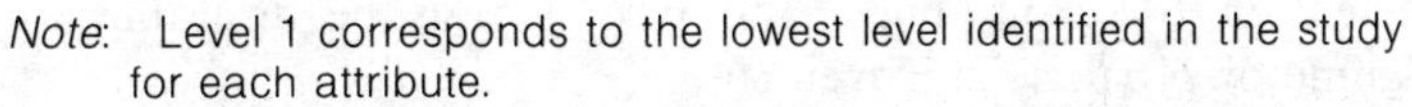

Note: Level 1 corresponds to the lowest level identified in the study for each attribute.

Figure 12.4 Graphical output of conjoint analysis

by the customer, the demand curve is, in effect, shifted to the right, as in Figure 12.5.

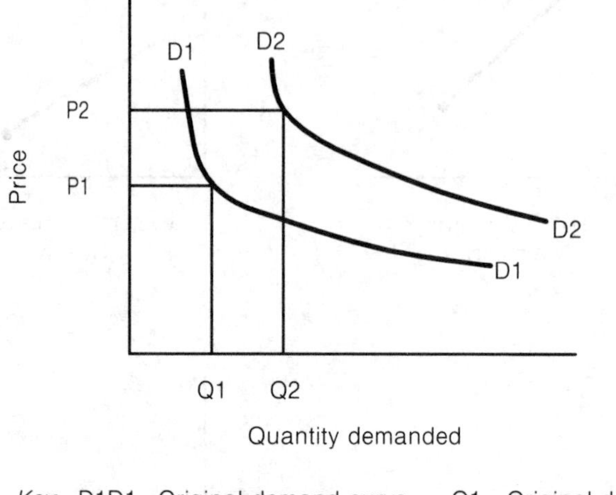

Key: D1D1 Original demand curve Q1 Original demand
D2D2 New demand curve P2 New price
P1 Original price Q2 New demand

Figure 12.5 The effect of perceived added-values on the demand curve

So in this particular case the effect of these heightened perceptions of customer values has been to stimulate greater demand but at a higher price.

To make use of this fundamental model for profit improvement we must recognise two basic factors:

- *Perception*: to what extent does the customer/potential customer perceive that our product embodies certain attributes?
- *Value/utility*: to what extent does the customer/potential customer consider these attributes to be important in the purchase decision?

In the first case, if the perception of product performance falls below that of competitive products, what can be done? It may be that the problem is largely one of communication. Perhaps we have not been forceful enough in our attempts to inform the market about the strengths of our product or, if we have, the message still has not come across. Alternatively, it may be that our product is deficient in these attributes and it may thus be desirable to institute a programme of product improvement.

If, on the other hand, we identify that our product scores highly, but on attributes that are perhaps given less weight by the customer (that is, their value/utility is lower), then we could downgrade the product on these attributes to improve overall profitability, or indeed reduce the price if appropriate. Likewise, recognising the value/utility placed upon the various product attributes should be of great help in designing and introducing new products or in reformulating old ones.

From the point of view of marketing strategy, value-in-use can become the basis of a more effective segmentation strategy. Because different customers will have different perceptions of a product's attributes and will also differ in the value/utility they place upon those attributes, it will often be possible to target products to specific groups, or segments, in the market. Price is one of the simplest ways of segmenting markets but price segmentation can become far more effective when based upon value-in-use.

Competitive Pricing Strategy

Most marketing activity takes place within the context of some level of competitive activity. Thus pricing decisions must clearly reflect competitive positioning and the customer's perception of any differential values that are embodied in competitive offerings.

At one extreme is a market with one dominant supplier – say 40 per cent market share to the nearest rival with 15 per cent – and where that dominant supplier has an offer that is high in perceived added values then it is likely that a substantial price differential should be obtained. On the other hand if there is no one dominant player in market share terms, and the market is effectively a 'commodity' market with no perceived product differences, then it is highly unlikely that any one supplier could command a higher price.

In any competitive market place the following relationship will normally hold:

$$\frac{\text{Perceived benefits (market leader)}}{\text{Price (market leader)}} \geqslant \frac{\text{Perceived benefits (competitor)}}{\text{Price (competitor)}}$$

In other words to maintain a position of market share leadership the ratio of price to perceived benefits must exceed that of the competition. Using this relationship it will be recognised that it is not sufficient to have a high level of perceived benefits if the competition has a substantially lower price. It will sometimes be the case that a supplier may develop an offer with substantial added values and sell it at a high price, but in so doing will provide competitors with a price umbrella under which they can shelter whilst developing 'me too' products. The success of the so-called IBM-PC clones in the personal computer market provides a testament to this.

The position of the product in relation to the market life-cycle will also be important in determining pricing strategy. Given the importance of maintaining or increasing market share in the early stages of the life cycle as a means of increasing the speed of movement down the experience curve – to ensure both higher profitability and cash flow as the market matures – careful attention must be paid to the benefit/price ratio.

In the past, marketing authors have distinguished between *skimming* strategies and *penetration* strategies, particularly in the context of pricing new products. It has been suggested that a penetration strategy (that is, a low relative price) is a route to early gains in market share if:

- Demand is price sensitive.
- Economies of scale exist.
- Competitive imitation is not difficult.

An example of such a pricing strategy might be the low price established initially for the sale of domestic TV satellite dishes.

Alternatively a skimming strategy (that is, a high relative price) could be appropriate, it is argued, where:

- Demand is not particularly price sensitive.
- There is a relatively flat cost curve (that is, unit costs at low volumes are not so much higher than unit costs at higher volumes).
- There is limited danger of competitive imitation.

The pricing policy adopted by Rolex watches is perhaps an example of this approach.

Figure 12.6 suggests the possible pricing strategies that may be appropriate given the opportunities for value enhancement or cost reduction. Value enhancement is a strategy based upon building perceived benefits, whilst cost reduction can provide the basis for successful price competition.

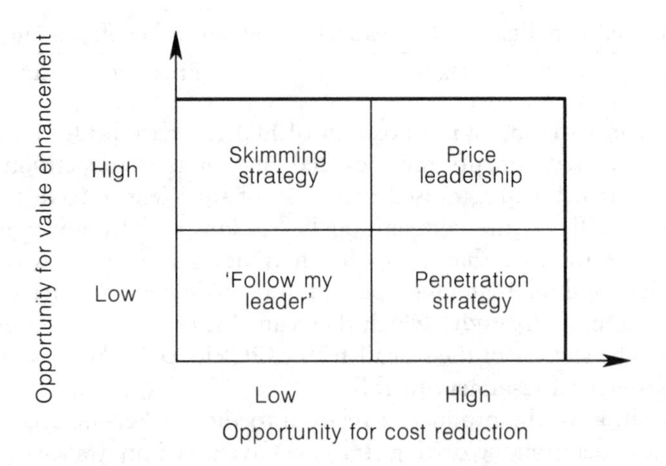

Figure 12.6 Appropriate pricing strategies

The rationale behind each of these options can be demonstrated by the use of the experience curve concept. As we have seen, it is usually the case that penetration strategies are more appropriate where the opportunity for cost reduction is greatest, that is, rapid movement down a steeply sloping experience curve can be achieved.

On the other hand a skimming strategy is more likely to be appropriate where rapid cost reductions are unlikely, that is, the experience curve is less steep. Figure 12.7 outlines the logic of each of the four pricing options.

Ultimately, however, neither a skimming nor a penetration policy will lead to a position of substantial market leadership unless the benefit price ratio is maintained at a higher level than that of the competition. The achievement of a favourite ratio is obviously not down to pricing strategy alone, but can only come about through a total focus of the marketing mix upon differentiation whilst managing the operations of the business to provide a cost advantage.

■ International Pricing Management

One of the most striking trends in recent years has been the rapid increase in the globalisation of markets. Not only is this true in the case of well-established brands such as Coca-Cola, Marlboro and Gucci, but it is also apparent in markets as diverse as computing, motor cars and consumer electronics. Nor is the trend towards globalisation confined only to products, we see similar transformations in services, whether it be banking, retailing or satellite TV.

At the same time, the corporations that have created and developed these global brands are refocusing their operations so that they too are global in their scope. What this means is that an electronics company, for example, may source some of its components in one country, subassemble in another, with final assembly taking place in a third country. Managing these complex global networks becomes one of the prime challenges to the achievement of profitability.

The impact of this move towards the globalisation of business on the pricing decision is substantial. Firstly there are implications for the cost of the product or service and secondly, it is quite likely that there will be significant differences from country to country in the price sensitivity of demand. Let us consider both of these issues in turn.

■ Cost Implications of Global Sourcing

As we have noted, there is an increasing tendency for organisations to source materials, assemble and manufacture items off-shore. The motivation for this is largely economic, based upon the search for cost reductions. These lower costs may be available through lower labour rates, lower costs of material, lower taxes, lower costs of capital or government assistance. At the same time these

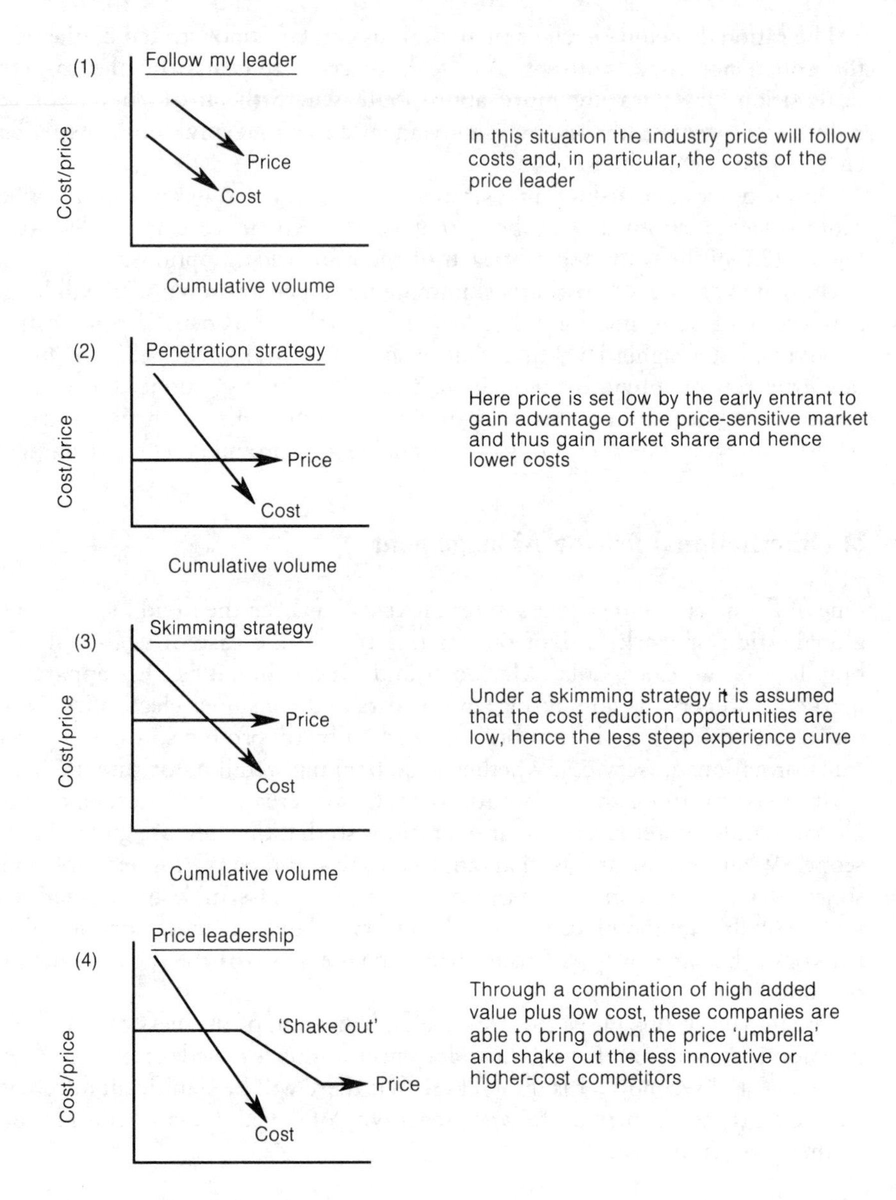

Note: All the above charts assume logarithmic scales, hence the experience 'curve' is shown as a straight line.

Figure 12.7 Price and the experience curve

organisations may also rationalise production so that individual country operations no longer produce a full range of products for their own national markets. Instead the company may now focus production on fewer factories making a limited range of items but for a regional or even global market. The opportunities for enhanced economies of scale in production through such strategies may be considerable. Companies such as Unilever, for example, which previously manufactured soups and detergents in local factories for local markets, have now rationalised their production on a regional basis with fewer factories producing for wider markets.

Whilst the advantages of such strategies seem to be readily apparent, there are a number of implications for pricing:

□ *Exchange-Rate Fluctuations*

Given the volatility of exchange rates between currencies, there is a considerable inherent risk in companies committing themselves to long-term off-shore supply arrangements. Companies with the ability to switch production from one location to another at short notice clearly have an advantage. For example Heinz can increase or decrease production of tomato ketchup in their regional plants with a high degree of flexibility in order to take advantage of exchange-rate fluctuations. Companies that lack this flexibility can often find themselves faced with substantial cost increases as a result of changes in exchange rates.

□ *Changes in Factor Costs*

Closely allied to the risk of exchange rate fluctuation is the problem of changes in factor costs such as labour, land or capital. Many companies decided to locate production in what were then perceived to be low-labour-cost countries, often in South-East Asia, only to find that with rapid economic development that advantage proved to be transitory. Also to be taken into account is the way in which the costs of transport from the source of supply to the end market can change, in some instances eliminating any production cost advantage.

□ *Transfer Pricing*

In complex, multilevel production and distribution systems within a single company, the issue of internal transfer pricing arises. In other words, at what internal price should products or supplies be 'sold' to the next stage in the chain? Sometimes these decisions will be determined by tax considerations, but often there will be other factors influencing the transfer price, such as internal accounting practices that might allocate overhead costs on some arbitrary basis, hence distorting the cost that is passed on down the chain. There are countless examples of companies that have been forced to charge higher prices in end markets because of an accumulated cost that reflects the real costs of supply.

□ *Parallel Imports*

Often the same product may be sold in different markets at different prices. This practice, known to economists as 'price discrimination', is made possible because of the different demand and supply characteristics in these different markets. However once the price difference between markets exceeds the cost of acquiring and transporting those products from one market to another then arbitrage or 'parallel imports' can become a serious problem for the company. This is a phenomenon that is frequently encountered in both consumer and industrial markets. One partial solution to this problem is to develop a unique brand for individual markets, but this may not allow economies of scale in sourcing, production and distribution to be achieved.

□ *Global/Regional Purchasing*

In the same way that suppliers are tending to operate on a global, or at least regional, basis, so too are their customers. If a major European retailer, for example, sees that a product is being sold by a manufacturer at a lower price in one market (because of supply/demand considerations) then that retailer may insist on buying that product at that price for all the markets in which it operates. This will become more of a problem for suppliers as more and more customers band together into regional or global buying groups. Across Europe a number of such groups already exist, particularly in grocery retailing.

A further challenge to international pricing management arises where the same brand may be positioned quite differently in different national markets. Stella Artois is a premium-priced lager in the UK, for example, whereas in its home country of Belgium it is seen as a 'regular' beer sold at standard prices.

Given these potential problems, what are the options for a company seeking to develop an international pricing strategy?

The overriding consideration, as with pricing decisions generally, is that the price must reflect the value proposition that is presented to the customer in each market in which the product is offered. Based upon this the 'target cost' for that market can be identified, that is, the achievable price less the desired profit margin. Decisions on sourcing must be taken in the context of that target cost, taking into account total supply chain costs – preferably undistorted by transfer pricing manipulations. No pricing strategy will eliminate the risks we have identified above, but careful and continuous management of the pricing decision on a global basis will help to minimise them.

■ Summary

The pricing decision is one of the most important issues to be faced by the marketing manager. Almost every market is influenced to some extent or another by the relative price of the products that compete in that market.

When customers buy products they are making choices based upon their perception of the relative value of competing offers. The maximum price at which a product or service can be sold can be no greater than its perceived value.

In this chapter we have proposed that price should be related to the value of benefits that our product or service delivers. Techniques such as trade-off analysis can be utilised to assist in the pricing decisions, particularly in the valuation of benefits.

CHAPTER 13

Communications Strategy

Open any newspaper or magazine and you are confronted with advertisements of all shapes, sizes and colours exhorting you to buy this, try that, save money with this product or win a free holiday with that product. Switch on the radio or TV and the story is much the same. Go to the cinema or drive down the High Street and you are bombarded by similar messages, be they off the screen or from billboards.

What is going on? What is it all about? Clearly hundreds of very intelligent people are spending millions of pounds trying to make contact with us. Are they getting value for money?

'I know half the money I spend on advertising is wasted; but I can never find out which half.' This poignant cri de coeur, attributed to the first Lord Leverhulme, aptly sums up the feelings of many marketers.

In this chapter, we will examine the various ways that potential and current customers and/or consumers receive communications about our products or services. We will also look at how best to develop a communications mix that will help us to achieve our marketing objectives. Finally, we will consider how the communications mix can be planned and managed. At the end of the day we want to ensure that, as marketers, we get good value from the money, energy, time and brainpower that is devoted to this important aspect of marketing.

Communication Methods

Companies have at their disposal an armoury of communication techniques that might be used singly, or in a combination we call the *communications mix*. Those with acknowledged expertise in the area of communicating with customers are continually experimenting with the communications mix they employ as they strive to become more cost-effective in this area. The techniques they use fall under two broad headings: personal communications and impersonal communications.

Personal communications mean just that: they are addressed to the individual, generally in a face-to-face situation such as a salesman's visit or a demonstration. Impersonal communications cover such topics as advertising, point-of-sale displays, various types of sales promotions and public relations, although with the advent of word processors and desktop publishing many companies are now attempting to personalise what were previously impersonal communications – mailshots, for example.

Here then are some of the communication mechanisms by which information, beliefs and intentions can be sown in the customer's mind.

■ Word of Mouth

Most customers and consumers will readily agree that word of mouth is one of the most influential of all communication channels. Human nature being what it is, we know we will hear tales of woe from friends and acquaintances who have had bad experiences with certain products or services. Conversely, they may be enthusiastic about their bargains and good experiences. 'I was really pleased with the work the garage did on my car'; 'If I were you, I'd try that shop in the High Street, they are always so helpful'; 'Don't buy any of these, it's the biggest mistake I've ever made' – all these are persuasive marketing communications.

Good or bad, such comments have tremendous impact on us because we value their independent origin and we believe that the supplying company trying to influence us has no control over these messages.

But is the marketer impotent to influence these word-of-mouth messages? We believe not, for when a company develops a communications strategy all the different audiences that it should address can contribute to a positive image of the company. Figure 13.1 shows some of the communication channels that might have an effect on word of mouth. By genuinely striving to provide and communicate its intentions to each audience group, the organisation can expect to earn a positive response in terms of word of mouth.

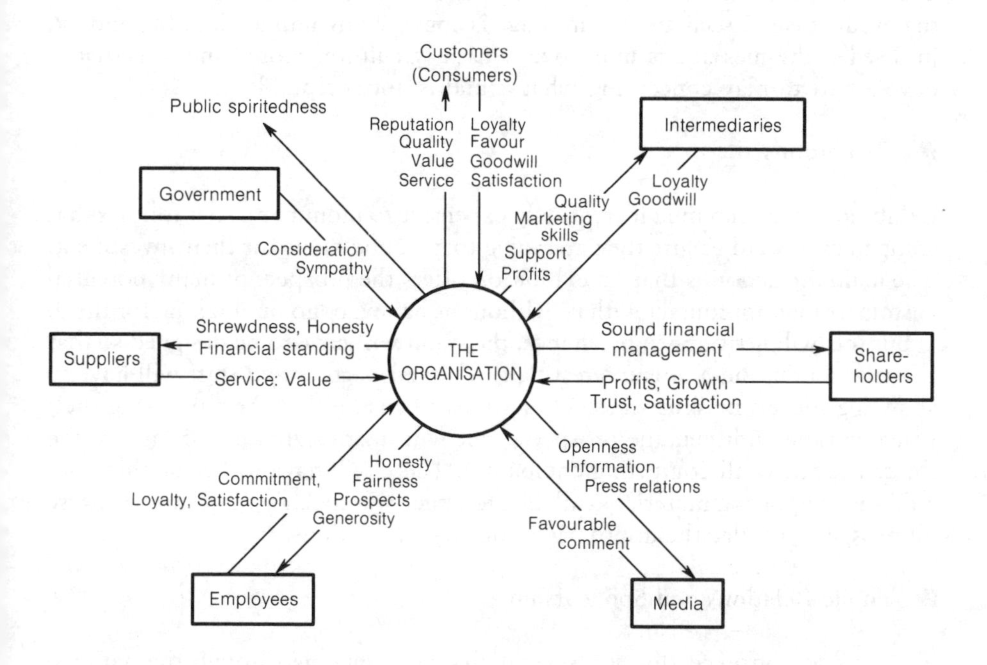

Figure 13.1 Communication relationships of an organisation

Advertising

Advertising is an integral part of the marketing effort and must never be seen as an isolated activity. Its effectiveness will depend not only upon the persuasiveness of the message being conveyed to customers and consumers but also on the accuracy with which the target audience has been selected. Clearly any product or service can offer several different benefits; for example, it can be newer, safer, cheaper, more efficient or unique. Each of these benefits will have more, or less, appeal to different customer groups. Targeting the right message to the right people is the key to successful advertising.

However, the most impressive, elaborate and indulgent campaign will not convince customers and consumers to buy again if the product or service, whose virtues the advertising extols, is non-competitive. Advertising alone rarely produces long-lasting market success. Whilst it will encourage, reinforce a message and perhaps even help to develop a loyalty to a particular product or service, it will be no substitute for an offering that fails to bestow the necessary benefits on a customer.

It must be remembered also that advertising can be subject to controls or constraints from one country to another. For example, in the Netherlands confectionery advertisements must be followed by exhortations to brush one's teeth. Cigarette advertising is banned in many countries. In the wake of AIDS the advertising of condoms is only beginning to be allowed in some countries and even so there are considerable differences in what is permissible. In the UK the product is not seen and the message is conveyed by implication. In contrast, in Sweden the message is more overt. Clearly cultural mores and sensitivities have a part to play concerning what is and is not acceptable.

Exhibitions

Exhibitions are becoming increasingly expensive to mount and so it follows that companies have to ensure they are going to get good value for their investment. The main attraction is that an exhibition offers the prospect of many potential customers making contact with us without us having to go out looking for them.

But this will not happen by chance; the stand will have to be designed so that it attracts attention and is interesting to visit. Also, the stand staff will have to show high levels of skill and ask questions to ensure that they are using their valuable time with genuine prospects, not with mere sightseers or, as is often the case, staff from competing companies. There will have to be suitable sales aids and supporting material available, together with back-up systems to ensure all prospects receive the appropriate follow-up.

Public Relations and Sponsorship

This can be conveyed through several channels, such as through the national and regional press, trade and professional magazines, direct mail, exhibitions and seminars. Increasingly the public relations function is becoming as much a part of the personal communications function as it is an impersonal communications function. Nowadays as many publicity and public relations activities are used as opportunities for stimulating personal contact with customers as they are for attracting an impersonal response.

The company that sponsors a golf tournament does so primarily to be able to invite key customers to meet its executives in unusual and interesting circumstances. Both parties should be aware of this underlying purpose. However, it is also the intention of the sponsor to attract as many people as possible to the golf tournament, even if many of the visitors will not be potential customers.

Many companies are moving away from the traditional techniques of press releases and conferences as a means of communicating their marketing message to clients. They are beginning to explore new channels, as the growth in sponsorship in sport, the arts and inner-city renewal projects indicates.

■ Personal Contact

For many years salesmen and women have been criticised by some as being 'people who spend their time trying to get others to buy things that they do not really need'. The classic example is perhaps the door-to-door insurance sales representative who, it is alleged, persuades the gullible to sink their savings into a policy they do not fully understand.

Perhaps such salesmen do exist, but which profession doesn't have the occasional, unscrupulous 'rotten apple'? Today many safeguards help to protect us from such unsavoury characters, but what about all the other salespeople who are proudly and legitimately going about their business? What are they doing?

When we stop and think about it, we learn a tremendous amount about products and services from personal contact with sales representatives. We find out how the product works; how it has been modified to give even greater efficiency; how and when it has to be serviced and what back-up services are available. It is quite possible that some of this information could be found in brochures and information sheets, but tracking it down takes time and we are all busy people. The sales representative can make it easy for us; he can respond to all our queries and more. He or she can encourage us, overcome our doubts and uncertainties, widen our horizons and steer us towards that purchase decision. Little wonder personal contact can play such an important role in the communications mix.

■ Sales Promotions

As we shall see, these can take many different shapes and forms: for example, two for the price of one; coupons to get a price reduction on the next purchase; purchase of product or service gives you a free entry in a prize draw. Sales promotions are essentially short-lived, aimed to achieve a particular objective that will contribute to the overall marketing objectives. As with advertising, sales promotions need careful planning and monitoring.

Point-of-Sale Displays

Sometimes called 'the silent salesman'. With suitably designed packaging and attractive dispensers in strategic locations, point-of-sale displays can communicate valuable marketing information and also contribute to sales.

Direct Mail

Modern technology makes direct mailing less haphazard than it once was. However, any campaign has to be carefully thought out to stand any chance of being successful. Traditionally, direct approaches through the post have had very low response rates but in recent years, companies have become more and more successful in targeting their mailshots. One of the reasons for this is the fact that more sophisticated techniques have been used to analyse the location of target prospects.

Geodemographic classifications, as they are called, can be made available through specialist organizations. The best known and probably widest used classification in the UK is ACORN (A Classification Of Residential Neighbourhoods), which was developed in the mid-1970s. This works by segmenting the country, street by street, into eleven distinct housing groups, subdivided into thirty-eight different sociodemographic types. For instance, *J36* refers to affluent detached housing in exclusive suburbs where occupants have a high level of disposable income.

A more recent classification is PIN (Pinpoint Identified Neighbourhoods). This system uses the raw ingredients of census data and postal codes, from which it is able to produce revealing maps of any neighbourhood, complete with a profile of the inhabitants.

Other data bases exist to enable industrial marketing companies to target their messages in a highly effective way by direct mail. It is therefore not surprising that direct marketing has become one of the most powerful weapons in the communications mix in many countries today.

Brand Management and Company Image

Increasingly, corporate and brand image is being recognised as a major influence on sales. In the commercial world, where it is becoming increasingly easy from a technical point of view to duplicate a competitor's offering, the creation of a favourable or different image may give the company a competitive advantage.

The concept of brand management was created in the 1930s by Procter & Gamble, the giant Cincinnati soap and toiletries company. It came about as a result of the failure to launch successfully a new soap at that time, Camay. P&G's original market strength had been founded on a soap brand called Ivory and it was felt that the sales failure of the company was due to 'too much Ivory thinking'.

In a revolutionary step at that time, the Camay advertising account was switched from the agency that handled Ivory and the two brands were encouraged to compete. The brand management system was introduced slightly later and, far from being the disaster some P&G executives thought it would be, the company was soon reaping the rewards.

A strong brand reassures the customer; it gives confidence in terms of the quality and satisfaction that can be anticipated from buying it. From all of this comes the possibility of long-term profits. Many brands are household names today, but the concept of brand management has moved beyond the household goods categories.

People with brand-management experience in fast-moving consumer goods companies are now in demand by financial institutions, service organisations, retailers and new technology-based companies. Their marketing skills are being applied to 'own label' brands. For example, the Midland Bank has introduced new brands of accounts, with names such as Vector and Orchard, which have been strongly promoted. The Halifax Building Society is moving along similar lines with its 'Contents Xtra' insurance scheme.

Without a doubt, the concept of branding can fit in very well with the idea of the corporate image. Take British Airways, for example. At one time it was organised on the basis of a number of 'marketing centres', which were essentially geographical areas such as North America, Europe and Australia. With such an organisation, it was very difficult to get a focus on customer service and to track down the real needs of customers.

There is now an 'umbrella' or 'master brand', which is British Airways itself. Under this are seven 'pillar' brands: Concorde, First Class, Club World, Club Europe, World Traveller, Eurotraveller and Super Shuttle, each run by a brand manager and a group brand manager. Customer service and profitability have both improved under the new system.

■ Corporate Communications Audit

This technique provides a system whereby the image of the company as perceived by the management can be compared with that held by the public or a specified target group. Often there is a divergence, and as a result of the audit detailed recommendations can be made for bringing the differing views more closely into line with each other.

The audit also produces secondary advantages. By interviewing a cross-section of staff within the company, it soon becomes apparent if there are different perspectives on fundamental issues. Clearly it is to the company's advantage to take corrective action to clear up any real or imagined misunderstandings. When it comes to analysing the views held about the company by its external audiences, the divergencies of opinion are usually greater than internal differences. The audit therefore not only helps to identify inconsistencies, but, equally importantly, provides the clues for an improvement plan.

A powerful element in the corporate communications audit is the publications audit. This is a technique used to assess the effectiveness of printed material emanating from different parts of the company. The overall graphics layout and content are analysed in the light of their individual purposes and the overall communications strategies of the company.

The Communication Process

Essentially the marketer is faced with the same communication problems as those experienced by any two people talking. Figure 13.2 illustrates such a process.

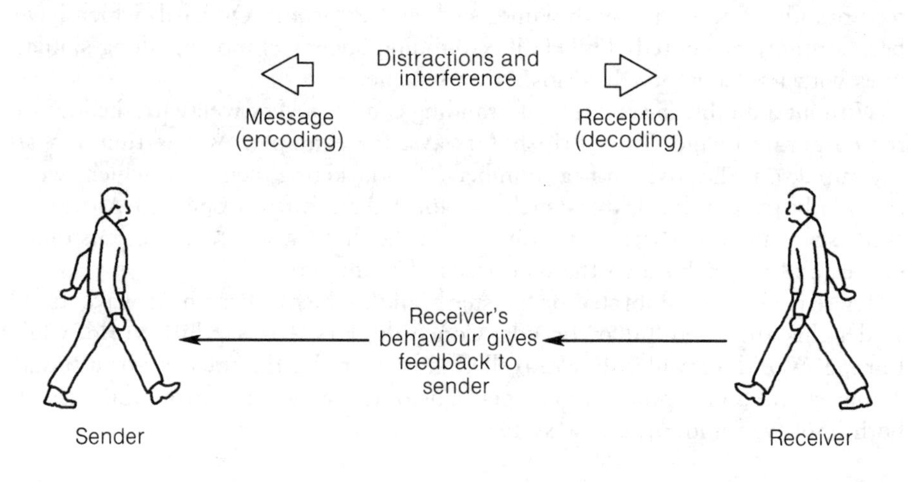

Figure 13.2 The communication process

The sender's message is determined largely by his or her values, knowledge, attitude and vocabulary. It could therefore be claimed to be worded in the sender's personal code. If the receiver is 'tuned in' to the sender's code, because he or she shares similar values and attitudes, then the 'decoding' process is relatively straightforward. If he or she is not attuned to the sender's wavelength then it is very difficult for the message to get through.

The communication process is further complicated by the 'interference' that can come between the two parties. For the marketer this can mean that the receiver's attention is focused on other matters, for example, or perhaps that the receiver is confused by conflicting messages from competing suppliers of products or services.

The lessons for the marketer that stem from this simple communication model are fourfold:

- Keep the marketing message relatively simple.
- Word it in the receiver's language.
- Choose a medium/mechanism for transmitting the message that gives minimal distortion and interference.
- Know the target audience.

■ The Receiver's Viewpoint

In the analysis of the communications process we must be concerned to understand the process from the receiver's point of view. What mental processes take place in the receiver's mind upon receipt of the message? There is evidence to suggest that the potential buyer goes through a thinking process something like this:

- Becoming aware and developing understanding and knowledge (about product or service).
- Developing interest, feelings, beliefs and preferences.
- Developing intentions, convictions and preparedness to try.

In other words the buyer goes through the 'thinking', 'feeling', 'acting' cycle that we mentioned earlier in the chapter on buyer behaviour.

A somewhat similar model of the buyer's thinking process is the AIDA model:

A = *Attention*: something has to happen to capture the buyer's attention from all other possible distractions.
I = *Interest*: the buyer's interest must now be hooked in order to progress to the next stage.
D = *Desire*: A desire to own or use the product or service is generated in the buyer.
A = *Action*: This is required on the buyer's part to ensure that the desire becomes reality.

It is a relatively small step to combine these ideas and come up with a fairly comprehensive model that provides some useful clues about appropriate marketing communication methods. Figure 13.3 provides a generalised model of the communications and purchase decision process.

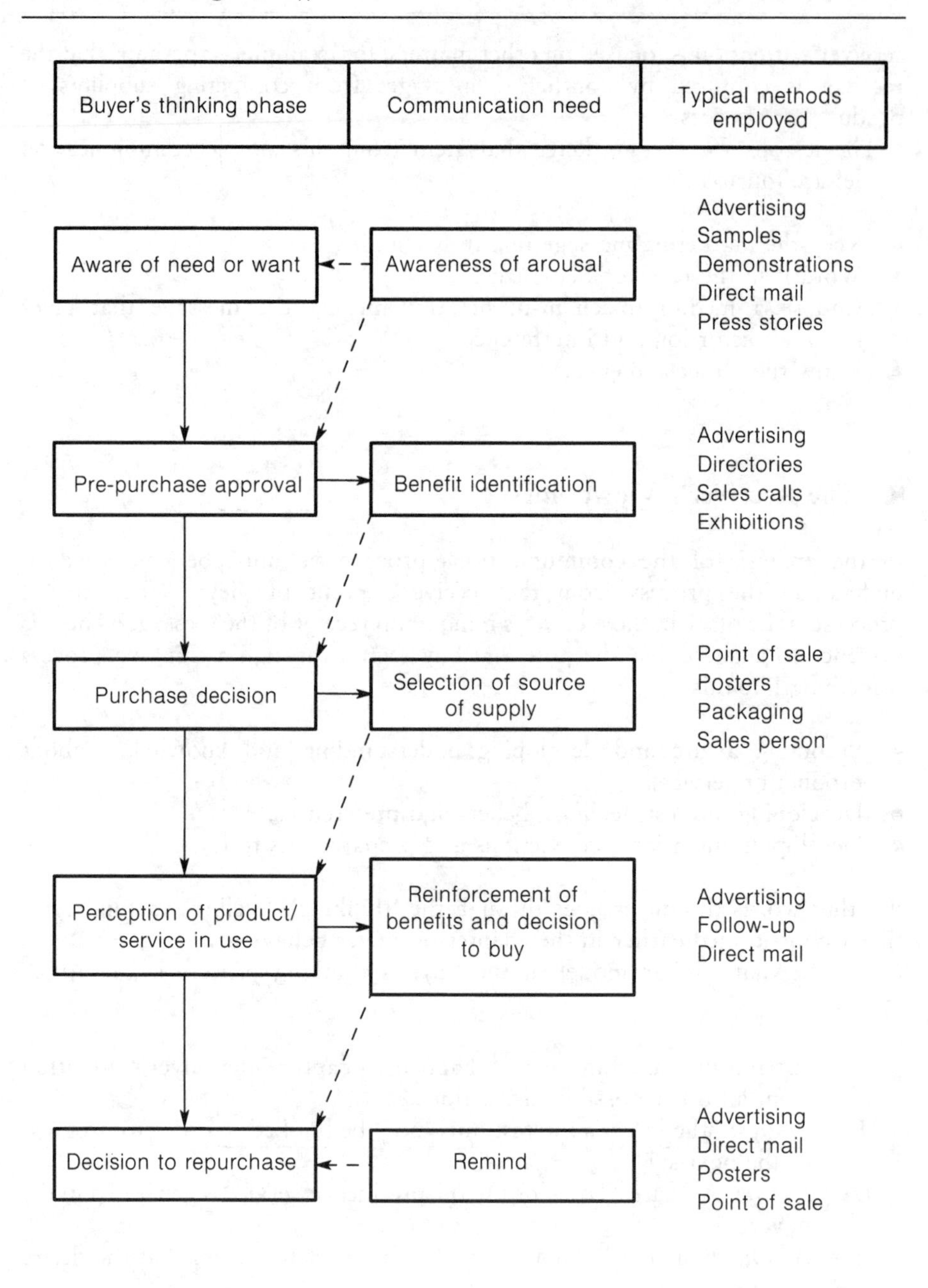

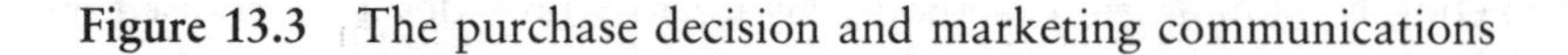

Figure 13.3 The purchase decision and marketing communications

Developing Communication Objectives

We have seen that not only is there a wide choice of communication techniques available to the marketer but also that some might be more effective at conveying certain types of messages than others. Their appropriateness depends to a large extent on the potential purchaser's frame of mind and the stage in the buying decision process he or she is at. We also observed that the choice of communication media had some bearing on the 'interference level' from extraneous 'noise'

What we now have to decide is *what* we want to communicate and how best to do it. There are a number of possible communication objectives, as indicated in Figure 13.4.

	To . . .	
Education and information	Create awareness Inform Generate enquiries	The chosen communication objective(s) must contribute towards a total marketing programme, the objective of which is to achieve profitable sales
Branding and image building	Build recognition of company name Create favourable image Reach personnel inaccessible to salesmen	
Affecting attitudes	Create desire Ease the selling task Achieve positive editorial coverage Overcome prejudices	
Loyalty and reminding	Remind about benefits Endorse the original choice decision (reassurance) Retain customer loyalty	

Figure 13.4 Some communication objectives

Marketing communication objectives should be a concise statement of exactly what we wish to convey to the intended recipients. It will be seen that these objectives are highly specific, and are not expressed in terms of sales results, which are themselves influenced by the combined effects of the marketing mix and not just by the communications programme.

The Communications Plan

A major theme throughout this book has been the need to plan and integrate the marketing mix elements against defined objectives. Nowhere is this more important than in the context of the *communications plan*. Figure 13.5 shows the logical relationship between the communications plan and overall marketing objectives. It indicates that the communications plan is the blueprint for integrating the various components of the communications mix (or, in the language of the four 'P's, the promotional mix).

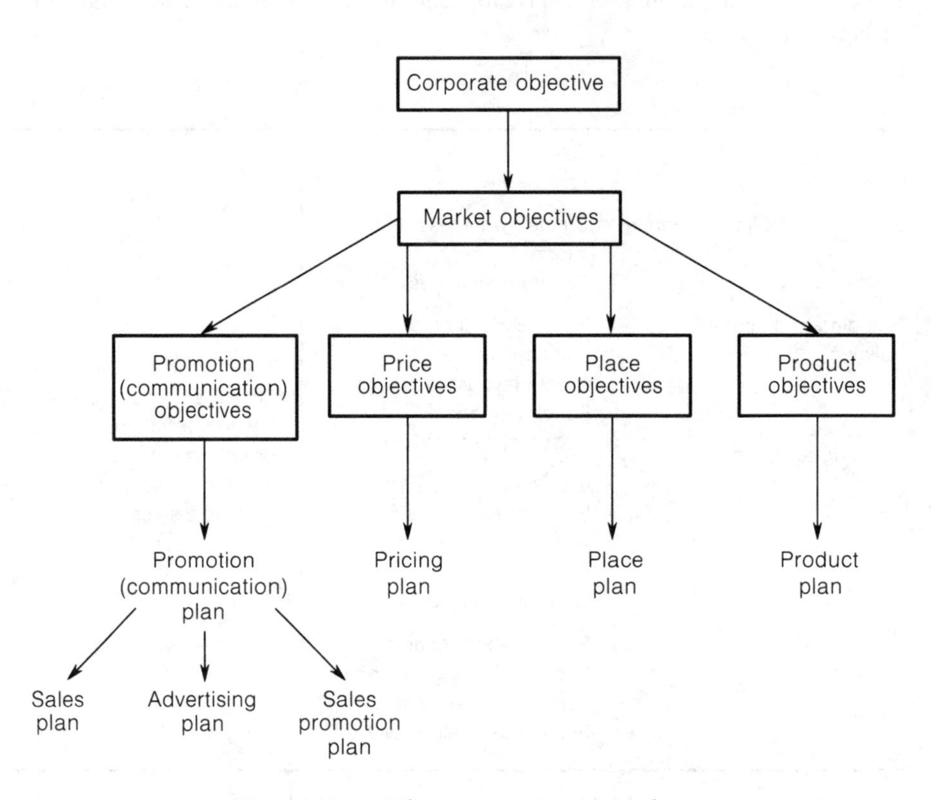

Figure 13.5 The communications plan

In fact the communications plan comprises three components: the *sales plan*, the *sales promotion plan* and the *advertising plan*. The two former components are dealt with in later chapters and we will deal here only with the advertising plan.

Advertising Plan

As with any plan, the advertising plan should be based around a clearly defined set of objectives. However, there can be a wide range of objectives for advertising. Naturally, we might hope that advertising will have an important influence on sales levels but it would be wrong to set objectives solely in terms of sales increases since so many other factors also influence sales. Having said this, what objectives should be set for advertising? We may start by agreeing that we need to set objectives for advertising for the following reasons:

- We need to set a budget for advertising.
- We need to determine who our target audience is.
- We need to determine the content of advertisements.
- We need to decide on what media to use.
- We need to decide on the frequency of advertising.
- We need to decide how to measure the effectiveness of our advertising.

These decisions can be summarised like this:

- Why (objectives)
- Who (target)
- What (message-copy platform)
- Where (media)
- How (creative platform)
- When (timing)
- How much (budget)
- Schedule (putting it all together)
- Response (how will it be measured?)
- Evaluation (did it work?)

Research has shown that many companies set advertising objectives that advertising by itself cannot achieve. A helpful starting point in setting an advertising objective is to ask the question: 'Is it possible to achieve this objective through advertising alone?' If the answer is no, then it cannot be a suitable objective. Try again until the answer is in the affirmative. All other steps in the process of putting an advertising plan together stem naturally from this beginning, as the list in Figure 13.6 shows.

It must be remembered that the role of advertising is never static. As we have seen, the recipient needs to receive new messages as his or her thought processes engage different phases of the buying sequence. Similarly, as the product or service moves through different stages in the life-cycle, so too must the advertising objectives reflect the changed priorities.

WHO ... is the target audience?
- What sort of people are they?
- How would we describe/identify them?
- What do they already know, feel or believe about us and our product/services?
- What do they know, feel or believe about the competition?

WHAT ... response do we wish to evoke from the target audience(s)?
... are these specific communication objectives?
... do we want to say, make them feel, believe, understand or know about buying our product or service?
... are we offering?
... are the priorities in terms of importance of our objectives?
... are our objectives? Can they be written down and agreed by ourselves and the advertising department or agency?

HOW ... will our objectives be embodied in an appealing form?
... is our creative strategy/platform going to look?
... do we know – what firm evidence is there – that this is acceptable and appropriate to our audience(s)?

WHERE ... is (are) the most cost-effective place(s) to expose our communications (in cost terms vis-à-vis our audience(s)?
... is (are) the most beneficial place(s) for our communications (in expected response terms *vis-à-vis* the 'quality' of channels available)?

WHEN ... are our communications to be displayed/conveyed to our audience(s)?
- What reasoning is behind our scheduling of advertisements/communications over the planning period?
- Do we have to fit in with other promotional activity on:
  - other products/services supplied by our company?
  - competitors' products/services?
  - seasonal trends?
  - special events in the market? for example, trade shows?

RESULTS ... What results do we expect?
... What will be our measures of success?
- If we are to measure results, is there anything we need to do beforehand (for example, measure starting position or organise a data collection system)?
- If we cannot say how we would measure precise results then:
  - are our objectives not sufficiently specific?
  - are they really communications objectives?
- How will we judge the relative success of our communications activities (good/bad/indifferent)?
- Should we have some intermediate 'milestones' so that corrective action can be taken if it looks as though the expected results will not be achieved?

BUDGET ... How much money do the intended activities need?
... How much money can we afford/make available?
... How will we control expenditure?

SCHEDULE ... Who is to do what and when?
... What is being spent on what, where and when?

Figure 13.6 Steps in the process of putting together an advertising plan

■ Selecting the Right Media

In choosing the most appropriate medium for your advertising message the company will need to take four main factors into account:

1. *The characteristic of the medium*. This describes the geographical coverage the medium gives; the types of audience it reaches; the frequency of publication or screening; its physical possibilities (such as colour, sound and movement) and its power to reach special groups.

2. *The 'atmosphere' of the medium*. The consistency with the image an organisation wishes to project. For example, an up-market beauty salon might choose to post a glossy brochure to potential clients rather than have cheap leaflets stuffed through all the letterboxes in the neighbourhood along with the newspaper delivery. Thus images can be of quality, élitism, popularity, fun – whatever the requirement, some media will convey the required image more effectively than others.

3. *The coverage of the medium*. The number of people exposed to the medium in terms of being aware of the content of the message. For example, a newspaper might be read by just two or three members of the family, whereas a technical journal might be circulated to a large number of specialists within a company or read in libraries. In contrast, a poster might be passed by thousands of people and yet only be noticed by a few.

4. *The comparative cost*. How much it will cost to reach a specific audience size. Cost per 1000 viewers/readers is often used as a comparative yardstick.

■ International Communications

Extending the communications strategy across countries has an enormous appeal to most international companies because of the cost savings associated with this approach. There are two principal sources of potential savings. The first is to do with spreading the costs arising from producing copy, particularly in respect of advertising. For a company with world-wide operations, the cost of preparing separate print and TV/cinema films for each market would be enormous. The second derives from bulk purchasing, a phenomenon that will become increasingly important as media ownership and coverage becomes more international. Castrol GTX, Marlboro, Coca-Cola and the like are, of course, well-known examples of truly global brands with global communications strategies.

Militating against this are the different functions and patterns of behaviour in different parts of the world, as well as differences in media availability in different countries.

For a fuller treatment of this topic, please refer to the sections on international market segmentation in Chapter 5, to the section on global brands in Chapter 11 and to the section on international product planning in Chapter 20.

■ Summary

We began this chapter by observing that, as customers and consumers, we are being bombarded incessantly with marketing communications. The 'noise' is at times almost overpowering. However, looking at the communication problem from the company's viewpoint, we can see that there is, or at least there ought to be, a logic behind what this noise is attempting to achieve.

In reality, the company has an armoury of communication techniques, which it can 'blend' together into an effective and persuasive communications mix. Essentially, the communications strategy can be summed up in a few words:

- What do we want to say?
- To whom do we want to say it?
- Why do we want to say it?
- How do we choose to say it?
- Where shall we communicate our message?
- When shall we say it?

Although these questions are deceptively simple, the skilled marketer doesn't fall into the trap of believing that the answers are equally easy. As we have seen, many important decisions and choices have to be made, sometimes affecting the organisation at all levels.

MODULE 5

Managing Marketing Relationships

CHAPTER 14

Sales Force Strategy

In this chapter we shall explore the role of direct selling in the marketing mix, and the sales process itself. We shall also discuss the role of sales promotion. For convenience, the words 'salesman' and 'he' have been used. The authors recognise that salespeople are frequently women and no offence is intended.

How Important is Personal Selling?

Most companies have an organised sales force long before they introduce a formal marketing activity of the kind described throughout this book. In spite of this, sales force management traditionally has been a neglected area of marketing management.

There are several possible reasons for this. One is that not all marketing and product managers have had experience in a personal selling or sales management role. Consequently, these managers often underestimate the importance of efficient personal selling.

Another reason for neglect of sales force management is that sales personnel themselves sometimes encourage an unhelpful distinction between sales and marketing by depicting themselves as 'the sharp end'. After all, isn't there something slightly daring about dealing with real customers as opposed to sitting in an office surrounded by marketing surveys, charts and plans? Such reasoning is dangerous, because unless a good deal of careful marketing planning has taken place before the salesman makes his effort to persuade the customer to place an order, the probability of a successful sale is much reduced. The suggested distinction between marketing 'theory' and sales 'practice' is further invalidated when we consider that profitable sales depend not just on individual customers and individual products, but on groups of customers (that is, market segments) and on the supportive relationship of products to each other (that is, carefully planned product portfolio). Another factor to be taken into account in this context is the constant need for the organisation to think in terms of where future sales will be coming from rather than to concentrate solely on present products, customers and problems.

Investigation of many European sales forces over the last decade has provided evidence that there remains an alarming lack of planning and professionalism in many cases. Frequently, salesmen have little idea of which products and which groups of customers to concentrate on, have too little knowledge about competitive activity, do not plan presentations well, rarely talk to customers in terms of *benefits*, make too little effort to close the sale and make many calls without any clear objectives. Even worse, marketing management is rarely aware that this important and expensive element of the marketing mix is not being managed effectively. The fact that many organisations have separate departments and directors for the marketing and sales activities increases the likelihood of such failures of communication.

Although its importance varies according to circumstances, in many businesses the sales force is the most important element of the marketing mix. In industrial goods companies, for example, it is not unusual to find very small amounts of money being spent on other forms of communication and very large sums being spent on the sales force in the form of salaries, cars and associated costs. Personal selling is also widely used in many service industries where customers are looking for very specific benefits. Insurance companies, for example, do use media advertising but rely for most of their sales on personal selling. Customers for insurance policies almost invariably need to discuss which policy would best fit their particular needs and circumstances. It is the task of the salesman to explain the choices available and to suggest the most appropriate policy.

Recent surveys show that more money is being spent by companies on their sales forces than on advertising and sales promotion combined. Personal selling, then, is a vital and expensive element in the marketing mix.

The solution to the problem of poor sales force management can only be found in the recognition that personal selling is indeed a crucial part of the marketing process and that it must be planned and considered as carefully as any other element. Indeed, it is an excellent idea for the manager responsible for marketing to go out into the territory for a few days each year and himself attempt to persuade customers to place orders. It is a good way of finding out what customers really think of the organisation's marketing policies!

■ The Role of Personal Selling

Personal selling can most usefully be seen as part of the *communications mix*. (Other common elements of the communications mix, it will be remembered, are advertising, sales promotion, public relations, direct mail and exhibitions.) In order to determine the precise role of personal selling in its communications mix, the company must identify the major influences in each purchase decision and find out what information they are likely to need at different stages of the buying process. Most institutional buying decisions can involve a large number of people and take a considerable amount of time. It is possible to split this decision-making process into a number of distinct steps, which are known as 'buy phases'.

- A problem (or need) is anticipated or recognised and a general solution worked out. For example, designers working on plans for a new plant or machine may decide a special component must be incorporated in the design.

- The characteristics and quantity of the required items are worked out. This, in the case of the machine component, would indicate the function and required performance of the component and any special design features (weight and size, for example).
- The specification and required quantity of the necessary items is determined.
- A search is made for potential sources of supply.
- Potential suppliers' tenders and design specifications are taken and scrutinised.
- Proposals are evaluated and a supplier selected.
- Orders are then placed.
- The supplier's components are subsequently monitored for such things as performance to specification and promptness of delivery.

Different people and different numbers of people are involved in each buy phase. A useful way of identifying who is likely to be involved in the purchase decision, and at what stages, is to look at the decision in terms of its 'newness' to the buying organisation. This 'newness' can be broken down into two parts:

- The complexity of the product.
- The degree of commercial risk or uncertainty surrounding the outcome of the purchase.

The higher the 'newness' in both these dimensions, the more people tend to be involved and the higher their status. If product complexity is high, but commercial uncertainty is low, then the design engineer and technologists have the more important role. If newness is low in both dimensions, purchasing officers tend to dominate the process. The higher the newness, the more activity is concentrated in the early phases and the more important it is for the salesman to involve himself at an early stage if he is to influence the outcome effectively. This is because a growing commitment operates throughout the decision process. Thus, early decisions are reinforced and become successively more and more difficult to change. The industrial salesperson, therefore, needs to know the degree of newness involved so that he can direct his efforts to the appropriate people.

■ The Buy Classes

In using this concept of newness in the purchase decision, the salesperson can divide the decision-making process of his prospects into what are called *buy classes*:

- New buy
- Straight rebuy
- Modified rebuy

New Buy

When the need results from a new task, all the buy phases will normally be followed. Several functional departments of the organisation will usually be involved: for example manufacturing, design, finance, the company board and the purchasing department. People in all these departments can be influenced during the decision-making process which, in the new buy context, takes the longest time to come to a conclusion.

Straight Rebuy

On the other hand, when the need arises for a straight rebuy – for example, reordering standard items for stock – the situation is quite different. Only one or two functional departments such as the user and purchasing department may be involved. The other buy phases do still apply in that they will have been followed in the initial purchase routine but, since the technical specification of the product is now known and unchanging, no further technical involvement is needed in the buying process. The only factors likely to worry the buyer, provided that quality is maintained, are price and delivery and these therefore become important negotiating points.

Modified Rebuy

Sometimes a change in the specification or some other parameter may be necessary; this gives rise to a modified rebuy. Changes in the specification may be initiated by a salesperson (for example, an offer of improved performance or a reduction in price) or by the purchasing company itself. The design and manufacturing functions may therefore become involved and most of the buy phases will once more apply.

The industrial salesperson should always endeavour to change a straight rebuy situation into a modified rebuy. When he or she succeeds, the commitment of existing customers may be strengthened and opportunities may be created to open new accounts with companies that have been using the products and services of competitors.

Pressure on the Individual Buyer

We know from our own personal experience how difficult it can be to agree on the colour of a new wallpaper; partners, friends and even what the neighbours possess all bring pressures to bear that may influence our personal decision. The buying decision-makers in the average company are subjected to many more pressures.

■ Pressures from Outside the Company

Buyers are subjected to a number of external pressures such as:

- *The economic situation.* Is it the best time for investment in new projects? What is the cost of credit? Can the company afford to proceed?
- *Political considerations.* Is it the time to embark on new projects, when demand is perhaps being squeezed and government expenditure being cut back?
- *Technology.* Does the necessary technology exist for the project? Will the proposed product be overtaken by new technology in the foreseeable future?
- *Environmental considerations.* Will the new project be acceptable or will conservationists' interests or pollution controls prevent us from going ahead?
- *The business climate.* How will profit levels, interest rates and the cost of labour, for example, influence the decision of whether or not to proceed?

■ Pressures from Within the Company

The way the buying department is organised and the number of people within it will affect the decision process. 'Internal politics', personal rivalries and vested interests will all put pressures on the buyer.

Individual status within the organisation will also affect the way in which the decision is reached and the degree to which other people within the company influence it.

There are further pressures from other parts of the organisation. The buyer may have to try to reconcile conflicting advice, resist pressure from vested interests and perhaps even act as referee in the final decision.

■ Individual Pressures

Even the buyer's own personality and past experience will influence the decision.

Past purchases will prejudice the buyer. For example, good experiences will be used to justify staying with a particular supplier even if a salesperson can show that his product offers benefits which prove that a change would make good sense.

Similarly, habit acts against the industrial salesperson who is trying to win a new order. Many buyers prefer to stay with known suppliers rather than risk the disruption of changing to another.

The buyer's perception of the situation may be different from that of other people. Other managers may rate a particular feature of a new product very highly, but the buyer may be obsessed with price, for example, and may therefore resist change, whatever the evidence of its desirability.

Allied to the perception 'barrier', there may be the difficulty of persuading the buyer to change because it takes him a long time to absorb new information.

What Does all this Mean to the Salesperson?

The way the buying process operates in different circumstances has several implications for the industrial salesman. He has to:

- Recognise the buying situation he faces, and the stage it is at, and determine how he will handle it;
- Identify those people in the organisation who are likely to be able to influence the purchase decision at that moment and during subsequent phases;
- Decide what benefits his product and his company can offer to each of these people and what technical help he can give in an attempt to influence the decision;
- Attempt to convert straight rebuys into modified rebuys by demonstrating that his product has additional benefits over those used at present.

It can be seen, then, that the large number of people to be influenced, and the extended time this process might take, means that the industrial salesperson has to adopt a much wider role than that of merely selling to his customers. Unlike in other forms of selling, he/she is as much a consultant as a salesperson. In industry, selling is a focal point in the dissemination of information (unlike in the consumer field, where advertising plays the major role). Many industrial salespeople have technical qualifications in chemistry, engineering, electronics or management, and most have considerable product knowledge. The industrial salesperson is thus able to help his customers in many ways – in fact, he will find that some customers rely on him to solve problems for them to help keep them up to date technically. Without the advice and guidance of industrial salesmen, many manufacturing projects would run into severe difficulties and would be considerably delayed.

Understanding the Salesperson's Role

The Consultant

When acting as a consultant, a salesman must understand the nature of this role and the way in which it must be performed. It is not necessarily difficult. The key to a successful relationship between consultant and consulted is mutual trust and respect. To perform this role the salesman will have to show (perhaps over a period of time) that his advice is reliable and given in the best interests of his client. To do this effectively he needs to listen to what the client wants, analyse his needs and recommend the best solution. He must be careful not to damage his company's reputation by giving bad advice to gain a quick sale. Above all he has to have an excellent understanding of his company's products.

However, this very knowledge causes problems if it is used incorrectly. Many industrial salesmen make the mistake of dulling the buyer's senses with sophisticated technical jargon. Years of training might have given the salesman a deep understanding of chemistry, electronics or engineering, every word of which, he believes, must be used to impress and to demonstrate to the buyer his complete grasp of his subject. Such displays can cause more problems than they solve. Buyers do not like to feel inferior in knowledge, even if they are, and when this happens at best they become bored and at worst annoyed. In either case, the sale is in danger.

Nevertheless, the industrial salesman can play an important part in helping his customers. He might work with design engineers to overcome problems associated with incorporating his product in the overall design, or with systems engineers in setting up procedures for using his product. In this way he is able to influence the decision-making process and build on the growing commitment that develops as time goes by.

■ The Salesman

The industrial salesman may believe that his value to buyers lies in his specialist knowledge rather than in his ability as a salesman. If he thinks in this way he is wrong. Only a few of today's salesmen will experience a seller's market. It is normally a buyer's market and there is plenty of competition from firms at home and abroad. This is the golden rule of selling:

- 'When all things are equal, the orders usually go to the salesman with the greatest SELLING skills.'

Much of the rest of this chapter is concerned with selling skills, and these are indeed vital to the salesman. However, selling ability is rarely enough to clinch a deal with the modern industrial buyer. Buyers today are better-equipped than ever before. They are better educated and have information about the market that is as accurate as the supplier's own information; they also understand finance – margins, liquidity, cash flows and returns on investment capital. Armed with this knowledge, the buyer will be in a position to negotiate every aspect of the proposed deal. Furthermore, in times of recession, buyers have power to back their demands.

■ The Negotiator

Faced with such knowledgeable buyers, the industrial salesman must therefore understand the difference between negotiating and selling. A combination of sales ability and determination, without negotiating skills, can be a positive disadvantage. The too-eager salesmen, using closing techniques to clinch the sale, can be a disaster when negotiation is needed.

Negotiating is quite different from selling. Negotiating begins when each party realises that the other has something that they want. Negotiation is about the art of manoeuvre in order to secure the best possible deal. The salesman therefore needs to be able to exert influence over his side of the deal.

He needs knowledge of costs and margins, measures of the profitability of his major customers, awareness of the impact of profit on minor variations in volume, price, costs and sales mix, and he has continually to improve his planning and handling of customer negotiations if he is to be truly effective.

■ Identifying the Buyer

The industrial salesman is faced with the problem of convincing a number of people or groups within an organisation over an extended period. He is also faced with the problem of finding who actually has the power to make or influence the purchase decision. It is very easy for him to waste his time attempting to achieve the impossible – selling to someone who cannot give a decision or who has no real influence on the decision process.

There can be two reasons for this failure: poor preparation and fear. Once he has done his preparatory homework the industrial salesman can, or should, approach his task with confidence. Even so, many salesmen prefer to meet in the organisation people with whom they are familiar and whom they count as friends, rather than risk meeting a buyer who holds an important position – such as a financial director, works director or managing director – even though they know the more senior executives have greater buying power.

These fears are groundless. Most senior managers are very reasonable people to deal with and few try to dominate the interview with questions to catch him out. In reality it is the assistant – the junior buyer, the secretary or local manager – who makes life difficult for the salesman. A buyer may be protected by a host of such people. It must be the salesman's objective to bypass these guards and to see the person who can really make or influence the decision.

We have stressed the importance of preparation. This means that a great deal of research may be needed into the whole organisation and product-design strategy of potential customer companies.

■ Basic Research

The industrial salesman must first find out as much as he can about his potential customers. He must also keep this information up to date:

- What sort of company is it and what is its business?
- What new businesses is it entering?
- What new products is it developing?
- How big is it?

- Is it part of a group?
- How is the buying done?
- Who within the organisation has the real authority to choose the supplier, and who influences him?
- What past relationships have there been between the vendor and purchaser companies?
- Is the company profitable? How is it doing at present?
- Is it in an expanding, declining or static industry?
- How strong is competition in the area (has a competitor an office close to the buyer's works)?
- Who supplies the company at present?
- Are the directors traditional or modern-minded businessmen? Have there been any changes at the top recently?
- Have representatives from the company ever visited the salesman's company exhibitions or showrooms?

Such information can be culled from many sources. For example:

- Past records of dealings with the company.
- Other salesmen.
- Other customers.
- The company itself – telephone inquiries and unofficial sources of information such as receptionists and gatekeepers.
- Chambers of trade.
- Productivity organisations.
- National and local newspapers.
- Trade press.
- Classified telephone directories.
- Trade directories.
- Exhibition catalogues.
- Association membership lists.
- *Kompass*;
- *Kelly*;
- *Extel* cards;
- The prospect's own literature.

A great deal of work is involved in this sort of basic research, but the salesman should consider the time this research can save if it ensures that he is able to see the right person and know all about his organisation and its products before he meets the buyer.

■ Identifying Who Has Influence

We have seen that a large number of people are involved in each buy phase and that many of them will be able to influence the decision process. The salesman will have to spend a lot of time selling to these people. Sound preparation will identify the influential; poor preparation may result in time being wasted on intermediaries who do not have influence.

Although the organisation of each manufacturer differs in some way from every other, a number of basic operations have to be performed irrespective of the size of the organisation or the nature of the end product. At one end of the spectrum there is the one-man firm, in which the proprietor may perform all the operations himself. At the other, each of the basic operations will be the concern of a separate, highly specialised department. In very large organisations the necessary operations may be further subdivided in an effort to increase efficiency by yet greater specialisation.

The industrial salesman must understand the elements of the typical manufacturing company, how these interact and how they depend upon each other to influence the final purchase decision. Armed with this knowledge a salesman will be able to decide when and where to concentrate his efforts for maximum effect. Typical activities of the various departments of a company are summarised below.

■ Marketing

An important task of the marketing department is to identify market needs and opportunities. A long and complex procedure is followed before full-scale design and production work can begin. This may involve a market survey, a design feasibility study, an evaluation of available manufacturing resources and a financial study. Assuming these studies are successful, the new project then becomes the responsibility of a design department. The industrial salesman can influence a prospective customer's marketing department by showing how his products can open up new market opportunities.

■ The Design Department

This department has many titles and many sections, for example dealing with development, research, design, engineering and drawing. The main task of the department is to design a product which will meet a specified market requirement. The starting point may be a sales specification and the theoretical finishing point may be the production of a prototype model, design drawings and a performance specification. During the design phase, designers will call upon other departments and also may have to seek specialist assistance from existing or potential component or material suppliers. The industrial salesman has a vital part to play at this stage.

■ Production Engineering Department

In broad terms, the function of the production engineering department is to specify how the product should be made and to provide the manufacturing departments with the equipment needed to make it. The department's responsibilities are very broad-ranging. They include resolving such matters as whether to purchase from outside or manufacture in-house, and whether to utilise existing plant as opposed to new acquisitions. It decides the source for the purchase of materials and provides estimates of manufacturing costs. The industrial salesman may well find some very powerful allies in this department.

■ Production Control Department

This department is responsible for the logistics of the manufacturing operation. The prime function is to ensure that men, materials and machines are all brought together at the right time to meet planned production programmes. Supplies of the majority of raw materials and components are usually secured well in advance and the department tries to maintain stock levels that provide the optimum balance between insufficient stock, which can create long delivery times, and excessive stocks which are expensive to maintain. Industrial salesmen will invariably work closely with this department.

■ Purchasing Department

This department buys little on its own behalf, but seeks and vets suppliers, negotiates contracts and monitors performance. On the face of it, one might think that purchasing departments play an important part in the selection of suppliers. However, in many cases, the selection of the supplier is more strongly influenced by other departments and the purchasing department's eventual selection is almost a formality. This is particularly the case when design or production engineering departments have received technical help or advice from a potential supplier at an early stage of development. If the supplier has been able to guide the design or manufacturing process towards the use of his product, then his chances of achieving a subsequent order are usually higher than that of competitors who have not been so involved. The purchasing department is not therefore necessarily the right place for the industrial salesman to direct his main effort. The salesman may negotiate and obtain the actual order from this department, but usually his real selling effort will have been directed elsewhere, long before reaching this final stage.

■ Territory Planning and Obtaining the Interview

Let us now turn our attention briefly to the sales process itself, starting with territory planning and obtaining the interview.

The industrial salesman must plan his life to ensure that maximum time is spent selling and minimum time is spent on travelling, administration, planning and other activities. A systematic approach to territory planning is needed to ensure that all customers receive regular visits.

Although some calls will be made 'on spec', the majority will be by appointment. Appointments between buyers and industrial salesmen are usually arranged on the telephone. Thorough preparation is needed before the call, to enable the salesman to decide who is to be spoken to, what is the objective of the call and what lever should be used to arouse the prospect's interest. It is not always easy to get through to the prospect or, once connected, to persuade him to agree to the interview. There is a range of techniques the salesman can use to persuade the telephone operator and the prospect's secretary to connect him with the prospect, and for persuading the prospect to agree to an interview. This process of persuasion is a form of selling, which is discussed later in this chapter.

The salesman should always try to suggest the times for his appointments. This will enable him to fit four or five appointments a day into a schedule that is economical in terms of travel and efficient in the use of time.

■ Opening Techniques

The salesman will only succeed if he handles his sales interviews effectively. He must establish clear objectives for each call and have a plan of how he intends to achieve these objectives.

A useful sequence to follow in any call is the 'ABC' sequence in order to achieve the required objectives. The salesman should arrest the prospect's attention (A), sell benefits (B) and move to a close (C). The sales offer has to be preplanned and the necessary facts, information and supporting sales-kit of literature, samples, data and other aids needed to achieve the interview objectives must be assembled.

It is essential to arrive in plenty of time for an interview. The salesman must be neat and tidy and he must preplan his opening remarks in order to create a good impression from the outset and secure the client's immediate interest. Pleasantries and social chat should be kept to the minimum. The salesman may open by asking a question, giving new information, quoting a reference, using a sales aid, demonstrating something or linking his visit with some previous business. The aim must be to arrest the prospect's interest from the very outset.

■ Benefit Selling

Throughout this book we have referred to the fact that customers do not buy products or services, but rather they seek to acquire benefits. Every product or service has its features, but the potential customer is only interested in the benefits that will accrue from these features. Since people buy products and services for what they will do for them – that is, the *benefits* of having those products or services – the salesman must sell these benefits rather than the features.

For the salesman, a simple formula to ensure this customer-orientated approach is adopted is always to use the phrase 'which means that' to link a feature to the benefit it brings.

The salesman must undertake a detailed analysis to underline the full range of benefits he has to offer his customers. He should seek to identify standard benefits (benefits that arise directly from the features of what he offers), company benefits (benefits offered by the salesman's company) and differential benefits (benefits that differentiate between the salesman's product or service and those of his competitors). A 'benefit analysis form' should be used to ensure a methodical analysis is conducted and proof should be given to substantiate every claim.

■ Dealing with Objections

The buyer will almost invariably raise objections during the sales interview. An objection is a statement or question that puts an obstacle in the path leading towards closure of the sale. A buyer may raise a fundamental objection when he cannot see a need for the product or service on offer. He may raise standard objections when he recognises his need but either wishes to delay a decision or needs further convincing before concluding a deal.

The salesman should always seek to forestall objections before they are raised. This can be done by identifying possible objections and 'answering them' in his offer. When faced with a fundamental objection, the salesman has to sell the need for the product in question rather than the benefits entailed. There is a range of techniques for dealing with standard objections but, if the buyer continues to raise objections without actually concluding the interview, there may be a hidden objection. It is often possible to discover what this is by asking an incomplete question, such as, 'and your other reason for not deciding is . . .?'

The salesman should not fear a price objection. This can usually be overcome by talking in terms of value rather than cost. Furthermore, the salesman is sometimes able to negotiate the price in order to secure an order.

■ Closing Techniques

The sale is closed when the buyer makes a firm commitment to place an order. The salesman should constantly look for opportunities to close the sale.

The buyer will often show interest, make committing statements and ask questions; these are buying signals, which the salesman should follow up by asking a question in order to confirm that he has correctly interpreted the buying signals.

Trial closes should be used throughout the sales offer to test the buyer's reactions, uncover objections, determine buyer interest and speed the sale. Trial closes also help the salesman retain the initiative and accumulate small commitments from the buyer. The salesman should use direct and indirect questions to obtain buyer commitment. It is sometimes possible to offer alternatives that lead the buyer into stating a preference, which, once expressed, can pave the way to an immediate close. Other opportunities to close can be created by the summary technique, giving a quotation or by offering a concession.

- The salesman will only achieve a final close if he *asks for an order.*

The successful close is the culmination of a great deal of preparation, planning and hard work. It is the moment that makes it all worthwhile. But the close is not the end of the matter, it is just a step in a continuous process. The salesman must always remember that his objective is not only to close the sale, but also to open up a lasting relationship with the customer. In the final analysis, this is what makes a successful salesman.

Advantages of Personal Selling

- It is a two-way form of communication, giving the prospective purchaser the opportunity to ask questions of the salesman about the product or service.
- The sales message itself can be made more flexible and therefore can be more closely tailored to the needs of individual customers.
- The salesmen and women can use in-depth product knowledge to relate their messages to the perceived needs of the buyers and to deal with objections as they arise.
- Most important of all, the sales representatives can ask for an order and perhaps negotiate on price, delivery or special requirements.

Once an order has been obtained from a customer, and there is a high probability of a rebuy occurring, the sales representative's task changes from persuasion to reinforcement. All communications at this stage should contribute to underlining the wisdom of the purchase.

Clearly, in different markets different weighting is given to the various forms of communication available. In the grocery business, for example, advertising and sales promotion are extremely important elements in the communications process. However, the food manufacturer must maintain an active sales force that keeps in close contact with the retail buyers. This retail contact ensures vigorous promotional activity within the chain. In the wholesale hardware business frequent and regular face-to-face contact with retail outlets through a sales force is the key determinant of success. In industries where there are few customers (such as capital goods and specialised process materials), and in-depth understanding of the customers' production processes has to be built up, personal contact is of paramount importance. In contrast, many fast-moving industrial goods are sold into fragmented markets for diverse uses. In this area, forms of communication other than personal selling take on added importance. One such form of communication is sales promotion.

Sales Promotion

The term *advertising* (often referred to as 'above-the-line expenditure') can be defined as all non-personal communication through media. This includes television, cinema, radio, print and outdoor media.

Sales promotion, for which the term 'below-the-line expenditure' is often used as a synonym, is not so easily defined. For example, the Americans use the term to describe all forms of communication, including advertising and personal selling. In the UK some use the term to describe any non-face-to-face activity concerned with the promotion of sales. Some people use it to describe any non-media expenditure, whilst others use it specifically to mean in-store merchandising. The fact that none of these definitions is an accurate reflection of how sales promotion works in practice is an indication of why there is so much confusion about many aspects of this important area of marketing activity.

In practice, sales promotion is a specific activity, which can be defined as the making of a featured offer to defined customers within a specific time limit. In other words, for an activity to qualify as a sales promotion, someone must be offered something that is 'featured' rather than just being an aspect of trade. Furthermore, the offer must include benefits not inherent in the product or service, as opposed to the intangible benefits offered in advertising (such as adding value through appeals to imagery). Seen this way, every other element of the marketing mix, including advertising, personal selling, point-of-sale material, pricing and after-sales service can be used as part of a structured activity in order to achieve specified objectives.

How can we use sales promotion? Essentially, this is a problem-solving activity designed to encourage customers to behave more in line with the economic interests of the company. Typical tasks for sales promotion are: encouraging stock movement; counteracting competitive activity; encouraging repeat purchase; securing marginal buyers; getting bills paid on time and inducing trial purchases. From this, it will be seen that sales promotion is not necessarily concerned with volume increases. For example, it is often used to assist production and distribution scheduling by persuading customers to bring forward their peak buying from one period to another.

To summarise, sales promotion seeks to influence:

- Salesmen – to sell
- Customers – to buy
- Customers – to sell
- Users – to buy
- Users – to use

} more, faster, earlier

Although in recent years sales promotion activity has increased to such an extent that it now accounts for as much expenditure as above-the-line advertising, it is important to realise that, on its own, sales promotion will not replace selling, change long-term trends or build up long-term customer loyalty. Nevertheless, whilst sales promotion is essentially a tactical device, it also has an important strategic role to play.

What different kinds of promotion are there? Many and varied types of sales promotions are listed in Table 14.1. Each of these different types are appropriate for different circumstances and each has advantages and disadvantages. For example, points schemes are flexible, have wide appeal, do not involve the company in holding stocks of gifts, prevent customers from easily valuing gifts and are easy to administer.

Preparing the Sales Promotion Plan

There is widespread acknowledgement that sales promotion is one of the most mismanaged of all marketing functions. This is mainly because of the confusion about what sales promotion is, which often results in expenditures not being properly recorded. Some companies include it in advertising; others as part of sales force expenditure; some as a general marketing expense and others as a manufacturing expense (as in the case of extra product, special labels or packaging); whilst the loss of revenue from special price reductions is often not recorded at all.

Such failures can be extremely damaging because sales promotion is such an important part of marketing strategy. Also, with increasing competition from EU countries, troubled economic conditions and growing pressures from the trade, sales promotion is becoming more widespread and more acceptable. This means that companies can no longer afford not to set objectives, nor to evaluate results after the event, nor to fail to have some company guidelines. For example, a £1 case allowance on a product with a contribution rate of £3 per case has to increase sales by 50 per cent just to maintain the level of contribution. Failure to realise this, or to set alternative objectives for the promotion, can easily result in loss of control and a consequent reduction of profits.

In order to manage a company's sales promotion expenditure effectively there is one essential step that must be taken. An objective for sales promotion must be established in the same way that an objective is developed for advertising, pricing or distribution and the objectives for each promotion should be clearly stated – such as trial, repeat purchase, distribution, display, a shift in buying peaks or combating competition. Thereafter, the following process should apply:

- Select the appropriate technique;
- Pretest;
- Mount the promotion;
- Evaluate in depth.

Spending must be analysed and categorised by type of activity (for example, special packaging, special point of sale material and loss of revenue through price reductions).

Table 14.1 Sales promotions

Target Market	*Money*		*Goods*		*Services*	
	Direct	*Indirect*	*Direct*	*Indirect*	*Direct*	*Indirect*
Consumer	Price reduction Dealer loaders Loyalty schemes Incentives Full range buying	Coupons Vouchers Money equivalent Competitions	Free goods Premium offers (e.g. 13 for 12) Free gifts Trade-in offers	Stamps Coupons Vouchers Money equivalent Competitions	Guarantees Group participation Special exhibitions and displays	Cooperative advertising Stamps, coupons Vouchers for services Competitions
Trade		Extended credit Delayed invoicing Sale or return Coupons Vouchers Money equivalent	Free gifts Trial offers Trade-in offers	Coupons Vouchers Money equivalent Competitions	Guarantees Group participation events Free services Risk reduction schemes Training Special exhibitions, displays Demonstrations Reciprocal trading schemes	Stamps, coupons Vouchers for services Competitions
Sales force	Bonus Commission	Coupons Vouchers Money equivalent Competitions	Free gifts	Coupons Vouchers Points systems Money equivalent	Free services Group participation events	Stamps, coupons Points systems for services Competitions

One company manufacturing self-assembly kitchens embarked on a heavy programme of sales promotion after a dramatic reduction in consumer demand. Whilst they managed to maintain turnover, they were worried that their sales promotional activities had been carried out in such a haphazard and piecemeal fashion that they were unable to evaluate the cost effectiveness of what they had done. They were also very concerned about its effect on company image and their long-term consumer franchise. So the company made a concentrated study of this area of expenditure, which now represented over half of their communication budget. Next time round they had clear objectives, a clear promotional plan properly integrated into the marketing plan, and an established means of assessment.

As for the sales promotional plan itself, the objectives, strategy and brief details of timing and costs should be included. It is important that too much detail should *not* appear in the sales promotional plan. Detailed promotional instructions will follow as the marketing plan is revealed. For example, the following checklist outlines the kind of detail that should eventually be circulated. However, only an outline of this should appear in the marketing plan itself.

Checklist for promotional instruction:

1.	*Introduction*	Briefly summarise content – What? Where? When?
2.	*Objectives*	Marketing and promotional objectives for new product launch.
3.	*Background*	Market data. Justification for technique. Other relevant matters.
4.	*Promotional Offer*	Detail the offer: special pricing structure; description of premium, etc. Be brief, precise and unambiguous.
5.	*Eligibility*	Who? Where?
6.	*Timing*	When is the offer available? Call, delivery or invoice dates?
7.	*Date Plan*	Assign dates and responsibilities for all aspects of plan prior to start date.
8.	*Support*	Special advertising. POS. Presenters. Leaflets. PR. Samples, etc.
9.	*Administration*	Invoicing activity. Free goods invoice lines. Depot stocks. Premium (re)ordering procedure. Cash drawing procedures.
10.	*Sales Plan*	Targets. Incentives. Effect on routing. Briefing meetings. Telephone sales.
11.	*Sales Presentation*	Points to be covered in call.
12.	*Sales Reporting*	Procedure for collection of required data not otherwise available.
13.	*Assessment*	How will the promotion be evaluated?

■ Summary

Sales and marketing are clearly linked yet require separate attention. The marketing process is only completed when a sale is made. It is essential that a sales strategy be developed that is closely integrated with the overall marketing strategy.

CHAPTER 15

Managing the Sales Force

In this chapter we turn our attention to methods of determining the size of the sales force, establishing sales territories, setting sales objectives and managing the sales force effort.

How Many Salesmen and Women do we Need?

The organisation should begin its consideration of how many sales representatives it needs by finding out exactly how work is allocated at the present time. Start by listing all the things the current sales force actually does. These might include opening new accounts, servicing existing accounts, demonstrating new products, taking repeat orders and debt collecting. This analysis should be utilised to investigate alternative ways of carrying out these responsibilities.

For example, telephone selling has been shown to be a perfectly acceptable alternative to personal visits, particularly in respect of repeat business. The sales force can thus be freed for pioneering work, which is not so susceptible to the telephone approach. Can debts be collected by mail or by telephone? Can products be demonstrated in showrooms or at exhibitions? It is only by asking these kinds of questions that we can be certain we have not fallen into the common trap of committing the company to a decision and then seeking data and reasons to justify the decision. At this stage, the manager should concentrate on collecting relevant, quantified data and then use judgement and experience to help him come to a decision.

Workload

Basically, all sales force activities can be categorised under three headings: making calls, travelling, and performing administrative functions. These tasks comprise the *workload*. If we first decide what constitutes a reasonable workload for a salesman, in hours per month, we can measure how long the current activities take and then work out the exact extent of the workload. There are, of course, several ways of measuring workload. One major consumer goods company used its Work Study department to measure sales force effectiveness. The results of this study are summarised in Figure 15.1, which shows how a salesman's time is spent and approximately how much of his time is actually available for selling. One immediate action taken by the company was to initiate a training programme, which led to more time being

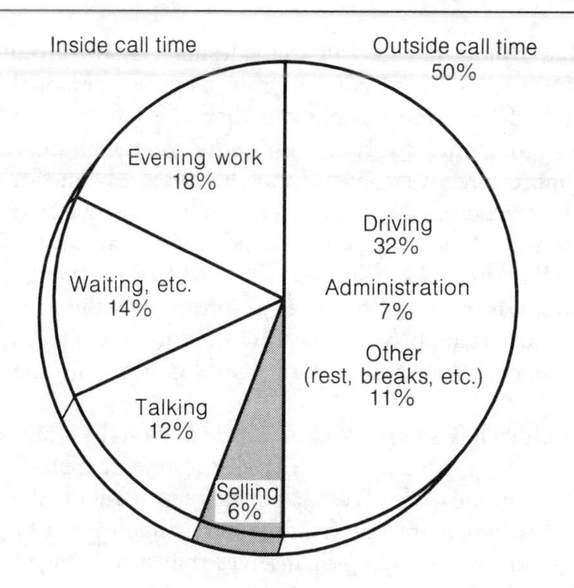

Figure 15.1 Breakdown of a salesman's total daily activity

spent on selling as a result of better planning. Another was to improve the quality of the sales performance whilst face-to-face with the customers.

There are, of course, other methods of measuring current sales force performance. One such method involves getting salesmen to carry out their own measurement. Research shows that salesmen carry out this measurement task diligently over the prescribed measurement period. The method involves recording their daily starting time and the miles on the car clock, and repeating this throughout the working day for all calls. The only additional information required is the account category called on, and the time in and time out.

From this, it is possible to calculate over a two-month period, for example, the *average* time it takes to make a particular type of call (such as to a wholesaler, a chemist, a doctor, a hospital or a consultant). It is also possible to measure, given the type of territory (for example, town or country), how long it takes in travel to cover a given territory size. Finally, since administration is likely to be a fixed period of time for everyone, the company now has in its possession the vital information to measure, *territory by territory*, the precise workload of every salesman. Territories can now be equitably allocated to all salesmen.

There are, of course, many methods of calculating workload, but there is one further factor that is worthy of consideration here. This is a subject we have researched over a number of years and which has proved extremely valuable in helping companies to allocate their salesmen more effectively.

During the 1970s, it was fashionable to predict the death of the salesman as a key component in commercial success. Enthusiasts predicted that marketing methods would become so sophisticated and precisely targeted that the need for personal selling would vanish. But the salesman is still around: indeed, even now, many companies spend considerably more on personal selling than on advertising and sales promotion put together.

The reason is not hard to find. Despite his very high cost, no one has yet discovered a more effective agency than the human being for communicating the full benefit of product offerings and for smoothing out customers' concerns. Moreover, research shows that, even in industries that doubt the usefulness of the personal selling process, customers take a different line. For example – and one that confounds popular belief – according to a recent survey medical representatives are actually welcomed by doctors and are considered a most valuable source of information about developments in the pharmaceutical industry.

As the pendulum has swung back towards personal selling, companies have invested heavily to improve the productivity of one of their scarcest resources: the group of individuals who have a direct interface with the customers. And indeed, today's salesmen are significantly better than those of a decade ago. But it is not the quality of the 'reps' themselves that has changed, so much as the quality of their direction and management. Creative, highly-motivated and productive salesmen could certainly be found in 1975; but, where excellence existed, it often stemmed from an individual's personal imagination and desire to excel rather than from the wherewithal provided by the company's training and management development processes. Some salesmen were excellent performers despite the firm's management, not because of it.

Clearly, this is a broad generalisation. Some companies were as excellent at selling a decade ago as the best performers today. But even now, despite the improvements, there are all too few companies that, on close reflection and with honest self-appraisal, can truly claim a level of salesmanship that exceeds the mediocre.

Increasing the productivity of a sales force is a major challenge for the most enlightened and results-oriented sales manager, well aware that an increased call rate, higher revenue targets, a larger client base and similar objectives are not the only yardsticks. It is becoming fully recognised that productivity calls for a combination of both quantitative and qualitative performance measures.

Some of the methods and ideas that have been used to improve the productivity of sales forces during the last decade have proved very useful. Among those that have become fairly standard in competently managed organisations are (1) the development of imaginative and thorough training modules covering areas such as communication techniques, body language, human behaviour and motivation, observation skills, transactional analysis and effective planning; (2) the introduction of performance measurement, supported by evaluation procedures; (3) the design of creative and productive sales aids; (4) the establishment of systems for tapping and cross-fertilising creative ideas generated by the firm's sales force; and (5) the development of effective incentive systems.

■ Directing the Sales Effort

Every company places a slightly different emphasis on each one of these items, making many interesting and creative variations. But direct observation of a large number of seemingly effective and productive sales forces over the last few years has revealed a serious weakness in the way the majority of them are directed in one important area: salesmen are rarely guided on how their communication effort should be changed when addressing loyal customers at one end of the spectrum and hostile customers at the other. For instance, one salesman on an in-company training programme proudly told a seminar that he was in the habit of calling on one outlet 135 times a year, on the grounds that the account was worth $500,000 and the client was so loyal that 'one needed to reciprocate'.

The fact is that a firm's clientele normally consists of many types of customer. Some are large and some are small. Some represent a high sales potential; others the opposite. Some clients are loyal to the point of folly; others are sufficiently cynical to change patronage at the slightest provocation. Yet others are almost phobic about the supplying company and need superhuman persuasion to change their attitude towards it. Sheer common sense demands that customers of different potential should have different amounts of sales time invested in them.

The trouble is that, understandably enough, the average salesman enjoys calling on the loyal customer and dislikes the prospect of being constantly rebuffed by the hostile one. The result, also understandably, is that salesmen tend to concentrate on loyal customers who will probably continue to buy from their company regardless. A simple analysis of a salesman's call record can highlight the incestuous relationship developing between reps and the buyer. Both sides are quite happy to fête each other at frequent intervals, although it is really a 'mutual admiration society' from which little additional commercial and marketing value can be derived.

The main difficulty is that if the salesman achieves his sales budget little notice is normally taken of the fact that a lot of his time is directed unproductively – towards a customer who is literally 'in the bag'. Salesmen would no doubt reply that, if they are neglected, even loyal customers may lose 'affection' for their pet supplier. This is obviously true. However, it is no less true that the main thrust of his communication with a very loyal customer should be quite different from that which takes place in front of a hostile prospect. In the former case, the main purpose of the sales call is to maintain contact; to reassure the customer that his loyalty is wise and to cement a happy relationship. In the latter case, the aim is to try to understand the reasons for the hostility, to attempt to remove them and then 'sell' the product. These are totally different tasks; they call for different approaches and should yield different results.

This notion can be taken a stage further. A firm's clientele can be divided into three major groupings: those who love the supplier (the 'Philes'); those who are totally indifferent to the identity of the supplier as long as the offering is right (the 'Promiscuous' companies); and those who are hostile to the selling company and reluctant to buy from it at all (the 'Phobes').

The point is that each of the three groups needs to be addressed with different selling and communication techniques. In fact, there is a strong case for developing individual sales aids for each case.

The situation is further complicated by the need to distinguish between the level of sales effort that is directed towards the large, medium and small potential customer. Since each of the three Phile, Promiscuous and Phobe groupings can represent a large, medium or small prospect, there are a possible nine types of customer. Obviously, some of the cells of the matrix represent better opportunities than others. A small Phobe is probably not worth bothering about, since the results of even a successful combating of the phobia will not justify the effort involved. A small Phile, on the other hand, will probably buy from the supplier anyway. Since it only represents a small potential, however, the right approach is for the supplier to call infrequently and then concentrate on assuring the customer that the affection is reciprocated. Spending any more time than the absolute minimum on such a client is unproductive.

Large Philes are both loyal and important. They should be handled with a maintenance policy, under which a representative should do only what is necessary to maintain the business. In practice, this might consist of a personal telephone call once a week only. The frequency of personal visits is a matter of management judgement, since there is always an element of vulnerability to strong competitive moves. The medium Philes can be handled according to the same principles, although obviously the call frequency will have to be less.

The most promising pay-off for the time invested by the representative clearly comes from the company that is both large and 'promiscuous'. The appropriate treatment here is an investment policy that might mean a much higher call frequency with additional support from the company in whatever ways are thought necessary. The objective, if possible, is to move it up to the status of Phile. Medium and small Promiscuous customers can be handled likewise, but with a decreasing call frequency.

Large Phobes are an interesting challenge. The first thing to establish here is the precise reason for the antipathy to the selling firm. If that can't be discovered, it may not be worth spending too much time on them.

To go into the suggested selling postures more deeply we will take the customer types one by one (Figure 15.2). First, Phile/Large (Box 1) – an important customer that has proved to be very loyal. The main selling task thus consists of: (1) maintaining contact – no more calls than are absolutely necessary; (2) communicating details of all new developments; (3) responding to complaints (if any); and (4) collecting information about general developments pertaining to the use of the product and/or competitive practices. It is important

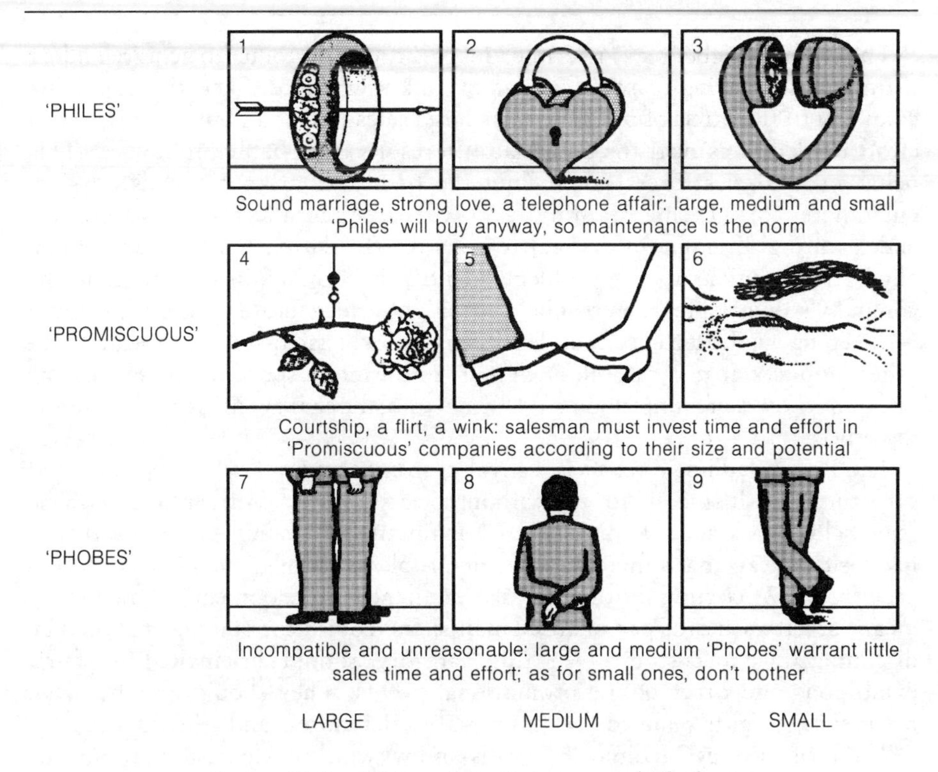

Figure 15.2 'Philes, Promiscuous and Phobes'

that the client receives a copy of the company's annual report – and that salesmen are authorised to spend £x twice a year on entertaining appropriate members of the client's organisation.

Promiscuous/Large (Box 4), on the other hand, is a fairly difficult customer, apt to change allegiance at the slightest opportunity and very sensitive to price. However, it is a large potential user and the business is worth having. So the main selling task consists of: (1) identifying the motivational stimuli of the members of the decision-making unit in such companies (what makes them tick?); (2) planning sales presentations capable of demonstrating the cost/benefit and 'value-in-use' of the product; (3) maintaining a careful record of competitive pressures likely to affect sales; (4) demonstrating the selling company's ability and willingness to respond to problems and queries at all times; and (5) endeavouring to change the attitude of the prospect from Promiscuous to Phile. Success in doing so will form part of the salesman's performance appraisal system. Salesmen can be authorised to spend £x on entertaining members of the client's decision-making unit provided they have identified the most appropriate person and they can see a probability of a pay-off.

The Phobe/Large (Box 7) is a much more difficult customer to acquire and/or maintain. For some reason, known or unknown, it dislikes the supplying company to the point of phobia. It has large sales potential, but the amount of effort needed to convert the potential into results is probably prohibitive. This being so, the sales force should limit the time and effort it spends on such customers to: (1) maintaining a low-profile contact, if possible; (2) endeavouring to diagnose the real reasons for the current hostility and trying alternative solutions to any problems identified; (3) monitoring changes in the company's ownership or personnel that might affect future relationships; and (4) keeping vigilant for serious let-downs or exhausted-stock problems with other suppliers. In general, salesmen must refrain from spending too much time or money on such unproductive clients until a change in attitude can be discerned.

The Phile/Medium (Box 2) is a loyal customer with a fairly good potential sales turnover. It is likely to buy without excessive sales effort. In this case, the main selling task should consist of: (1) maintaining contact – no more than a few visits a year unless there are specific problems (strong telephone contact is preferred); (2) communicating details of all new developments – mostly by means of letters and/or personalised mail-shots. Lavish entertainment should be discouraged, but customers in this category should be invited to fairs, exhibitions and other public promotional events. They should also be given preference for gifts planned for anniversary celebrations and Christmas.

The Promiscuous/Medium (Box 5) is an awkward, fickle customer, but one whose business is not insignificant. Beware of wasting too much time on penetrating such accounts. The main objective must be to 'flirt' with them in a fairly low-key attempt to persuade them to mend their ways. More specifically, the selling task is to: (1) identify the motivations of the decision-making unit to find what incentive is likely to convert its members from 'promiscuity' to loyalty; (2) communicate at frequent intervals (although not through personal visits) the great benefits of using the company's products. Emphasis here is to be through mail-shots, telephone calls and literature. Correspondingly, entertainment expenses must be kept to an absolute minimum and should only be used in exceptional circumstances.

The Phobe/Medium (Box 8), on the other hand, is a hostile customer with only medium purchasing potential. There is little justification for wasting too much selling effort on it. The selling task is limited to: (1) trying to determine the reason for the company's hostility; (2) tracking and recording changes in the organisation that might alleviate the phobia; (3) if the hostility stems from past mistakes, ensuring that any corrective measures are brought to the notice of the client; and (4) maintaining an up-to-date client dossier.

Now take the Phile/Small (Box 3). Although its loyalty is appreciated, the seller cannot reciprocate by giving it too much non-productive selling time. The selling emphasis should rather be placed on: (1) organising an annual meeting to inform all the small Philes of developments in both the industry and the selling company (the meeting is a good opportunity for the small Philes and their friends in the sales force to demonstrate their mutual admiration); (2) maintaining frequent (and less costly) telephone contact; (3) ensuring that the restricted contact does not make the small and loyal customers feel unwanted. Happy communication can often be maintained through members of the sales administration team, which should be trained accordingly.

Promiscuous/Small companies (Box 6) should mostly be ignored. They are small customers who feel that their limited purchasing power is sufficiently attractive to make selling organisations fight hard for their business. The only exceptions to this rule are when: (1) there are indications that the firm is likely to become big in the near future; (2) the customer is part of a larger organisation that the selling company would like to penetrate. In all other cases, very little time should be allocated to them. When they decide to become more loyal, they will receive more attention and affection. Finally, Phobe/Small (Box 9): forget it! This customer is more trouble than he is worth. Allow him to indulge his phobias in happy isolation.

■ What Do We Want Our Salesmen and Women To Do?

Whatever the method used to organise the salesman's day, there is always comparatively little time available for selling. In these circumstances, it is vital that a company should know as precisely as possible what it wants its sales force to do. Sales force objectives can be either *quantitative* or *qualitative*.

■ Quantitative Objectives

The principal quantitative objectives are concerned with the following measures:

- How much to sell (the value of unit sales volume).
- What to sell (the mix of unit sales volume).
- Where to sell (the markets and the individual customers that will take the company towards its marketing objectives).
- The desired profit contribution (where relevant and where the company is organised to compute this).
- Selling costs (in compensation, expenses and supervision).

The first three types of objectives are derived directly from the marketing objectives, which were discussed in an earlier question, and constitute the principal components of the sales plan. There are many other kinds of quantitative objectives that can be set for the sales force; these are summarised overleaf.

- Number of point-of-sale displays organised.
- Number of letters written to prospects.
- Number of telephone calls to prospects.
- Number of reports turned or not turned in.
- Number of trade meetings held.
- Use of sales aids in presentations.
- Number of service calls made.
- Number of customer complaints.
- Safety record.
- Collections made.
- Training meetings conducted.
- Competitive activity reports.
- General market condition reports.

Qualitative Objectives

These can be a potential source of problems if sales managers try to assess the performance of the sales force along dimensions that include abstract terms such as 'loyalty', 'enthusiasm' and 'cooperation', since such terms are difficult to measure objectively. *In seeking qualitative measurements of performance, managers often resort to highly subjective interpretations that cause resentment and frustration amongst those being assessed.*

However, managers can set and measure qualitative objectives that actually relate to the performance of the sales force on the job. It is possible, for example, to assess the skill with which a person applies their product knowledge on the job, the skill with which the work is planned or the skill with which objectives are overcome by the representative during a sales interview. While still qualitative in nature, these measures relate to standards of performance understood and accepted by the sales force.

Given such standards, it is not too difficult for a competent field sales manager to identify deficiencies; to get agreement on them; to coach in skills and techniques; to build attitudes of professionalism; to show how to self-train; to determine which training requirements cannot be tackled in the field and to evaluate improvements in performance and the effect of any past training.

One consumer goods company with thirty field sales managers discovered that most of them were spending much of the day in their offices engaged in administrative work, most of it self-made. The company proceeded to take their offices away and insisted that the sales managers spend most of their time in the field training their sales representatives. To assist them in this task they provided training on how to appraise and improve salesmen's performance in the field. As a result, there was a dramatic increase in sales and consequently in the sales managers' own earnings. This quite rapidly overcame their resentment at losing their offices.

■ How Should We Manage Our Sales Force?

Sales force motivation has received a great deal of attention in recent times, largely as a result of the work undertaken by psychologists in other fields of management. It is now widely accepted that it is not enough to give someone a title and an office and expect to achieve good sales results. Effective leadership is as much 'follower-determined' as it is determined by management, and so we shall mention briefly some important factors that contribute to effective sales force management.

If a sales manager's job is to improve the performance of his or her sales force, and if performance is a function of incentives minus 'disincentives', then the more he can increase incentives and reduce disincentives the better will be performance. Research has shown that an important element of sales force motivation is a sense of doing a worthwhile job. In other words, desire for praise and recognition, the avoidance of boredom and monotony, the enhancement of self-image, freedom from fear and worry and the desire to belong to something believed to be worthwhile all contribute to enhanced performance.

However, remuneration will always be a most important determinant of motivation. This does not necessarily mean paying the most money, although clearly unless there are significant financial motivations within a company it is unlikely that people will stay. In drawing up a remuneration plan, which would normally include a basic salary plus some element for special effort such as bonus or commission, the following objectives should be considered:

- To attract and keep effective salesmen.
- To remain competitive.
- To reward salesmen in accordance with their individual performance.
- To provide a guaranteed income plus an orderly individual growth rate.
- To generate individual sales initiative.
- To encourage teamwork.
- To encourage the performance of essential non-selling tasks.
- To ensure that management can fairly administer and adjust compensation levels as a means of achieving sales objectives.

A central concept of sales force motivation is that the individual salesperson will exert more effort if he is led to concentrate on:

- *expectations* of accomplishing the sales objectives and
- *personal benefits* derived from accomplishing those objectives.

The theory of sales force motivation is known as the *path-goal* approach because it is based on the particular path the sales representative follows to a particular sales objective – and the particular goals associated with successfully travelling down that path. Representatives estimate the probability of success of travelling down various paths or sales approaches and estimate the probability that their superiors will recognise their goal accomplishments and will reward them accordingly. Stated less formally, the motivational functions of the sales manager consist of increasing personal pay-offs to sales representatives for work-goal attainment, making the path to these pay-offs easier to travel by clarifying it, reducing road-blocks and pitfalls and increasing the opportunities for personal satisfaction *en route*.

■ Preparing the Sales Plan

No two sales plans will contain precisely the same headings. However, some general guidelines can be given. The following is an example of setting objectives for an individual sales representative. Clearly, these objectives will be the logical result of the breaking-down of the marketing objectives into actual sales targets.

All companies set themselves overall objectives, which in turn imply the development of specific marketing objectives. In this chapter we have discussed personal selling in the context of overall marketing activity. This approach leads us to the following hierarchy of objectives: *corporate objectives*, *marketing objectives* and *sales objectives*, as outlined in Figure 15.3.

■ Summary

The benefits to sales force management of following the approach detailed in this chapter can be determined as:

- Coordination of corporate and marketing objectives with actual sales effort.
- Establishment of a circular relationship between corporate objectives and customer wants.
- Improvement of sales effectiveness through an understanding of the corporate and marketing implications of sales decisions.

The sales force is a vital but very expensive element of the marketing mix and as much care should be devoted to its management as to any other area of marketing management. This is most likely to be achieved if intuitive sense, which is associated with experience, can be combined with the kind of logical framework suggested in this chapter and in Table 15.1.

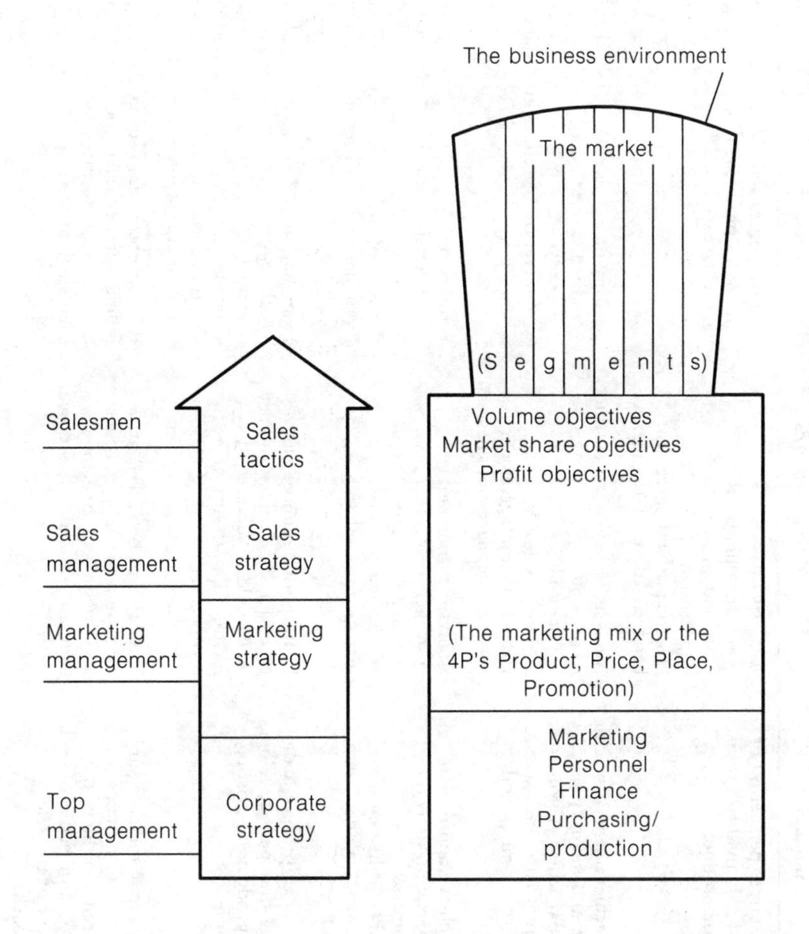

Figure 15.3 The link between corporate markets and sales objectives

Table 15.1 Setting objectives for an individual sales representative

Task	*Standard*	*How to set standards*	*How to measure performance*	*Performance shortfalls*
1. To achieve personal sales target.	Sales target per period of time for individual groups and/or products.	Analysis of – territory potential – individual customer's potential. Discussions and agreement between salesman and manager.	Comparison of individual salesman's product sales against targets.	Significant shortfall between target and achievement over a meaningful period.
2. To sell the required range and quantity to individual customers.	The achievement of specified range and quantity of sales to a particular customer or group of customers within an agreed time period.	Analysis of individual customer records of – potential – present sales. Discussion and agreement between manager and salesman.	Scrutiny of – individual customer records – observation of selling in the field.	Failure to achieve agreed objectives. Complacency with range of sales made to individual customers.
3. To plan journeys and call frequencies to achieve minimum practicable selling cost.	To achieve appropriate call frequency on individual customers. Number of live customer calls during a given time period.	Analysis of individual customer's potential. Analysis of order/call ratios. Discussion and agreement between manager and salesman.	Scrutiny of – individual customer records. Analysis of order/call ratio. Examination of call reports.	High ratio of calls to individual customer relative to that customer's yield. Shortfall on agreed total number of calls made over an agreed time period.
4. To acquire new customers.	Number of prospect calls during time period. Selling new products to existing customers.	Identify total number of potential and actual customers who could produce results. Identify opportunity areas for prospecting.	Examination of – call reports – records of new accounts opened – ratio of existing to potential customers.	Shortfall in number of prospect calls from agreed standard. Low ratio of existing to potential customers.
5. To make a sales approach of the required quality.	To exercise the necessary skills and techniques required to achieve the identified objective of each element of the sales approach.	Standards to be agreed in discussion between manager and salesman related to company standards laid down.	Regular observations of field selling using a systematic analysis of performance in each stage of the sales approach.	Failure to identify – objective of each stage of sales approach – specific areas of skill, weakness – use of support material.

CHAPTER 16

Marketing Channel Strategy

Channels of Distribution

Where our customers buy our products is logically determined by the outlets at which those products are made available. Typically, many companies will not give too much attention to the question of channel choice; it is not seen as being a variable in the marketing mix. More often than not the distribution channel will have taken its current form as a result of unplanned and haphazard development.

Such a disregard for this vital area of marketing discretion means that many opportunities for profitable market potential are passed over. For example, an international chemical company selling into Europe, using their own sales force to sell direct to customers, found that by using a chemical merchant, or middleman, they could reduce their own sales costs and take advantage of a ready-made sales organisation with a host of local contacts.

Another company, a British shoe manufacturer producing good quality shoes, found it possible to open up a new and profitable market segment in the catalogue of a national mail-order firm. This gave the company the facility to reach a wider audience without compromising on its traditional channels – upmarket, speciality shoe shops.

Another British company, a carpet manufacturer, was perplexed by its falling sales even though total carpet sales in the UK remained at a high level. It was felt that somehow the quality or the pricing must be wrong to achieve the poor results they were getting. In fact, a deeper examination of the company situation showed that it had continued to sell through the small, traditional High Street carpet shops. The new growth outlets were the edge-of-town carpet warehouses, often selling at a discount. These now accounted for the lion's share of carpet sales and the manufacturer had missed a wonderful opportunity by failing to recognise the change in distribution patterns.

These three examples demonstrate the benefits of taking a fresh look at marketing channels. They each involved a reappraisal of the route by which the customer acquired the product and a comparison of the costs and benefits of the alternative options.

Many companies do not rely on a single channel of distribution but prefer instead to use multiple channels. They may choose different channels to reach each different market segment, or alternatively they may approach a single market via a dual distribution channel. Whatever the situation, it is a necessary and valuable exercise to weigh up the costs and benefits accruing through the use of specific channels of distribution. As Figure 16.1 shows, each channel can have distinctly different costs and revenue profiles.

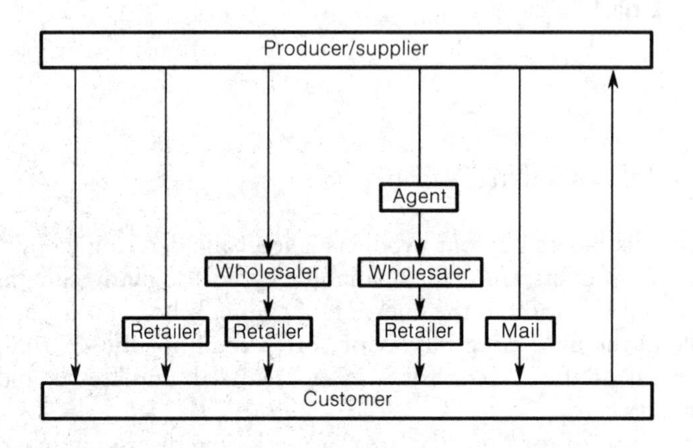

Figure 16.1 Alternative channels of distribution

The range of options here are not unlike those faced by Fruit Farms Ltd which will be described in Chapter 17. The company can distribute direct to the customer, work through one or more intermediaries, reach the customer by mail or even, in some instances, have the customer come to the factory to purchase and take away the product.

The channel decision has to be undertaken in the widest possible context. It needs to consider questions about the company's overall marketing strategy, the appropriateness of the channel to the product and its image, and customer requirements and preferences. These can be every bit as important as the comparative costs of selling and distribution.

Choosing the Channel

The underlying purpose of the marketing channel is to reach the customer in the most appropriate way. Whilst the requirements of the customer might vary from market to market, it is possible to generalise customer objectives relating to the decision of where to buy the product.

Price/Value

This dimension is present to a greater or lesser extent in all markets. It implies that the customer is seeking a certain level of value or utility from the product or service, but there is an implicit trade-off between that value and the price charged. In this way shoppers in the UK have a wide choice before them. At one end of the spectrum they can buy their groceries at Harrods; at the other end they can choose the no-frills approach of Kwik-Save or Price-Rite.

In industrial service markets the same principles of price/value optimisation apply; the only difference is that professional buyers are likely to use formalised evaluation techniques, such as *value analysis* to help them to reach their purchase decision.

■ Convenience/Availability

It has long been recognised that these factors can play a key role in competitive markets. For example, in the UK, estate agents, who traditionally played the role of a 'marriage broker' between seller and buyer, now offer a complete range of ancillary services. The prospective property buyer can now literally complete his transaction by convenient 'one-stop shopping'. The recognition of this simple truth has led to many major financial service companies buying into estate agencies as distribution outlets for their products.

On the industrial front, manufacturers of high-density polyurethane foam plastic, which is used extensively in furniture upholstery, often set up plants where there is a high concentration of furniture manufacturers. Not only does this reduce the high transport costs of shipping 'bubbles of air' around the country, which would be the case if they were to move blocks of plastic foam great distances, but it also virtually guarantees supplies 'on tap' for the furniture companies.

■ Company Objectives

The selection of marketing channels must fit the requirements and capabilities of the company in addition to meeting the objectives of the customer. Essentially, we can look at two major aspects of the firm's viewpoint on its channel decision: the *market* and *institutional considerations*.

Here is an example of how market considerations might influence the choice of channel. Suppose we were marketing financial services to individuals in the high tax bracket. It would not be appropriate to set up a network of door-to-door salesmen and women. Instead we would be likely to choose an indirect channel of distribution that might rely upon intermediaries such as accountants and bank managers to connect us with our target customers. Clearly we would also be faced with making decisions regarding geographical coverage and penetration of our market, but these decisions are far less difficult to make once we are clear about our distribution channels.

Institutionally, we should be concerned with issues such as image and appropriateness of the channel. For example, if we produced top-quality goods with a somewhat élitist image, then we will be obliged to seek distribution channels that are consistent with this image. It would be counterproductive to do anything less.

Marketing Strategies

Let us consider the simple distribution channel shown below:

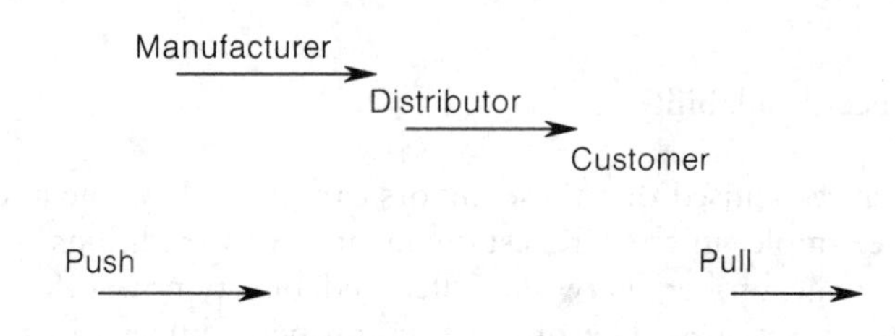

The manufacturer has two main marketing strategies open to him if he wants to maximise the flow of his goods through the channel.

1. *Push strategy*: here the manufacturer focuses his attention on the distributor and uses an armoury of different approaches to 'sell-in' more of his products. He might use his field sales force, advertising and special promotions aimed at the distributor and his special incentive schemes. The use of 'trade marketing', whereby the manufacturer works closely with the distributor in developing joint marketing programmes, has become widespread in recent years.

2. *Pull strategy*: here the focus of attention is the customer, and the objective of the strategy is to stimulate the level of demand so that the distributor is encouraged to stock the product. Marketing techniques used could include TV advertising, national press advertising and promotions, and in-store demonstrations and exhibitions.

In practice, most manufacturers would probably use a combination of push and pull strategies consistent with their marketing objectives and their capabilities.

Working with Intermediaries

One of the problems with indirect marketing channels – that is, those which involve intermediaries – is that they generally lead to a loss of close contact with the market place and some loss of control over key areas such as customer service policy. Also, by implication, there is a loss of margin for the firm in that intermediaries absorb some of the margin that otherwise could have been available to either the company or the customer.

On the other hand, intermediaries are often the only means of providing wider distribution without incurring the considerable costs of maintaining a direct marketing channel. The middleman performs a very necessary function in many markets by consolidating what might be many small shipments, comprising the products of several producers, to multiple customers. This important role is illustrated in Figure 16.2.

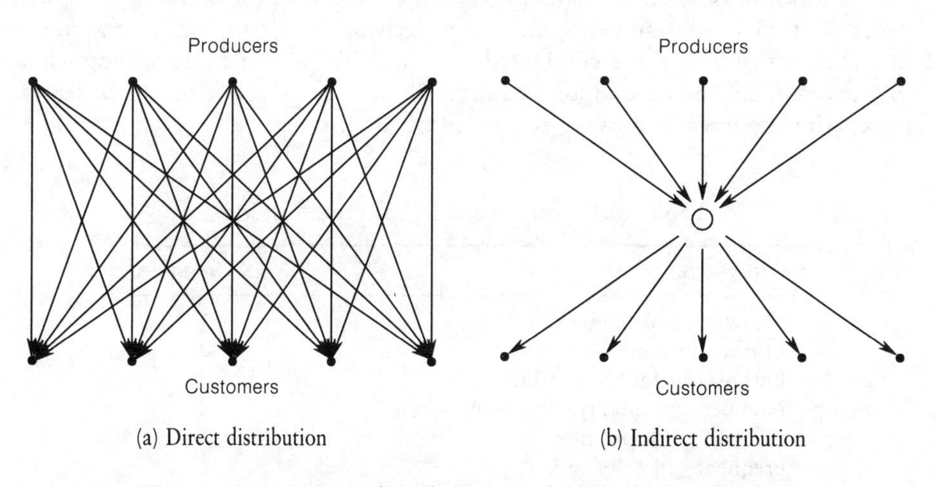

Figure 16.2 Direct distribution and indirect distribution. Direct and indirect modes of shipments

Figure 16.2(a) represents a 'nightmare' in terms of transport costs alone, regardless of the additional administrative costs for handling a multitude of paperwork. In contrast, Figure 16.2(b) provides a more economic model. Moreover, the intermediary can often generate extra sales. He could, for example, be an electrical wholesaler who buys in cable of all types and ratings, plugs and sockets, electrical fittings, tools and accessories – everything in fact, that the local electrical contractors could require. When the customer orders he specifies a job lot – the requirements to rewire a row of houses, for example – and the wholesaler assembles this 'package'. In doing so he adds value. This is the concept of a 'value-added distributor'. Another example would be an office furnishings distributor who buys in cupboards and desks as 'flat-pack' units and assembles them before delivery to his customers. Clearly the manufacturer is saved the costs of running an assembly department and he can ship flat-packs far more economically than he could assembled furniture. By taking over assembly functions and reducing transport costs the intermediary can justify a larger margin on his transactions with the manufacturer.

The intermediary is not always a wholesaler, and sometimes this function is performed by a distribution service company. Such specialist companies, for example NFC and TNT in the UK and Europe, will provide the means of gaining the benefits of large-scale distribution at a fraction of the cost of going it alone.

Selecting an Intermediary

For many companies this could prove to be one of the most important decisions they will ever make. Without doubt, an efficient and motivated intermediary can be a priceless asset; a lacklustre also-ran could ruin the company. A wide range of factors could influence the choice decision. Table 16.1 shows the result of a recent survey that was conducted in a sample of UK firms, regarding what influenced their choice of intermediary. These factors are listed in order of rank, with the most important at the top of the list.

Table 16.1 Intermediary selection criteria

Criteria	*UK ranking*
Knowledge of the market	1
Market coverage	2
Enthusiasm for the product	3
Number and quality of sales personnel	4
Knowledge of product	5
Frequency of sales calls	6
Previous success/track record	7
Costs involved	8
Extent of dealing with competitors	9
Service and stocking facilities	10
Quality of service staff	11
Executive's career history	12

Clearly, these results underline the fact that many of the key selection criteria relate to the intermediaries' marketing expertise and strength 'on the ground'. However, others would add the following considerations to this list and suggest that they should also figure in any selection process:

- Is the intermediary creditworthy?
- Does he create the right image?
- Are his policies regarding inventory and customer service compatible with ours?
- Are his total promotion activities and budgets what we would expect for success?
- Is his location consistent with our overall distribution strategy?

And perhaps the most important of all:

- Is he someone we can trust and with whom we could develop a good working relationship?

If the answer to the last question is negative then all the other criteria are largely redundant, because the secret of success is to select intermediaries who in effect become business partners. Implicit in this is that the relationship between the parties be conducted in an open and mature manner.

■ Relationships with Intermediaries

At a recent company conference, to which, for the first time, a manufacturer's overseas agents had been invited, discussion focused on communications. It is sad to report that the agents, to a man, claimed that the only time they ever had a visit from representatives of the British company was 'when things went wrong'. Not only that, they also felt that they were kept 'in the dark' regarding future plans and new products.

The company in question was to be commended for taking such a bold step in organising this conference as a means of integrating the agents more fully into the organisation. Before they could begin to improve relationships they had to discover how they were perceived by the agents. The impression created by the company was not what they intended and, by seeming to focus on negative parts of the relationship, they had caused the agents to develop a defensive attitude. Instead of trust, they had bred distrust.

The conference did in fact provide both the company and the agents with the opportunity to bring many issues into the open and to work through them amicably. Indeed, the event proved to be a watershed in the company's relationship with its overseas representatives.

So how can a company build a good relationship with an intermediary? Here are some tried and tested suggestions:

- *Understand the distributor's needs and problems* : this means getting out and talking to them, and not just when things go wrong. One company insists that its own sales representatives spend a set number of days 'working on the counter' in the distributors.
- *Learn from distributors' experiences*: monitor and feed back the information about common problems, market information, current trends and so on.
- *Conduct market research studies*: get distributors to provide annual appraisals of the service you provide them with and make recommendations about improvements. Alternatively, conduct customer surveys and share results with distributors to enable them to increase sales.
- *Create a distributor panel*: have a small group of specially selected distributors meet at regular intervals to use as a sounding board for future policies and to get feedback on current issues.
- *Involve distributors in inputs to company's marketing plan*: this is likely to get them committed to those parts of the plan that make an impact upon distribution.

- *Establish two-way communications* – at many different levels, for example director to director, salesman to salesman, clerk to clerk.
- *Demonstrate commitment to distributor*: refer customer enquiries and requests to the distributor and don't open up competing distributorships in his territory.

■ Effectiveness of Channel Intermediaries

Since the success of the manufacturer is heavily dependent on the effective performance of the intermediary, it is necessary to have a general framework against which to assess performance. In recent years the concept of *performance auditing* of distributors has been increasingly used by marketers. One way of doing this is to monitor outlets on a day-to-day basis, keeping check of their sales, either in total or through the range. This information can be useful as a rough control mechanism for management, but a detailed performance audit will go further than this. Some of the elements that should be reviewed are as follows:

- Sales performance:
  - Current sales compared with historical sales.
  - Sales compared with other channel members.
  - Sales compared with target sales.
  - Sales growth trends.
- Inventory maintenance:
  - Levels compared with contractual (if any) arrangements.
  - Levels through the range.
  - Levels compared with market trends.
  - Number of 'stock-out' situations.
  - Levels of competing stocks.
  - Condition of inventory and facilities.
  - Old stock on hand/attempts to shift it.
  - Stockkeeping records/control efficiency.
- Attitude:
  - Enthusiasm/motivation of staff.
  - General housekeeping.
  - Displays of products/sales material.
  - Number of suggestions/queries initiated by distributor.
- Competition:
  - Competition from other intermediaries compared with sales figures.
  - Competition from other product lines stocked by intermediary.
- General growth prospects:
  - Does track record indicate future growth? In pace with that projected for region, trade area, etc?
  - How does current performance compare with local yardsticks?
  - Is intermediary's organisation expanding/shrinking? Why?

- What record of investment in his business does intermediary have?
- What are the qualifications/experience of his staff?
- What continuity is likely? For example, through management succession plans and health of key staff members.
- What evidence of adaptability to change?
- What are the intermediary's own business plans? How does he see the future outlook?

Having developed a set of criteria such as these, it ought to be possible to evaluate the performance and longer-term prospects of any distributor. More accurate assessment, for comparative purposes, can be attained by weighting the individual criteria according to their importance. Also 'point-scoring' techniques can be used in conjunction with the weighting if they serve a clear purpose.

The performance audit not only provides the marketer with valuable information about the current effectiveness of the distribution channel, but it also establishes the basis upon which a distributor development strategy can be formed.

Dealer Development Strategy

Too often a manufacturer sees himself as *selling to* rather than *selling through* the intermediary. No small wonder then that, with this perception, manufacturers are frequently dissatisfied with distributor performance.

Four areas have been identified as being sources and symptoms of problems common amongst various types of intermediaries. These should be closely monitored by the manufacturer, and are as follows:

- *Diversification*: the intermediary is spreading his limited resources over too wide a range of products or markets.
- *Capitalisation*: there is inadequate funding/cash flow to sustain the business unless tough management decisions are made.
- *Market Share*: falling market share can be a valuable pointer to the fact that the intermediary is failing to be competitive.
- *Attitude*: how positive is the attitude of the intermediary to our company and its products?

In addition, field sales personnel should monitor the dealer's performance in:

- Financial management
- Sales personnel training
- Planning
- Network management
- Market development
- Sales management

It is in these areas that huge strides can be made in terms of dealer development. However, few manufacturers have a sales force of sufficient calibre to play this role, either to identify needs or to provide business counselling.

Some enlightened manufacturers have set up separate specialist teams of advisers to fulfil the dealer development role, thereby overcoming what might be seen in some quarters as a dilution of the field sales activity. The results stemming from this type of investment indicate that distributors become more flexible, adaptive and successful, thus safeguarding the manufacturer's longer-term strategic interests. In addition, considerable goodwill can be generated by this approach to dealer development.

It must be remembered that dealer development can be costly, and the decisions regarding the depth and breadth of such improvement activities should not be taken lightly. However, there is an alternative approach to securing more effective control of a distribution channel and this is through a process called *vertical integration.*

■ Vertical Integration

This is a common phenomenon in marketing channels. Such integration could involve a company merging with or absorbing those firms who are its sources of supply (*backward integration*), or taking similar steps to gain control of those intermediaries closer to its markets (*forward integration*). Such a movement, either forward or backward, can sometimes be accomplished without taking over the ownership of the firms involved.

For example, Marks & Spencer, the retail organisation in the UK, can, through its massive buying power, exert considerable control over its suppliers. When you sell 100 per cent of your output to one customer, you are to all intents and purposes owned by them. The motor-car industry has a similar relationship with some of its component suppliers.

Even where integration through ownership or control does not exist, institutional pressures within the channel can be considerable. Who should hold the inventory? In what quantities? How should the available margin be split? Can intermediaries lower down the chain be relied upon to follow through on the desired marketing strategy and promotional plans? The possibilities for conflict are considerable, and prospects are very much enhanced if each level of the channel attempts to maximise its own return. In situations like this, maximisation of one's return can only be achieved at the expense of others.

Conflict, and the resulting likelihood of a reduced return being experienced by all, can to a large extent be eliminated if someone within the distribution chain exercises a leadership role. It can therefore be in the manufacturer's interest to set out deliberately to take the initiative and strive for channel leadership, thereby bringing a sense of order and fairness to what could be a volatile and mutually destructive situation. However, leadership can only be sustained if the manufacturer can back up his stance with economic power, or with a unique, highly desirable product that is in great demand.

It is quite conceivable that channel leadership can pass to anyone else in the chain. The example of Marks & Spencer mentioned above demonstrates how a retailer can take the leadership role. Similarly wholesalers, distributors or agents can, if they exploit their power according to their circumstances, influence the channel 'politics' to their advantage.

■ Summary

Getting products or services to the market is a regulated dimension of the marketing mix. It is vital for the success of the company that customers should have access to the product or service through channels that meet their requirements as well as the company's.

Development relationships with channel intermediaries based on partnership can be a powerful means of building competitive advantage. The aim should be to develop marketing programmes that are attractive to all members of the distribution channel and not just to end users.

CHAPTER 17

Distribution and Logistics Strategy

Distribution and the Marketing Mix

Making sure that products reach customers cannot be regarded by marketing managers as simply the concern of someone else. The distribution activity is as much part of the company's marketing mix as are product, pricing and promotion decisions. In fact in some markets, the impact of the distribution element on sales can exceed that of the other mix elements. Seen in this light, the means whereby the product reaches the customer assumes a vital importance in marketing strategy. The implications of this view of distribution's marketing role are therefore far-reaching, and can involve a considerable reappraisal of attitudes as well as of the means of distribution used. Moreover, as studies have estimated that the average European manufacturing company spends 15 per cent of its sales revenue on distribution-related activities, it is not difficult to contemplate the benefits of such a reappraisal.

Although *place* is a convenient shorthand description used to define one of the quartet of 'P's' that go to make up the marketing mix, it represents the means whereby the needs of the market and the offering of the company are physically matched. As such it provides the addition of time- and place-utility to the product. Without this added value the product is worthless.

An Overview

Many of the issues we need to address as marketers can be demonstrated by considering the following example.

Fruit Farms Ltd is a small company based in the South Midlands that grows and sells its fruit produce. In getting its fruit to the customer it has a number of quite different options. It can:

- Advertise and get people to come and pick their own fruit;
- Sell the produce at its own farm shop.
- Sell to local fruiterers.
- Sell to supermarket chains.
- Sell to local restaurants and hotels.
- Sell to manufacturers of, for example, jams, pies, or frozen foods.

- Transform its product into jams, pies or frozen packs and sell these direct through retail outlets and mail order catalogues.
- Use a combination of some of the above.

Which is the best distribution channel to select? The short and easy answer is the one which helps to make the business most profitable – but which one would that be?

- If the company wanted to keep its costs down it could let customers pick their own fruit. Would it sell enough?

If it sold through intermediaries it would then have to provide them with a profit margin and this could represent lost profits for the company. Then again, it would cost money to staff and run its own farm shop.

If it sold to local restaurants and hotels would it have to deliver, or would they collect? More cost considerations.

If it sold to supermarkets then it would have to package the fruit in their containers and to their standards. Could it do this? At what cost?

If it sold to manufacturers it could sell in bulk orders, but they would probably demand a lower unit price – so would the company be better off?

As we can see, it is easier to come up with the questions than it is the answers.

As more and more companies take a new look at the role of distribution in their marketing effort they also are coming to similar conclusions. While there is considerable scope for profit enhancement through distribution improvement, it isn't always immediately obvious where to make the improvements. Nor is it always a cost-saving benefit that pays off. Sometimes profitability can be improved by spending more on some aspects of distribution, rather than less.

For example, Rank Xerox has found that it pays to ship high-value spares to European customers by air express, rather than by less expensive surface transport. Although some savings are made on packaging and insurance, the main benefit is that faster deliveries mean lower inventory carrying costs for goods in transit. In addition, this means that customers can be involved more quickly, which has the effect of improving cash flow and, of course, enhancing service levels to customers.

This example shows how important it is for the marketer to have an overview of the whole distribution process and not to see it merely as a means of transporting the product from A to B in the cheapest possible way. Indeed, in many companies the marketing department is seen to be responsible only for demand *creation* rather than demand *satisfaction*. The costs of distribution are often pushed into someone else's cost centre. Not surprisingly in such circumstances, it becomes exceedingly difficult to achieve a situation in which marketing and distribution work closely together.

To overcome these problems of compartmentalisation of the company's effort, a new integrative approach to marketing and distribution has been introduced.

■ The Logistics Concept

The emphasis behind this approach is to view the movement of products, as they pass through the manufacturing process and eventually to the customer, as a total system. Thus instead of marketing, production, distribution and purchasing – all working away oblivious to the others and each trying to optimise their individual efforts – the logistics concept suggests that it may be necessary for some or all of these areas to operate suboptimally in order that the whole system may be more effective.

So, for example, the marketing manager might have to be prepared to accept a lower level of customer service than he would like; or alternatively the production manager might have to schedule shorter runs with more frequent tool changes if the overall effectiveness of the system is to be maximised.

In practice there are five areas of concern that have to be addressed in logistics management. These key decision areas constitute the logistics mix.

■ Logistics Mix

This comprises *facility*, *inventory*, *communication*, *unitisation* and *transport decisions*. Let us look at each of these decision areas in turn.

□ *Facility Decisions*

These are concerned with how many warehouses and plants we should have, and with where they should be located in order to optimise the customer service/cost equation. For a majority of companies it is necessary to take the location of existing facilities as a *fait accompli* in the short term. However, taking a longer-term perspective, companies often have alternative options and opportunities opening up from them regarding how they plan their facilities.

□ *Inventory Decisions*

The cost of holding stock can be a major element in many companies' total distribution costs. Decisions about how much stock to hold, where to hold it and what quantities to order therefore become vital in the logistics mix. Inventory levels, as we shall see later, are also instrumental in determining the level of service that a company can offer its customers.

□ *Communication Decisions*

Logistics is not only about the flow of materials or products through the distribution system; it is also about the efficient flow of information. Here we are concerned with the order-processing system, the invoicing system and the demand forecasting system. Without effective communications support the logistics system will never be capable of sustaining a satisfactory customer service at an acceptable cost.

□ *'Unitisation' Decisions*

The way in which goods are individually packaged and then subsequently assembled in larger batches can have a major bearing on logistics economics. For example, two competing companies made fertiliser for sale to farmers. Traditionally the product was supplied in plastic sacks, but farmers found these to be very labour-intensive to load, unload and transport around their farms. Company A responded to the farmers' criticism by supplying multiple bags on wooden pallets which, incidentally, reduced their own handling costs in their factory and warehouses. Company B responded by packaging the fertiliser in a 'Jumbo Bag', equivalent to many ordinary sacks. A key feature of this giant bag was the provision of a loop that enabled it to be carried by a hook on a tractor arm.

Company B increased its sales because its new bulk packaging could be easily handled by farmers with tractors; in contrast fewer farmers had fork-lift trucks to handle the pallets of Company A. Moreover, fork-lift trucks with heavy loads could be unstable on uneven terrain, and the farm environment was very different from the flat concrete floors of the factory and warehouse.

□ *Transport Decisions*

These are the decisions surrounding the transport function of the company. They are likely to be concerned about such issues as: 'What mode of transport should be used? Should we use our own vehicles or use an outside contractor? How should we route our deliveries? How frequently should we deliver?'

Of the five decision areas, the transport decision has received perhaps the greatest attention in most companies, in that it is one of the more obvious facets of the distribution task. Certainly in recent years there have been many changes in this area, some of which are just gathering momentum. One of the most significant has been the growth of the specialist carrier, to replace the company's own transport service. However, we must remember that, taken in the total logistics context, transport might only account for a small proportion of the total costs.

Together, these five areas constitute the total costs of distribution within a company. Furthermore, it is frequently the case that a decision made in one area will have an effect on the other four. Thus it may be that a decision to open or close a depot will affect transport costs (longer or shorter travelling distances), inventory (stock levels at factory and other depots have to change) and possibly data-processing costs (for installing and operating new system requirements).

This is the idea of a *cost trade-off*. Managing the logistics function involves a continuous search for such trade-offs, the intention being to secure a reduction in total costs by changing the cost structure in one or more areas. Alternatively, investment in one of the logistic decision areas might be vindicated if it can be shown to differentiate the product from its competitors in a way that can bring increased sales revenue or improve the market share through better service.

The Service-Level Decision

One of the fundamental cost trade-offs in logistics that has an impact upon marketing performance is the question of *service levels*. The level of service is a measure of the extent to which the organisation plans to make the product available and to support it in use, for example with the provision of after-sales service.

The simplest measure of service is stock availability, usually measured as the percentage of demand that can be met from stock. Clearly there is more to service than this, as we shall explore in Chapter 19. However, it can be regarded as the foundation of the service 'package'.

Naturally the customer seeks maximum availability and the company will normally endeavour to supply it. However, the problem is that as we increase the planned level of availability, the necessary investment in inventory rises more than proportionately. Figure 17.1 highlights the relationship between inventory and service levels.

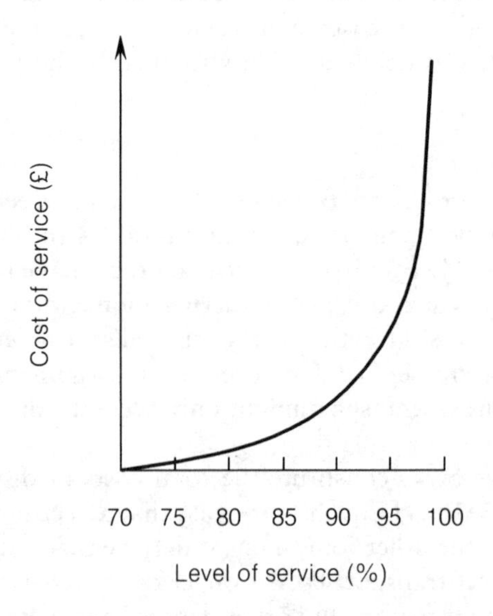

Figure 17.1 The cost of 'availability'

The reason the curve rises so steeply as the planned level of availability increases is that, even though the chance of running out of stock may be remote, additional safety stock must be held to cater for that possibility.

Many companies frequently underestimate the true costs of holding stock. It is a fair estimate to account for a 25 per cent per annum holding cost for inventory (that is, 25 per cent of the book value of stock) if we include the cost of capital, storage, obsolescence and insurance. Since most medium-to-large organisations carry millions of pounds of stock at any time, the annual cost at 25 per cent is clearly substantial.

The trade-off that has to be considered, therefore, is: 'What is the cost of holding stock compared with the cost of running out?' If stock runs out too frequently the outcome can be a substantial fall in sales revenue. At best, the company will forfeit the immediate contribution to its cash flow, whilst at the same time incurring some degree of customer hostility. At worst, the customer will not delay his purchase but will buy from a competitor instead. Clearly the cost of running out of stock will vary from product to product and will to some extent be dependent upon the nature and availability of competing products.

Poor stock availability also antagonises channel intermediaries. In a recent survey carried out in the USA, it was estimated that if a supplier decreased his stock availability by 5 per cent, nearly a quarter of intermediaries indicated they would purchase elsewhere. Oblivious of this reaction, supplying companies estimated that such a reduction of service would at worst lose them 'only about 9 per cent' of their outlets!

■ Establishing the Profit Consequences of a Running Out of Stock

Because we are dealing with aspects of human behaviour as well as economics when faced with an out-of-stock situation, there is no precise way of measuring the impact on profit. Instead we have to evaluate the probabilities of stock-exhaustion consequences, estimate the frequency at which each of these consequences is likely to occur and make a weighted judgement about the financial consequences. Below is an example of how this might be done:

Consequence of service	*Failure profit penalty*
• Loss of sale to competitor	• Gross margin of item
• Customer re-ordering	• Order-processing cost
• Loss of sale on related items	• Gross margin on all items
• Shipment of goods from other depots	• Expediting and transport cost
• Expediting of rush orders at factory	• Non-standard procedure cost
• Customer's ill-will	• Possible lost customer

Ideally, a market experiment should be conducted to measure more precisely the effect of non-availability on market share. There have been a number of reported studies that suggest that over a certain range of service improvement there can be a significant impact on sales. However, once a certain 'saturation' level is reached – the customer may find it difficult to distinguish between small improvements in stock availability. Thus, as in Figure 17.2, it is suggested that there comes a point where diminishing returns to service improvement are encountered.

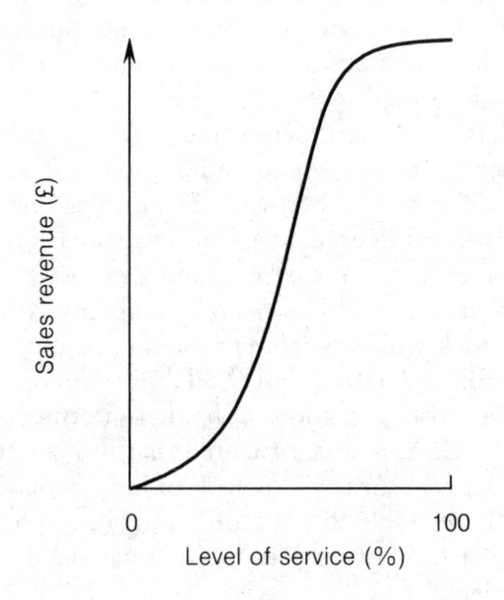

Figure 17.2 The market response to service

The task of marketing management when seeking to develop appropriate levels of stock availability is to balance the known cost of service against the estimated market response. Figure 17.3 depicts the basic trade-off between the cost function and the response function.

Bringing the Logistics Mix Together

One of the major problems with conventional approaches to distribution is that responsibility for it is spread over too many discrete functional areas; that is, there is a high degree of 'compartmentalisation'.

In one engineering company, responsibility for stock levels throughout the system was in the hands of the production department. Yet, *at the same time*, the purchasing manager was pursuing policies that conflicted with the production policy and the distribution manager operated an inflexible delivery system. Little wonder the marketing manager was driven to despair by the erratic service levels customers received.

The acceptance of an integrated systems-based approach lies at the very heart of the logistics concept. This, together with the recognition that the

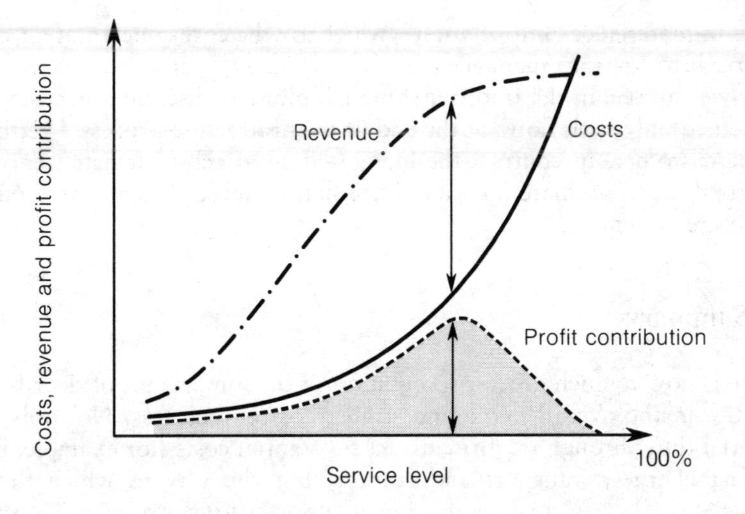

Figure 17.3 The cost/benefit of service

interrelationship of the component parts of the mix makes them mutually dependent, should be the cornerstone of the marketer's philosophy.

Somehow the distribution planner must unite the interlinked subsystems that together form the company. With his logistics orientation he must be concerned with the flow of materials through the whole business process, from raw material through to the finished goods shipped to the customer. Figure 17.4 brings together those aspects of the company's operations involving flows –

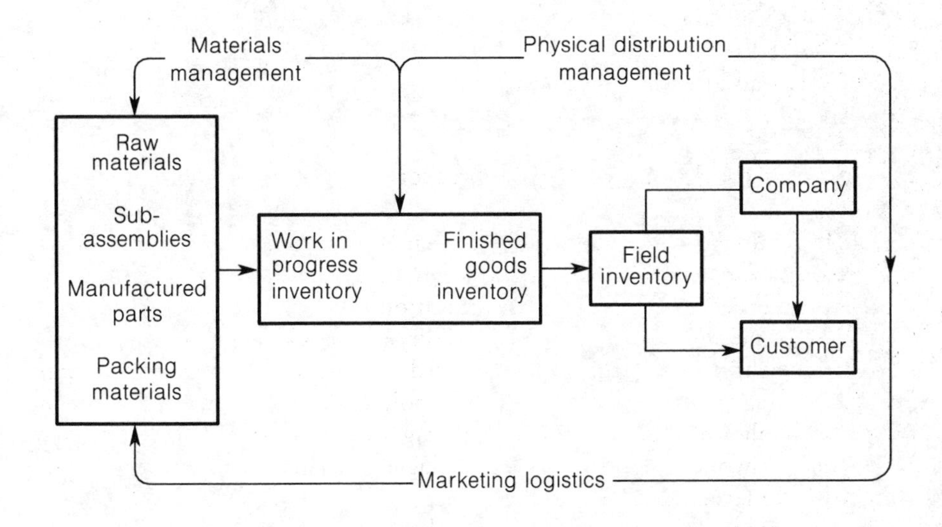

Figure 17.4 The logistics systems concept

either of materials or information – which are the core concern of an integrated approach to logistics management.

As we can see, in the traditional model, physical distribution management is concerned only with flows at the end of the production process – getting goods to the customer. In contrast the integrated approach to logistics encompasses the total flow of materials and information into, through and out of the corporate system.

■ Summary

There is now a much greater recognition of the importance of distribution and logistics in the overall marketing strategy of the business. Not only does the material flow through the firm attract substantial costs (for example, inventory holding charges, transport and storage) but the way in which the flow is managed can have a considerable impact upon customer service. Thus there is a need for a complex trade-off between the costs and benefits attached to different market strategies.

CHAPTER 18

Customer Retention Strategies

It has been suggested that it costs up to five times as much to win a new customer as it does to retain an existing customer. The costs of capturing market share are not always easy to gauge, but there are many companies who now regret earlier strategies based upon the blind pursuit of volume. Whilst there is strong evidence for the link between market share and profitability there is equally strong evidence to show that it is the *quality* of that market share that counts. In other words, does our customer base comprise, in the main, long-established, loyal customers or is there a high degree of turnover or 'churn'? If the latter is the case then the chances are that we are not as profitable as we might be.

The international consulting company, Bain & Company, has suggested that even a relatively small improvement in the customer retention rate (measured as the percentage of retained business from one period to another) can have a marked impact upon profitability. They suggest that, on average, an improvement of five percentage points in customer retention can lead to profit improvements of between 25 per cent and 85 per cent in the net present value of the future flow of earnings.

Why should a retained customer be more profitable than a new one? Firstly, because of the costs of acquiring new business in the first place, it might take time to bring a new customer into profit. Secondly, the more satisfied customers are with the relationship the more likely they are to place a bigger proportion of their total purchase with us, even to the extent of 'single sourcing' from us. Thirdly, these retained customers become easier to sell to, with consequent lower costs; also they are more likely to be willing to integrate their systems (for example their planning, scheduling and ordering systems) with ours, leading to further cost reductions. In some markets satisfied customers may also refer others to us, leading to a further enhancement of profitability. Finally, Bain and Company suggested that loyal customers are often less price sensitive and less inclined to switch suppliers because of price rises.

All of these elements combine to lead to the conclusion that retained customers generate considerably more profit than new ones. Figure 18.1 summarises this relationship.

A study of the North American car industry suggested that a satisfied customer is likely to stay with the same supplier for a further twelve years after the first satisfactory purchase, and during that period will buy four more cars of

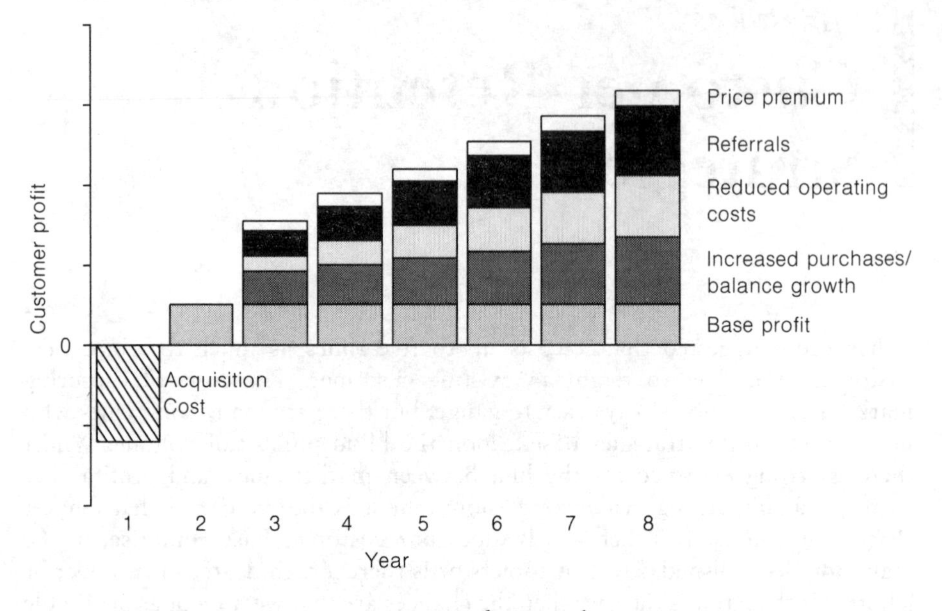

Figure 18.1 Customer profit contribution over time

the same make. It is estimated that, to a car manufacturer, this level of customer retention is worth $400 million in new car sales annually.

There is a direct linkage between the customer retention rate and the average lifetime of a customer. For example, if the customer retention rate is 90 per cent per annum (meaning that we lose 10 per cent of our existing customer base each year) then the average customer lifetime will be ten years. If, on the other hand, we manage to improve the retention rate to 95 per cent per annum (meaning that we lose 5 per cent of our customers each year) then the average customer life will be twenty years. In other words a doubling of the average customer life is achieved for a relatively small improvement in the retention rate. Figure 18.2 illustrates the relationship between the retention rate and the customer lifetime.

An important statistic that is not always measured is the *lifetime value of a customer*. Put very simply, this is a measure of the financial worth to the organisation of a retained customer. If customers are loyal and continue to spend money with us into the future then clearly their lifetime value is greater than that of a customer who buys only once or twice then switches to another brand or supplier.

Measuring the lifetime value of a customer requires an estimation of the likely cash flow to be provided by that customer if he or she achieves an average loyalty level. In other words, if a typical account lasts for ten years then we need to calculate the net present value of the profits that would flow from that customer over ten years. We are now in a position to calculate the impact that increasing the retention rate of customers will have upon profitability, and also

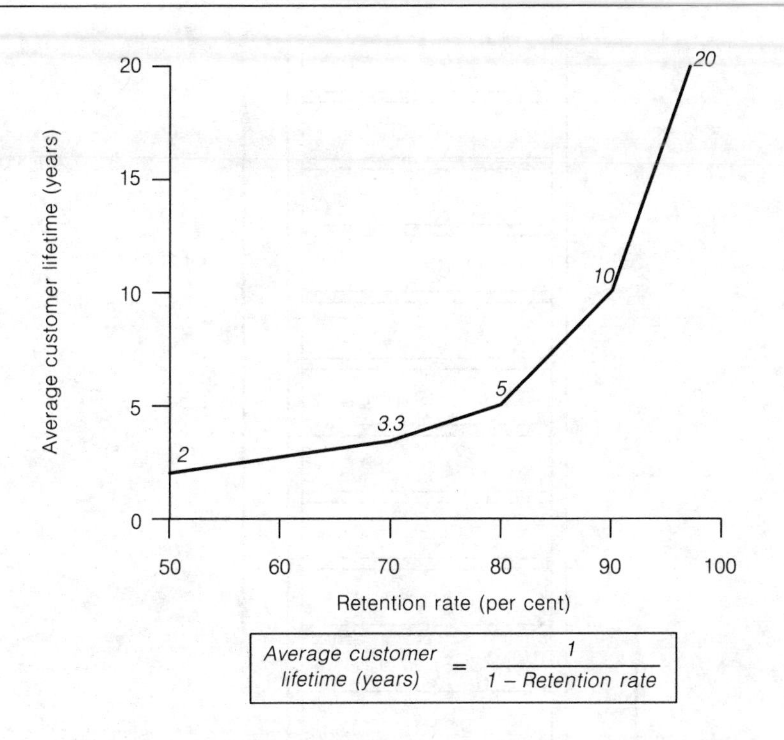

Figure 18.2 Impact of customer retention rate on customer lifetime

what the effect of extending the customer lifetime by a given amount will be. This information provides a good basis for marketing investment decision making; in other words, how much is it worth spending, either to improve the retention rate or to extend the life of a customer relationship?

The Ladder of Loyalty

It will be apparent from the previous comments that customer loyalty must become one of the principal objectives of marketing strategy. Customer loyalty is defined as a commitment to continue to do business with a company on an on-going basis. In other words we are seeking to create *committed* customers, not customers who are 'locked in'. A customer who is locked in is a 'prisoner' and is unlikely to stay with us if an alternative supplier makes a satisfactory offer.

To help us in the development of customer-loyalty building strategies it is useful to think in terms of a supplier taking a customer up a 'ladder of loyalty' (Figure 18.3).

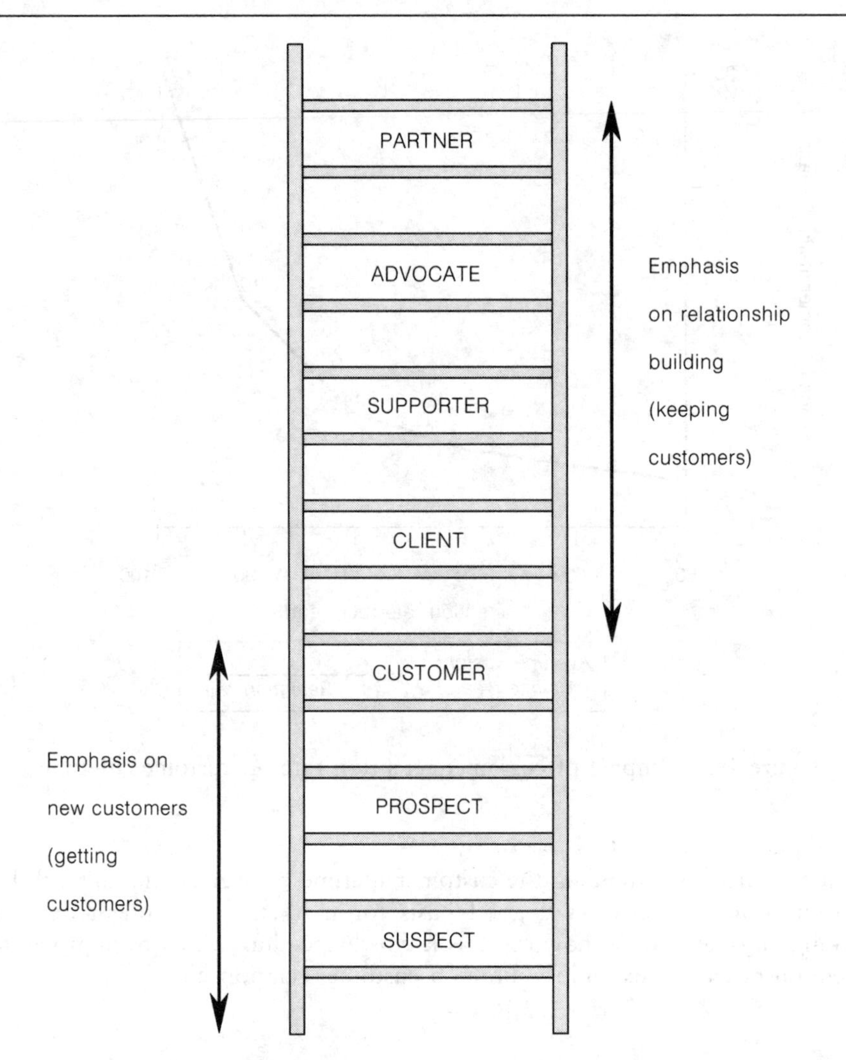

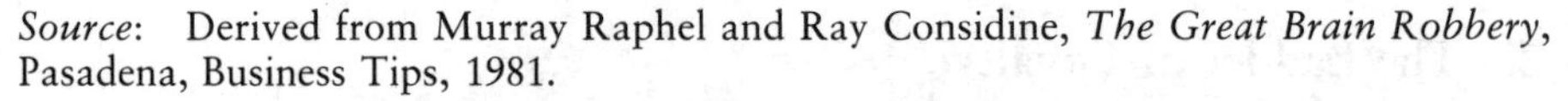
Source: Derived from Murray Raphel and Ray Considine, *The Great Brain Robbery*, Pasadena, Business Tips, 1981.

Figure 18.3 The ladder of loyalty

The bottom rung of the ladder represents the potential market for our product or service. At this stage we do not know the precise identity of these people (or companies) but we hopefully know something of their characteristics – for example demographic profile, life-style and so on. The use of marketing databases (which will be discussed later in this chapter) may well be a valuable means of targeting 'prospects' for our offer. Once prospects have been identified, the sales process proper begins. These prospects may first need to be 'qualified' to identify those most likely to be in the market for our product or service. This can be achieved by a number of means, including direct mail, telephone interviews or even field sales visits, although the latter is usually reserved for use as a follow-up once enquiries have been received via other, more cost-effective, means.

Once a sale has been made, then we have a customer. For many companies this is seen as the culmination of the marketing process. However, under the new paradigm of relationship marketing, this should be seen as only the start of a process of building customer loyalty.

To convert the customer into a 'client' requires that we establish a pattern of repeat buying by making it easy for the customer to do business with us. Being a client does not necessarily signal *commitment* however. For example banks have regular customers who might be termed clients. However many of those clients may well express quite high levels of dissatisfaction with the service they receive, and if it were possible for them to move accounts easily, they would. What is required is for us to develop such a customer-oriented approach that these clients become 'supporters' – meaning they are pleased with the service they receive. In fact, if they are really impressed with the quality of the relationship, they may well become 'advocates' – meaning they tell others about their satisfaction with our offer. Given the power of word-of-mouth, this type of advocacy can be worth more than any advertising.

The final rung on the ladder of loyalty is the customer as 'partner'. Here we have achieved a mutually rewarding relationship where neither party intends to leave the other. Increasingly we are starting to see the acceptance of the concept of 'partnership' as a desirable goal of business relationships. This is particularly the case in industrial marketing and business-to-business marketing.

The ladder of loyalty, whilst a simple idea, can provide a practical framework around which to build specific customer retention strategies.

■ Developing a Customer Retention Strategy

In Chapter 3 we discussed the concept of relationship marketing, where it was suggested that the goal of marketing activity should be not only to win customers but to keep them. This begs the question: 'What does it take to keep a customer?'

Customers continue to buy from a particular supplier because they perceive that the total 'value' they gain from the relationship is greater than the total cost that they incur. The challenge to the supplier, therefore, is to seek continually to improve the ratio between the perceived value the customer derives from our offer and the perceived cost. These costs, by the way, include not only price, but switching costs and on-going costs such as maintenance or servicing, running costs and so on.

If we wish to strengthen the relationship with our customers it can be helpful to look more closely at their *value chains*. In other words to understand their own processes and to identify where in those processes it is possible for us as a supplier to have a positive impact. For example, if we identify that currently some customers are carrying high levels of inventory – say stocks of spares – then the implementation of a rapid-response logistics programme might enable them to carry less inventory, thus their costs will be reduced and they will run out of stock less often. Such an initiative could both raise customer value and lower their costs.

In marketing to end-users a similar approach can often be applied. For example, many of today's consumers are 'time-sensitive' and products that can be augmented by a service dimension, for example home delivery, can lead to a strengthened customer relationship. Domino's Pizza, a North American company, took a big share of the massive US market for pizza by basing its entire business philosophy around providing a reliable, speedy home delivery service in less than an hour from the customer's telephone call.

■ Customer Retention Programmes

Besides continually striving to offer a superior product at a competitive price, with strong brand values (or corporate image), what else can a company do to keep its customers from defecting to the competition? Increasingly organisations are realising that they need to develop *active* customer retention strategies in contrast with the more conventional *passive* approach to retention. As we have noted several times elsewhere in this book, today's market place – whether we are talking about consumer, service or industrial markets – is much more volatile than hitherto and is characterised by a greater willingness on the part of customers to switch brands or suppliers. Hence the need to develop explicit programmes for customer retention.

Figure 18.4 outlines an approach to developing a customer retention programme which is based around understanding not just what motivates customers to stay, but also what prompts them to leave.

Firstly, let us examine the issues surrounding customer defection. Why do customers leave us? Surprisingly few companies carry out formal follow-up research amongst lapsed customers. There are many reasons why customers depart but normally the 80/20, or Pareto Rule, will be evident. That is, 80 per cent of customers leave for the same 20 per cent of reasons. The purpose of customer defection research is to get at the root causes of customer loss.

Research into lost customers can be carried out through telephone interviews or postal questionnaires, and even in-depth interviews and focus groups may be appropriate. The objective of this research is to dig as deeply as possible below the surface to identify the real reasons for defection. For instance many customers may cite 'price' as the reason for leaving, but that might simply be a 'top of the head' response and there may well be underlying reasons to do with customer service, lack of responsiveness, unreliability and so on.

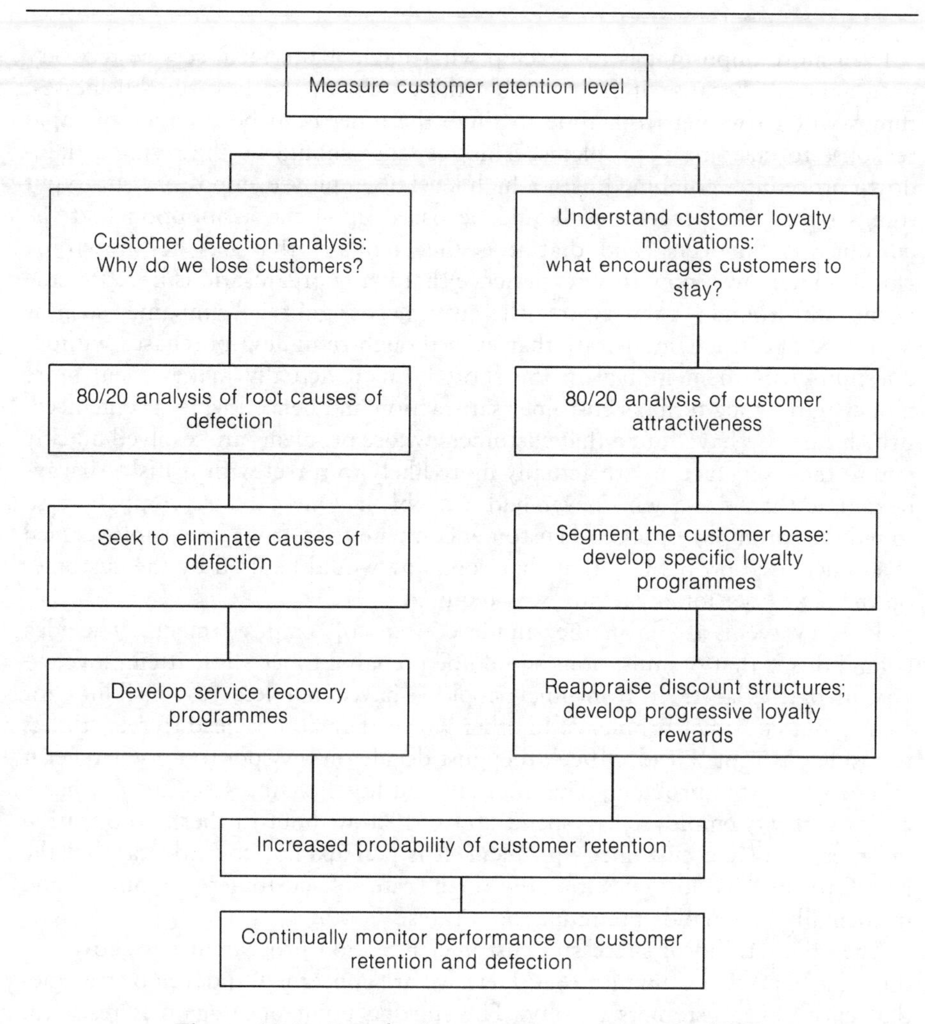

Figure 18.4 Developing a customer retention level

Because the decision to change suppliers or brands is not taken lightly by most customers, it will usually be cumulative dissatisfaction that triggers the decision. It follows therefore that if we can pin down the causes of dissatisfaction then specific actions can be taken to remove them.

Often customer complaints will provide an indication of the source of dissatisfaction but it must be remembered that only a minority of customers complain – the rest just vote with their feet. There is something to be said for actively seeking criticism from customers. Regular feedback through formal questionnaires and focus groups is a prerequisite for a continuous programme of improvement in customer relations.

Even more important is to develop what might be termed 'service recovery programmes'. Because it is inevitable that, even in the best-run businesses, things will go wrong from time to time, there needs to be a policy of rapid response to customers' problems. This response should be the result of laid-down procedures combined with a high level of employee empowerment to put things right. The procedures should be based upon the assumption that the customer is 'innocent' and that it is the company that has got it wrong. Unfortunately we know from experience that many organisations have this the wrong way round – they assume the customer is 'guilty'. Companies such as Marks & Spencer demonstrate that even though refunding purchases without question costs them money in the short term, it actually makes them more money in the long term as customer satisfaction and hence loyalty is enhanced. British Airways have found that customers whose problems are resolved quickly and to their satisfaction are actually more likely to travel with British Airways next time than those who never had a problem. One car hire company also found that prompt response to customer complaints by front-line employees led to an increased probability that that company would be used by the customer on the next occasion a car hire was required.

The key seems to be in the simple concept of 'empowerment'. The idea behind this is that organisations should be prepared to let all their employees – and in particular their front-line people – have complete responsibility for sorting out customer problems. In other words they do not need to refer things to a supervisor or 'Head Office', they just decide on the spot to do whatever it takes to solve the problem. The international hotel chain, Ritz-Carlton, has a policy that *any* employee can spend up to $1000 without further authorisation in order to solve a customer's problem. It is perhaps not coincidental that the Ritz-Carlton has an exceptionally high rate of customer retention, and incidentally commands premium room rates.

The other strand of successful customer retention programmes is shown on the right hand side of Figure 18.4. Here we are concerned to develop strategies that encourage customers to stay. The starting point once again is research. What is it that motivates customers to buy from us rather than from competitors? These are the critical success factors that need to be understood, developed and honed so that they will withstand any competitive comparison. Clearly there will normally be more than one determinant of supplier or brand choice and they may well differ by customer. Indeed a viable and often powerful means of market segmentation is to group customers according to their choice criteria.

It should also be noted that not every customer is equally attractive to the organisation. Once again the 80/20 rule is evident and it makes good sense to ensure that retention rates are highest amongst the 20 per cent of customers who provide us with 80 per cent of total profit. Many 'frequent flyer' programmes are based upon recognition of the existence of a small core of customers who travel the most miles, usually paying the full (undiscounted) fare. For these 'Gold' customers there will be red-carpet treatment, upgrades, personalised service and tailored promotions. Whilst the aim is to improve retention rates amongst all groups of profitable customers, it is inevitable that there will always be a core group of customers providing the greatest profit.

Rover, the car company, has developed a communications channel to its most important customers and seeks to maintain the closest possible contact with them. Its glossy magazine, *Catalyst*, is tailored to the specific interests of each recipient. Thus people who register their sporting interests as golf and fishing, for example, receive a version of the magazine that places greater emphasis on those sports and less on other things.

A traditional way of incentivising customers to stay loyal and to buy more is through discounts, in particular volume-related and retrospective discounts. There is no point in a discount system that encourages 'forward buying' only, what the organisation should seek is the increased volume that comes from a customer choosing you as preferred supplier rather than purchasing from several suppliers. Also, discounts should reward loyalty through retrospective bonuses and should be structured to encourage 'cross-buying' of other products from the supplier's range.

Structured programmes such as the British Airways Executive Club encourage customers to aim for the next level of 'reward' through a three-tier membership: Blue, Silver and Gold, based upon the number of miles travelled and the class of travel. General Motors is currently having some success with its GM credit card, a card with a difference. Every time it is used to purchase goods or services, 5 per cent of the transaction value is awarded in the form of a rebate against the future purchase of a GM car.

The important point to remember about any of these loyalty programmes is that they should not be designed to 'lock the customer in' – this inevitably leads to resentment on the part of the customer – but instead should be seen by the customer as a reward for loyalty.

In summary, if customer retention strategies are to succeed then they should focus upon the two related, but separate, issues of customer defection and customer loyalty. If these two parallel strands of the retention strategies can be successfully managed then the probability of an improved customer retention rate will almost certainly increase.

■ DataBase Marketing

DataBase Marketing (DBM) is a powerful tool that has recently become available to organisations seeking to forge stronger relationships with existing customers and find new customers with similar profiles. DBM is not the same as 'direct marketing' but rather direct marketing is a channel of communication that is often used in conjunction with DBM.

By making use of computerised customer information files that are constructed on a 'relational' basis (that is, different elements of information can be brought together from separate files) the marketer is able to target more precisely the message to the individual customer or prospective customer. The opportunity now exists to develop marketing strategies that are focused more upon the individual. Instead of the traditional concept of 'mass marketing', the emphasis will increasingly become one of 'micromarketing'.

It is not just computer technology that has made DBM a reality, it is also the rapid growth in the availability of detailed information on individual customers in many markets. A major spur to the use of DBM in consumer markets particularly has come through the rapidly developing field of *geodemographics*.

Geodemographics is the generic term applied to the construction of relational databases that draw together data on demographic variables (for example age, gender, location), socioeconomic variables (for example occupation, income), purchase behaviour, life-style information and indeed any data that might usefully describe the characteristics of an individual customer.

Much of this information is available through sources such as the Census of Population, electoral rolls, Target Group Index (TGI), National Shoppers' Survey (NSS), credit card purchase data and so on, all of which can be related to postcode areas and, in some cases, to individuals.

Commercially available geodemographic databases such as ACORN, PINPOINT and MOSAIC can greatly assist marketing to target far more precisely the appropriate audience. It is now possible to identify with a high level of accuracy the characteristics of every one of the UK's fifteen million postcodes – each with a maximum of about fifteen addresses.

One of the major opportunities that DBM provides is the facility to profile the organisation's existing customer base and then to seek other potential customers with similar profiles. Similarly the increasingly detailed information of individuals' purchase behaviour that is now available makes it much easier to target them with appropriate communications for products or services.

DBM also facilitates a much greater degree of personalisation on customer contact. Direct mail can be made more specific to the recipient. Catalogues, newsletters – even magazines – can be tailored to the known interests and preferences of the individual. One company in the USA, Donnelly, provides a specialised printing service so that many different versions of a single magazine can be printed with tailored editorial and advertising content to small groups of subscribers. One magazine, *Farm Journal*, is printed in 8000 different editions, each one of which goes to a specific category of reader, according to their demographic profile, from size, type of crop or livestock, and so on.

Retailers have been amongst the first to recognise the marketing opportunities for building customer loyalty provided by DBM. Customers are encouraged to register for 'frequent shopper' programmes and to benefit from discounts and special promotions if they present their card at the checkout counter when making their purchases. As a result customers' precise purchasing histories can be recorded along with their demographic profiles, lifestyles and other details. This enables tailored promotions to be offered, cross-selling to be facilitated and, importantly, the merchandise mix in that store to be matched more precisely to customers' requirements. Already many retail chains are developing specific merchandise and marketing strategies for individual stores so that a store patronised by shoppers with particular demographic profiles and known purchasing preferences will carry a mix of products appropriate to the customer base.

The use of DBM is spreading widely in the service industry. Frequent-flyer schemes and hotel club schemes have been around for some time, but now their potential is being more fully utilised. Thus not only is the individual's preference behaviour known, but this can be correlated with the background information previously collected on that individual. Relationships can thus be enhanced because it becomes possible to customise the service, for example seating and food preferences on an airline, room preferences in an hotel and so forth can be easily catered for.

Financial service companies are using databases to explore the opportunities for much more selective promotion amongst target groups for the products. Knowing the characteristics of existing customers for specific financial services makes it possible, using geodemographic databases, to find potential customers with similar characteristics. One UK bank has targeted customers selected from its credit card operations who have used their card frequently for travel to and from France and/or have used their card to make purchases in France. They have combined this information with their knowledge of those customers' incomes and lifestyles (information that is made available through data provided by customers when they apply for the card and through an analysis of their purchases) to identify those most likely to be interested in buying property in France. They have then targeted these prospects with a mortgage scheme specifically designed for such customers. The success of the product has been exceptional.

Fast-moving consumer goods (FMCG) companies are increasingly able to pinpoint likely targets for their products through the use of DBM, but more importantly they can use it to strengthen relationships with key customers by designing promotions and incentives that will bind customers more closely to the company. Surveys such as the National Shoppers' Survey have provided data on over three million individual customers in the UK for example, enabling marketers to target heavy users of their product category, or to select users of competitive products for targeted promotions.

In consumer durables more and more car companies are using DBM to improve customer retention rates. Saab, for example, collects a great deal of detail on each of its customers at the time they buy a car, then they update it every six months. Using this information, Saab can design appropriate joint promotions with other companies with a high level of potential appeal to Saab customers – recent examples include Bang & Olufsen and Laurent Perrier Champagne. As the time approaches when existing customers are likely to be in the market for a new car, an individually focused marketing programme begins. Clearly if the company knows who the key prospects are, it can afford to spend a lot more on sales and marketing per individual and that sales and marketing effort will be much more effective because it is specific to an individual.

In case it is thought that DBM can only be applied to consumer and service marketing, a growing number of industrial marketing companies have also become aware of its potential. Texas Instruments, for example, maintains a detailed database on its customers. It organises technical seminars and provides high-level technology-focused newsletters, both of which are targeted at specific end-user types.

Many business-to-business marketing companies have yet to appreciate the opportunity that DBM presents. It is often the case that they are not aware of the amount of data that exists about their clients or potential clients. Some of the leaders in the use of DBM began by widening the scope of their existing customer enquiry systems. Thus CSX, a major North American transport company, tracks every one of its customers' shipments, firstly so that it can provide status reports to customers on the location of a particular shipment, but secondly so that it can tailor its services more precisely to individual customer's requirements.

Whilst the technology and users' experience of DBM is still in its infancy, and whilst there are some concerns about data protection and individual privacy, there can be no doubt that it is rapidly becoming one of the most powerful means available for improving customer retention. DBM provides a viable means for making individual marketing a reality.

Summary

It will be apparent from what has been said that customer retention is critical to the long-term profitability of the business. Because of the impact that even small changes in the rate of customer defection can have, it is imperative that we have a defined strategy for retention. In other words we must formally map out exactly how defection is to be reduced and retention enhanced. This implies that there must be clear organisational responsibilities for managing customer retention and measuring performance.

We have previously noted that 'what gets measured, gets managed'. The implication of this is that there must be continuous monitoring of customer satisfaction, since it is a critical force behind improved customer retention. Measures of customer satisfaction should be developed and regularly fed back throughout the organisation. Many enlightened companies are already putting customer satisfaction measures at the top of their list of 'key performance indicators' (KPIs). In other words, issues such as on-time delivery performance, customer complaint analysis and response times are regularly reported and provide the basis for continuous improvement programmes within the business.

The recognition that customer retention is a key concern of everyone within the business will eventually lead to a much sharper focus on the process of building long-term relationships with customers. Nothing less should be accepted as the ultimate goal of marketing strategy.

CHAPTER 19

Customer Service Strategy

One of the best-selling management books of recent years, *In Search of Excellence* by T. J. Peters and R. H. Waterman, has alerted managers and others to the simple truth that customers create sales, and that the most successful companies are those that create the most customers *and keep them*. It may seem strange that such obvious axioms should provide the basis for a book that appears on executives' shelves around the world. Nevertheless, it has taken a major recession to focus many organisations' attention upon the customer more sharply than was often the case in the past. The lessons of *In Search of Excellence* extend beyond a concern for customer relations, but it is perhaps in this field that the greatest scope for improvement lies for the 'non-excellent' company.

Two factors have perhaps contributed more than anything else to the growing importance of customer service as a competitive weapon. One is the continual development of customer expectations: in almost every market the customer is now more demanding, more 'sophisticated' than he or she was, say, thirty years ago. Likewise in industrial purchasing situations we find that buyers expect higher levels of service from vendors, particularly as more manufacturers convert to 'Just-in-Time' manufacturing systems.

The second factor is the slow but inexorable transition towards 'commodity' type markets. By this we mean that the power of the 'brand' is increasingly diminishing as the technologies of competing products converge, thus making product differences difficult to perceive – at least to the average buyer. Take for example the current state of the personal computer market. There are so many competing models, and these are substitutable as far as most would-be purchasers are concerned. Unless one is particularly expert it is difficult to use product features as the basis for choice.

Faced with a situation such as this, the customer may be influenced by price or by 'image' perceptions, but overriding these aspects may well be 'availability' – in other words, 'Is the product in stock; can I have it now?' Since availability is clearly one aspect of customer service, we are in effect saying that the power of customer service is paramount in a situation such as this. Nor is it only in consumer markets that we are encountering the force of customer service as a determinant of purchase; as we shall note shortly, there is much evidence from industrial markets of the same phenomenon. On top of all this we have seen the growth of the 'service' sector in many western economies. Over 50 per cent of the GNP of the UK is derived from the non-manufacturing sector and every year the percentage increases. The marketing of services should not call for any different philosophy from that underlying the marketing of physical products. Rather it calls for an even greater emphasis upon availability, particularly given the 'perishability' of the service product. Nevertheless, both service and tangible products are increasingly dependent for their success upon suppliers' ability to enhance their appeal through the 'added value' of customer service.

■ What is Customer Service?

It is sometimes suggested that the role of customer service is to provide 'time and place utility' in the transfer of goods and services between buyer and seller. Put another way, there is no value in a product or service until it is in the hands of the customer or consumer. It follows that making the product or service 'available' is what, in essence, the distribution function of the business is all about. *Availability* is in itself a complex concept, affected by a galaxy of factors that together constitute customer service. For example, these factors might include delivery frequency and reliability, stock levels and order cycle time as they have an impact upon availability. Indeed, it could be said that customer service is ultimately determined by the interaction of all those factors that affect the process of making products and services available to the buyer.

In practice, many companies have varying views of customer service. A major study of customer service practices found that, in the industries surveyed, a range of views existed as to what constituted 'customer service'. Some of the definitions of service they encountered are shown below:

- All activities required to accept, process, deliver and bill customer orders and to follow up on any activity that erred.
- Timeliness and reliability of getting materials to customers in accordance with the customers' expectations.
- A complex range of activities involving all areas of the business which combine to deliver and invoice the company's products in a fashion that is perceived as satisfactory by the customer and which advances our company's objectives.
- Total order entry, all communications with customers, all shipping, all freight, all invoicing and total control of repair of products.
- Timely and accurate delivery of products ordered by customers with accurate follow-up and enquiry response, including timely delivery of invoice.

What all these definitions have in common is that they are concerned with relationships at the buyer/seller interface. This same study suggested that customer service could be examined under three headings:

- Pre-transaction elements
- Transaction elements
- Post-transaction elements.

The *pre-transaction* elements of customer service relate to corporate policies or programmes; for example, written statements of service policy, adequacy of organisational structure and system flexibility. The *transaction* elements are those customer service variables directly involved in performing the physical distribution function: for example, product availability, order cycle time, order status information and delivery reliability. The *post-transaction* elements of customer service are generally supportive of the product while in use: for instance, product warranty, parts and repair service, procedures for customer complaints and product replacement.

Many commentators have defined various elements of customer service, but the most commonly occurring seem to be:

- Order cycle time
- Consistency and reliability of delivery
- Inventory availability
- Order-size constraints
- Ordering convenience
- Delivery times and flexibility
- Invoicing procedures and accuracy
- Claims procedure
- Condition of goods
- Salesman's visits
- Order status information

In any particular product/market situation some of these elements will be more important than others, and there may be factors other than those listed above which have a significance in a specific market. Indeed, it is essential to understand customer service in terms of the differing requirements of different market segments and to recognise that no universally appropriate list of elements exists; each market serviced by the company will attach different importance to different service elements.

It is because of the multivariate nature of customer service and because of the widely differing requirements of specific markets that it is essential for any business to have a clearly identified policy towards customer service. It is surprising perhaps that so few companies have defined policies on customer service – let alone an organisation flexible enough to manage and control that service – when it is considered that service can be the most important element in the company's marketing mix. A considerable body of evidence exists to support the view that if the product or service is not available at the time the customer requires it, and a close substitute is available, then the sale will be lost to the competition. Even in markets where brand loyalty is strong, running out of stock might be sufficient to trigger off brand switching. In industrial markets, too, the same pressures on purchasing-source loyalty seem to be at work. One survey of industrial purchasing officers found that distribution service was considered second in importance only to product quality as a deciding criterion for vendor selection. Moreover, more than one-third of these purchasing officers indicated that they would cancel the order if it were not available for shipment when ordered.

In the light of this and other evidence it is suggested that three basic actions are required for the management of customer service:

- Define an overall company philosophy of customer service in terms of attitude, organisation and responsibilities.
- Develop internal standards for customer service based on careful studies that have explored the quantitative trade-offs between various levels of customer service and the costs of achieving such levels, so as to identify the most profitable policy for each customer segment.
- Inform customers what they might expect by way of customer service (perhaps in more general terms than the company defines its policies internally).

To achieve the most effective deployment of corporate resources in developing a customer service policy along the lines broadly defined above, a number of prerequisites exist:

- The differing perceptions of the various parties to the purchasing decision in terms of customer service must be recognised.
- The trade-off potential between the various components of the customer service mix must be evaluated.
- The unique customer service requirement of each product/channel/market segment must be identified.

If cost-effective customer service policies are to be successfully developed and implemented within the firm it is imperative that a formalised logic is adopted and closely followed. Customer service is too important and too costly to be left to chance.

■ The Components of Customer Service

It is a common fault in marketing to fail to realise that customers do not always attach the same importance to product attributes as the vendor. Thus it sometimes happens that products are promoted on attributes or features that in reality are less important to the customer than other aspects. A floor cleaner that is sold on its ease of application, for example, will not succeed unless 'ease of application' is a salient benefit sought by the customer. If 'shine' or the need for less frequent cleaning are important to the customer then we might be better advised to feature those aspects in our promotion. The same principle applies in customer service: which aspects of service are rated most highly by the customer? If a company places its emphasis upon stock availability, but the customer regards delivery reliability more highly, it may not be allocating its resources in a way likely to maximise sales. Alternatively, a company that realises that its customers place a higher value on completeness of orders than they do on, say, regular scheduled deliveries could develop this to its advantage.

Thus there is a great premium to be placed on gaining an insight into the factors that influence buyer behaviour and, in the context of customer service, which particular elements are seen by the customer to be the most important. The use of market research techniques in customer service has lagged behind their application in such areas as product testing and advertising research, yet the importance of researching the service needs of customers is just as great as, for example, the need to understand the market reaction to price. In fact, it is possible to apply standard, proven market research methods to gain considerable insight into the ways that customers will react to customer service.

The first step in research of this type is to identify the relative source of influence on the purchase decision. If we are selling components to a manufacturer, for example, who will make the decision on the source of supply? This is not always an easy question to answer as, in many cases, there will be several people involved. The purchasing manager of the company to whom we are selling may only be acting as an agent for others within the firm. In other cases his influence will be much greater. Alternatively, if we are manufacturing products for sale through retail outlets, is the decision to stock made centrally by a retail chain or by individual store managers? The answers to these questions can often by supplied by the sales force. The sales representative should know from experience who the decision-makers are.

Given that a clear indication of the source of decision-making power can be gained, the customer service researcher at least knows *who* to research. The question still remains, however: which elements of the vendor's total marketing offering have what effect on the purchase decision? Ideally, once the decision-making unit in a specific market has been identified, an initial, small-scale research programme should be initiated, based on personal interviews with a representative sample of buyers. The purpose of these interviews is to elicit, *in the language of the customer*, first, the importance they attach to customer service *vis-à-vis* the other marketing mix elements such as price, product quality and promotion, and second, the specific importance they attach to the individual components of customer service.

■ Customer Service Trade-Offs

Given that through research we can identify the appropriate elements of the customer service mix for the specific market segments we are targeting, how do we decide on where to place the emphasis?

Whilst ideally the customer would like to have the best of everything, for example 100 per cent availability from stock, twenty-four-hour delivery, reliable on-time deliveries and emergency ordering, it will probably not be cost-effective for the supplier to offer such a service.

In the customer service decision, therefore, we are forced to make *trade-offs*. The question is which elements of service do we trade off against each other? A simple analogy is the decision to buy a car. One person might ideally like a car with the appearance of a Lamborghini and the performance of a Ferrari, but with the miles-per-gallon of a Fiat, the spaciousness of a Volvo estate and perhaps at the price of a Nissan! Clearly not all these things are achievable in one car. The actual purchase decision has to be based upon a trade-off, or a series of trade-offs. The final purchase decision can be viewed, therefore, as a reflection of the importance that an individual attaches to each aspect of the purchase, that is, appearance, performance and price.

The technique of trade-off measurement was discussed more fully in Chapter 12, where pricing decisions were discussed. However, the analogy with the customer service decision is a good one. The marketing decision-maker needs to research the service priorities of the company's target markets and to assemble a customer service package that is optimal for that market and for the company.

■ Designing the Customer Service Package

To compete effectively in any market requires the ability to develop some differential advantage over competing companies and their product or service offerings. Sometimes the differential advantage may be in terms of distinctive product attributes or related benefits as perceived by the customer. On other occasions it may be price, or alternatively the product may be promoted in such a way that it acquires a distinctive image in the eyes of the market. In just the same way, customer service can be used to develop a differential advantage, and indeed there can be a major benefit to the company in using customer service in this way. For example in competitive markets, where real product differentiation may be difficult to establish and where to compete on price would only lead to profit erosion, it makes sense to switch the marketing emphasis to customer service.

The current battle in the office copier market provides a case in point. Xerox, the early leader in this field, has found that competition has become increasingly severe from products that, to the potential customer at least, seem to offer the same product benefits. Pressure on margins is considerable and price cutting would not provide a lasting solution for Xerox, which instead switched its emphasis to service. Its advertisements underline this point. A recent advertisement in the business press for Xerox copiers stated:

- 'Because the best way to get new customers is to keep your current ones happy, Xerox offers the largest service force in the business. Over 30,000 men and women worldwide.'
- 'Parts inventories and parts distribution systems are all part of our job. That's why we have distribution centres around the globe.'

- 'So, chances are, our technical representatives will always have what you need where you need it. Whenever possible, we standardize parts so that they're interchangeable from country to country. That way we can take better care of our copiers and our customers.'

Similar use of service as a marketing tool has been made by companies such as Digital Equipment and Caterpillar, who have built up commanding positions in their markets and maintained them through the effective use of customer service.

Earlier it was stressed that it is important to establish those components of the total customer service mix that have the greatest impact on the buyer's perception of us as a supplier. This thinking needs to be carried right through into design of the customer service offering. This offering can best be described as the customer service 'package', for it will most likely contain more than one component.

The design of the package will need to take account of the differing needs of different market segments so that the resources allocated to customer service can be used in the most cost-effective way. Too often a uniform, blanket approach to service is adopted by companies, which does not distinguish between the real requirements of different customer types. This can lead to customers being offered too little service or too much.

The precise composition of the customer service package for any market segment should depend on the results of the market research described earlier. It will be determined by budgetary and cost constraints. If alternative packages can be identified that seem to be equally acceptable to the buyer, it makes sense to choose the least costly alternative. For example, it may be possible to identify a highly acceptable customer service package that enables the emphasis to be switched away from a high level of inventory availability towards improved customer communication. Once a cost-effective package has been identified in this way it should become a major part of the company's marketing mix – 'using service to sell' is the message here. If the market segments we serve are sensitive to service, then the service package must be actively promoted. One way in which this can be achieved with great effect is by stressing the impact on the *customer's* costs of the improved service package: for example, what improved reliability will do for his own stock planning; what shorter lead times will do for his inventory levels and how improved ordering and invoicing systems will lead to fewer errors. All too often the customer will not appreciate the impact that improved service offered by the supplier can have on his, the customer's, 'bottom line'.

■ Strategies for Service

Beyond the simple presentation of a marketing message based around an improved customer service package lies the opportunity to develop tailor-made service offerings, particularly to key accounts, based on 'negotiated' service levels. The idea here is that no two customers are alike, either in terms of their requirements or, specifically, in terms of their profitability to the supplier. One UK-based company in the consumer electronics field identified that whilst three of its major customers were roughly equivalent in terms of their annual sales value, there were considerable differences in the costs generated by each. For example, one customer required delivery to each of its 300-plus retail outlets, whilst the others took delivery at one central warehouse. Similarly, one company paid within thirty days of receiving the invoice; the others took nearer to forty days to pay. Again, one of the three was found to place twice as many 'emergency' orders as the others. Careful analysis of the true costs showed that the profitability of the three customers differed by over 20 per cent. Yet each customer received the same value-related discounts and the same level of customer service!

Conducting such a 'customer account profitability' analysis can provide the supplier with not only the basis upon which to negotiate price but also a basis for 'negotiating' service. Whilst companies in the USA tend to be familiar with the importance of relating price discounts to customer-related costs, because of the Robinson-Patman legislation, it is rarely used elsewhere in a positive way. Thus, whilst the concept of paying more for an airmail letter than a surface letter is well established, it is less common to find a supplier offering different 'qualities' of service at different prices. Interestingly enough, the business manager who accepts the difference between First Class, Business Class and Tourist Class on the plane he flies in to see his customer might never think of how that same principle could be applied to his own business!

■ Developing a Customer Service Culture

In our eagerness to develop a customer service strategy it would be a mistake to focus exclusively on the 'external' dimension of service, that is, customer perceptions. Of equal importance is the 'internal' dimension, that is, how do our own people, our managers and workforce, view service? What is their attitude to customers? Do they share the same concept and definition of service as our customers?

It would be a truism to suggest that ultimately a company's performance is limited more by the vision and the quality of its people than it is by market factors or competitive forces. However it is perhaps only belatedly that we have come to recognise this.

Much has been written and spoken about 'corporate culture'. We have come to recognise that the shared values held throughout the organisation can provide a powerful driving force and focus for all its actions. More often than not, though, we have to admit that most organisations lack a cohesive and communicated culture. Even if there is a defined philosophy of the business, it may be little understood. This lack of shared values can have an impact upon the company in many ways and particularly upon its approach to customer service.

One viable way to assess the customer 'climate' within the firm is to take the temperature by means of an employee survey. One such approach that has been developed begins with identifying all personnel who have a direct or indirect impact upon customer service. A useful device here is to consider the complete 'order to cash' cycle and to ensure that we have identified all those people involved in all the different departments that influence the order flow. The focus of the survey should be upon these key people's perceptions of service: what do *they* think is important to the customers? And how do they think we perform, service-wise?

What quite often emerges from these internal surveys is that different employees hold quite different views as to what constitutes customer service. Similarly, they may often overrate the company's actual performance compared with the customer's own rating. Making such comparisons between customers' perceptions and the employees' perceptions can provide a powerful means of identifying customer service problems and their sources.

This 'audit' of internal perceptions and attitudes towards service can form the basis of a programme of action aimed at developing a customer service culture. However, such a process, which almost inevitably will involve a major reorientation within the firm, cannot work without the total commitment of top management. The service culture must grow outwards from the boardroom and the chief executive must be its greatest champion.

Within the customer service function one very practical step is to set up the equivalent of a 'quality circle'. Such a scheme might involve looking at the total order-processing and invoicing cycle and selecting individuals from all the departments or sections involved. This group would meet at least once a week with the expressed objective of seeking improvements to customer service from whatever possible source. A further task that might usefully be given to this group is the handling of all customer complaints that relate to service.

Underpinning all these initiatives should be a company-wide education programme. Increasingly, more and more organisations have come to recognise the key role that in-company education can have in developing a sense of shared values. Furthermore, because it is a basic tenet of psychology that attitude change must precede behavioural change, education can lead to a measurably improved performance. One of the best examples recently has come from British Airways, whose 'Putting People First' campaign has resulted in a significant change in employee behaviour and thus in the company's performance in the market place.

■ Summary

Customer service is perhaps the most powerful dimension in the marketing mix of any company. In one sense the development of targeted customer service strategies is only the logical extension of the marketing concept. In other words customer service is about recognising the specific needs of the customer and developing a strategy that focuses the resources of the organisation towards meeting those needs.

As such, the development of a customer service strategy requires a corporate culture that extends beyond slogans and involves all levels of the organisation in working together to ensure that, for customers, doing business with your company becomes a regular habit.

MODULE 6

Planning and Control

CHAPTER 20

Marketing Planning

What is Marketing Planning?

In this chapter we shall consider one of the most difficult aspects of the marketing task – actually making it all work in practice by means of a system within the company. This is something that many people seem to overlook. Yet no investigation of marketing management can be complete without a fairly detailed consideration of how all the structures and frameworks presented in the earlier chapters are to be effectively implemented.

To make marketing work, it is necessary to have available a logical 'common format' for the implementation of strategy, that is, a *marketing plan.* In effect the planner is attempting to manage the future by deciding *what to do about the possible different trading environments.*

Let us now remind ourselves what marketing planning is about. It is a logical sequence and a series of activities leading to the setting of marketing objectives and the formulation of plans for achieving them. It is a management *process.* Formalised marketing planning by means of a planning system is, *per se*, little more than a structured way of identifying a range of options for the company, making them explicit in writing, formulating marketing objectives that are consistent with the company's overall objectives and scheduling and costing the specific activities most likely to bring about the achievement of the objectives.

Issues to be considered in marketing planning are:

- When should it be done; how often; by whom and how?
- Is it different in a large and a small company?
- Is it different in a diversified and an undiversified company?
- Is it different in an international and a domestic company?
- What is the role of the chief executive?
- What is the role of the planning department?
- Should marketing planning be 'top down' or 'bottom up'?
- What is the relationship between operational (one year) and strategic (longer-term) planning?

Benefits of formalised marketing planning

In one study, 90 per cent of the industrial goods companies involved did not, by their own admission, produce anything approximating to an integrated, coordinated and internally consistent plan for their marketing activities. This included a substantial number of companies that had highly formalised procedures for marketing planning. Certainly, few of these companies enjoyed the following benefits of formalised marketing planning:

- Coordination of the activities of many individuals whose actions are interrelated over time.
- Identification of expected developments.
- Preparedness to meet changes when they occur.
- Minimisation of non-rational responses to the unexpected.
- Better communication among executives.
- Minimisation of conflict among individuals that might result in a subordination of the goals of the company to those of the individual.

■ Why is Marketing Planning Essential?

There can be little doubt that marketing planning is essential when we consider the increasingly hostile and complex environment in which companies operate. Hundreds of external and internal factors interact in a bafflingly complex way to affect our ability to achieve profitable sales. Also, let us consider for a moment the four typical objectives of companies

- The maximisation of revenue.
- The maximisation of profit.
- The maximisation of return on investment.
- The minimisation of costs.

Each one of these has its own special appeal to different managers within the company, depending on the nature of their particular function. In reality, the best that can ever be achieved is a kind of optimal compromise, because each of these objectives is often in conflict with another.

Managers of a company have to understand, or at least have a view of, how all these variables interact; and managers try to be rational about their business decisions no matter how important intuition, feel and experience are as contributory factors in the process of rationality. Most managers accept that some kind of formalised procedure for marketing planning is desirable because it may help to reduce the complexity of business operations and add a dimension of realism to the company's hopes for the future. Without some procedures for dealing with these issues there is a danger that the company will exhaust much of its energies in mutually destructive disputes, whilst its marketing is at risk of becoming little more than an uncoordinated mixture of interesting bits and pieces.

Ideally, what is required is some kind of institutionalised process designed to work out and write down in advance the particular competitive stance that the company plans to take. This should be communicated throughout the company so that everyone is conscious of what has to be done to take the company towards its objectives. A useful way of achieving this synergy is through the marketing planning process.

The Marketing Planning Process

Figure 20.1 illustrates the several stages that have to be worked through in order to arrive at a marketing plan. The dotted lines joining up steps 5, 6 and 7 are meant to indicate the reality of the planning process in that each of these steps is likely to have been worked through more than once before the final programmes could be written.

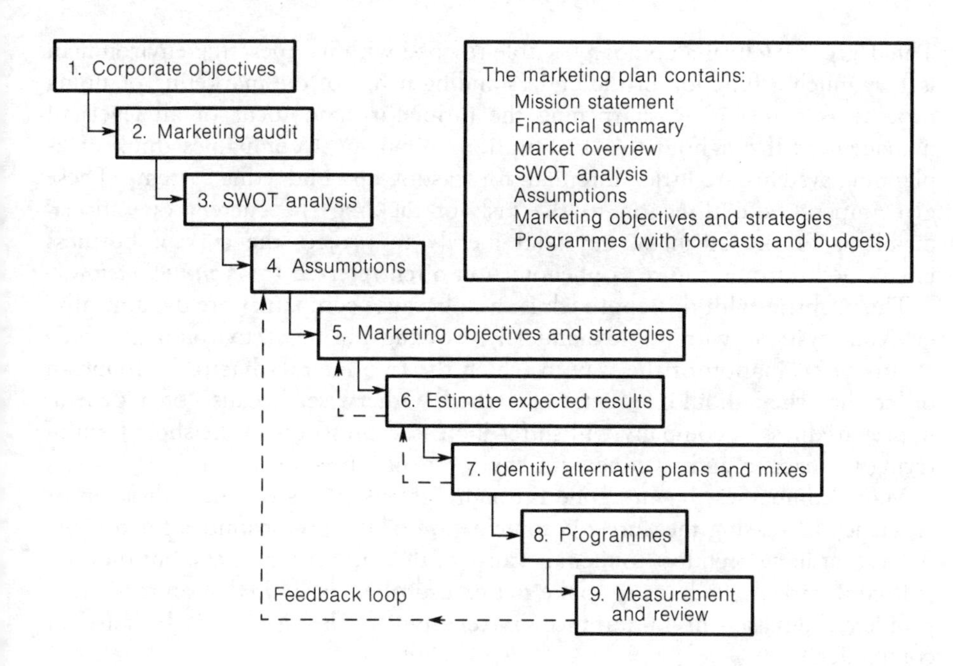

Figure 20.1 The marketing planning process

Although it is generally accepted that each of the marketing planning steps is applicable in most cases, the degree to which each of the separate steps in the diagram needs to be formalised depends to a large extent on the size and nature of the company.

For example, an *undiversified* company generally uses less formalised procedures, since top management tends to have greater functional knowledge and expertise than subordinates and because the lack of diversity of operations enables direct control to be exercised over most of the key determinants of success. Thus situation reviews or the setting of marketing objectives, for example, are not always made explicit in writing, although these steps still have to be considered.

In contrast, in a *diversified* company it is usually not possible for top management to have greater functional knowledge and expertise than subordinate management, hence the whole planning process tends to be formalised in order to provide a consistent discipline for those who have to make the decisions throughout the organization.

Problems Associated with Marketing Planning Ignorance

The degree to which a company is able to cope with its operating environment is very much a function of the understanding it has of the marketing planning process as a means of sharpening the rationality and focus of all levels of management throughout the organisation. What most companies think of as planning systems are little more than forecasting and budgeting systems. These give impetus and direction to the task of tackling the current operational problems of the business, but tend merely to project the current business unchanged into the future, a phenomenon often referred to as *tunnel vision*.

The problem with this approach is that, because companies are dynamically-evolving systems within a dynamically-evolving business environment, some means of evaluation of the way in which the two interact has to be found in order that they should be better matched. Otherwise, because of a general unpreparedness, a company will suffer increased pressures in the short term in trying to react to and to cope with environmental pressures.

Many companies, having gone through various forms of rationalisation or efficiency-increasing measures, become aware of the opportunities for making profit that have been lost to them because of their unpreparedness, but they are still confused about how to make better use of their limited resources. This problem increases in importance in relation to the size and diversity of companies.

In other words, there is widespread awareness of lost market opportunities through unpreparedness and real confusion over what to do about it. Also, there is a strong relationship between these two problems and the techniques most widely used in place of formal marketing planning – that is, *sales forecasting* and *budgeting systems*. Following is a list of the most frequently observed operating problems resulting from a reliance on traditional sales forecasting and budgeting procedure in the absence of a marketing planning system:

- Lost opportunities for profit.
- Meaningless numbers in long-range plans.

- Unrealistic objectives.
- Lack of actionable market information.
- Interfunctional strife.
- Management frustration.
- Proliferation of products and markets.
- Wasted promotional expenditure.
- Pricing confusion.
- Growing vulnerability to environmental change.
- Loss of control over the business.

It is not difficult to see the connection between all of these problems. Perhaps what is not apparent is that each is in fact a symptom of a much larger problem emanating from the way in which a company sets its objectives. The eventual effectiveness of any objective is dependent upon the quality of the informational inputs about the business environment. However, objectives also need to be realistic, and to be realistic they have to be closely related to the company's particular capabilities in the form of its assets, competences and reputation that have evolved over a number of years.

Some kind of appropriate system has to be used to enable meaningful and realistic marketing objectives to be set. A frequent complaint is that there is preoccupation with short-term thinking and an almost total lack of what has been referred to as *strategic* thinking. Another complaint is that plans consist largely of numbers, which are difficult to evaluate in any meaningful way, since they do not highlight and quantify opportunities, emphasise the key issues, show the company's position clearly in its markets, nor delineate the means of achieving the sales forecasts. Indeed, very often the actual numbers that are written down bear little relationship to any of these things. Sales targets for the sales force are often inflated in order to motivate them to higher achievement, whilst the actual budgets are deflated in order to provide a safety net against shortfall. Both act as demotivators and both lead to the frequent use of expressions such as 'ritual' and the 'numbers game'. It is easy to see how the problems listed above begin to manifest themselves in this sort of environment. Closely allied to this is the frequent reference to profit as being the only objective necessary to successful business performance.

However, even though many British companies have made the making of profit almost the sole objective, many of them have gone into decline.

Why should this be so? It is partly because some senior managers believe that all they have to do is to set profit targets and that middle managers will somehow make everything come right. Financial objectives, whilst being essential measures of the desired performance of a company, are of little practical help since they say nothing about *how* the results are to be achieved. The same applies to sales forecasts and budgets, which are *not* marketing objectives and strategies.

To summarize, a structured approach to the situation is necessary, irrespective of the size or complexity of the organisation. Such a system should:

- Ensure that comprehensive consideration is given to the definition of strengths and weaknesses and to problems and opportunities.
- Ensure that a logical framework is used for the presentation of the key issues arising from this analysis.

Very few companies in Britain have planning systems that possess these characteristics. Those that do manage to cope with their environment more effectively than those that do not. They find it easier to set meaningful marketing objectives; are more confident about their future; enjoy greater control over their business and react less on a piecemeal basis to ongoing events. In short, they suffer less operational problems and as a result are more effective.

The characteristics of companies with effective marketing planning systems are:

- Widely understood objectives.
- Highly motivated employees.
- High levels of actionable market information.
- Greater interfunctional coordination.
- Minimum waste and duplication of resources.
- Acceptance of the need for continuous change.
- A clear understanding of priorities.
- Greater control over the business and less vulnerability from the unexpected.

In the case of companies without effective marketing planning systems, whilst it is possible to be profitable over a number of years, especially in high-growth markets, such companies will tend to be less profitable over time and to suffer problems that are the very opposite of the benefits referred to above. Furthermore, companies without effective marketing planning systems tend to suffer more serious commercial and organisational consequences when environmental and competitive conditions become hostile and unstable.

■ How to Prepare a Marketing Plan

So far we have discussed the total marketing planning process and in Chapter 8 we considered one of the most important steps in the planning process – the marketing audit. Before turning our attention to the other important steps in the marketing planning process, it will be useful to discuss how marketing planning relates to the corporate planning process. Table 20.1 shows five steps in this process.

As we can see, the starting point is usually a statement of corporate financial objectives for the long-term planning period of the company; these are often expressed in terms of turnover, profit before tax and return on investment.

Table 20.1 Steps in the corporate planning process

Step 1	*Step 2*	*Step 3*	*Step 4*	*Step 5*
Corporate financial objectives	*Management audit* *Marketing audit* Marketing *Distribition audit* Stocks and control; transportation; warehousing *Production audit* Value analysis; engineering development; work study; quality control; labour; materials, plant and space utilisation; production planning; factories *Financial audit* Credit, debt, cash flow and budgetary control; resource allocation; CAPEX; long term finance *Personnel audit* Management, technical and administrative ability, etc.	*Objective strategy setting* Marketing, distribution, production, financial and personnel objectives and strategies	*Plans* Marketing, distribution, production and financial plans	*Corporate plans* Issue of corporate plan, to include corporate objectives and strategies, production objectives and strategies, etc.; long-range P&L accounts and balance sheets

More often than not the long-term planning horizon spans five years; but the precise period should be determined by the nature of the markets in which the company operates. For example, five years would not be a long enough period for a glass manufacturer, since it takes that amount of time to commission a new furnace; whereas in some fashion industries five years would be too long a period. A useful guideline in determining the planning horizon is that there should be a market for the company products for long enough at least to depreciate any capital investment associated with those products.

At this stage it is worth pointing out that one of the main purposes of the corporate plan is to provide a long-term vision of what the company is – or is striving to become – taking into account shareholder expectations, environmental trends, resource market trends, consumption market trends and the distinctive competence of the company as revealed by the management audit. What this means in practice is that the corporate plan will contain the following elements:

- Desired level of profitability.
- Business boundaries:
  - What kinds of products will be sold to what kinds of market(s);
  - What kinds of facilities will be developed (production and logistics);
  - The size and character of the labour force (personnel);
  - Funding (finance).
- Other corporate objectives such as social responsibility, corporate image, stock market image, employee image.

Such a corporate plan, containing projected profit-and-loss accounts and balance sheets – being the result of the process described above – is more likely to provide long-term stability for a company than plans based on a more intuitive process and containing forecasts that tend to be little more than extrapolations of previous trends.

The headquarters of a major multinational company, with a sophisticated budgeting system, used to receive plans from all over the world and coordinate them in quantitative and cross-functional terms (such as number of employees, units of sale, items of plant and square feet of production area) together with the associated financial implications. The trouble was that this complicated edifice was built on initial sales forecasts, which were themselves little more than a time-consuming numbers game. The really key strategic issues relating to products and markets were lost in all the financial activity, which eventually resulted in grave operational and profitability problems.

■ The Steps in the Planning Process

Let us briefly remind ourselves of some of the principal points made about the *marketing audit* in Chapter 8.

- A checklist of questions must be agreed and issued.
- Checklists need to be customised according to level in the organisation to make them meaningful/relevant.
- It is essentially a data base of all relevant company/market related issues.
- It should be continuous/dynamic.
- Do not hide behind vague terms, for example 'poor economic conditions'.
- Do incorporate PLCs and portfolio matrices. (see Chapters 9 and 10). Diagrams and corresponding words should match.
- It is a valuable 'transfer device' for incoming personnel

Compiling the SWOT Analysis

To decide on marketing objectives and future strategy, it is first necessary to summarise the unit's *present* position in its market(s). The marketing audit must now be summarised in the form of a SWOT analysis, which was mentioned briefly in Chapter 8. The word SWOT derives from the initial letters of the words *strengths*, *weaknesses*, *opportunities* and *threats*. In simple terms:

- What are the opportunities?
- What are the present and future threats to the unit's business in each of the segments which have been identified as being of importance?
- What are the unit's *differential* strengths and weaknesses *vis-à-vis* competitors? In other words, why should potential customers in the target markets prefer to deal with you rather than with any of your competitors?

Guidelines for completing the SWOT Analysis

The marketing audit will have identified what are considered to be the key markets upon which the company should focus. For presentation purposes, it is helpful to prepare a SWOT for each of these key products. Each of these SWOTs should be brief and interesting to read.

Point 1 below indicates how the *opportunities* and *threats* section of the SWOT should be completed. Point 2 concerns *strengths* and *weaknesses*.

1. *Summary of outside influences and their implications* This should include a brief statement about how important environmental influences, such as technology, government policies and regulations and the economy have affected this segment. There will obviously be some opportunities and some threats.

2. *Some important factors for success in this business* How does a competitor wishing to provide products in the same segment succeed? Relatively few factors determine success: factors such as product performance, quality of software, breadth of services, speed of service and low costs are often the most important ones.

A brief statement should now be made about the company's strengths and weaknesses in relation to the most important factors for success that have been identified. To do this, it will probably be necessary to consider other specialist suppliers to the same segment in order to identify why your company can succeed and what weaknesses must be addressed in the long-term plan.

■ Planning Assumptions

Having completed our marketing audit and SWOT analysis, assumptions now have to be made and explicitly written down. There are certain key determinants of success in all companies about which assumptions have to be made before the planning process can proceed. For example, it would be no good receiving plans from two product managers, one of whom believed the economy was going into decline by 2 per cent whilst the other believed the economy was about to grow by 10 per cent.

An example of presented assumptions might be:

- 'With respect to the company's industrial climate, it is assumed that:
  1. Industrial overcapacity will increase from 105 per cent to 115 per cent as new industrial plants come into operation;
  2. price competition will force price levels down by 10 per cent across the board;
  3. a new product will be introduced by our major competitor before the end of the second quarter.'

Assumptions should be few in number, and if a plan is robust – that is, possible irrespective of any assumption made, then so much the better.

■ Marketing Objectives and Strategies

The next step in marketing planning is the writing of marketing objectives and strategies, the key step in the whole process.

- *Objectives* are what you want to achieve.
- *Strategies* are how you plan to achieve your objectives.

Therefore, there can be objectives and strategies at all levels in marketing. For example, there can be advertising objectives and strategies, and pricing objectives and strategies.

However, it is important to remember that marketing objectives are about *products and markets only*. Common sense will confirm that it is only by selling something to someone that the company's financial goals can be achieved, and that advertising, pricing and service levels are the means (or strategies) by which we might succeed in doing this. Thus pricing objectives, sales-promotion objectives and advertising objectives should not be confused with marketing objectives. In other words, we can say that marketing objectives are about one or more of the following:

- Existing products in existing markets.
- New products for existing markets.
- Existing products for new markets.
- New products for new markets.

They should be capable of measurement, otherwise they are not objectives. Directional terms such as 'maximise', 'minimise', 'penetrate' and 'increase' are only acceptable if quantitative measurement can be attached to them over the planning period. Measurement should be in terms of sales volume, money value (pounds, francs or dollars, for example), market share and percentage penetration of outlets.

Marketing strategies are the means by which marketing objectives will be achieved and are generally concerned with the four Ps – that is product, pricing, place and promotion decisions. Having completed this major planning task, it is normal at this stage to employ judgement, experience and field tests to assess the feasibility of the objectives and strategies in terms of market share, sales, costs and profits.

■ Programmes

The general marketing strategies are now developed into specific 'sub-objectives', each supported by more detailed strategy and action statements, with timings and responsibilities clearly indicated.

■ Use of Marketing Plans

A written marketing plan is the background against which operational decisions are taken on an ongoing basis; consequently too much detail should not be included. We should remember that its major function is to determine where the company is *now*, where it wants to *go* and *how* to get there. This is central to the company's revenue-generating activities, and from it flow all other corporate activities, such as the timing of the cash flow and the size and character of the labour force. Finally, the marketing plan should be distributed to those who need to know what is going on, since its purpose is as an aid to effective management.

■ International Marketing Planning

The process of marketing planning outlined in this chapter is universally applicable, irrespective of company size and complexity. The only real difference concerns the degree of formality of the processes and procedures.

In the case of a company operating internationally, a more formalised approach is advisable in order to gain the economies of scale and scope that give international organisations their competitive edge. For example, in order to create a truly international brand such as Perrier or Castrol GTX, the kind of issues outlined in the section on global branding in Chapter 10 must obviously be planned centrally. Perhaps it is worth repeating the definition of a global brand given there:

- A global brand is a product that bears the same name and logo and presents the same or similar message all over the world. Usually the product is aimed at the same target market and is promoted and presented in much the same way.

Consequently it is clear that the brand's positioning must be planned and controlled centrally. This will embrace the channels used to reach the target market, the price position within the market and, of course, the way it is promoted.

In many organisations product planning needs to be centrally controlled in order to ensure a balanced portfolio globally. This will entail an understanding of a product's position in its life-cycle in each country and region of the world in order to ensure that appropriate objectives and strategies are set for it, together with the decision when and how to allocate R&D resources.

In respect of the process of international product planning itself, the following section outlines the issues that are important.

International Product Planning

Inadequate product planning is a major factor inhibiting successful international marketing operations. The stories of product failures, once an organisation steps outside its home territory, are legion.

One of the better known stories concerns Campbell Soup, which tried to sell its US tomato soup formulation to the British, only to discover, after incurring considerable losses, that the British prefer a more bitter taste. Even the great Philip Morris did not understand sufficiently well that Canadians prefer a Virginia tobacco and failed with their blended tobacco.

In general, the three most important questions to be answered in the domain of international product planning are:

- Do I need to adapt my national products when I sell them abroad?
- What product line should I sell in world markets?
- How do I develop products for international markets?

In many markets the product application is not universal. Additionally there are legal/semi-legal requirements that must be satisfied. All of this, of course, is in addition to the normal needs/wants analysis by means of market research. Yet other obstacles to overcome, however, are those concerned with production and distribution complexities not encountered in home markets.

If a similar product or service already exists in the target country, there is likely to be a standard for it. So, under the product itself, we need to look for:

- Legal requirements (such as environment/pollution legislation).
- Mandatory standards (such as electrical safety standards).
- Industry standards (such as light alloy wheels in Germany).
- Voluntary standards (such as paper size).

One major problem is that, whereas standards are always well defined, they tend to be:

- Different by country.
- Many in number and coverage (measurement, quality, material properties, performance, safety and so on).
- Different in legal backing/adherence and rationale (protectionism, tradition and so on).

Figure 20.2 shows some of the physical product characteristics that need to be most carefully researched in all target countries.

For example, in respect of raw material input, paper size is different in photocopiers in different markets; different flour quality affects the design of baking machinery. In the case of size, there are different generator sizes in different countries. In the case of application, tyre requirements differ significantly in hot countries, although the product is essentially the same. In the case of packaging, codes, symbols, languages, protective requirements and the like differ from country to country.

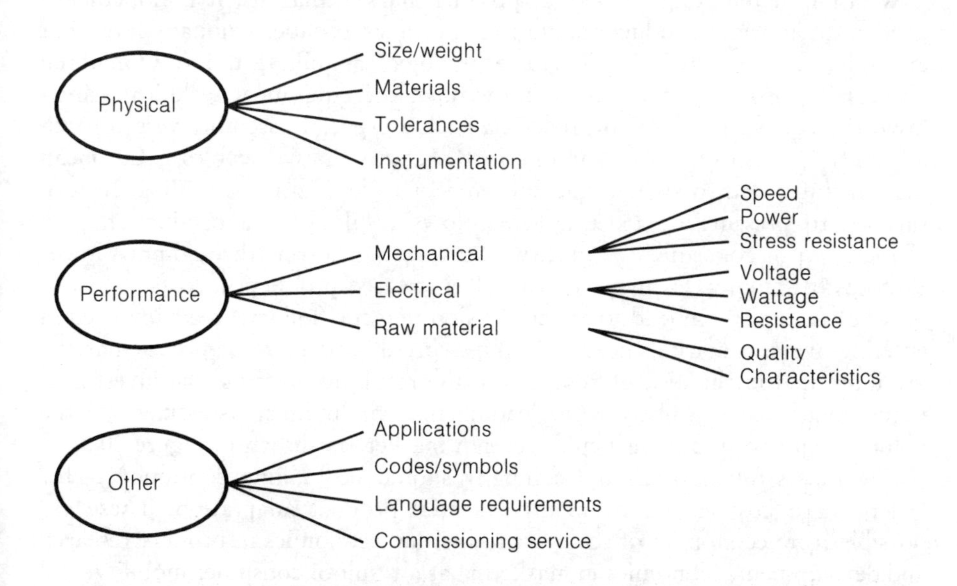

Figure 20.2 Product characteristics in respect of foreign markets

Not all of this, however, is bad. In the case of one boiler manufacturer, who discovered that stainless steel lining became furred up by the high chalk content of German water and that copper piping suffered from a chemical reaction in Germany, changed the basic product design for the home market, as well as for the German market, saved 24 per cent on costs and opened up a much larger market for its boilers as a result.

Understanding market characteristics, then, involves several stages, as shown in Table 20.2.

Table 20.2 Understanding market characteristics

Analysis	*Seeking answers*
Competitive product performance	Why is their product made the way it is?
Market usage patterns	*How* are the products used? *Where* will they be applied?
Customer-specific expectations	*How* does the foreign customer's process differ from the home market? *What* do they expect from the product?
Product trials/test	Where are the likely weaknesses of the product in use?

Whilst is it tempting to stop at product/market analysis, it is nonetheless prudent to consider product adaptation at a much broader company level. For example, do we have the design/technology capability, the raw material processing capability, the labour know-how, the equipment/technical know-how, the correct production processes, such as special assembly versus batch assembly, and so on? For example, in the case of power cables a European manufacturer had to switch machines and provide additional tooling. In turn this led to pressure on existing work-flows resulting in a production plan change, with consequent capacity constraints, slower throughput, lower earnings for employees and, worst of all, increased production costs.

Issues such as these lead to the conclusion that the financial risks involved in entering overseas markets need to be most carefully evaluated. In particular, we are interested in the cost of adaptation, the resulting margins, the investment requirement and the likely ROI, leading to a preliminary assessment of the volume required in any particular foreign market, as shown in Figure 20.3.

The successful international company should be looking continuously for synergy and cost saving from any essential product adaptation. These are possible from economies of scale in production, economies in product research and development, economies in marketing as a result of consumer mobility, and the impact of technology.

PRODUCT/ PRODUCT GROUP	COUNTRY (note others where same specification for these products apply)	CURRENT STATUS OF APPROVALS IN THIS PRODUCT/ MARKET SECTOR	SPECIFIC CHANGES TO MEET SPECIFICATION	TIME AND COST TO GET APPROVAL					TOTAL COST	Minimum volume required
				Technical changes	Production trials	Approval authority test	Cost of application	Other		

Figure 20.3 Specifications implications analysis

To summarise, international product planning involves the following:

- The product itself:
  - standardisation;
  - adaptation;
- Packaging and labelling:
  - protection/security;
  - promotional/channel aspects;
  - cultural factors;
  - package size;
  - language;
  - government.
- Brands and trademarks:
  - global or national;
  - legal;
  - cultural;
  - other marketing considerations.
- Warranty and service:
  - international customers;
  - safety;
  - varying quality control standards internationally;
  - varying use conditions;
  - promotion;
  - service networks.

To achieve all these things successfully the organisation needs a marketing planning system that is consistent across each of the countries and regions in which it does business. Whilst this will clearly be more difficult in the case of trading carried out through third parties such as agents and distributors, it should, nonetheless, still be the goal in order to exercise international control.

In summary, each management decision must resolve the issues illustrated in Figure 20.4.

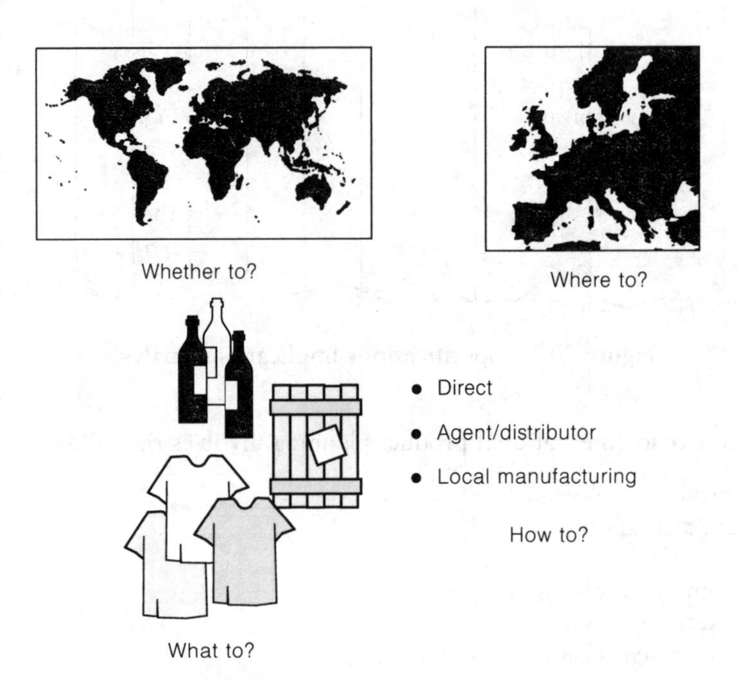

Figure 20.4 The key questions to international marketing

Whether to market abroad: geographical extension may be more desirable than product diversification, depending, of course, on circumstances. However the decision to sell abroad should not be taken lightly.

Where to market abroad: this is one of the major decisions for international marketing. Choosing foreign markets on the basis merely of proximity and similarity is not necessarily the most profitable option to go for.

What to market abroad: the degree to which products should be altered to suit foreign needs is a fundamental problem in international marketing, as can be seen from the section on international product management above.

How to market abroad: this is concerned not just with the issue of how to enter a foreign market, but also with the management of the four 'P's once a company arrives. Finally, there is the difficult question of how to coordinate the international effort in many foreign markets in order to gain competitive advantage.

■ Can Marketing Planning Fail?

As a rule, formalised marketing planning procedures result in greater profitability and stability in the long term and also help to reduce friction and operational difficulties within organisations.

When marketing planning fails, it is generally because companies place too much emphasis on the procedures and the resulting paperwork, rather than on generating information useful to and consumable by management. Also, when companies relegate marketing planning to a 'planner' it invariably fails, for the simple reason that planning for line management cannot be delegated to a third party. The real role of the planner should be to help those responsible for implementation to plan. Failure to recognise this simple fact can be disastrous. Equally, planning failures often result from companies trying too much too quickly and without training staff in the use of procedures.

One Swedish company selling batteries internationally tried unsuccessfully four times to introduce a marketing planning system, each one failing because management throughout the organisation was confused by what was being asked of them. Furthermore not only did they not understand the need for the new systems, but they were also not provided with the necessary resources to make the system work effectively.

Training of managers and careful thought about resource requirements would have overcome this particular company's problems to a great extent.

In contrast, a major multinational company, having suffered grave profitability and operational difficulties through not having an effective marketing planning system, introduced one over a three-year period. It included a training programme in the use of new procedures and the provision of adequate resources to make them work effectively. This company is now firmly in control of its diverse activities and has recovered its confidence and profitability.

■ Summary

There are a number of points to be watched for that may signal the beginning of a marketing plan failure. Recognition of these will reinforce the purpose of a marketing plan, which is to aid effective management. It cannot be a substitute. These points are summarised below.

There is a process for marketing planning, the formalisation of which is a function of size and product market complexity. This process is no different in an international context. The choice of product strategy in international markets is a function of three key factors:

- The product itself, defined in terms of the function or need it serves.
- The market, defined in terms of the conditions under which the product is used, including the preferences of potential customers and their ability to buy the products in question.
- The costs of adaptation to the company.

■ Marketing Planning Systems Design and Implementation Problems

- Weak support from chief executive and top management.
- Lack of a plan for planning.
- Lack of line management support:
  - hostility;
  - lack of skills;
  - lack of information;
  - lack of resources;
  - inadequate organisational structure.
- Confusion over planning terms.
- Numbers in lieu of written objectives and strategies.
- Too much detail, too far ahead.
- Once-a-year ritual.
- Separation of operational planning from strategic planning.
- Failure to integrate marketing planning into a total corporate planning system.
- Delegation of planning to a planner.

■ What Goes Into a Marketing Plan?

- Only the SWOT (not the audit) goes in a marketing plan.
- A summary emanating from the marketing audit.
- A brief, interesting, concise commentary.
- Focus on *key* factors only.
- List *differential* strengths and weaknesses *vis-à-vis* competitors.
- List *key* external opportunities and threats.
- Identify and pin down the *real issues*; not a list of unrelated points.
- The reader should be able to grasp instantly the main thrust of the business; he should even be able to write your marketing objectives.
- Follow the implied question, 'which means that . . .?' to get to the real implications.
- Do not over-abbreviate.
- Spend time on the SWOT. It is worth it.

■ Assumptions

- Must be few in number.
- If a plan can happen irrespective of the assumption, the assumption is unnecessary.

Marketing Objectives

- Products/services and markets only.
- They articulate what we are committing ourselves to, and the corresponding resource implications.
- They flow from the SWOT and must be compatible.
- They should be quantifiable and measureable. Avoid directional terms such as 'increase', 'improve' and so on
- There will be a hierarchy of objectives throughout the organisation.
- Set priorities for the chosen marketing objectives.
- Do not mix up objectives and strategies (objectives – what we want to achieve; strategies – how).

Marketing Strategies

- Product, pricing, place and promotion policies.
- Marketing strategies must eventually be transformed into detailed marketing actions.

Programmes

- Forecasts come last (not simple extrapolations), they are not objectives.
- Specific subobjectives for products and segments, with detailed strategy and action statements (what, where, when, costs and so on).
- Include budgets and forecasts and a consolidated budget.
- Budgets and forecasts *must* reflect marketing objectives. Objectives, strategies and programmes *must* reflect agreed budgets and sales forecasts.

CHAPTER 21

Organisation and Control of Marketing

Organisation

Organisation for effective marketing is a subject that is fraught with difficulty, largely because all companies and all markets are different. The complexities arising from the possible combinations of product, market, geography, function and size make it impossible to be prescriptive about the way a company should organise for marketing. Nonetheless, there are some abiding general principles.

At a 'macro' level, there are basically two kinds of organisation, which can be described as decentralised or centralised. In *decentralised* organisations, the company frequently has a strategic level of management at headquarters, supported by a number of managers making up central services such as product development, finance, personnel and production. At the divisional or subsidiary level there is often a similar kind of organisation, with each divisional chief in charge of his own area of responsibility, being largely independent as long as profits are satisfactory.

The point about this kind of decentralised organisational structure is that it inevitably leads to duplication of effort and differentiation of strategies, with all the consequent problems, unless a major effort is made to get some synergy out of the several systems by means of a company-wide planning system. One company in the telecommunications industry had a range of 1500 products and one of those products had 1300 different variations; all of which was the result of a totally decentralised marketing-orientated approach in the subsidiary companies. It is not surprising that any sensible economies of scale in production were virtually impossible, with the result that the company made a substantial loss. The same problems apply to marketing research, advertising, pricing, distribution and other business areas. When someone takes the trouble to find out, it is often very salutary to see the reaction of senior managers at headquarters when they are told, for example, that the very same market problem is being researched in many different countries around the world, all at enormous expense.

It is this kind of organisational structure that, above all others, requires strong central coordination by means of some kind of planning system; otherwise everyone wastes enormous amounts of corporate resources in striving to maximise their own small part of the business. If, however, some system can be found of gaining synergy from all the energy expended, then the rewards are great indeed.

In a *centrally* controlled company there is often no strategic level of management in the subsidiary units, particularly in respect of new product introductions. This kind of organisational form tends to lead to standardised strategies, particularly in respect of product management. For example, when a new product is introduced it tends to be designed at the outset with as many markets as possible in mind, while the benefits from market research in one area are passed on to other areas, and so on. The problem here, of course, is that unless great care is exercised the company can easily become less sensitive to the needs of individual markets, and hence lose flexibility in reacting to competitive moves. The point is that marketing in this kind of system means something different from marketing in the kind of system described above.

There is a difference between financial manipulation and business management in respect of the headquarters role. There is a difference between a corporation and its individual components, and often there is confusion about what kind of planning should be done by managers at varying levels in the organisation, such confusion arising because the chief executive has not made it clear what kind of business he is managing.

We have looked briefly at two principal organisational forms, both of which consist essentially of a central office and various decentralised divisions, each with its own unique products, processes and markets, which complement the others in the group. In enterprises of this type, planning within the divisions applies to the exploration of markets and improved efficiency within the boundaries laid down by headquarters,. The problems and opportunities that this method throws up tend to make the role of headquarters one of classifying the boundaries for the enterprise as a whole in relation to new products and markets that do not appear to fall within the scope of one of the divisions.

In this type of organisation, the managers of affiliated companies are normally required to produce the level of profit set by headquarters management within the constraints imposed on them. Such companies need to institutionalise this process by providing a formal structure of ideas and systems so that operating management know what they are expected to do and whether they are doing the essential things. The point about these kinds of organisation seems to be that some method has to be found of planning and controlling the growth of the business in order to utilise effectively the evolving skills and growing reputation of the firm, and so avoid an uncontrolled dissipation of energy. It is probably easier to do this in a centrally-organised firm, but, as we have pointed out, both forms of organisation have their disadvantages.

Finally, the financial trust type of organisation needs to be mentioned briefly. The primary concern of its central management is the investment of shareholders' capital in various businesses. The buying and selling of interests in various firms is done for appreciation of capital rather than for building an enterprise with any logic of its own. Planning in this type of operation requires different knowledge and skills, and addresses itself to different kinds of problems from those of the two organisational forms described above.

There are two further points worth making briefly about organising for marketing. The first is that where marketing and sales are separated at board level, marketing planning is going to be a very different kind of activity from a situation in which both functions are coordinated at board level. Figure 21.1 illustrates these two different situations.

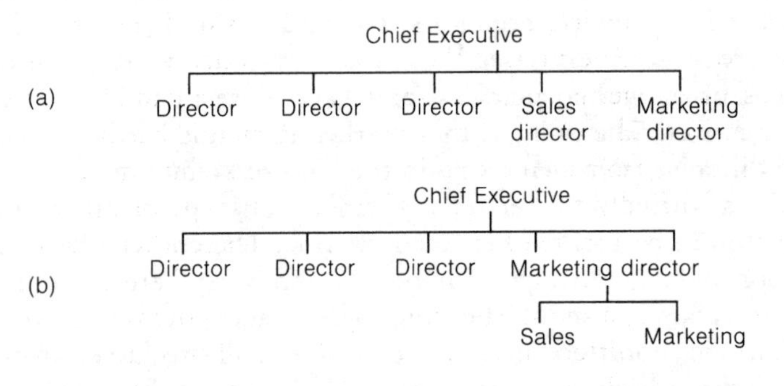

Figure 21.1 Alternative marketing/sales organisations

In the first of these organisational forms, marketing is very much a staff activity, with the real power vested in the sales organisation. While a strong chief executive can ensure that the two activities are sensibly coordinated, unfortunately this rarely happens because he is often too busy with production, distribution, personnel and financial issues to devote enough of his time to sales and marketing. The point here is that a sales force is quite correctly concerned with today's products, problems and customers, while the marketing manager needs to be thinking about the future. The sales force is also quite correctly concerned mainly with individual products, problems and customers, while a marketing manager needs to be thinking about groups of products and customers (portfolio management and market segmentation). The two jobs are closely connected, but fundamentally different, and great care is necessary to ensure that what the marketing department is planning is the same as what the sales force is actually doing in the field. All too often it is not.

The second kind of organisational form tends to make it easier to ensure a sensible coordination between planning and doing.

Whatever the marketing organisational form, there are a number of issues that all firms have to address. These are:

- Functions (such as advertising, market research, pricing)
- Products
- Markets
- Geographical locations
- Channels

Of these, most firms would readily agree that in most cases the two main issues are products and markets, which is why many companies have what are called 'product managers' and/or 'market managers'. There can be no right or wrong answer to the question of which of these is the better, and commonsense will dictate that market circumstances alone will determine which is most appropriate for any one company.

Each has its strengths and weaknesses. A product-manager-orientated system will ensure good strong product orientation, but can also easily lead to superficial market knowledge. Many a company has been caught out by subtle changes in their several markets, causing a product to become practically redundant. In consumer goods, for example, many companies are beginning to admit that their rigid product/brand management system has allowed their major customers, for example retail chains, to take the initiative; and many are now changing belatedly to a system in which the focus of marketing activity revolves around major customer/market groups rather than individual products.

On the other hand, a market-manager-orientated system can easily result in unnecessary product differentiation and poor overall product development.

Ideally, therefore, whatever organisational form is adopted, the two central issues of products and markets constantly need to be addressed. This conundrum is summarized in the following brief case study.

Wessol Ltd manufactures two basic types of machinery, mechanical and electrical, that are supplied to a number of markets, principally oil, gas, water, automotive and farming.

Wessol has both a product management and a market management structure (Figure 21.2). The basic role of the product manager is to ensure that the

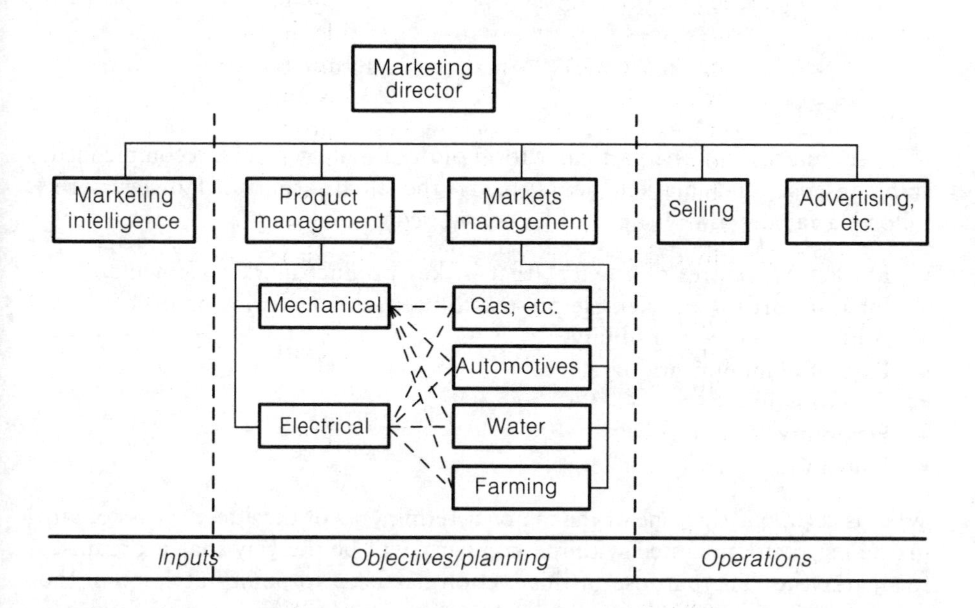

Figure 21.2 Wessol's product/market management structure

product is properly managed, while the role of the market manager is to pay particular attention to the needs of the market. Close liaison between the two is obviously necessary, and a basic principle of this kind of organisation is that ultimate authority for the final decision must be vested in either one or the other. Even when this is done, however, communications can still be difficult, and great care is necessary to ensure that vested interests are not allowed to dominate the real product/market issues.

This is the basis of the classic matrix organisation which in the case of Wessol can be represented as in Figure 21.3.

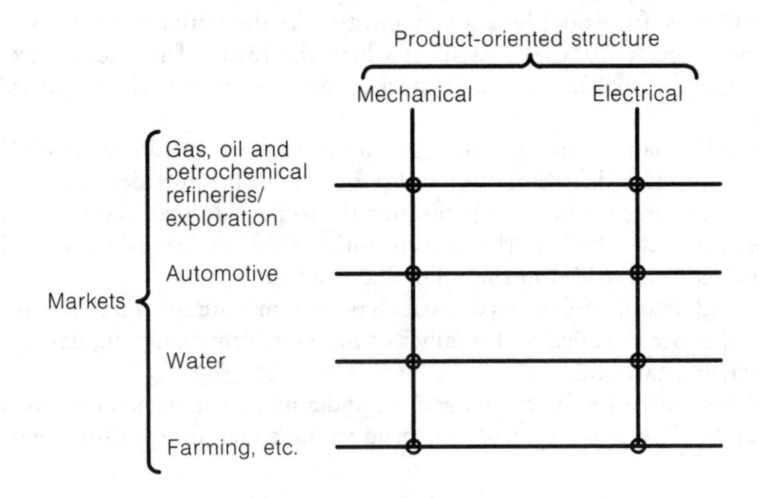

Figure 21.3 A matrix organisation

To summarise, no one particular form of organisation can be recommended, commonsense and market needs being the final arbiters. However, the following factors always need to be considered:

- Marketing 'centres of gravity' (that is, key product/market segments).
- Interface areas (for example present/future; salesmen/drawing office).
- Authority and responsibility.
- Ease of communication.
- Coordination.
- Flexibility.
- Human factors.

What is certain is that one of the major determinants of the effectiveness of any marketing plan attempted within a company will be the way that it organises for marketing. The purpose of this section has been to point out some of the more obvious issues and pitfalls before outlining a number of approaches to control, to which we will now turn.

Control

Just as there is a hierarchy of objectives, so there has to be a hierarchy of information and control data. For example, at the *macro* level in a company information will have to be generated to show overall sales volume; whilst at the *micro* level varying degrees of individual account detail will have to be generated according to the needs of the company.

At the next level down, each department will need to generate its own specific control data, so that, for example, if an advertising objective is to achieve an attitude change over a given period, then it will require an attitude survey in order to ascertain whether this particular objective has been achieved. Or, if the objective was to convey a particular piece of information to a specific target market, then again research will be necessary to establish whether this objective was achieved. The same principle would also apply to the sales department, which ideally will have a series of control data generated and distributed according to need, as well as establishing its own specialised control procedures when circumstances demand information that cannot be generated by the general company information and control system.

Any information system should be closely related to the company's organisation and objectives so that relevant information for decision-making can be presented to each level of management. Thus, the objective of a company's sales information and control system may include some or all of the following objectives:

- To provide a weekly guide to sales performance indicating any likely budget shortfalls.
- To review, each period, product performance in total and within each category of trade, providing comparison against last year and against sales forecast.
- To examine the contribution of each product to both sales and gross profit and to assess the effect of 'mix' on the overall profit percentage of each market.
- To provide for marketing management information that allows them to identify strengths and weaknesses by product, by market and by geographical region.
- To provide sales-operating statements for senior management.
- To provide information by geographical unit for the use of sales and distribution management in restructuring territories and redefining distribution boundaries.
- To enable sales management to review the trading situation of any customer in terms of profit.
- To encourage development of profitable accounts not only through greater sales but also increased delivery drop size and more relevant discounts.
- To enable sales management to monitor trading agreements.

- To enable salesmen to schedule their work according to a predetermined calling cycle.
- To ensure that, in the call, the salesman is equipped with accurate and up-to-date information on the customer's order pattern, overall sales performance, and mix of sales.
- To analyse for sales management the productivity of salesmen in terms of calling rate and product placement.
- To identify by type of outlet and product the penetration achieved and the potential in existing accounts.

These and many more are the kind of objectives that result in the detailed output a system will produce, such as brand performance.

The important fact that emerges from any review of information and control procedures is that its purpose should be to provide management with the necessary information to enable it to monitor its progress towards its predetermined objectives, thus providing the necessary loop in the planning cycle.

Nonetheless, the basic tool for controlling the marketing effort is the budget, which itself derives from the marketing plan.

■ Setting the Marketing Budget

Perhaps the most central and frequent question asked in respect of a marketing programme is, 'how much should we spend?' Certainly, this is one of the most difficult problems facing any marketing manager. It may also explain why relatively little attention is given to this problem, compared with other aspects of marketing. However, before we decide how much we should spend, it is worth trying to isolate those costs that are justifiable marketing costs.

■ Identifying Marketing Costs

Many people contend that the marketing budget is an unambiguous concept – it is quite simply a statement of marketing costs. However, in practice the marketing budget should be much more than this. Strictly, a comprehensive marketing budget will include all direct and indirect costs of the marketing organisation, such as those outlined below:

- Staff costs.
- Office and equipment expenses.
- Marketing mix costs:
  - product policy (packaging, new product lauches, modification lauches and so on);
  - pricing (discounts given, price lists, commissions, and so on);

- communications (advertising media and production costs, sales promotions, public relations, sales force office and field costs, and so on);
- distribution (transport of finished goods, storage, warehousing, special deals with distributors, and so on).

However, this is not normal practice and there are a number of reasons for this. First, there is often some reluctance to identify marketing as a cost centre. It is easier, given the problems of cause and effect analysis, to consider marketing as little more than an overhead, or a charge against profits, rather than a revenue creator and profit maker.

The list above falls into the trap of combining *controllable* and *uncontrollable* costs; this inevitably invalidates the use of the budget as a planning and a control mechanism. For example, in one European company the largest component of the marketing budget was *distributor commission*; that is, the difference between sales value at list prices and revenues received from distributors. In fact, since commission rates were set by the finance department and senior management, this was to a great extent an 'uncontrollable factor' for the marketing department and sales managers.

Another related problem is the danger of confusing *overheads* with direct or *incremental* costs. A product manager may plan sales promotions and construct a budget for them, but he is unlikely to be involved in determining the costs of administering the sales office and order processing system.

Even more difficult – yet essential if one is to improve the productivity of the sales effort – is to attempt to allocate costs right down to individual customer accounts in order to determine the true costs associated with dealing with specific outlets.

Such an approach is based on the principle that the individual customer is the ultimate profit centre and that costs incurred after production are primarily related to the customer and the unique factors associated with serving him, such as order size, sales discounts, returned goods, promotional items and delivery costs. A customer profitability model is given in Table 21.1. This is followed by a worked example.

The *comprehensive budget* implies a particular form of marketing organisation and a particular type and degree of marketing management responsibility. Empirical studies have shown that it is all too easy to exaggerate the real responsibilities of the marketing manager. At its simplest, for instance, if the marketing department has no responsibility for physical distribution, then it has no real place in the budget. This then highlights the whole question of what is, and what is not, a marketing cost.

Let us take the example of an Anglo-Arab joint publishing venture operating in the Middle East. This was a comparatively infant enterprise employing expatriate staff whose general manager reported to the parent company in England as well as to the local Arab directors. The marketing function of the company embraced a sales force of six, headed by a marketing manager. The production function of the company was subcontracted to the British parent

Table 21.1 Customer profitability model

	£	£
Gross sales value		80 000
Less discounts	8 000	
Net sales values		72 000
Less production costs	44 000	
Gross profits		28 000
Less sales and distribution costs:		
1. Selling cost	9 000	
2. Order processing	6 500	
3. Warehousing and order assembly	6 400	
4. Cost of holding stock	800	
5. Inbound freight	1 600	
6. Outbound freight	2 700	
7. Returns	250	
8. Merchandising	4 500	
9. Cost of credit	1 100	
TOTAL	32 850	
Net contribution		(4 850)

Notes

1. *Selling*: includes costs of sales force (including sales management) and sales administration, allocated according to visit frequency and call duration.
2. *Order processing*: includes costs relating to credit rating, stock checking, processing the order, raising invoices, and the accounts and credit control departments, allocated according to turnover.
3. *Warehousing and order assembly*: includes warehousing, fixed costs, order picking, assembly and loading, allocated on the basis of work study measurements.
4. *Cost of holding stock*: includes credit, insurance, shrinkage, pilferage, staff.
5. *Inbound freight*: costs of transport from factory to warehouse, allocated according to order size.
6. *Freight out*: costs of transport from warehouse to customer. A standard unit of cost.
7. *Returns*: includes cost of returned goods, plus returns of packaging materials.
8. *Merchandising*: cost of merchandising, i.e. price marking, shelf stacking, displays, etc.
9. *Cost of credit*: cost of credit over the average period of outstanding debts.

company, and the editorial policy and financial functions, whilst run from the Middle East base, were controlled also by the parent company. In practice, the two line managers, the company accountant and the marketing manager reported to the general manager and were concerned only with the marketing income and expenditure of the company. This covered not only the costs of the sales team, marketing channels, advertising and promotion, but also the costs of inventory storage and shipment, together with all the fixed overheads of the Middle East operation. Equally, the company's sources of income were derived solely through publication and advertising-space sales achieved by the marketing department. In effect the planning and control of the marketing budget was the company's profit and loss account.

In other words, it is necessary to accept that the components of the marketing budget vary very greatly between companies. It is not the place in a book of this nature to give step-by-step guidelines for all the principal permutations. Rather, we consider as many elements and models for approaching the marketing budget process as possible, so that you can apply the most appropriate to your own particular circumstances.

Such is the ambiguity on the subject that one management accountant was recorded recently as saying:

> 'Unfortunately, it may well be that many controllers have resigned themselves to assuming that marketing cost is an impossible area to analyse and control.'

Fortunately, however, all is not gloom and disarray! An American survey has demonstrated that three-quarters of a sample of large industrial companies in the USA budgeted around the following concepts – and successfully:

- *Order-filling activities* – mainly concentrated on physical distribution costs such as transport, warehousing, order handling, credit and stocking.
- *Order-getting activities* – mainly centred upon advertising, sales promotion and merchandising.

In many companies the marketing budget is in effect the budget for advertising and promotion. The substantive control of an important budget may, in organisational terms, be both a source of power and a sign of that power to others. It has been noted, for instance, that in companies with a large TV advertising budget, real control has passed from the marketing department to general managers and company directors.

Budgets as Managerial Tools

All budgets, no matter how they are constructed, still serve the original purpose. That is, they enable managers to pull together their commitments, their plans and projects, and all the costs involved into one comprehensive document – in this case a marketing budget. Above all it is a managerial tool, not just a financial device. One of the best ways to approach a marketing budget is to ask the simple question: 'What are the expected results?'

Budgets are expressed in monetary terms, but we should regard monetary terms as a kind of shorthand for the actual efforts needed. They should be based on real values. In other words, the marketing budget should be a tool by which we can think through the relationship between desired results and available means. Whatever we do, we should avoid the worst pitfall of all, that is, a tendency to regard last year's expenditure as being 'about right' and to project this into the new budget.

Budget Alternatives

It is important that each manager responsible for the marketing function should identify the costs and revenue for which he or she is accountable. As we mentioned earlier, care must be taken to assess the relevance of including the following in a marketing budget:

- Fixed costs.
- Variable costs.
- Controllable costs.
- Uncontrollable costs.

It will be all too easy for the marketing department to find itself responsible for certain capital investment costs, depreciation of equipment costs, research and development expenditure and public relations activity, when, in reality, the demarcation as to which item belongs to which department is a grey area because it has never been correctly allocated. Until this is clear, marketing objectives and strategies cannot be quantified in terms of expected results.

Zero-based Budgeting

Zero-based budgeting is growing in popularity, since, rather than starting with last year's expenditure, new targets and objectives are the primary concern. Questions are asked such as: 'Are we operating in the right area? Is the area a priority?'

The marketing director is asked to justify his marketing expenditure each year from a zero base against the tasks he wishes to perform, and for which he can forecast revenue expectations, rather than starting with last year's budget and adding a percentage.

This should not be too difficult if the procedures outlined in Chapter 20 are adhered to; a hierarchy of objectives will be built up in such a way that every item of budget expenditure can be related back directly to its own specific objective and ultimately to the corporate financial objectives. Thus, having identified sales promotion as a major promotional strategy for achieving an objective in a particular market – when sales promotional items appear in the programme – each one has a specific purpose that can be related back to a major objective.

Doing it this way not only ensures that every item of expenditure is fully accounted for as part of a rational objective and task approach, but also that when changes have to be made during the period to which the plan relates they can be made in a way that causes least damage to the company's long-term objectives.

Zero-based budgeting can, and should, be used by every organisation as a tool for the periodic systematic review of all products, markets and related activities, so helping the systematic abandonment of the obsolescent, the unproductive, and above all the unnecessary.

□ *Life-cycle Budgeting*

Life-cycle budgeting is based on the principle that the budget should start out with the appropriate time cycle. What portion of the expenditure needed over this time cycle belongs in this current budgeting period? This will be particularly relevant to marketing operations where product life-cycles have to be viewed in relation to the phasing-in of new products and the phasing-out of those that have reached maturity or decline. This will also allow for other expenditure such as pilot testing of new products, marketing research and the projected cash-generation life of cash cows and stars.

One of the best-known examples of life-cycle budgeting is that which Robert McNamara introduced into the American defence budget while secretary of defence under President Kennedy's administration in the early 1960s. Under the budgeting process of the US government, as it had been practised earlier, the armed services submitted their requests for money for the development of a new weapon, such as a new fighter plane, on an annual basis. In other words, they asked for enough money to get a project started without disclosing how much money it would take to get the project finished. Then, when the first few hundred million dollars had been spent, they always argued that to abandon a product because its costs were rising sharply (as the new plan moved from drawing board into production) would lead to a waste of money already spent. When the first prototype of the plane rolled off the production line and when it became apparent that there would be need for an expensive and extensive training programme (and also for very large sums of money to buy replacement parts for the plane) they could argue that not to provide these sums in the future budget would mean a waste of very large sums already spent.

Under life-cycle costing the armed services are supposed to present total cost estimates over the life of the proposed weapon, including the training expenses and the expense for maintaining, repairing, and replacing equipment. This, in theory at least, enables the secretary of defence, the president and the Congress to know in advance the size of the commitment and its impact on future budgets.

Life-cycle costing, or some variant of it, is increasingly standard practice in many companies. In fact, it is now regarded as poor budgeting practice to assume that a new product – whether involving capital investment or an activity such as an advertising campaign – will cost less in the future. In other words, marketing managers should always think through the implications of how much more money will be required to run with success.

□ *Operating Budget and Opportunities Budget*

Many companies nowadays separate their budgets into two parts. One is the *operating budget*, which deals with all the things that are already being done. The other is sometimes called the *opportunities budget*, which deals with new products, development, research and testing.

In terms of the operating budget the marketing manager should ask questions such as:

- What is the minimum that needs to be done in this area to prevent damage?
- How much effort and resources do we need to keep this activity operational?
- What are the minimum requirements needed to prevent unacceptable performance?

In respect of the opportunities budget, the first question should be:

- Is this the right opportunity?

If the answer is yes, then the next questions must be:

- What is the optimum, in terms of resources and money, that this opportunity can absorb at the present level?
- Can we hope to speed up the development process of a badly needed new product by putting more people to work on it?
- Will this create confusion?

□ *Human Resources Budgeting*

Most budgets provide only for money and specify where it should be spent. They do not contain the necessary provisions to make reasonably sure that the expected results can be obtained. They do not provide for the only resource that can produce results: accomplished people. This is particularly relevant to marketing managers, where skilled sales representatives, market researchers, advertising personnel and public relations executives are crucial to the survival of the company. Recruitment and training must be accounted for both in terms of time and money resources.

□ *Sales Budget*

Whilst the overall marketing commitment is the responsibility of any marketing manager, it may be that in smaller companies considerations such as product research and development, testing and extensive marketing research are not relevant in terms of a young or comparatively small operation. It may be that the sales budget will be central to the marketing manager's objectives.

■ Summary

Whilst this chapter has not attempted to address specific financial questions, it has demonstrated the issues and problems associated with marketing budgeting before any 'numbers are crunched'. The numbers can be worked out with comparative ease once the criteria for expected results been explored fully and marketing management have a clear brief as to what they are accountable for and what marketing objectives must be satisfied.

The essential feature of marketing organisation and control is that it 'closes the loop' and connects marketing plans to marketing actions. Ultimately, therefore, the way we manage marketing is the major determinant of commercial success or failure.

Further Reading

Baker, M., *Marketing Strategy and Management* (Macmillan, 1985)
Christopher, M. *et al.*, *Strategy: A Guide to Marketing for Senior Executives* (Gower Press, 1989)
Davidson, H., *Offensive Marketing* (Penguin, 1987)
Day, G. S., *Analysis for Strategic Market Decisions* (West Publishing Co., 1986)
Levitt, T., *The Marketing Imagination* (Free Press, 1983)
McDonald, M. H. B., *Marketing Plans: How to Prepare Them, How to Use Them* (Heinemann, 1988)
Ohmae, K., *The Mind of the Strategist* (Penguin, 1985)
Oliver, G., *Marketing Today* (Prentice-Hall International, 1986)
O'Shaughnessy, J., *Competitive Marketing: A Strategic Approach* (Unwin Hyman, 1989)
Peters, T. J. and Waterman, R. H., *In Search of Excellence* (Harper & Row, 1982)
Porter, M. E., *Competitive Strategy* (Free Press, 1980)

Index